Osborne's
CNE® NetWare® 5
Test Yourself
Practice Exams

CERTIFIED NOVELL ENGINEER℠

Osborne's CNE® NetWare® 5 Test Yourself Practice Exams

Syngress Media, Inc.

Osborne McGraw-Hill

Berkeley New York St. Louis San Francisco Auckland Bogotá Hamburg London Madrid Mexico City
Milan Montreal New Delhi Panama City Paris São Paulo Singapore Sydney Tokyo Toronto

Osborne McGraw-Hill
2600 Tenth Street
Berkeley, California 94710
U.S.A.

For information on translations or book distributors outside the U.S.A., or to
arrange bulk purchase discounts for sales promotions, premiums, or fund-raisers,
please contact Osborne/**McGraw-Hill** at the above address.

Osborne's CNE® NetWare® 5 Test Yourself Practice Exams

1234567890 AGM AGM 90198765432109

ISBN 0-07-212107-6

Publisher	**Technical Editor**
Brandon A. Nordin	Justin Grant
Associate Publisher and	**Copy Editor**
Editor-in-Chief	Nancy Faughnan
Scott Rogers	
	Proofreader
Acquisitions Editor	Doug Robert
Gareth Hancock	
	Computer Designer
Editorial Management	Roberta Steele
Syngress Media, Inc.	Jani Beckwith
Project Editor	**Illustrator**
Carolyn Welch	Beth Young
Editorial Assistant	**Series Design**
Tara Davis	Roberta Steele
Series Editor	**Cover Design**
Daniel Cheung	Regan Honda

From Global Knowledge

At Global Knowledge we strive to support the multiplicity of learning styles required by our students to achieve success as technical professionals. In this series of books, it is our intention to offer the reader a valuable tool for successful completion of the CNE NetWare® 5 Exams.

As the world's largest IT training company, Global Knowledge is uniquely positioned to offer these books. The expertise gained each year from providing instructor-led training to hundreds of thousands of students worldwide has been captured in book form to enhance your learning experience. We hope that the quality of these books demonstrates our commitment to your lifelong learning success. Whether you choose to learn through the written word, computer-based training, Web delivery, or instructor-led training, Global Knowledge is committed to providing you the very best in each of those categories. For those of you who know Global Knowledge, or those of you who have just found us for the first time, our goal is to be your lifelong competency partner.

Thank you for the opportunity to serve you. We look forward to serving your needs again in the future.

Warmest regards,

Duncan Anderson
President and Chief Executive Officer, Global Knowledge

The Global Knowledge Advantage

Global Knowledge has a global delivery system for its products and services. The company has 28 subsidiaries, and offers its programs through a total of 60+ locations. No other vendor can provide consistent services across a geographic area this large. Global Knowledge is the largest independent information technology education provider, offering programs on a variety of platforms. This enables our multi-platform and multi-national customers to obtain all of their programs from a single vendor. The company has developed the unique CompetusTM Framework software tool and methodology which can quickly reconfigure courseware to the proficiency level of a student on an interactive basis. Combined with self-paced and on-line programs, this technology can reduce the time required for training by prescribing content in only the deficient skills areas. The company has fully automated every aspect of the education process, from registration and follow-up, to "just-in-time" production of courseware. Global Knowledge, through its Enterprise Services Consultancy, can customize programs and products to suit the needs of an individual customer.

Global Knowledge Classroom Education Programs

The backbone of our delivery options is classroom-based education. Our modern, well-equipped facilities staffed with the finest instructors offer programs in a wide variety of information technology topics, many of which lead to professional certifications.

Custom Learning Solutions

This delivery option has been created for companies and governments that value customized learning solutions. For them, our consultancy-based approach of developing targeted education solutions is most effective at helping them meet specific objectives.

Self-Paced and Multimedia Products

This delivery option offers self-paced program titles in interactive CD-ROM, videotape and audio tape programs. In addition, we offer custom development of interactive multimedia courseware to customers and partners. Call us at 1 (888) 427-4228.

Electronic Delivery of Training

Our network-based training service delivers efficient competency-based, interactive training via the World Wide Web and organizational intranets. This leading-edge delivery option provides a custom learning path and "just-in-time" training for maximum convenience to students.

ARG

American Research Group (ARG), a wholly-owned subsidiary of Global Knowledge, one of the largest worldwide training partners of Cisco Systems, offers a wide range of internetworking, LAN/WAN, Bay Networks, FORE Systems, IBM, and UNIX courses. ARG offers hands on network training in both instructor-led classes and self-paced PC-based training.

Global Knowledge Courses Available

Network Fundamentals
- Understanding Computer Networks
- Telecommunications Fundamentals I
- Telecommunications Fundamentals II
- Understanding Networking Fundamentals
- Implementing Computer Telephony Integration
- Introduction to Voice Over IP
- Introduction to Wide Area Networking
- Cabling Voice and Data Networks
- Introduction to LAN/WAN protocols
- Virtual Private Networks
- ATM Essentials

Network Security & Management
- Troubleshooting TCP/IP Networks
- Network Management
- Network Troubleshooting
- IP Address Management
- Network Security Administration
- Web Security
- Implementing UNIX Security
- Managing Cisco Network Security
- Windows NT 4.0 Security

IT Professional Skills
- Project Management for IT Professionals
- Advanced Project Management for IT Professionals
- Survival Skills for the New IT Manager
- Making IT Teams Work

LAN/WAN Internetworking
- Frame Relay Internetworking
- Implementing T1/T3 Services
- Understanding Digital Subscriber Line (xDSL)
- Internetworking with Routers and Switches
- Advanced Routing and Switching
- Multi-Layer Switching and Wire-Speed Routing
- Internetworking with TCP/IP
- ATM Internetworking
- OSPF Design and Configuration
- Border Gateway Protocol (BGP) Configuration

Authorized Vendor Training

Cisco Systems
- Introduction to Cisco Router Configuration
- Advanced Cisco Router Configuration
- Installation and Maintenance of Cisco Routers
- Cisco Internetwork Troubleshooting
- Cisco Internetwork Design
- Cisco Routers and LAN Switches
- Catalyst 5000 Series Configuration
- Cisco LAN Switch Configuration
- Managing Cisco Switched Internetworks
- Configuring, Monitoring, and Troubleshooting Dial-Up Services
- Cisco AS5200 Installation and Configuration
- Cisco Campus ATM Solutions

Bay Networks
- Bay Networks Accelerated Router Configuration
- Bay Networks Advanced IP Routing
- Bay Networks Hub Connectivity
- Bay Networks Accelar 1xxx Installation and Basic Configuration
- Bay Networks Centillion Switching

FORE Systems
- FORE ATM Enterprise Core Products
- FORE ATM Enterprise Edge Products
- FORE ATM Theory
- FORE LAN Certification

Operating Systems & Programming

Microsoft
- Introduction to Windows NT
- Microsoft Networking Essentials
- Windows NT 4.0 Workstation
- Windows NT 4.0 Server
- Advanced Windows NT 4.0 Server
- Windows NT Networking with TCP/IP
- Introduction to Microsoft Web Tools
- Windows NT Troubleshooting
- Windows Registry Configuration

UNIX
- UNIX Level I
- UNIX Level II
- Essentials of UNIX and NT Integration

Programming
- Introduction to JavaScript
- Java Programming
- PERL Programming
- Advanced PERL with CGI for the Web

Web Site Management & Development
- Building a Web Site
- Web Site Management and Performance
- Web Development Fundamentals

High Speed Networking
- Essentials of Wide Area Networking
- Integrating ISDN
- Fiber Optic Network Design
- Fiber Optic Network Installation
- Migrating to High Performance Ethernet

DIGITAL UNIX
- UNIX Utilities and Commands
- DIGITAL UNIX v4.0 System Administration
- DIGITAL UNIX v4.0 (TCP/IP) Network Management
- AdvFS, LSM, and RAID Configuration and Management
- DIGITAL UNIX TruCluster Software Configuration and Management
- UNIX Shell Programming Featuring Kornshell
- DIGITAL UNIX v4.0 Security Management
- DIGITAL UNIX v4.0 Performance Management
- DIGITAL UNIX v4.0 Intervals Overview

DIGITAL OpenVMS
- OpenVMS Skills for Users
- OpenVMS System and Network Node Management I
- OpenVMS System and Network Node Management II
- OpenVMS System and Network Node Management III
- OpenVMS System and Network Node Operations
- OpenVMS for Programmers
- OpenVMS System Troubleshooting for Systems Managers
- Configuring and Managing Complex VMScluster Systems
- Utilizing OpenVMS Features from C
- OpenVMS Performance Management
- Managing DEC TCP/IP Services for OpenVMS
- Programming in C

Hardware Courses
- AlphaServer 1000/1000A Installation, Configuration and Maintenance
- AlphaServer 2100 Server Maintenance
- AlphaServer 4100, Troubleshooting Techniques and Problem Solving

About Syngress Media

Syngress Media creates books and software for Information Technology professionals seeking skill enhancement and career advancement. Its products are designed to comply with vendor and industry standard course curricula, and are optimized for certification exam preparation. Visit the Syngress Web site at www.syngress.com.

About the Contributors

Melissa Craft (MCNE, CCNA, MCSE, CCP) is a Senior Consulting Engineer for MicroAge. MicroAge is a global systems integrator headquartered in Tempe, Arizona. MicroAge provides IT design, project management and support for distributed computing systems. Melissa develops enterprise-wide technology solutions and methodologies for client organizations. These technology solutions touch every part of a system's lifecycle—from network design, testing and implementation to operational management and strategic planning. Aside from earning a bachelor's degree from the University of Michigan, Melissa has several technical certifications including Microsoft's MCSE, Cisco's CCNA, Novell's Master CNE and Citrix's CCP. Melissa is a member of the IEEE, the Society of Women Engineers and American MENSA, Ltd. Melissa Craft currently resides in Phoenix, Arizona with her family, Dan, Justine and Taylor, and her two dogs, Marmaduke and Pooka. She can be contacted at mmcraft@compuserve.com.

    Todd Meadors (CNE, MCSE) is a Computer Information Systems (CIS) Instructor for DeKalb Technical Institute, a technical school located close to Atlanta, Georgia. He teaches courses in networking and programming. Todd has a Master of Science (MS) degree in Computer Information Systems from Georgia State University. He also has a Master of Business Administration (MBA) degree and Bachelor of Business Administration (BBA) degree from Mercer University. Todd holds Microsoft Certified Systems Engineer (MCSE) and Certified NetWare Engineer (CNE) certifications. For fun, he enjoys weight lifting, playing with his kids, watching movies, and reading non-computer stuff. He can be contacted by e-mail at LTMEADORS@YAHOO.COM.

Brian Frederick (MCSE, ASE, MCNE, Network+) is a Systems Engineer with over seven years of technical background. Brian started working with computers with an Apple II+. Brian attended the University of Northern Iowa and is married with two adorable children. Brian's hobbies include his kids, family, and golfing. Brian is a Systems Engineer for Entre Information Systems, a leading Novell Platinum Partner and Microsoft Certified Solution Provider. Entre is a sister company with New Horizons Computer Learning Company, a premier Microsoft ATEC and Novell Authorized Training Partner. Brian owes his success to his parents and brother for their support and backing during his Apple days and in college, and to his wife and children for their support and understanding when Dad spends many hours in front of their computer.

Jim Queen (MCNE) is the President of Network Data Services, Inc, a network consulting firm based in Dallas, Texas. Jim is an MCNE with 15 years of experience in NetWare networking. He is an author and contributor to several books, and has written numerous network-related articles for various computer publications. Jim's e-mail address is jqueen@ndsvcs.com.

James Vogan Tysinger holds CNE, CNA, and A+ certifications, and lives in Sacramento, California with his wife Kathleen, son Connor, and daughter Grace. He is also a private pilot and enjoys flying on his time off from working on Novell, NT, and Macintosh networks for a national telecommunications firm.

Series Editor

Daniel Y. Cheung (CNI, CNE, MCNE, MCP, MCT) has been a networking consultant since 1996 and a technical trainer since 1995. Daniel is currently an instructor in computer networking at University of New England–Westbrook College, Portland, Maine, as well as a freelance writer and editor. Dan spent ten years working in bank financial accounting systems and served six years on active duty as a Captain in the United States Army. He has a BA from Cornell University, Ithaca, NY, and has also attended Northwestern University–University College, Evanston, IL, and the University of Alaska-Anchorage, Anchorage, AK. Dan is also a competitive rower (sculling).

Technical Reviewer

Justin Grant (MCNE, CNE, CNA, CNI) is the Network Technology Consultant for Health Care Excel. Health Care Excel is a private not-for-profit organization and a federally designated Medicare Utilization and Quality Control Peer Review Organization (PRO) holding the Indiana and Kentucky PRO contracts with the Health Care Financing Administration (HCFA). Justin holds certifications in all versions of NetWare from 3.1x to 5.0, as well as holding several Master CNE certifications and a CNI. Justin can be reached at justin@alexander-grant.com.

ACKNOWLEDGMENTS

e would like to thank the following people:

- Richard Kristof of Global Knowledge for championing the series and providing us access to some great people and information.

- To all the incredibly hard-working folks at Osborne/McGraw-Hill: Brandon Nordin, Scott Rogers, and Gareth Hancock for their help in launching a great series and being solid team players. In addition, Carolyn Welch and Tara Davis for their help in fine-tuning the book.

- Marci Shanti of Novell, Inc., for her assistance and support.

CONTENTS

Foreword . . . . *v*

About the Contributors . . . . *ix*

Acknowledgments . . . . *xiii*

Preface . . . . *xxvii*

Introduction . . . . *xxxi*

Part I
NetWare® 5 Administration (Exam 50-639)

NetWare 5 Administration Questions 3

Introduction to NetWare 4

Enabling Network Access 7

Managing User Accounts 10

Managing Network Printing 13

Managing the File System 16

Managing File System Security 18

Creating Login Scripts 21

Remote Management of Workstations (NEBO) 25

Configuring Network Applications for Users 27

Using Workstation Manager to Manage Workstations 30

Managing NDS Security 33

Managing Resources in a Multicontext Environment 36

Performing a Simple Installation 39

NetWare 5 Administration Answers 43

Introduction to NetWare 44

Enabling Network Access 47

Managing User Accounts 51

Managing Network Printing 54

Managing the File System 57
Managing File System Security 61
Creating Login Scripts 64
Remote Management of Workstations (NEBO) 66
Configuring Network Applications for Users 68
Using Workstation Manager to Manage Workstations 69
Managing NDS Security 71
Managing Resources in a Multicontext Environment 73
Performing a Simple Installation 75

Part 2
NetWare® 5 Advanced Administration (Exam 50-640)

NetWare 5 Advanced
Administration Questions 81

Upgrading NetWare 3.1x to NetWare 5 Server 82
Upgrading from Queue-Based Printing to NDPS 85
Performing a Custom Installation 88
Setting Up the Network File System 89
Using the Server Console 91
Optimizing the Network and Server 93
Backing Up Servers and Workstations 95
Using DNS/DHCP Services 97
Installing a Web Server 100
Securing the Directory Tree 102
Maintaining NDS 105
Mobile Clients 108

NetWare 5 Advanced
Administration Answers 111

Upgrading NetWare 3.1x to NetWare 5 Server 112
Upgrading from Queue-Based Printing to NDPS 115
Performing a Custom Installation 118
Setting Up the Network File System 119

Using the Server Console 122
Optimizing the Network and Server 124
Backing Up Servers and Workstations 127
Using DNS/DHCP Services 129
Installing a Web Server 131
Securing the Directory Tree 133
Maintaining NDS 135
Mobile Clients 137

Part 3
Networking Technologies (Exam 50-632)

Networking Technologies Questions **141**
Network Services 142
Transmission Media and Connections 145
The OSI Model's Lower Layers 148
The OSI Model's Middle Layers 151
The OSI Model's Upper Layers 156
Networking Technologies Answers **161**
Network Services 162
Transmission Media and Connections 167
The OSI Model's Lower Layers 171
The OSI Model's Middle Layers 175
The OSI Model's Upper Layers 180

Part 4
Novell Directory Services® (NDS) Design and Implementation (Exam 50-634)

NDS™ Design and Implementation Questions **187**
Assessing the Network 188
Defining and Justifying the Network Solution 191

Designing the Directory Tree 194

Implementing Time-Synchronization Strategies 201

Creating an Accessibility Plan 205

Conducting a NetWare Implementation 209

NDS™ Design and Implementation Answers   217

Assessing the Network 218

Defining and Justifying the Network Solution 222

Designing the Directory Tree 226

Implementing Time-Synchronization Strategies 231

Creating an Accessibility Plan 235

Conducting a NetWare Implementation 240

Part 5
NetWare Service and Support (Exam 50-635)

NetWare Service and Support Questions ...   247

Network Troubleshooting 248

Installing and Troubleshooting Network Interface
    Cards and Cables 252

Installing and Troubleshooting Network Storage Devices . 255

Troubleshooting the DOS Workstation 260

Troubleshooting Network Printing 264

Troubleshooting and Optimizing the Network 268

NetWare Service and Support Answers ...   273

Network Troubleshooting 274

Installing and Troubleshooting Network Interface
    Cards and Cables 276

Installing and Troubleshooting Network Storage Devices .. 277

Troubleshooting the DOS Workstation 280

Troubleshooting Network Printing 283

Troubleshooting and Optimizing the Network 285

Part 6
NetWare: Integrating Windows NT (Exam 50-644)

NetWare: Integrating Windows NT Questions **291**

Introduction to Windows NT 292
Introduction to Windows NT Networking 294
Windows NT Domain Networking 298
Managing Windows NT Security 302
Integrating Windows NT Workstations 304
Multiple Domain Windows NT Networking 307
Integrating NetWare and Windows NT Domains 310
Designing, Implementing, and Maintaining an
    Integrated Network 313
Implementing and Maintaining Accessibility in an
    Integrated Network 313

NetWare: Integrating Windows NT Answers **315**

Introduction to Windows NT 316
Introduction to Windows NT Networking 320
Windows NT Domain Networking 325
Managing Windows NT Security 330
Integrating Windows NT Workstations 334
Multiple Domain Windows NT Networking 337
Integrating NetWare and Windows NT Domains 341
Designing, Implementing, and Maintaining an
    Integrated Network 345
Implementing and Maintaining Accessibility in an
    Integrated Network 346

Part 7
Test Yourself: Practice Exam 1: NetWare 5 Administration (Exam 50-639)

Test Yourself: Practice Exam 1 Questions .. **349**
Practice Exam 1 Questions 350
Test Yourself: Practice Exam 1 Answers **371**
Practice Exam 1 Answers 372

Part 8
Test Yourself: Practice Exam 2: NetWare 5 Advanced Administration (Exam 50-640)

Test Yourself: Practice Exam 2 Questions .. **411**
Practice Exam 2 Questions 412
Test Yourself: Practice Exam 2 Answers **433**
Practice Exam 2 Anwers 434

Part 9
Test Yourself: Practice Exam 3: Networking Technologies (Exam 50-632)

Test Yourself: Practice Exam 3 Questions .. **465**
Practice Exam 3 Questions 466
Test Yourself: Practice Exam 3 Answers **489**
Practice Exam 3 Answers 490

Part 10
Test Yourself: Practice Exam 4: NDS™ Design and Implementation (Exam 50-634)

Test Yourself: Practice Exam 4 Questions .. **521**
Practice Exam 4 Questions 522
Test Yourself: Practice Exam 4 Answers **543**
Practice Exam 4 Answers 544

Part 11
Test Yourself: Practice Exam 5: NetWare Service and Support (Exam 50-635)

Test Yourself: Practice Exam 5 Questions .. **573**

Practice Exam 5 Questions 574

Test Yourself: Practice Exam 5 Answers **601**

Practice Exam 5 Answers 602

Part 12
Test Yourself: Practice Exam 6: NetWare: Integrating Windows NT (Exam 50-644)

Test Yourself: Practice Exam 6 Questions .. **625**

Practice Exam 6 Questions 626

Test Yourself: Practice Exam 6 Answers **643**

Practice Exam 6 Answers 644

Appendix A
About the Web Site **669**

Access Global Knowledge 670

What You'll Find There... 670

Glossary **671**

W e built this book for a specific reason. Every time we asked NetWare technicians and CNE candidates what they wanted in their study materials, they answered "More questions!" Based on that resounding request, we built a book full of questions on the CNE exams so you can test yourself to your heart's desire.

In This Book

This book is organized in sections that correspond to the 5 core exams and the Integrating Windows NT elective exam for CNE NetWare 5 certification. We cover topics on each of the exams in a separate module of questions and answers, and we also have a separate "Test Yourself" Practice Exam for each of the CNE exams.

The Q&A Chapters

You will find one Q&A chapter for each exam, from NetWare 5 Administration to NetWare Service and Support. Each question section has original questions, followed by an answer section that has full explanations of the correct choices and the incorrect choices.

Each chapter is divided into categories, so you will cover every topic tested by Novell. Each topic is a heading within the chapter, so you can study by topic if you like. If you need further review on any particular topic, you will find that the topic headings correspond to the chapters of Osborne/McGraw-Hill's *CNE NetWare 5 Study Guide.* Want to simulate an actual exam? The section "The Test Yourself Practice Exams" below explains how.

In addition, throughout the Q&A chapters, we have sprinkled helpful notes in the form of Exam Watches and Q&A scenarios:

- **Exam Watch** notes call attention to information about, and potential pitfalls in, the exam. These helpful hints are written by Cisco certified technicians who have taken the exams and have received their certification—who better to tell you what to worry about? They know what you're about to go through!

- **Q & A** sections lay out problems and solutions in a quick-read format.

QUESTIONS AND ANSWERS

Jenny has just completed a course in network administration and has decided to create a new login script that contains the following line: `#MAP R G:=SYS:PUBLIC.` The login script executes, but instead of a smooth drive mapping within the login window, a DOS window pops up. Why?	Jenny has erroneously invoked the external MAP command instead of the login script version. She should remove the # sign from the MAP statement.

The Test Yourself Practice Exams

If you have had your fill of exam questions, answers, and explanations, the time has come to test your knowledge. Or maybe, you want to start with one of the Test Yourself Practice Exams to see where your strengths and weaknesses are, and then review only certain topics. Either way, turn to the final section of the book, the Test Yourself chapters. In this section we actually simulate the exams. We have given you one practice test for each of the exams, with the number of questions corresponding to the actual exams in random order. Lock yourself in your office or clear the kitchen table, set a timer, and jump in.

The Global Knowledge Web Site

Global Knowledge invites you to become an active member of the Access Global Web site. This site is an online mall and an information repository that you'll find invaluable. You can access many types of products to assist you in your preparation for the exams, and you'll be able to participate in forums, on-line discussions, and threaded discussions. No other book brings you unlimited access to such a resource. You'll find more information about this site in Appendix A.Introduction

How to Take a Novell CNE Certification Examination

Good News and Bad News

If you are new to Novell certification, we have some good news and some bad news. The good news is that Novell's CNE certification is one of the most highly recognized and respected IT credentials you can earn. It sets you apart from the crowd and marks you as a valuable asset to your employer and customers. Not only will you gain the respect of your peers, the CNE certification can have a positive effect on your income potential.

The bad news is that CNE certification tests are not easy. You may think you can read through some study materials, memorize a few facts, and pass the examinations. After all, these certification exams are just computer-based, multiple-choice tests, so they must be easy. If you believe this, you are wrong. Unlike many standardized tests you may have been exposed to in school, the questions on CNE certification exams go beyond merely processing factual knowledge.

The purpose of this introduction is to teach you how to take a CNE certification exam. To be successful, you need to know something about the purpose and structure of these tests. We will also look at the latest testing methodologies used in Novell testing. Using simulations and adaptive testing, Novell is enhancing both the validity and security of the certification process. These factors have some important effects on how you should prepare for an exam, as well as your approach to each question during the test.

We'll start by looking at the purpose, focus, and structure of Novell certification tests, and examine the effect these factors have on the kinds of questions you will see. We will define the structure of examination questions, and investigate some common formats. Next, we will present a strategy for answering these questions. Finally, we will give some specific guidelines on what you should do on the day of your test.

Why Vendor Certification?

The Novell CNE program, like the certification programs from Lotus, Microsoft, Oracle, and other software vendors, is maintained for the ultimate purpose of increasing an organization's profits and/or maximizing their productivity and efficiency. A successful vendor certification program accomplishes this goal by helping to create a pool of experts in a company's software, and by "branding" these experts so that companies using the software can identify them and be assured of a baseline level of knowledge, albeit a rather high one.

We know that vendor certifications have become increasingly popular in the last few years because it helps employers find qualified workers, and because it helps software vendors, like Novell, to sell their products. But why should you be interested in vendor certification rather than a more traditional approach like a college or professional degree in computer science? A college education is a broadening and enriching experience, but a degree in computer science does not prepare students for most jobs in the IT industry.

Computer and telecommunications technology have been developing at a rapid pace. The problem is that, if a first-year student learns about a specific computer program, it probably will no longer be in wide use when he or she graduates. Although some colleges are trying to integrate vendor certification into their curriculum, the problem is not really a flaw in higher education, but a characteristic of the IT industry. Computer software is changing so rapidly that a four-year college just can't always keep up. Most of the jobs today in the IT industry did not even exist five years ago.

A characteristic of the Novell certification program is an emphasis on understanding fundamental concepts and then applying them to specific job tasks rather than merely gathering knowledge. It should not come as a surprise, but most potential employers do not care how much you know about the theory of operating systems, testing, or software design. As one IT Manager Put It, "I don't really care what my employees know about the theory of our network. We don't need someone to sit at a desk and think about it. We need people who can actually do something to make it work better."

You should not think that this attitude is some kind of anti-intellectual revolt against book learning. Knowledge is a necessary prerequisite, but it is not enough. More than one company has hired a computer science graduate as a network administrator only to learn that the new employee has no idea how to add users, assign permissions, or perform the other everyday tasks necessary to maintain a network. One must be able to apply that knowledge to making the network work for the benefit of the organization that it supports. In addition to being up-to-date on technical developments, Novell certification is also job-task oriented.

The timeliness of Novell's certification program is obvious, and is inherent in the fact that you will be tested on current versions of software in wide use today. The job-task orientation of Novell certification is almost as obvious, but testing real-world job skills using a computer-based test is not easy.

Computerized Testing

Considering the popularity of Novell certification, and the fact that certification candidates are spread around the world, the only practical way to administer tests for the certification program is through Sylvan Prometric and Virtual University Enterprises (VUE) testing centers. Sylvan Prometric and VUE provide proctored testing services for Novell, Oracle, Lotus, and Comptia certifications. Although the IT industry accounts for much of Sylvan's revenue, the company provides services for a number of other businesses and organizations, such as FAA preflight pilot tests. In fact, most companies that need secure test delivery over a wide geographic area use the services of Sylvan Prometric. In addition to delivery, Sylvan Prometric also scores the tests and provides statistical feedback on the performance of each test question to the companies and organizations that use their services.

Typically, several hundred questions are developed for a new Novell certification exam. The questions are first reviewed by a number of subject-matter experts for technical accuracy, and then are presented in a beta test. The beta test may last for several hours, due to the large number of questions. After a few weeks, Novell Education uses the statistical feedback from the testing services to check the validity of the beta questions.

Questions are discarded if most test takers get them right (too easy) or wrong (too difficult), and a number of other statistical measures are taken of each question. Although the scope of our discussion precludes a rigorous treatment of question analysis, you should be aware that Novell and other vendors spend a great deal of time and effort making sure their examination questions are valid and relevant to today's IT needs. In addition to the obvious desire for quality, the fairness of a vendor's certification program must be legally defensible.

The questions that survive statistical analysis form the pool of questions for the final certification exam.

Test Structure

The kind of test we are most familiar with is known as a *form* test. For Novell certification, a form test usually consists of 50–80 questions and takes 60–105 minutes to complete, depending on the test. If there are 240 questions in the final pool for an examination, then four forms can be created. Thus, candidates who retake the test probably will not see the same questions. Until recently, form tests did not allow you to mark questions and go back to review it. Some of the newer form tests allow you to revisit a question and even change your response. Be careful not to waste time "retaking" the test, but do take the opportunity to make sure you marked "A" and not "B." The temptation to reread and change is great, but avoid it.

Eventually, when enough people sit for the exam, adaptive tests are developed and administered. *Adaptive tests* are also drawn from a pool of different versions. An adaptive test will have a minimum of 15 questions and a maximum of 25. The time limit varies from test to test; however, most of the tests are 30 minutes in duration, with the Service and Support test being close to two hours. You must mark a response for each question; otherwise, you will be prompted to do so and the test will not give you the next question until you do. Just as important, don't exceed the time limit; if you do, the test will be marked as "failed" due to exceeding the time limit even if you have accumulated enough points to pass. Novell Education endeavors to have every CNE test become adaptive, although, some tests, due to the low number of candidates taking them, may remain as form tests.

The questions in a Novell adaptive test are assigned weighted values. The more difficult questions or ones that require more complex actions and analysis are given a greater weight in computing your final score. When you finish all the questions, your test is scored and you will see a message that tells you how you scored and whether you passed.

When an adaptive test begins, you are first given a simple or moderately simple question. If it is answered correctly, a more difficult question or action requiring more complex actions is presented. An incorrect response results in a question from the next lower level. When 15–20 questions have been answered in this manner, the scoring algorithm is able to predict, with a high degree of statistical certainty, whether you would pass or fail if all the questions in the form were answered. When the required degree of certainty is attained, the test ends, gets scored, and you receive either a pass or fail based on the total points achieved.

CNE adaptive tests also generally have five categories of questions. Typically, in order to pass, correct responses must be given in three out of the five categories. If you are pursuing a CNI certification, you must give correct responses in all of the categories. Be careful which version of the test you register for. The CNI version of the test asks identical questions as the CNE version; however, a higher passing threshold score is required, and even if you score high enough to pass the CNE version of the test, your test will be scored as "failed" with no credit applied toward CNE certification.

Adaptive testing has some definite advantages for everyone involved in the certification process. Adaptive tests allow Sylvan Prometric to deliver more tests with the same resources, as certification candidates often are in and out in 30 minutes or less. For Novell, adaptive testing means that fewer test questions are exposed to each candidate, and this can enhance the security, thus safeguarding the validity of certification tests.

One possible problem you may have with adaptive testing is that you are not allowed to mark and revisit questions. Since the adaptive algorithm is interactive, and all questions but the first are selected on the basis of your response to the previous question, it is not possible to skip a particular question or change an answer.

Question Types

Computerized test questions can be presented in a number of ways. Some of the possible formats are used on Novell certification examinations, and some are not.

True/False

We are all familiar with true/false questions, and the inherent 50 percent chance of guessing the correct answer.

Multiple Choice

The majority of Novell certification questions are in the multiple-choice format, with either a single correct answer or multiple correct answers. There is an interesting variation on multiple-choice questions with multiple correct answers and you are asked to select *all that apply*, and you are not told how many to choose. These tend to be the most challenging.

Example:

Which two of the following are Leaf objects? (Choose two.)

Or

Which of the following commands can be used at the server console? (Choose all that apply.)

You may see both variations on Novell certification examinations, but the trend seems to be toward the first type, where candidates are told explicitly how many answers are correct. Questions of the "choose all that apply" variety are more difficult, and can be confusing.

Graphical Questions

One or more graphical elements are sometimes used as exhibits to help present or clarify an exam question. These elements may take the form of a database diagram, flow charts, or screenshots from the software on which you are being tested. It is often easier to present the concepts required for a complex performance-based scenario with a graphic than with words.

Test questions called *performance-based*, actually incorporate simulated graphical utilities as part of the answer. These questions ask the certification candidate to perform administrative tasks on the simulated utility to answer the question. For example, you might be asked to grant NDS object rights to a User object. The answer is correct if any combination of steps will lead to the desired result. These questions do not necessarily test which technique you used, but rather, whether the task was accomplished.

Short-Answer Questions

Another kind of question you sometimes see on Novell certification examinations requires a typed-in answer. An example of this type of question might be to type in a server console command, a text box in a dialogue box, or even to complete a statement's blank spaces.

Knowledge-Based and Performance-Based Questions

Novell Education develops a blueprint for each Novell certification examination with input from Novell's internal personnel, current CNEs and MCNEs (Master Certified Novell Engineers), managers at some of Novell's biggest customers, and CNIs (Certified Novell Instructors). This blueprint defines the content areas and objectives for each test, and each test question is created to test a specific objective. The objectives for each test can be found at Novell Education's Web site.

Some objectives demand a knowledge-based question. For example, objectives that use verbs like *list* and *identify* tend to test only what you know, not what you can do.

Example: Objective: Explain how file system security works.

Which two of the following are file system rights that allows a user to run an executable file with an EXE extension?

(Choose two.)

A. Access Control

B. Read

C. Modify

D. File Scan

E. Browse

Correct answers: B and D

Other objectives use action verbs like *connect, configure,* and *troubleshoot* to define job tasks. These objectives can often be tested with either a knowledge-based question or a performance-based question.

Example: Objective: Troubleshoot NDS database inconsistencies.
Knowledge-based question:
Which of the following symptoms might indicate that replicas are out of synchronization?
A. Dirty Cache Buffers are consistently at 90.
B. Client login takes dramatically longer than usual.
C. The SYSCON utility is no longer available.
D. An SNMP Trap message is received.
Correct answer: B

Performance-based questions typically require an action done on a simulated GUI-based utility, such as NetWare Administrator, to perform a task, such as granting object rights to a user. However, the functions are limited to the task at hand, and the <Help> button is disabled.

Even in this simple example, the superiority of the performance-based question is obvious. Whereas the knowledge-based question asks for a single fact, the performance-based question presents a real-life situation and requires that you make a decision based on this scenario. Thus, performance-based questions give more bang (validity) for the test author's buck (individual question).

Testing Job Performance

We have said that Novell certification focuses on timeliness and the ability to perform job tasks. We have also introduced the concept of performance-based questions, but even performance-based, multiple-choice questions do not really measure performance. Another strategy is needed to test job skills.

Given unlimited resources, it is not difficult to test job skills. In an ideal world, Novell would fly CNE candidates to one of their sites, place them in a controlled environment with a team of experts, and ask them to plan, set up, administer, and document a network. In a few days at most, the experts could reach a valid decision as to whether each candidate should be granted CNE status. Obviously, this is not likely to happen.

Closer to reality, another way to test performance is by using the actual software, and creating a testing program to present tasks and automatically grade a candidate's performance when the tasks are completed. This *cooperative* approach would be practical in some testing situations, but the same test that is presented to CNE candidates in Chicago must also be available in Tokyo and Sydney. Many Sylvan Prometric testing locations around the world do not have all of the equipment needed to set up a complete NetWare network, much less provide the complex networked solutions required by cooperative testing applications.

The most workable solution for measuring performance in today's testing environment is a *simulation* program. When the program is launched during a test, the candidate sees a simulation of the actual software that looks and behaves just like the real thing. When the testing software presents a task, the simulation program is launched and the candidate performs the required task. The testing software then grades the candidate's performance on the required task and moves to the next question. In this way, a Windows 3.1 simulation program can mimic the look and feel of a network operating system, a Windows NT Workstation, a complicated network, or even the entire Internet.

Novell has included simulation questions on the certification since the first tests for the earlier CNE4 certification tests. Simulation questions provide many advantages over other testing methodologies, and simulations are expected to become increasingly important in the Novell CNE Program. For example, studies have shown that there is a very high correlation between the ability to perform simulated tasks on a computer-based test and the ability to perform the actual job tasks. Thus, simulations enhance the validity of the certification process.

Another benefit of simulations is in the area of test security. It is just not possible to cheat on a simulation question. In fact, you will be told exactly what tasks you are expected to perform on the test.

Study Strategies

There are appropriate ways to study for the different types of questions you will see on a Novell certification examination.

Knowledge-Based Questions

Knowledge-based questions require that you memorize facts. There are hundreds of facts inherent in every content area of every Novell certification examination. There are several keys to memorizing facts:

- *Repetition.* The more times your brain is exposed to a fact, the more likely you are to remember it.

- *Association.* Connecting facts within a logical framework makes them easier to remember.

- *Motor Association.* It is often easier to remember something if you write it down or perform some other physical act, like clicking a practice test answer.

We have said that the emphasis of Novell certification is job performance; however, there are many knowledge-based questions on Novell certification exams. A few of the CNE tests contain nearly all knowledge-based questions. The Networking Technologies and Fundamentals of Internetworking (not required for CNE) tests are prime examples of tests that test your ability to recall technical minutiae.

Simulations

Simulation questions really do measure your ability to perform job tasks. You *must* be able to perform the specified tasks. There are two ways to prepare for simulation questions:

1. Get experience with the actual software. If you have the resources, this is a great way to prepare for simulation questions.

2. Use practice tests. Practice tests are available that provide practice with the same simulation engine used on Novell certification exams. This approach has the added advantage of grading your efforts.

Using Practice Tests

Practice tests are invaluable aids to help you prepare for the real thing. They are very helpful in giving you an idea of the type of questions that you might encounter on the test and the depth of knowledge required. Use practice tests to get an idea of what topics you should concentrate on in your preparation. Most practice tests will give you an analysis of the question and cite specific references, which you can look up. One common pitfall is to memorize the answers to practice tests. This can lead to disastrous test scores, since you can be lulled into a false sense of security. If you use practice tests, analyze the questions and topics that you scored poorly on, and actually go to the cited reference. Also, don't forget to analyze those questions you answered correctly, and check to see if you answered the question correctly because you truly understood the concepts presented, or if you just got lucky.

Signing Up

Signing up to take a Novell certification examination is easy. Sylvan operators in each country can schedule tests at any testing center. There are, however, a few things you should know:

- If you call Sylvan during a busy time period, you may be in for a long wait. Sylvan does an excellent job, but everyone in the world seems to want to sign up for a test on Monday morning.

- You will need your Social Security number or some other unique identifier to sign up for a Sylvan test, so have it at hand.

- Pay for your test by credit card if at all possible. This makes things easier, and you can even schedule tests for the same day you call, if space is available at your local testing center.

- Know the number and title of the test you want to take before you call. This is not essential, and the Sylvan operators will help you if they can. Having this information in advance, however, speeds up the registration process and reduces the risk that you will accidentally register for the wrong test.

Taking the Test

Teachers have always told you not to try to cram for examinations, because it usually does no good. If you are faced with a knowledge-based test requiring only that you regurgitate facts, cramming can mean the difference between passing and failing. This is not the case, however, with Novell certification exams. If you don't know it the night before, don't bother to stay up and cram.

Instead, create a schedule and stick to it. Follow these guidelines on the day of your exam:

1. Get a good night's sleep. The scenario questions you will face on a Novell certification examination require a clear head.

2. Remember to take two forms of identification—at least one with a picture. A driver's license with your picture, and Social Security or credit cards are acceptable.

3. Leave home in time to arrive at your testing center a few minutes early. It is not a good idea to feel rushed as you begin your exam.

4. If you are given a practice exam when you register on the testing workstation, take the 15-minute exam. It is a good way to check the "feel" of the mouse and keyboard, or to find out if they work properly at all. If nothing else, you have the opportunity to score 100% at least once that day.

5. Do not spend too much time on any one question. If you are taking a form test, take your best guess and mark the question so you can come back to it if you have time. You cannot mark and revisit questions on an adaptive test, so you must do your best on each question as you go.

6. If you do not know the answer to a question, try to eliminate the obviously wrong answers and guess from the rest. If you can eliminate two out of four options, you have a 50 percent chance of guessing the correct answer.

7. For all questions, read the question carefully to ensure you understand what is being asked, look over all the answers, before selecting an answer, re-read the question, then mark your answer.

8. Keep track of the time on the computer. Anyone not completing all questions will get a failing score.

9. If the test is adaptive and you are at question #25, check how much time you have left and use as much of it as possible to think about the question before selecting your answer. If you have gotten this far, it is your last chance to pass. The adaptive testing algorithm has calculated that you have a chance to pass, if you answer the question correctly.

Finally, I would advise anyone attempting to earn Novell certification to adopt a philosophical attitude. Even if you are the kind of person who never fails a test, you are likely to fail at least one Novell certification test somewhere along the way. Do not get discouraged. If Novell certification were easy to obtain, more people would have it, and it would not be so respected and valuable to your future in the IT industry.

Part I

NetWare® 5 Administration (Exam 50-639)

EXAM TOPICS

Introduction to NetWare

Enabling Network Access

Managing User Accounts

Managing Network Printing

Managing the File System

Managing File System Security

Creating Login Scripts

Remote Management of Workstations (NEBO)

Configuring Network Applications for Users

Using Workstation Manager to Manage Workstations

Managing NDS™ Security

Managing Resources in a Multicontext Environment

Performing a Simple Installation

NetWare® 5 Administration Questions

Q&A

I n this chapter we will pose various questions, as well as offer various scenarios about how to manage Novell® NetWare® 5 Administration. Even the most experienced Network Administrator has room to learn new topics or approach old ones from different angles. This chapter discusses Novell Directory Services® (NDS), protocol and client installation, user account management, and network printing. We also explore questions and answers on file systems, security, creating login scripts, remote access, configuring network application, NDS security, NDS multicontext environments, and finally, performing a simple installation.

Introduction to NetWare

1. The services in a Novell NetWare network are typically provided through certain programs that only run a NetWare server. What are these programs called?

A. Virtual Loadable Modules (VLMs)

B. Dynamic Link Libraries (DLLs)

C. Network Interface Cards (NICs)

D. NetWare Loadable Modules (NLMs)

Refer to the Following Scenario and Illustration for Questions 2–3

Jessie is a Network Engineer and she works for a medium-sized firm, Short Stuff Enterprises, outside of Atlanta, GA. The structure of the company is organized with various users in the following departments: Accounting, Engineering, Information Technology, and Human Resources. The organization of the NDS for SSE is displayed in the following illustration.

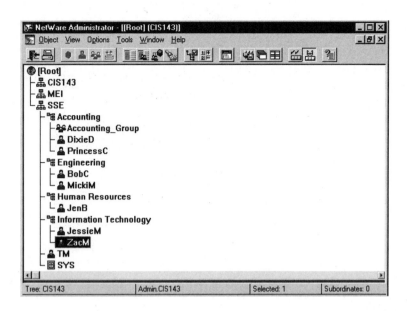

2. How many additional [Root] objects can Jessie create in this NDS tree for her company?

A. Zero

B. One

C. Two

D. Unlimited

3. What is the context for the User object MickiM in the illustration?

A. Accounting

B. [Root]

C. SSE

D. Engineering

4. What types of information are stored in the NDS schema? Choose all that apply.

   A. Attribute

   B. Inheritance

   C. Context

   D. Subordination

5. What type of NDS right enables a trustee to access the values of the property information for an NDS object?

   A. Property

   B. Object

   C. Inherited Rights Filter (IRF)

   D. Effective Rights

Enabling Network Access

Refer to the Following Scenario for Questions 1–5

Zac works as a Network Administrator for a large international firm. He is installing the client software for NetWare 5 on various computers in his organization. Logon security will be an issue. Also, Zac needs to automate the logon process for the computers so the users are able to access applications and printers.

1. Zac is attempting to install NetWare Client 32 software on the computers. What operating systems can support Client 32 software? Choose all that apply.

A. DOS/Windows 3.1

B. OS/2

C. Microsoft Windows 95/98

D. Microsoft Windows NT 4

2. What are the methods Zac can use to install Client 32 on a workstation? Choose all that apply.

A. Zac can install Client 32 over the network in attended mode.

B. Zac can install Client 32 from Novell's Web site.

C. He can install Client 32 over the network in unattended mode.

D. He can use the NetWare 5 installation CD.

exam
ⓦatch

The four components needed to supply client access to NetWare's ODI specification are, in this order, MLID, LSLC32.NLM, IPX.NLM/IPHLPR.NLM, and CLIENT32.NLM.

3. What optional components can Zac load on a Windows 95 Client 32? Choose all that apply.

A. Novell Workstation Manager

B. Novell Distributed Print Services (NDPS)

C. Novell SNMP Agent

D. Novell Remote Server Agent

4. Todd is going on vacation and Zac wants to make sure nobody can log on using Todd's User name. What should Zac do to implement this?

A. Zac should disable the group to which Todd belongs.

B. He should delete the Todd User and recreate the User when Todd comes back from his vacation.

C. Zac should limit the number of concurrent sessions Todd has to one.

D. Zac should disable Todd's User object.

5. Zac has set the network address for a user named TM. The following illustration gives a sample screenshot of the network address restrictions for this user. From which protocols and workstation nodes can this user log on? Choose all that apply.

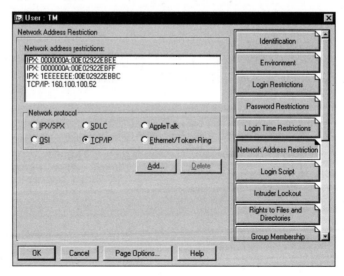

A. The user can log on from all workstations.

B. The user can use the TCP/IP protocol and log on from any machine except the one with IP address 160.100.100.52.

C. The user can log on to a server running IPX as long as the user is logging on from the node with the address of 00E02922EBEE on network address A.

D. The user can log on to a server from network address B from a node with the address 00E02922EBFF.

6. What installation file installs Netscape Navigator's Web browser?

A. N32E404.COM

B. N32E404.EXE

C. INSTALL.COM

D. NWADMIN.EXE

QUESTIONS AND ANSWERS

Justine is the administrator of a NetWare 5 network. She has created a Profile script that runs a CAPTURE command for the Graphics Department's color laser printer. Justine then assigns the Profile script to the users within the Graphics Department. There is no Container script or User script being run. When Justine tests the script, she gets an error that the external command CAPTURE cannot be executed. CAPTURE is in the Public directory, and when Justine checks, there is a mapping to SYS:PUBLIC. Why does she get this error and how can she fix it?

Justine was depending on the default login script to provide the mapping to the Public directory. However, because the Profile script executes before the default login script, it did not have a mapping to SYS:PUBLIC when it was trying to find the CAPTURE command. In order to fix this, Justine can add the Search drive mapping to the Profile script. Or, to prevent errors like this from happening in the future, she can place the commands she wants to have in the Container script for all users and add the NO DEFAULT line so that the default script will not run for users in that container.

Managing User Accounts

Refer to the Following Scenario for Questions 1–6

Todd is a LAN Manager for a small firm. He must set up users accounts for all the employees in Meadors Enterprises Incorporated. There are 125 users who work in Production, Accounting, Sales and Engineering. The user objects must reside in the correct container in the NDS tree.

1. Todd is attempting to create a user object in the top level [Root] object. He is running into problems doing this. Why is he getting a problem creating the user object?

   A. Todd can create a user object only in an Organization.
   B. Todd can create a user object only in another leaf object.
   C. Todd cannot create a user object in [Root].
   D. Todd has no permissions to create the user object.

2. At Meadors Enterprise Incorporated, there are three shifts that work in the Production department. The users need logon access only during their shift. Todd needs to add 25 users with first-shift hours, 20 users with second-shift hours, and 10 users with third-shift hours. What is the most efficient method Todd could use to create this many users and fulfill their shift hour requirements?

   A. Todd should assign them all a group by adding all the users as members of the group.
   B. Todd should create separate containers for each of the shifts and add the users to each of the container objects.
   C. Todd should set up a user template object for each shift, which has the logon time hours defined for that shift. Then, he could create the user objects by using the user template.
   D. Todd should set up a user template object for each user. Then, the logon time hours could be defined for that user template object. The user will then be able to log on using the user template object.

3. Todd is trying to add licenses to the NetWare 5 server. What is the name of the program that allows him to add a license?

A. NLS.EXE

B. NLSMAN32.EXE

C. NDS Partition Manager

D. NetAdmin

4. Todd and a coworker are discussing the types of network security available in Novell. What are the types of NetWare network security? Choose all that apply.

A. Server security

B. Logon security

C. File system security

D. NDS object security

E. Workstation security

QUESTIONS AND ANSWERS

Jeff is from Phoenix and is visiting the New York branch office. He borrows a workstation that is set to access the New York context. Jeff tries to log on the same way he does in the Phoenix office, by inputting his username and password. The login fails. Why?	The NDS tree looked for Jeff's ID in the borrowed workstation's context, but Jeff's ID is located in the Phoenix context. The Phoenix user must know his user account's context for the login program to find it in NDS.

5. MEI is hiring 20 temporary workers that will work in their production department. They will only work for three months. What should Todd do in order to make sure the users' accounts are no longer valid after the three months?

A. Todd should require a unique password for each user.

B. Todd should check the Account Disabled box for each temporary user.

C. Todd should set an expiration date on the user accounts.

D. Todd should limit the number of concurrent restrictions.

exam
Ⓦatch   *A distinguished name will always be able to find a resource regardless of the current context.*

6. MEI is expanding and will have a new department called Customer Service. The company will hire 50 employees in this new department. From a security standpoint, what are the best options for him to use in order to give all 50 users similar access rights to a container or folder? Choose all that apply.

A. He should create access rights using a user template and set the group membership on the user property sheet.

B. He should create a group and then trustee rights to the group.

C. He must use NetWare Administrator to manually add all the user property information.

D. He should make sure their account balance is not too high.

exam
Ⓦatch   *User objects cannot be created in the [Root] object.*

QUESTIONS AND ANSWERS

Jane created a User object in the NDS tree. She named the object JL4788, which was the end user's employee ID. The user's name is Taylor Meyer. Jane instructed Taylor to log on as Tmeyer, but Taylor was unable to log on. What went wrong?	Jane had named the User object JL4788. In NDS, the name of the User object is the login name. Jane can either instruct Taylor to log on as JL4788, or rename the User object to Tmeyer.

Managing Network Printing

1. What are the objects used to implement network printing? Choose all that apply.

  A. Print Queue object

  B. Print Server object

  C. Print Volume object

  D. Printer object

exam
Ⓦatch

A NetWare print queue object represents a subdirectory under the volume_name:QUEUES\ directory, which gets created when the first Queue object is created. The individual queue directories are assigned hexadecimal numbers as directory names so they may appear as seemingly random numerals and letters.

2. In order for a client computer to use a network printer that is attached to a server, what must occur at the client?

  A. The local printer port on the client must be assigned to the Print Server object.

  B. The client computer must be running NPTWIN95.EXE.

  C. The local printer port on the client must be captured.

  D. The local printer port must have a printer attached to it.

QUESTIONS AND ANSWERS

Taylor has created an automated installation for the NetWare Client 32 that specifies some of the default settings for printers, including a banner page and notification for users. She then automatically updates all workstations through the addition of an ACU Setup command in the login script. A few days after the clients are updated, Taylor receives a complaint from a user that he has captured a printer and reconfigured the capture settings for the banner and notification, but each time he logs in, the capture settings go back to where they were. What's going on?

Taylor had configured the default capture settings for the client. When the files installed, they updated the user's workstation settings. The default capture settings are inherited by each new print capture performed at the workstation. The only way to change this for the user is to have him go into the Default Capture settings page for the NetWare Client 32 properties and change to the preferred settings there.

3. What are the parts of the NDPS broker? Choose all that apply.

    A. Service Registry Service (SRS)
    B. Event Notification Service (ENS)
    C. Novell Directory Services (NDS)
    D. Resource Management Service (RMS)

QUESTIONS AND ANSWERS

Justine is an engineer who is migrating an Enterprise network from a mixed legacy NetWare 3.x and NetWare 4.x network to NetWare 5. The internetwork includes an Ethernet segment that historically performs poorly during main business hours. Justine notes that this segment includes a large number of printers and decides to migrate the servers that manage those printers first. Why would she decide to do this?

Justine knew that in migrating the servers, she could also migrate the printers to NDPS and immediately receive a performance bonus on that segment of the network since NDPS does not need to use SAP, whereas legacy printing is known to consume excess traffic due to SAP usage.

4. What must be done in order to set up NDPS? Choose all that apply.

A. The NDPS files must be installed on a NetWare server.

B. The NDPS files must be installed on a networked printer.

C. The printers must be set up and shared at a workstation.

D. INSTALL.NLM must be loaded on the NetWare 5 server.

exam
ⓦatch   *The NDPS NLMs, as well as most of the NLM files for NetWare, are stored in the SYS:SYSTEM directory or in the C:\NWSERVER directory. The server will search the NWSERVER and SYSTEM directories first for NLMs. If an NLM is moved to another directory, the LOAD command must include the path to the NLM file. Or the administrator can execute a SEARCH ADD <volume:path> command on the console so that all subsequent LOAD commands will also search that path for the NLM file before reporting that the file is not found.*

5. What are the names of the NLMs that run on the server? Choose all that apply.

A. BROKER

B. MODULES

C. NDPSM

D. RSPX

QUESTIONS AND ANSWERS

Dan, the CEO, calls up Cheryl, his network administrator, and explains that he was in the Windows 95 Explorer and pressed the Delete key when he meant to press the Home key. Now, all his files in his home directory have disappeared. Dan is worried that all his data is gone and that he won't be able to get it back before his meeting in half an hour because he knows it takes much longer than that to restore data from tape. What can Cheryl do to reassure Dan?	Cheryl can tell Dan that she will run FILER and salvage his deleted files. It should take her no more than a few minutes.

Managing the File System

1. What is the name of the file system management utility that allows you to search for NDS objects and also show volume information?

A. NLIST

B. CX

C. VOLUMES

D. WHOAMI

2. What is the Windows-based utility that allows you to administer the NDS objects, files, and folders?

A. NWCONFIG

B. NetWare Administrator

C. LOGIN

D. NDIR

Refer to the Following Scenario for Questions 3–5

Mack is a network administrator who has several users who need access to an application called TOUR on a Novell server named BOSS. The TOUR.EXE program is stored on a folder called SOUTH, on a volume called APPS.

3. The users Mack supports need to have a search drive mapped to the folder in which SOUTH is located. The search drive needs to be added at the end of the current search-drive list. What is the command-line syntax to accomplish this?

A. MAP NEXT BOSS\APPS:\SOUTH

B. MAP INS S16:=BOSS\APPS:\SOUTH

C. MAP S1:=BOSS\APPS:\SOUTH

D. MAP DEL BOSS\APPS:\SOUTH

<table>
<tr><td>exam
ⓦatch</td><td>Directories can be restricted from growing in size by checking the Restrict Size check box in the directory's Facts property page and then typing in the maximum size the directory should reach.</td></tr>
</table>

4. Now, Mack wants to create a regular drive mapping to the folder where TOURS.EXE is located. What command would do this for Mack?

A. MAP NEXT BOSS\APPS:\SOUTH

B. MAP INS S16:=BOSS\APPS:\SOUTH

C. MAP S1:=BOSS\APPS:\SOUTH

D. MAP DEL BOSS\APPS:\SOUTH

5. Mack notices many users are downloading files from the Internet and placing them on the APPS volume. What proactive approach should he take in order to minimize this problem?

A. He should set a search drive mapping.

B. He should delete all the files each time the users download files.

C. He should restrict a user's volume-space usage.

D. He should delete the user's account.

QUESTIONS AND ANSWERS

Jesse was browsing through her Network Neighborhood and attempted to execute the GLOW.EXE file. The file returned an error that the BRITE.DLL could not be found, but Jesse can see the BRITE.DLL file in the GLO directory. What can Jesse do to fix this problem?	The GLOW program requires the ability to search its local drive for the BRITE.DLL by referencing the current drive letter. To make the GLOW.EXE file execute, Jesse can map a drive.

Managing File System Security

Refer to the Following Scenario for Questions 1–6

Zac Meadors is a Network Administrator who works for a small firm. The firm is concerned about security and Zac has the job of implementing security for the departments.

1. Ralph has Read and File Scan rights to a folder called Payroll on a server called Accounting. Zac wants to also give Ralph the Write, Create, and Erase rights to this folder. Zac's NDS context is in the container with Ralph's username. What command should he type to give Ralph these additional rights?

   A. RIGHTS PAYROLL WCE /NAME=RALPH

   B. RIGHTS PAYROLL +WCE

   C. RIGHTS PAYROLL +WCE /NAME=RALPH

   D. RIGHTS WCE PAYROLL /NAME=ZAC

---

exam
ⓦatch

The minimal rights required to both list files and execute them are Read and File Scan. In order to remember the trustee rights, remember the words FEW SCRAM. F-file scan E-erase W-write S-supervisor C-create R-read A-access control M-modify.

---

2. Zac is working on the Help Desk and he gets a call from a customer. The customer is trying to create a folder in a directory and is getting an Access Denied error. Zac finds that the user has Read and File Scan rights. What additional right is needed to be able to make a directory?

   A. Access Control

   B. Rename Inhibit

   C. Create

   D. Write

3. Zac also supports Mary who is an employee in the Production department. In the following file-system structure, Mary is a member of the Production group and both user and group trustee assignments have been made by Zac. What are Mary's effective rights to the folder called ProjectB?

```
\   (DOS root)
|____ Projects          Inherited from above:   [          ]
   |          IRF:                          [SRWCEMFA]
   |          Mary:                         [ RW    F ]
   |          Effective Rights:             [ RW    F ]
   |__ProjectB Inherited from above:        [ RW    F ]
              IRF:                          [SRWCEMFA]
              Mary:                [ R    F ]
              Production:          [  WCEM  ]
              Effective Rights:    [   ?    ]
```

A. WCEM

B. RF

C. SRWCEMFA

D. RWCEMF

When planning rights to the file system, keep in mind how inheritance works. It is best not to grant users rights at the root of a volume or high-level directory. Granting users rights at a lower level is easier to control when adding directories later on. Give each trustee only the rights needed at each level.

---

4. A user attempts to delete a file using the DOS DEL command. She gets an error indicating she cannot. What right should Zac give the user in order to allow the user to remove the file?

A. Delete

B. Erase

C. Access Control

D. Modify

exam
ⓌatcH
Security equivalence is not transferable; e.g., if User Bob has been made a trustee of the SYS:ANSEU directory with Read, Write, Create, Erase, Modify and File scan [-RWCEMF-] rights granted, and User Tom has been granted only Read and File scan [-R----F-] rights, and is later made Security Equivalent to User Bob, then Tom gets [-RWCEMF-] rights. If User Bruce is made Security Equivalent to Tom, Bruce does not get the same rights to SYS:ANSEU, as Bob [-RWCEMF-], he gets the same rights as Tom, [-R----F-], because those were the rights granted to the trustee Tom.

5. Zac has hired a new employee, Jack, to help him out. Jack recently went to a NetWare Administration class and is a little confused about file system security rights and attributes. Which of the following are attributes? Choose all that apply.

   A. Copy Inhibit
   B. Rename Inhibit
   C. Erase
   D. Modify
   E. Purge

exam
ⓌatcH
Effective rights are calculated from the explicitly granted rights, plus those granted through security equivalence, group membership, and container membership, plus those inherited from upper directories minus those filtered by the IRF. The NetWare exams always include a couple of questions about determining the effective rights of users and planning the rights for the NetWare file system.

6. Zac and Jack are discussing the purpose of the Inherited Rights Filter (IRF). What could you tell them?

A. The IRF equals your effective rights.

B. The IRF is what is used to set trustee assignments.

C. The IRF can be used to block inherited rights.

D. The IRF blocks attributes.

QUESTIONS AND ANSWERS

Stephanie is an administrator of a NetWare network. She has a group of graphics design users that print very large files. Whenever Stephanie wants to salvage a file, she finds that only the most recently deleted files are available to be salvaged. When she browses through the files, she finds many extremely large files available in the Queues directory. What can Stephanie do to manage her file system?

Stephanie can flag the Queues directory to be purged immediately. This will keep the large print jobs from taking up space in the deleted files area in the NetWare file system.

Creating Login Scripts

1. If you wanted to have a login script execute only for one person, what type of login script would be used?

A. Single reference time server

B. User

C. Group

D. Container

2. What statement will prevent the default login script from being executed?

A. DO_NO_RUN_DEFAULT

B. NO_DEFAULT

C. USER_LOGIN_SCRIPT_ONLY

D. STOP_RUN

Refer to the Following Scenario for Questions 3–6

Scott is on a team of network engineers that is building login scripts for a set of users. They will create container profile and user login scripts. They have an Organization called MEADORS-CORP and several Organizational Units called Accounting, Information Technology (It), Sales, and Engineering.

3. Scott needs to show a reminder document to all users each Friday. The document is located on SERVER_A\SYS:PUBLIC\REMIND.TXT. How should he construct his login script?

A. He should use an IF test for the day of the week and use the DIR command to display REMIND.TXT.

B. He should use the WRITE command to display the document each Friday.

C. He should use an IF test for the day of the week and use the FDISPLAY command to show the document on the screen.

D. He should use the CASE statement and use the CAT command to see the document.

exam
ⓦatch

Knowing which directories are mapped in the default login script is critical to designing effective container and profile login scripts. If there is a drive letter conflict between the different login scripts, then the last executed script will determine which directory path gets mapped.

4. Scott wants a login script to add a search drive mapping to the SERVER_A\VOL2:APPS2\SALES folder. This needs to be appended to the end of the current drive mappings. What statement should he place in a login script in order for this mapping to take place?

A. MAP INS S1:=SERVER_A\VOL2:APPS2\SALES

B. MAP ROOT SERVER_A\VOL2:APPS2\SALES

C. MAP NEXT SERVER_A\VOL2:APPS2\SALES

D. MAP INS S16:=SERVER_A\VOL2:APPS2\SALES

QUESTIONS AND ANSWERS

Stacy is designing a login script system for an enterprise network, and has decided to utilize only the container script. She has a requirement to make sure that no one has drive mappings to the SYS: volume through the login script. Stacy creates a short container script that consists of one line: MAP R:=VOL1:GROUP, and then she tests it. When she types the MAP command at the prompt, she sees that the F: and Z: drives have been mapped to SYS:. What can Stacy do to meet the requirement to not map drives to SYS?

The extra SYS: drive mappings are from the default login script. Stacy needs to add the NO_DEFAULT command to the container script to avoid executing the default script.

5. Scott wants to be able to alter the sound that the FIRE PHASERS command uses when it executes in a GUI environment. What must he do?

A. He must replace PHASERS.WAV with the sound file of choice.

B. He must use the NO_DEFAULT statement.

C. He must add PHASERS.WAV to his login script using the # sign.

D. He must create a batch file and place the entry FIRE PHASERS in the batch file.

e x a m

ⓦatch *Login script variables, such as %HOME_DIRECTORY or %DAY_OF_WEEK, are used to extend the way a container script can be used. Usually, each user is granted a home directory that is completely separate from all other users' home directories. In order to map each home directory correctly, the administrator can use the %HOME_DIRECTORY variable with the MAP command in the container login script.*

6. Scott needs to make every user aware of the expiration date of their password each time they log on. He does not have the time to call each and every user. How could he distribute this information to each user in the company?

   A. Send them a post card in the mail.
   B. E-mail them each day.
   C. Create a login script that uses the %PASSWORD_EXPIRES variable.
   D. Create a login script that uses the %LAST_NAME variable.

QUESTIONS AND ANSWERS

Jenny has just completed a course in network administration and has decided to create a new login script that contains the following line:

`#MAP R G:=SYS:PUBLIC.`

The login script executes, but instead of a smooth drive mapping within the login window, a DOS window pops up. Why?

Jenny has erroneously invoked the external MAP command instead of the login script version. She should remove the # sign from the MAP statement.

Remote Management
of Workstations (NEBO)

I. Concerning NEBO, what can you say about security, bandwidth, and ease of use? Choose all that apply.

A. Users do not need appropriate rights.

B. NEBO uses a tremendous amount of bandwidth.

C. NEBO is easy to use.

D. NEBO uses little bandwidth.

E. Users do need appropriate rights in order to access it.

QUESTIONS AND ANSWERS

Heather has installed Z.E.N.works to a server located in .OU=ACCT.OU=LON.O=MA. When she was prompted for the container, she selected that server's container, then completed the installation. When Heather added the WSREG32.EXE file to the login script, her end users in the .OU=ENG.OU=LON.O=MA container complained that they were receiving errors during login. Why?

Heather did not run the WSRIGHTS.EXE file or the Prepare Workstation Registration utility from NetWare Administrator on the .ENG.LON.MA context.

2. What is the name of the command that registers a Windows 3.1x workstation?

A. WSRIGHTS.EXE

B. WSREG32.EXE

C. WSREG16.EXE

D. NWADMIN.EXE

The NTASCFG.EXE file is the installation file for the Novell WUser Service in NT. It can be found in the NT Control Panel Services icon, and runs at the operating system initialization.

3. What is the name of the Remote Control Agent service that is loaded for a Windows NT workstation?

A. WUSER.EXE

B. NAL.EXE

C. NTSTACFG.EXE

D. CX

4. What is the executable that runs the Help Request application on a Windows 95 workstation?

A. HLPREQ16.EXE

B. HLPREQ32.EXE

C. NTASCFG.EXE

D. WUSER.EXE

5. What is the process that synchronizes the workstation and the NDS workstation object?

A. Workstation import

B. Workstation registration

C. Remote-control agent

D. Help Request application

Configuring Network Applications for Users

1. What is meant by pushing an application in NAL?

A. When you push an application, you are setting up security at the workstation.

B. When you push an application, you are installing an application over the network by requiring user input to the application.

C. When you push an application, you are installing an application over the network to a workstation in an unattended fashion.

D. Pushing an application is setting the context in NDS.

2. What is the purpose of the snAppShot program?

A. To push an application to a user's desktop

B. To pull an application to a user's desktop

C. To create a baseline of a workstation before and after an application has been installed

D. It is only used to take a picture of a workstation after an application has been installed.

---

e x a m
Ⓦa t c h   *An .AOT file is an Application Object Template written in binary format and created by snAppShot. An .AOT file represents the changes made to the configuration files of a workstation during an applications installation.*

---

3. What is the difference between a simple and a complex application? Choose all that apply.

A. Simple applications don't require snAppShot to be run.

B. Simple applications do require snAppShot to be run.

C. Complex applications don't require snAppShot to be run.

D. Complex applications do require snAppShot to be run.

exam

Ⓦatch *snAppShot performs a baseline discovery, the application installation, a post-installation discovery, and a comparison of the discoveries, and writes an .AOT file with the configuration changes.*

4. What are the two NAL objects in the NDS schema? Choose all that apply.

   A. Application executables
   B. Application folders
   C. Application objects
   D. Application icons

exam

Ⓦatch *When an application is associated with a container object, or with a Group object, any user objects added later as members of the container object or the group automatically are granted access to the network application object through inheritance.*

5. What rights are needed to execute NAL? Choose all that apply.

   A. Read
   B. Write
   C. Execute
   D. File Scan
   E. Supervisor

QUESTIONS AND ANSWERS

An end-user has called the network administrator and complained that her workstation is running an application on startup and it is hanging her PC. How can the administrator check for the application that is running, and how can he fix it?

After checking the login scripts, the administrator would open NetWare Administrator and highlight the user object, then select Tools | Application Launcher Tools | Show Inherited Applications. The administrator would look for applications that are shown in the Force Run area for each container. Then, the administrator would open the User object and select the Launcher Configuration property page. The administrator would edit the Set Application Inheritance Level option to a number that does not reach the container level that has the offending application object in it, or to a 0 to avoid all application objects.

Read and File Scan rights are required to execute NAL.EXE.
NAL is installed to the SYS:PUBLIC directory by default during
Z.E.N.works installation.

QUESTIONS AND ANSWERS

Tyler has implemented NAL on his network, and has created a container login script with the line: NAL /C="NetWare Secured Programs for Tyler". An error occurs with the line, and when Tyler fixes that error he finds that everyone has his name on his or her title bar. What did Tyler do to fix the original error, and how can he fix the name problem?

Tyler realized that NAL was not being executed as an external command. He changed the line to @\\SERVER\SYS\PUBLIC\NAL /C="NetWare Secured Programs for Tyler". In order to change the name problem, Tyler should write the following command: @\\SERVER\SYS\PUBLIC\NAL /C="NetWare Secured Programs for %FULL_NAME".

Using Workstation Manager to Manage Workstations

1. Which policy will allow you to configure the protocol and components of a Novell Client?

   A. Novell login configuration

   B. Novell Client configuration

   C. Workstation inventory

   D. NT computer system policies

QUESTIONS AND ANSWERS

Jerry is a network administrator for two business units within a large network environment. Both of the business units exist in a single container, of which Jerry is the sole administrator. The network planning group is implementing Workstation Manager and has distributed a policy to Jerry that all workstations must use the business unit as part of the workstation's name to comply with the naming standards. They have asked Jerry to implement Workstation Manager. Jerry wants to create a separate container for one of the business units, move all the user objects, and change the context on their workstations. Is this necessary, and why or why not?

No, it is not necessary to create another container. Jerry can implement Workstation Manager through two user policy packages, one created for each business unit. He can associate the packages to the appropriate users. In each user policy package, he would create a workstation import policy with a custom naming convention using the business unit name. Then, Jerry would create a login script to register workstations upon a user's login. The import process would pull the correct naming convention from the workstation import policy.

2. Which statements are true? Choose all that apply.

A. A user policy package will follow a user who moves around on the network.

B. A workstation policy package will follow a user who moves around on the network.

C. A user policy package will be applied to the same workstation regardless of what user logs on.

D. A workstation policy package will be applied to the same workstation regardless of what user logs on.

QUESTIONS AND ANSWERS

Gail is planning an upgrade of all seven NetWare 4.11 servers to NetWare 5, the addition of twelve new NetWare 5 servers, and a full Z.E.N.works installation. This upgrade and these additions will include a full redesign of the NDS tree; no user will be in the same context. Gail is not sure whether she should implement Z.E.N.works with Workstation Manager first, or as part of the server upgrade. What will Gail gain by implementing Z.E.N.works first?

If Gail implements Z.E.N.works first, the installation of the clients and the importing of the workstations objects can all be done through the login script. When the servers are upgraded and the tree redesigned, the Novell client configuration policy for the workstations can automatically push out the new context to the workstations.
An alias in the old context can help the first login for users in order to implement the new context through the workstation Novell client configuration policy. If Gail does not implement Z.E.N.works first, she may have to visit each of the workstations to make the changes.

3. What is the best way to configure the user's desktop on Windows NT so he can move around to different machines and still get the same desktop appearance?

A. Go into the Registry on a Windows 95 or Windows NT machine and change the HKEY_LOCAL_MACHINE hive to mobile computing.

B. Go to each NT machine and create a user profile for that user.

C. Change the User policy package in the Desktop Preferences policy and create a roaming user profile.

D. Change NTCONFIG.POL to NTCONFIG.MAN.

---

exam
Ⓦatch

The workstation inventory policy schedules when the inventory updates will be sent to Novell Directory Services. All inventory information is stored within the Workstation objects.

---

4. What is true about scheduling actions for users and workstations? Choose all that apply.

A. When an action is scheduled for a user, it applies no matter what workstation that user logs on to.

B. An action is scheduled for a workstation only if a user with Supervisor rights logs on to the workstation.

C. When an action is scheduled for a user, it only applies to the workstation defined in the system policy file.

D. When an action is scheduled for a workstation, it applies no matter what users logs on.

---

exam
Ⓦatch

When an action is scheduled for a user, it will apply to that user wherever the user logs in on the network. When an action is scheduled for a workstation, it will apply to the workstation, regardless of which user logs in.

---

5. How would a user be configured so that a user account will be created temporarily and removed when the user logs out?

    A. Create an NTUSER.DAT file for the user.

    B. Check the Enable Dynamic Local User box on the Windows NT.

    C. Check the Use NetWare credentials and then the Volatile User boxes.

    D. Check the Use NetWare credentials only.

Managing NDS Security

1. What term describes an object that has been granted a right to another object?

    A. RIGHTS.EXE

    B. Trustee

    C. Container

    D. Property right

e x a m

ⓦ a t c h   *The administrator can change object rights by selecting either "Rights to Other Objects" or "Trustees of this Object." The Rights to Other Objects will show the NDS rights that the current object has granted to other objects in the tree. The Trustees of this Object will display the objects that have been granted rights to the currently selected object in the tree.*

2. What NDS object right allows a user to have complete control over an object?

    A. Supervisor

    B. Rename

    C. Create

    D. Delete

By default, NDS objects are not automatically granted full rights to their own properties.

3. What trustee is equivalent by default to the security of all users?

   A. The user template

   B. Their parent container

   C. Their volume object

   D. [Public]

QUESTIONS AND ANSWERS

Janet is the network administrator for an aeronautical design firm. The research and development business unit of the firm works on some projects that are considered top secret within the company. Janet has been informed that all resources within the R&D organizational unit are to be hidden from all other users. How can Janet achieve this but still be able to manage it herself?

The R&D organiztional unit will require Browse object rights and Supervisor object rights (since it implies the Browse right) to be filtered for all objects in the tree. Before filtering the Browse right, Janet will need to explicitly grant her own User object the Browse and Supervisor rights to that container unit.

4. You are going on vacation and you want one of the staff members to have the same permissions you have. They need to be able to perform your same job functions. What is the best thing you can do to give the user the same job function?

A. Give them your user name and password.

B. Make them security equivalent to you.

C. Disable your account but create a special account for them.

D. Make an explicit trustee assignment for every object to which you have rights.

---

exam
ⓦatch

Effective rights = (inherited rights – IRF) + explicit trustee assignments + security equivalence rights.

---

5. What is true about a trustee's effective rights? Choose all that apply.

A. Effective rights must account for the IRF.

B. Effective rights must account for trustee assignments.

C. Effective rights do not need to account for group trustee assignments.

D. Effective rights must account for security equivalence.

QUESTIONS AND ANSWERS

Marian is a network administrator who has been tasked with ensuring that the printers on F3 are not able to be seen by any users except those on that floor. However, both Marian and the president on Floor2 need supervisor access to the printer. The NDS tree has two organizational units beneath the SEC organization: EastBldg and WestBldg. Beneath EastBldg, there are three organizational units: Floor1, Floor2, and Floor3. Beneath WestBldg, there are three organizational units: Basement, Floor1, and Floor2. How can Marian set this up?

Marian granted the Floor3.EastBldg.SEC container object explicit Browse rights to the Printer objects. Since all users within the container object are implied security equivalent, they were able to access the printers. Marian also created a group that contained her own User object and the president's User object, and granted explicit Browse and Supervisor rights to the printers. Finally, Marian created an IRF on each Printer object that filtered out the Browse object rights.

Managing Resources in a Multicontext Environment

1. What are the main types of objects you can create in NDS? Choose all that apply.

   A. Container objects
   B. [Root] objects
   C. Leaf objects
   D. Last Name property objects

---

exam
Ⓦatch   *Volume objects and Group objects are not containers; they are leaf objects. [Root] is not a container either; it is the demarcation between the NDS tree and the rest of the world. The only container objects are Country, Organization, and Organizational Unit; this is a point of confusion for most students and can cause incorrect answers on Novell tests.*

---

2. Which of the following items are appropriate to review when planning your NDS directory tree? Choose all that apply.

   A. The number of leaf objects
   B. The number of container objects
   C. The number of [Root] objects
   D. The grouping of NDS objects

---

exam
Ⓦatch   *Context and the immediate parent container of the object are synonymous. It should also be stressed that both leaf and container objects have a context. Some students walk away with the notion that only leaf objects can have a context.*

---

3. What facility is used for the new feature in NetWare 5 that allows you to log on by simply typing in the user name and password and not having to enter the user's context?

A. Distinguished Name

B. Catalog Services

C. Context Service Management

D. Simple Login Management Services

exam
ⓦatch

This concept is critical to understand correctly. A common classroom analogy is stated like this: "Current context is like perspective, it is your view of where other objects are in relation to your current position. In other words, think of how you give directions to 123 Main if you were standing at 345 Main, versus if you were standing at 678 Elm and you had to give instruction in terms of left or right turns and distance only."

4. Which of the following statements is true regarding leading and trailing dots on an NDS name?

A. Leading dots are required on distinguished names and trailing dots are required on distinguished names; this indicates they begin at [Root].

B. Trailing dots are required on distinguished names and on relative distinguished names; leading dots are only required on relative distinguished names.

C. Leading dots are required on distinguished names, meaning they begin at [Root]. Trailing dots are only used on relative distinguished names.

D. Trailing dots are required on distinguished names, meaning they begin at [Root]. Leading dots are only used on relative distinguished names.

exam
ⓦatch

To keep the various naming concepts straight, remember this formula: Relative Distinguished Name + Current Context = Distinguished Name.

5. Jane works in the HQ office, located in Claxton, Georgia, and uses the HQ office most often. However, she needs occasional access to three branch offices, which have printers located in geographically dispersed cities. The branch offices are located in Macon, Lawrenceville, and Warner Robbins, Georgia. Assuming each city has an NDS Organizational Unit by the same name, in what context should her User object be located?

A. Claxton

B. Macon

C. Lawrenceville

D. Warner Robbins

---

e x a m
Ⓦa t c h

Naming concepts and dots can be somewhat confusing, so be sure you are clear on this for the exam. For the exam you may see at least one, maybe even two questions in regards to naming concepts. Review this material and make sure you understand the naming concepts. You will be asked, for example, which of the following is the Typeful Distinguished Name for user JSMITH. Then you will be given a directory tree to look at and some choices to choose from. Use the scratch paper you are given during the exam to draw out the complete name on paper if that is easier for you.

---

6. What is wrong with the entry in the following logon script?

```
#CAPTURE S=PRINT_Server.Payroll.Meadors-Corp
Q=Print_que.Payroll.Meadors-Corp
```

A. It does not need the name of the print queue.

B. It is not a distinguished name because the leading dot is missing.

C. It does not need the dots between the object levels.

D. It does not use typeful names and they are required.

exam
ⓦatch

Profile login scripts tend to confuse many people, especially those who have NetWare 3.x experience. Profile login scripts are a way to add additional login script commands for selected users. A profile login script can be used by multiple users who are not members of the same group.

Performing a Simple Installation

Refer to the Following Scenario for Questions 1–5

Todd is a LAN Manager whose job it is to install NetWare 5. His company receives the computers, his department loads NetWare 5 on them and ships them out to remote sites for the company. They also have an internal LAN that must be supported. The internal LAN has a 100BaseT network connected with 100 MBps hubs, and the cabling is Category 5.

1. James is installing NetWare 5 on a server that has 45MB of RAM available and a low processor speed. What type of installation will be used?

A. GUI

B. Text

C. Custom

D. Typical

2. James is installing a server and has a question about the default volume. What is the name and purpose of the default volume created during installation time?

A. The default volume is called VOL: and is used to hold the system files.

B. The default volume is SYS and is used to hold the DOS partition.

C. The default volume is SYS: and is used to hold system files.

D. The default volume is APPS and is used to hold application files.

The GUI installation looks at processor speed and RAM. If your processor does not rate at least a 1500, and you do not have a minimum of 47 MB of RAM, the server installation program runs only in text mode.

3. Todd is working on a computer that needs to connect to the Internet and also needs to connect to another internal server running Novell's native protocol. Todd just received a page from a customer and had to go help out. Todd instructs James to go ahead and install the server using the protocol(s) required. What protocols should James install to meet the connectivity needs of the Internet and of the internal Novell server?

   A. James should load IPX only.
   B. James should load IP only.
   C. James should load both IP and IPX.
   D. James should load NetBEUI.

QUESTIONS AND ANSWERS

I have the minimum amount of RAM and I want to increase performance.	Set your volume block size to a larger limit.
I only have 32 MB of RAM.	You need a minimum of 64 MB to install the server.
The server installation did not detect all of my hardware.	Supply the driver from the device manufacturer.

4. James and Todd have a computer that will be a print server in the company's current environment. This server will take some of the burden off one of the other servers. When installing this computer in the current environment, what should they do? Choose all that apply.

A. The computer will need a network adapter and the TP cable should connect to a hub that is on the network.

B. They should not connect this computer in the current local network.

C. They should install IPX.

D. They should install this server in the existing NDS tree.

---

exam
ⓦatch

By default NetWare 5 sets a compatibility mode. This allows IPX clients to work with an IP server. You can change this option to allow only one protocol.

---

5. James is installing a new computer at his local site. Todd is installing three computers to be shipped to a customer in Perth, Australia. This computer needs to get its time from another server. How should James install this server?

A. James should install this computer in its own NDS tree.

B. James should make this server a single reference time server.

C. James should install this computer in the current NDS tree.

D. James must load the TCP/IP protocol because it will be used to connect to the customer machines in Perth.

NetWare® 5
Administration
Answers

Q & A

T he answers to the questions are in boldface, followed by a brief explanation. Some of the explanations detail the logic you should use to choose the correct answer, while others give factual reasons why the answer is correct. If you miss several questions on a similar topic, you should review the corresponding section in the *CNE® NetWare® 5 Study Guide* before taking the NetWare 5 Administration test.

Introduction to NetWare

1. ☑ **D. NetWare Loadable Modules (NLMs).** NLMs are software programs that only run on the server. These NLMs provide services for various NetWare resources. In Novell® terms, a resource is an object or entity that exists somewhere in the network. Generally, both the service and resource must be available in order for the resource to be actually utilized. An example of a resource is a printer; it is an entity that physically exists on the network. In NetWare 5, the service that allows one to print to the printer is Novell Distributed Printing Services (NDPS). Therefore, in order to print on the printer, the printer must be powered on, contain paper and NDPS must be loaded. On the file server console, you would load the NDPSM.NLM in order to provide NDPS functionality. For example, to load this module on a file server named DEKALBTECH, you would enter the following: LOAD NDPS. You could omit typing in the text LOAD and merely type in the actual NLM name. To run the NDPSM.NLM at a server named DEKALBTECH, enter the following: NDPSM

   ☒ **A.** Virtual Loadable Modules (VLMs) is incorrect because they are a set of software modules that run on a DOS clieNT Workstation. **B.** Dynamic Link Libraries (DLLs) is not correct since DLLs are library routines that get pulled into an executable when it is run. **C.** Network Interface Card (NIC), is completely wrong because the NIC is a piece of hardware that fits into an expansion slot on the PC.

2. ☑ **A. Zero.** NDS™ creates the [Root] object when the initial server is installed. All other objects in the NDS tree stem from this top-level

container object. The [Root] object can contain only Country container objects or Organization container objects. The [Root] container object cannot contain any leaf objects. You can, however, have multiple trees and each tree will have a separate [Root]. There are four different types of container objects: [Root], Country, Organization and Organizational Unit. The [Root] object is the top object in the NDS tree and all others stem from it. There can be only one [Root] object and it is created at server installation time. They cannot contain leaf objects. A Country object represents the various country locations of an organization. It can only be two characters in length and can only be in the [Root] object. Organization objects typically represent the company or organization and are just under the [Root] or Country object. An Organizational Unit container object represents a division or department of a company or organization. Usually, leaf objects are placed in these containers.

☒ **B, C, D.** are incorrect since there can be only one [Root] created for a given NDS tree.

3. ☑ **D.** The User object MickiM is located in the Engineering Organizational Unit. NDS allows you to organize your leaf objects into container objects. The User object, MickiM, is a leaf object and that object is located in the Engineering Organizational Unit container object; the location of an NDS object in the directory tree is called its *context*. MickiM is a child of Engineering, and you can also say that Engineering is the parent container object of the User object MickiM. NDS only allows you to put leaf objects in Organization or Organizational Units objects. You cannot put a leaf object, such as a User object, in the [Root] object. NDS will only allow you to put a Country or an Organization object in the [Root] object.

☒ **A.** Accounting is incorrect because MickiM is not in the Accounting Organizational Unit. Although Accounting can hold User objects, it just so happens that the MickiM User object does not exist in the Accounting Organizational Unit. **B.** [Root] is incorrect since the [Root] object cannot contain any leaf objects. **C.** SSE is wrong because it is not the correct location, or context, for the MickiM object.

4. ☑ **A, B, D.** Attribute, Inheritance, and Subordination are all part of the NDS schema. Also included in the schema is Name information. The NDS schema is the skeleton, or structure, that describes all of the NDS objects that can be contained in an NDS tree. The schema contains the following type of information:

- Attribute information   the property information that is either required or optional about an object. For example, a User object is required to have a Login name and Last name but a Description is optional.

- Inheritance information   describes how rights and properties may be inherited from objects.

- Name information   the actual name of the object used when the object is created.

- Subordination   states that the object is either leaf or container.

☒ **C.** Context is incorrect because the context information is not held within the schema. This is held within the NDS tree. The schema only describes the type of information regarding an object, not the location of the object.

5. ☑ **A.** Property rights allow a trustee to access the values of an object's property. The property rights are: Compare, Read, Write, Add Self, Inheritable and Supervisor. Compare means you can compare the values of two properties. It will return either *true* or *false* indicating whether they are equal or not. Compare will not let you see the values in the properties. Read lets you see the value of a property. Write allows you to change the value of a property. Add Self gives you the ability to add or remove the object from the property list. Inheritable lets object trustees of a container inherit property rights to a container's child objects. Supervisor provides complete control over the properties. Supervisor can be blocked on the IRF for an object. When assigning the property rights, you can select All Properties or choose Selected Properties if you want to selectively make assignments to each property.

☒ **B.** Object is incorrect because Objects rights determine what you can to with the object, not the properties of the object. **C.** Inherited Rights Filter (IRF) is not correct because the IRF is used to filter out unwanted rights from flowing down in the NDS Directory tree. **D.** Effective Rights, is not right because effective rights are the true rights a trustee can use. Effective rights are what you can do after your NDS rights have been passed through the IRF or rights that have been explicitly granted.

Enabling Network Access

1. ☑ **A, B, C, D.** Because NetWare was designed to integrate dissimilar operating systems into a single network, they support other vender client machines. Therefore, Novell has Client 32 bit support for DOS clients, OS/2 clients, and of course, Microsoft Windows 3.1, Microsoft Windows 95, Microsoft Windows 98 and Microsoft Windows NT clients. IBM developed the OS/2 multitasking operating system. This means that all these client machines can access resources on a Novell server. As a matter of fact, you can even access a Novell server from a Windows NT server when it runs Novell's client software. Novell does not make a full-blown version of a client operating system. Instead, they depend upon the client software to already be present and then they allow an administrator to add their client software on top of the client, so to speak. Therefore, all the answers are correct.

2. ☑ **A, C, D.** Zac could install the Client 32 software over the network in attended mode. The NetWare 5 installation CD would be copied to a server directory. He could then boot up a DOS client. The DOS client software will fit on a single floppy. He could attach to the server, get logged on, map a drive to the server's directory that has the installation program and run it from there. Depending upon the traffic and speed of the network, an over-the-network installation could be tremendously faster. He could in also install it over the network in unattended mode. In order to do this, Zac would have to use SETUP /ACU and he may have to edit some configuration files to set PREFERRED SERVER or NAME CONTEXT. The /ACU switch stands

for Automatic Client Update. He could also install with the NetWare 5 installation CD.

☒   **B.** Zac cannot install from Novell's Web site. This is not a method that Novell uses to install software.

3.   ☑   **A, B, C.** Zac can install the Novell Workstation Manager, Novell Distributed Print Servers (NDPS), and the Novell SNMP Agent. The following table lists optional components that can be installed on a Windows 95 Client 32 computer.

Optional component	Description
Novell Workstation Manager	A program for managing user and desktop appearances
Novell Distributed Print Servers (NDPS)	Software new to NetWare 5 that allows real-time communication with network printers
Novell NetWare/IP Protocol	Provides support for NetWare/IP requestor
Novell Simple Network Management Protocol (SNMP)	This agent works on both IPX and IP networks for network monitoring
Novell Resources Management Information Base (MIB)	Allows a console to check on SNMP clients
Network Management Responder (NMR)	Gives operating, BIOS, and other information to the management console
Novell Target Service Agent (TSA)	Allows you to backup client computers
Novell NDS Provider – ADSI	Enables Active Directory Services Interfaces (ADSI) client applications to access the NDS Directory
Novell Remote Control Agent	Allows you to take control of other workstations

☒   **D.** Novell Remote Server Agent is a non-existent piece of software. You can remotely access a server by running the RCONSOLE command on a workstation. You would have to load REMOTE.NLM and RSPX.NLM on the server prior to running RCONSOLE on the workstation. Your workstation then becomes the server console.

4. ☑ **D.** Zac should disable Todd's User object. Zac can effectively handle Todd being on vacation by just disabling Todd's User account. Zac would go into NetWare Administrator and click on the User object. Then he'd go to Login Restrictions and check the Account disabled checkbox. This will prevent anyone, even Todd, from using Todd's account until he gets back from vacation.

☒ **A.** Zac cannot disable the group that Todd belongs to since there is no such mechanism. Anyway, the group is not a User object and nobody can log on using a Group object. **B.** Zac should not delete the User and recreate the User when that user gets back from vacation. This would actually cause more problems. By removing the User object, you would have to recreate other things, such as Login Time Restrictions, Login Script, and other User properties that would have been removed. **C.** Limiting the number of concurrent sessions Todd has to one does not prevent another user from logging on with Todd's User object and password while he's on vacation.

5. ☑ **C, D.** The user can only log on from the protocols, networks, and nodes that are listed in the illustration shown in the question (repeated below). Therefore, the user can log on to an IPX network as long as the network address is A and the node address is 00E02922EBEE. Also, the user can log on to an IPX network as long as it is on network address B and the node is address 00E02922EBFF. The node address is commonly called the hardware address, or the Media Access Control (MAC) address. This fits in Layer 2, the data-link layer, of the OSI model. The node address is placed on the Network Interface Card (NIC) by the card's manufacturer and is held in the card's firmware. You can retrieve the node address and network address for a user by issuing the NLIST USER /A command at a workstation. The network address for an IPX network is created on the server during installation time. It can be found in the AUTOEXEC.NCF file when the IPX protocol is loaded. By the way, the user could also log on to network address 1EEEEEEE from node 02E02922EBBC.

☒ **A.** The user cannot log on to all workstations since there are restrictions here. If the list in the illustration were empty, the user would have no restrictions as to the protocol, network, and node address; they could log on from anywhere. The user can log on to a TCP/IP network from any machine except the one with address 160.100.100.52. **B.** is incorrect because the user can use TCP/IP as long as it has IP address 160.100.100.52.

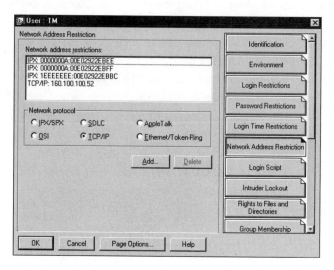

6. ☑ **B.** N32E404.EXE. A Web browser comes on the NetWare 5 CD. This is needed because the Novell documentation now comes on in HyperText Markup Language (HTML) format. So, a Web browser is needed. The steps to install this browser are:

1. Open Network Neighborhood and access the CD-ROM with the NetWare 5 Installation CD.
2. Go to the Products\Netscape\Win32\English folder.
3. Double-click on N32E404.EXE.

☒ **A.** N32E404.COM is the incorrect name due to the COM extension. **C.** INSTALL.COM is incorrect due to the wrong name. **D.** NWADMIN.EXE is the name of the NetWare Administrator utility that is used to manage NDS.

Managing User Accounts

1. ☑   **C.** A user cannot be created in the [Root] container object. It can be created under an Organizational Unit or an Organization. So, Todd cannot create the user object in [Root] because the system will not allow him. In NetWare Administrator, the user object will not be available; it will not even show up as a valid user type that can be created in the [Root].

☒   **A.** Todd can create a user object only in an Organization. This is not correct because a user object can be created in an Organizational Unit and in an Organization. **B.** Todd can create a user object only in another leaf object. This is not correct because no leaf object can be created in another leaf object. A user object is a leaf object, and so it cannot be created in another user object. **D.** Todd has no permissions to create the user object. This is incorrect because Todd is the LAN Manager. Being LAN Manager most likely gives Todd access to the Admin user. This user would have Supervisory rights to any object in NDS by default.

2. ☑   **C.** The most efficient method for Todd to create a large number of users that has characteristics that are identical, such as login time restrictions, is to create a user template. Todd could create a user template for the first shift and have their logon hours set to be Monday–Friday, 8 am–5 pm. The second-shift user template could have logon hours set to Monday–Friday, 3 pm–12 am. The third-shift user template could have logon hours set to 12 am–8 am. When creating the user objects, Todd could just check the check box for User Template, and then click the browse button to locate the template he needed. This way, Todd has to set up the login hours only once. Once the users are created using the user template, the template properties are copied to the new user properties. This saves a lot of time.

☒   **A.** Todd should assign the users to a group. This is incorrect for creating a lot of users with the same property characteristics. However, setting up groups is a useful security tool. You could add the users to a group, assign the group rights to folder, files, or even NDS objects. Using groups is more efficient than assigning a lot of rights to a large number of users. **B.** Todd should create a separate container for each shift and then add the users to each of the containers. This is incorrect for this question. However, setting up a container for each user in the shift is a good idea for managing the user objects in NDS. **D.** Todd should set up a user template object for each user. This is an incorrect answer since a user cannot log on using a user template.

3. ☑ **B.** The name of the utility program that allows one to add a license to NetWare 5 is NLSMAN32.EXE. It is located in the PUBLIC\WIN32 folder. NetWare Licensing Services (NLS) provides the following:

■ Provisions for any products meeting NLS specifications

■ Consistent licensing across Novell products

■ One utility for Novell license management

The program can be run on a 32-bit operating system such as Windows 95 and 98 as well as Windows NT.

☒ **A.** NLS.EXE is not a product. **C.** NDS Partition Manager is a tool that allows you to manage and create NDS partitions. Partitions are created on servers, which will hold a replica or copy of the NDS database. This is used for fault tolerance and performance over a WAN. **D.** NetAdmin is not the correct utility. NetAdmin is used to manage NDS not the license manager.

4. ☑ **A, B, C, D.** Novell NetWare is concerned with all of these types of security. These types of security all share the goal of control over network resources. Server security deals with how accessible is the server. For example, where is the server located? Ideally, the server should be in a room that is kept under lock and key. This would protect it from physical harm. You can access the server from a workstation but you would need to run REMOTE.NLM and RSPX.NLM on the server. You would run RCONSOLE.EXE on the workstation. The REMOTE.NLM requires a password and you would need that password when connecting via RCONSOLE. Therefore, this makes access to the server via a workstation secure. Logon security is concerned with users being able to log on to the server. Examples include login time restrictions,

network address restrictions and password requirement. File system security handles the access a user can have over files and folders. In terms of NDS security, there is object and property security. A trustee is typically a user object that has rights to an object or property. Object security is what a trustee can do with respect to an object. For example, can a user create a user object in a container? Property security is what a trustee can do to the properties of the objects. For example, can a user read the contents of the phone number property of the User object

☒ **E.** Novell does not have a term called workstation security. However, all resources on a network should be subject to scrutiny.

5. ☑ **C.** Todd could set the expiration date on the user accounts for three months. It is a good idea to create a user template and set the expiration date on the template. Then use this template to create all of the other user objects. By expiring the accounts on a certain date, Todd does not have to be concerned with a possible security breach with one of the temporary user accounts.

☒ **A.** It is advisable to require a password for each user; Novell does not require you to give a user a password. However, requiring a password does not limit access to the account after the 3 months. **B.** If Todd checks the Account Disabled box right now, the temporary users will not be able to do any work. **D.** Although limiting the number of concurrent connections is probably a good idea, it says nothing about disabling the user account after three months.

6. ☑ **A, B.** In order to efficiently implement a security scheme for users requiring similar rights, it is best to create a group, add all the users to the group, and make the security assignment to the group. One can implement group-level security with NDS object and property security as well as with file system security. Todd should consider creating the group with the name Customer Service since the group name should represent the department's function. The best way to set this up for all 50 users is to first create the group, then the template, and assign the group to that template. Then, create all the users using the user template by checking the Use user template box and browsing for the template. Then, when all the users are created, they will be members of the group. Finally, add the appropriate group trustee assignments for NDS, and file system security.

☒ **C.** is incorrect because you can use NetWare Administrator to manually create all the property information, including group assignment, but this would be too time consuming. **D.** Making sure the account balance is not too high says nothing about creating group assignments and making trustee group assignments.

Managing Network Printing

1. ☑ **A, B, D.** In order to implement network printing, you must create the following three objects:

   ■ Print Queue object

   ■ Print Server object

   ■ Printer object

   The Print Queue object is the object that represents a folder that takes the name Volume_name:QUEUES\directory, where Volume_name is the name of the volume that is assigned to the queue. The name QUEUES is a default system-assigned name that holds all print-queue directories. The directory is a hexadecimal number that randomly gets assigned to the queue. This is to preserve uniqueness for Print Queue object names. You can have two identically named Print Queue objects as long as they are in different containers. The Print Server object is the workhorse of the printing process. It is executed on the server and the program name is called PSERVER.NLM. The Print Server will look in the Print Queue for jobs ready to print and forward them to the correct Printer object. The Printer object represents the physical print device. If the printer is attached to a workstation, a program called NPRINTER.EXE is executed at the workstation. This tells the Print Server where the print device is physically located. If the printer is attached to a server, NPRINTER.NLM is automatically loaded when PSERVER.NLM is kicked off.

   ☒ **C.** There is no such object as Print Volume object, so this is incorrect.

2. ☑ **C.** In order for a client computer to be able to use a network printer, the local printer port must be captured. Capturing is the process of tricking the local printer port, such as LPT1 or LPT2, into thinking it has a print device attached to it when it actually does not. When issuing the CAPTURE command, you assign the local printer port on the client computer to a print queue that is located on a server's volume. When the PRINT command is later issued, instead of the print job going directly to the printer port, the print job will be sent over the network to the queue specified on the capture command.

☒ **A.** The local printer port on the client can be assigned to either a print server or a print queue. But the port does not have to be assigned to a print server. **B.** The client will only run NPTWIN95.EXE if the client has a network printer that needs to be shared by other users. **D.** The reason for network printing is to reduce the number of print devices that are in an actual network. We can share the network printer and wait our turn. So, attaching a printer to the client computer will not allow you to print to a printer attached to the server.

3. ☑ **A, B, D.** The NDPS broker is composed of the following components:

■ Service Registry Service (SRS)

■ Event Notification Service (ENS)

■ Resource Management Service (RMS)

The Service Registry Service will let public-access printers advertise their presence so users can locate the printers. One goal of NDPS is to reduce overall network traffic by having NDPS printers register themselves. In non-NDPS printing, the printers will use Service Advertising Protocol (SAP) to advertise themselves on the network. Advertising is necessary so client users are aware of the printers. However, with this method, the advertising process is placing unnecessary traffic on the network. NDPS printers don't use SAP. They register with the Service Registry Service. SRS will have information about the print device name, type of printer, and vendor information. Event Notification Service will allow printers to send messages in the form of log files, pop-up windows or GroupWise® e-mail messages to users informing the user about the status of the print job. The Resource Management Service lets printer resources be stored in a central location. These resources will be downloaded to clients and printers as needed. With RMS, you can add, list, and replace printer drivers, printer definition files, banners, and fonts.

☒   **C.** Novell Directory Services® (NDS) has nothing to do with NDPS printing. NDS is the database that contains all of the network resource objects such as servers, volumes, users, groups, and it does contain printer objects.

4.   ☑   **A, C.** In order to set up NDPS, you must install NDPS on the NetWare server. This is done with the NWCONFIG NetWare Loadable Module (NLM). You can no longer use LOAD INSTALL as you could on a pre-5.0 version of NetWare. After installing NDPS on the server, you will need to set up the NDPS object in NetWare Administrator.

☒   **B.** is incorrect since the NDSP files are not loaded on a network printer. They are loaded on the server. **D.** You can no longer use LOAD INSTALL to install products or to perform other functions. The INSTALL.NLM has been replaced by NWCONFIG.NLM.

5.   ☑   **A, C.** The BROKER and NDPSM modules are loaded on a NetWare server. NDPSM is the NDPS Manager NLM. It allows several options for printer management. You can check the status of the printer and of a print job. The BROKER is loaded to provide for Service Registry Service (SRS), Event Notification Service (ENS) and Resource Management Service (RMS). Both of these NLMs are located in SYS:SYSTEM.

☒   **B.** The MODULES command only shows you what modules are loaded on the server. It does not provide any NDPS printer management support. **D.** Remote Sequenced Packet eXchange (RSPX) is the version of Novell's IPX/SPX protocol, which allows you to administer the server from a workstation. This answer is incorrect since it does not deal with the printer.

Managing the File System

1. ☑ **A.** NLIST is the correct command line utility that will allow you to search for NDS objects. You can find useful information about the NDS objects in your NDS tree. The following illustration shows a sample screenshot of NLIST showing server information.

☒ **B.** The CX command is not used to search for NDS objects and show volume information. CX is used to show and change to an NDS context. **C.** The VOLUMES command is used to show what volumes are mounted and the name space the volume has loaded. This command is run at the NetWare server. It is incorrect. **D.** The WHOAMI command lists your current logon name and is incorrect.

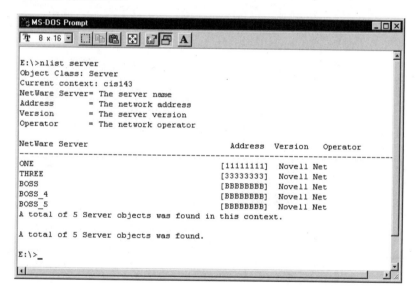

2. ☑ **B.** NetWare Administrator allows you to fully administer NDS objects and DOS-based files and folders. It is a powerful tool, which allows for the creation, deletion, and management of NDS objects such as users and printers, and it also allows you to create folders on NetWare volumes. You can also administer file system security within NetWare Administrator and it is all Windows-based. The following illustration shows a screenshot of NetWare Administrator.

☒   **A.** is incorrect. NWCONFIG is the new NetWare 5-based utility that is replacing INSTALL on earlier versions of NetWare. It is not used to administer files and folders. But it can be used to manage NetWare volumes and mirrors. **C.** The LOGIN command is used to log a user onto a Novell server. **D.** The NDIR command is used to list files and folders, but it does not allow you to administer NDS objects.

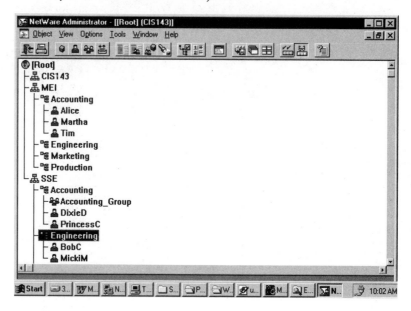

3. ☑   **B.** MAP INS S16:=BOSS\APPS:\SOUTH. The map command is run on a DOS workstation and it will allow you to set a search drive to a folder stored on a NetWare volume. The two types of drive mapping are regular/ standard drive mapping and search-drive mappings. You can map up to 26 drive letters on a NetWare Client. These are logical pointers to either local disks or network disks. The most common drive letter is *C.* A search drive is used to insert a network driver into the DOS path. The path is searched when a program is executed. The search order first looks in RAM, then in the current directory, then it looks down the path. Once found, the program executes and the search stops. If the program is not found, then an error occurs. When referring to the network drive, you must name it as follows: SERVER\VOLUME_NAME:\FOLDER_NAME. In order to map a search drive, you would need to use an *Sn*, where *S* = Search and *n* = a search-drive number. In order to insert it into the DOS path at the end, you would need MAP INS S16:=*Server\Volume_name:\Folder_name.*

☒   **A.** is incorrect because it is mapping a regular/standard drive mapping. A regular/standard drive mapping does not get inserted into the DOS path and is therefore not searched. This is an ordinary drive that would use the CD command or to which you would copy files. By the way, you can use the CD command on a search drive but it is not advised because if you change to another folder while on the drive mapping, you will change the search pointer, and will effectively lose your search mapping. Your programs may not run after that. The following illustration shows a sample of drive-mapping commands. **C.** is a search-drive mapping inserted at the beginning of the search list. It is advisable not to insert a search-drive mapping at the beginning, as this example shows. You can have up to 16 search drives, from S1 through S16. S1 is at the beginning while S16 is at the end. By placing the search drive at the end, you don't destroy the existing search order. **D.** is incorrect because this deletes a drive mapping.

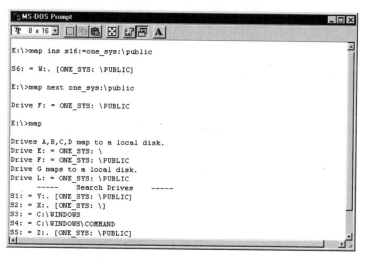

4. ☑ **A.** MAP NEXT BOSS\APPS:\SOUTH. Using MAP with the NEXT option will use the next available drive letter to map a drive. You can choose your own drive letter by typing in a valid drive letter from A: to Z: or you could let the MAP command do it for you by using NEXT. If Mack wanted L: drive to be mapped to the same folder, he would use: MAP L:=BOSS\APPS:\SOUTH. ☒ **B.** is incorrect because it maps a search drive. A search drive is used by DOS to locate the folder in which a program resides. **C.** is incorrect because it also maps a search drive. **D.** is incorrect because it deletes a drive mapping.

5. ☑ **C.** In order to minimize the impact of storing files on a volume, Mack can restrict the amount of disk space to which a user can save files. This should allow the user to store some things if necessary, but it will restrict the amount of space the user has. The following illustration shows a screenshot of restricting volume usage.
☒ **A, B, D.** are all incorrect since they don't accomplish the goal of minimizing the amount of disk space for a user. **B.** will accomplish the task, but it is a manually tedious process and not proactive.

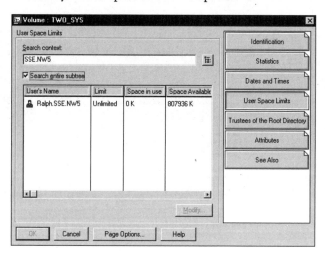

Managing File System Security

I. ☑ **C.** RIGHTS PAYROLL +WCE /NAME=RALPH. In order to manage trustee assignments such as adding and removing trustees, you would use the DOS-based RIGHTS command. You could also do this with NetWare Administrator; however, the RIGHTS command gives you a nice list of inheritance flowing down through folders, while NetWare Administrator does not. The following illustration shows use of the RIGHTS command showing inheritance. In order to give Ralph additional rights, Zac would need to enter the following command at a DOS prompt on a workstation:

F:\PRODUCTION\SHIFT1\PROJECTA>RIGHTS PAYROLL +WCE /NAME=RALPH

The plus sign before the rights (+WCE) is used to add to the current list of rights already available to the user.

☒ **A.** This command will not add the WCE rights to the list of current rights, but replaces any existing rights with just WCE. So, previous rights would be lost. Remember, Zac wants to keep R and F. **B.** This command will add WCE rights (+WCE) to the list of current rights but when the /Name parameter is left off, it assumes the currently logged on user is the default. So, Zac is logged on and would have given himself WCE if he were to do this command. **D.** This is an incorrect answer as the rights and the path are backwards and Zac is giving the rights to his own user name.

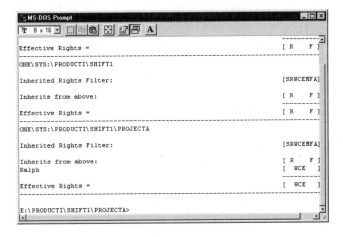

2. ☑ **C.** In order to create a new file or folder directory, a trustee must have the Create right. Read will allow the user to open a file and see the contents. File Scan will allow the user to perform a directory listing. The user is getting the Access Denied error because the user does not have the Create trustee right assigned to his username for the parent folder. Zac could give this user the Create right if necessary. He could use the DOS-based RIGHTS command or accomplish the same task in NetWare Administrator.

☒ **A.** Access Control is not the correct right to be able to create a folder. Access Control lets a trustee grant and revoke rights to other trustees. **B.** Rename Inhibit is not a trustee right, but an attribute. Attributes override effective rights on files and folders and are set with the FLAG command. Attributes can also be set in NetWare Administrator. **D.** The Write right is used to write data to an existing file. It does not allow you to create a new folder.

3. ☑ **D.** RWCEMF. Mary will get the effective rights of Read, Write, Create, Erase, Modify and File Scan. When a user is a member of a group and the group has been made a trustee, the user will receive the rights of the user trustee assignment and the rights of the group trustee assignment. Mary's user trustee assignment is Read and File Scan. She is a member of the Production group, which has Write, Create, Erase and Modify rights. Thus, she will get effective rights that are in both trustee assignments. If Mary was not a member of the group or the group was not a trustee, she would end up with just her user trustee assignment as effective rights. Keep in mind, if a trustee assignment is made, then the inherited rights don't get blocked with the IRF. The trustee assignment overrides inheritance and the IRF concept.

☒ **A.** is incorrect since Mary will get more than WCEM which happens to be the group rights. **B.** Mary will get more than what is in her user trustee assignment of Read and File Scan. **C.** is incorrect because Mary does not get Supervisor and Access Control rights.

4. ☑ **B.** In order to allow a user the right to delete a file, the user would need the Erase right. With this right, the user can delete an existing file or a directory. That means she could use the DOS-based DEL command to delete the file. With the Erase right, the user could also delete a directory with the DOS-based RD command. The user could also delete a file or folder in Windows with the Erase right.

☒   **A.** This is incorrect because there is no Delete right. **C.** Access Control gives the user the right to make trustee assignments. **D.** is incorrect since the Modify right allows a user to change a file's name or change file attributes.

5.   ☑   **A, B, E.** The following are attributes: Copy Inhibit, Rename Inhibit and Purge. Copy Inhibit will prevent a trustee from copying a file. This might be useful if the file has sensitive information such as payroll data. Rename Inhibit will not allow the trustee to rename a file even if he has the Modify right. Purge is an attribute that causes a file to be erased after it is deleted. Any possibility of recovery of the file is gone since it is deleted right away. If Purge was not set, then the file could be recovered with FILER, if deleted.

☒   **C, D.** Erase is a right, not an attribute. Erase gives the user the ability to delete a file. But, if the Delete Inhibit attribute is set, then this attribute overrides any effective right; the result is the user cannot delete the file even with the Erase right. The Modify right is not an attribute. Modify allows you to rename and change attributes. However, if Rename Inhibit is set, you cannot change a file's name even with Modify.

6.   ☑   **C.** The IRF is used to block inherited rights. In the absence of trustee assignments, inherited rights are sent through the IRF. If the inherited right is also on the IRF, then it is allowed. If the inherited right is not on the IRF, then it is not allowed. If a right is not inherited and not on the IRF, then it is not allowed. If the right is not inherited but on the IRF, it is not allowed. The IRF is used to block or filter unwanted rights from passing to lower levels in the DOS tree.

☒   **A.** is incorrect since the IRF does not equal your effective rights. **B.** The IRF is not used to set trustee assignment. **D.** The IRF is not used to block attributes. As a matter of fact, attributes override the effective rights in a folder.

Creating Login Scripts

1. ☑ **B.** The user login script is the last login script to be executed of all the login scripts. User login scripts are the most difficult to maintain because they have to be managed for all users. Also, they override settings in previous login scripts. However, they are useful if, for instance, you want to get one or two users a few additional drive mappings. Ideally, it is best to use a container login script because this will be executed for all users. You just have to change it once instead of a number of times.

   ☒ **A, C, D.** These are all incorrect answers. A single reference time server is not a login script but a server that is the time manager of the network. There is no group login script; earlier versions of NetWare had a group login script but it's been replaced by a profile login script. A profile login script will be executed for a grouping of users. A container login script will be executed for the masses.

2. ☑ **B. NO_DEFAULT.** If a user login script is not present, then the default login script will be executed. You can stop the default login script from being executed by placing the statement NO_DEFAULT in either a container or profile login script. This setting stops the default login script from running. The default login script is built into the LOGIN.EXE program and you cannot modify it. You can only prevent its execution.

   ☒ **A, C, D.** These are all incorrect because they are invalid statements.

3. ☑ **C.** In order for Scott to display the document on the screen, he must use the FDISPLAY statement. He will also need to test for the day of the week. He should write his login script to look something like the following:

```
IF %DAY_OF_WEEK = "FRIDAY" THEN
   FDISPLAY SERVER_A\SYS:PUBLIC\REMIND.TXT
END
```

The IF test will check to make sure the day of the week is Friday and if so, the reminder document will display on the screen. There is a DISPLAY and an FDISPLAY statement. The DISPLAY statement shows all the text in what is called raw format. The FDISPLAY statement filters out the unprintable control characters that are in a document that tell the printer how to print.

☒ **A. B, D.** are all incorrect statements. The DIR command will not display the output of a text document. The WRITE command is not used to display the file's contents. CASE and CAT are invalid commands.

4. ☑ **D. MAP INS S16:=SERVER_A\VOL2:APPS2\SALES.** In order to map a drive to the folder, Scott will need to create a search-drive mapping using INS. He also needs to add it to the end of the current drive mappings so he will need to use S16. There are 16 total search drives that can be used. A total of 26 total drive letters. The correct path name for the folder is given by SERVER_NAME\VOLUME_NAME:FOLDER\FOLDER.

☒ **A.** This is incorrect because it places the search-drive mapping at the beginning of the search list. It must be at the end. **B.** This statement creates a virtual root-drive mapping to the folder. A root-drive mapping creates an artificial root ceiling but does not create a search-drive mapping. **C.** creates a regular/standard drive mapping but not a search-drive mapping. A search-drive mapping is used to point to folders that contain executable programs. A regular/standard drive mapping does not do that.

5. ☑ **A.** He must replace PHASERS.WAV with the sound file of choice. In a GUI environment, the FIRE PHASERS command will use the PHASERS.WAV file by default. This file is located on the clieNT Workstation and can be replaced with another sound file. In a GUI environment, FIRE PHASERS does not use the machine's beep like it does in a text-based login. If you were to login in text mode and then in GUI mode, the beep emitted from your computer would sound different.

☒ **B.** The NO_DEFAULT statement will not run the default login script. **C.** Placing the # sign in front of a program will execute it; however, this is not how you run a sound wave file. **D.** Scott cannot put the FIRE PHASER command in a batch file because the batch file will not recognize the command. FIRE PHASERS is only a NetWare login script command.

6. ☑ **C.** Create a login script that uses the %PASSWORD_EXPIRES variable. Scott could create a login script that has an entry to display the expiration date of their password on the screen. Then at logon the user would know when the password expired. The %PASSWORD_EXPIRES variable returns the number of days left before the password will expire. Scott could set an entry such as:

```
WRITE "Your password expires in %PASSWORD_EXPIRES days"
```

☒ **A, B, D.** These are all incorrect answers because they don't address the requirement of knowing when the password will expire each time the user logs in. The %LAST_NAME variable will just show the user's last name that is on the Last Name property of the user object.

Remote Management of Workstations (NEBO)

1. ☑ **C, D, E.** Z.E.N.works uses NDS and is secured through logon authentication. NEBO will only work if the user has appropriate object rights to the workstation object. There is no excessive traffic caused by Z.E.N.works. This is because a Remote Control Agent is not required to broadcast all the time; the IP and IPX workstation addresses are stored in NDS, which reduces broadcasts. It is easy to use because you traverse it like you would a Windows folder or NDS objects in NWADMIN.
☒ **A, B.** These are incorrect answers because users need appropriate rights and NEBO does not use a lot of bandwidth.

2. ☑ **C.** The WSREG16.EXE command is used to register a Windows 3.1x workstation to NEBO. WSREG32.EXE is used to register it with Windows 95/98 and Windows NT Workstations. You could also do the same thing in NAL.
☒ **A.** The WSRIGHTS.EXE command is located in SYS\PUBLIC\WIN32 and it is used to grant the appropriate rights for NEBO. **B.** The WSREG32.EXE command is used to register Windows 95/98 and NT Workstations, so it is also incorrect. **D.** NWADMIN.EXE is used to manage NDS and is incorrect.

3. ☑ C. NTSTACFG.EXE. To remotely administer a workstation, there are certain agents that must be loaded on the workstation platforms. They are as follows:

- Windows 3.1 requires the WSUSER.EXE application agent.
- Windows 95/98 requires WSUER.EXE application agent.
- Windows NT 4 requires the NTSTACFG.EXE service agent.

☒ **A.** The WSUER.EXE Remote Control Agent is executed on Windows 3.1 and Windows 95/98 workstations. **B.** The NetWare Application Launcher (NAL) is not one of the Remote Control Agents. **D.** The CX command is used to change your NDS context.

4. ☑ **B.** HLPREQ32.EXE. It is located in SYS\PUBLIC. Users can use the Help Request application to contact a network administrator about a problem. The Help Request application is added to NAL as an object. Before a user can launch the Help Request program, a Help Desk policy needs to be set up for the users in an NDS policy package.
☒ **A.** The HLPREQ16.EXE program is the Help Requester program for a Windows 3.1 and DOS workstation. **C.** The NTASCFG.EXE is the Remote Control Agent that runs as a service on an NT workstation. **D.** The WUSER command is the Remote Control Agent for Windows 95/98 clients.

5. ☑ **B.** The workstation registration process is used to synchronize the workstation and the NDS workstation object. Z.E.N.works has a workstation inventory policy in NDS. The policy checks the workstation for information and then stores this as properties in the NDS workstation object. The workstation must first be imported and then registered. After the workstation has been imported and each time the registration program runs, the workstation will notify the workstation object of any updated inventory, then the NDS workstation object and the actual workstation agree and are in sync.
☒ **A.** The workstation import program will place a workstation object in the NDS tree. This is done before registration. You need to periodically import the workstations to keep their network addresses current within

NDS. You can schedule this with NAL. **C.** The Remote Control Agent must be run on a workstation in order to remotely connect to that workstation. **D.** The Help Request application program is used for problem reporting and notification, and is incorrect.

Configuring Network Applications for Users

1. ☑ **C.** When you push an application using NAL, you install an application over the LAN to a workstation in an unattended manner. This means there is no user input. This provides a great benefit because software can be distributed to a workstation automatically. Pulling an application means installing the application to a workstation over the LAN in an attended manner, so users sitting at the workstation would have to answer questions during the installation.
   ☒ **A.** When you push, you are not setting up security. **B.** is incorrect because it is the definition of pulling an application. **D.** is incorrect because you are not setting a context in NDS when you push an application.

2. ☑ **C.** The snAppShot utility program will take a snapshot of your workstation by recording the changes made to the workstation's configuration files, such as .INI files and Registry modifications. It creates a .AOT file that has information about the changes made by the application installation; this is a binary file. You could create a text version of the .AOT file in NetWare Administrator. The text version is called the .AXT file and it can be edited. Once the .AOT file is created, it can be imported into NDS and associated to a Container, Group or User object.
   ☒ **A, B.** are incorrect because the snAppShot utility does not push or pull an application to a workstation. **D.** is incorrect because it takes a snapshot before and after the installation, then it creates the .AOT file that can be imported into NDS.

3. ☑ **B, D.** Simple applications are defined as those not requiring any configuration changes to files such as the .INI files and Registry. A

snAppShot is not needed so you only have to create an Application object in NDS and then associate it to a Container, Group or User object. Complex applications, on the other hand, do require changes to the .INI files and the Registry. It would then require snAppShot to be executed so it could detect the changes and place them in the .AOT file.

☒ **A, C.** are incorrect because the opposite is true.

4. ☑ **B, C.** The NDS schema will be have two NAL object types. They are:

■ Application folders

■ Application objects

You can create Application folder objects that will organize the applications that are alike. This is how Windows organizes folders and files. Then, you could create Application objects that represent programs.

☒ **A, D.** are incorrect answers because these objects do no exist in the NDS schema.

5. ☑ **A, D.** The required file system rights needed to run NAL.EXE are Read and File Scan. Users need Read and File Scan rights to a server directory that has Read and File Scan. Z.E.N.works installation will place NAL and its files in SYS:PUBLIC with Read and File Scan. However, if you move it, then you'll need to make sure Read and File Scan are on the directory that has NAL.EXE. Read is needed to see and run executables and File Scan is needed to take a directory listing in a directory.

☒ **B, C, E.** are incorrect because they grant either insufficient or excessive rights. Supervisor rights, for example, should not be granted to typical users.

Using Workstation Manager to Manage Workstations

1. ☑ **B.** Novell Client configuration. Workstation Manager uses objects called policy package options. The policy packages are:

■ NT User Package

■ NT Workstation Package

■ 95 User Package

■ 95 Workstation Package

In order to configure the Novell protocol on the Novell Client, the Novell Client Configuration policy is used; it is applicable to NT Workstation Package and 95 Workstation Package.

☒ **A, C, D.** are incorrect. There is no Novell login configuration. The Workstation Inventory is used to manage an inventory of workstation software and hardware. The NT Computer System Policies manage NT system policies.

2. ☑ **A, D.** To use Workstation Manager, NetWare Administrator will need to have policy packages built and linked to the appropriate workstations and users. A workstation policy follows a roaming user on the network. No matter what workstation they log onto, they will get the same policy. A workstation policy, on the other hand, is strictly dedicated to the workstation regardless of what user logs on to the workstation.

☒ **B, C.** are false, and the inverse of the correct answers.

3. ☑ **C.** For Windows NT and Windows 95 you can change the desktop appearance for a user. You would set up a roaming profile for a user who needs the same desktop appearance no matter what computer he logs on. On the NT Desktop Preferences page, you would check Roaming Profile. You could then store the profile on either the User's home directory or in a NetWare File System directory. If you do set up a roaming profile, you don't need to go to each workstation and store the user profile there. If you are concerned about disk space on the workstation, setting up a roaming profile stored on the network will minimize any disk use.

☒ **A.** Going to the Registry is not advised unless absolutely necessary. For this scenario, you don't need to go to the Registry and you don't need to change any setting related to mobile computing. **B.** Going to each NT machine and making a user profile is impractical and not the best answer. **D.** Changing NTCONFIG.POL to NTCONFIG.MAN won't enable a roaming user profile. On an NT computer, this will not allow a user to change his desktop's appearance.

4. ☑ **A, D.** An application can be scheduled to be executed for any user or workstation; you do this in the user policy or workstation policy package. When an action is scheduled for a user, the action occurs for that user regardless of the workstation from which they logged on. Also, when an action is scheduled for a workstation, the action occurs on that workstation, regardless of what user logs on to that workstation.

☒ **B, C.** are incorrect. A user does not have to have Supervisor rights for the action to occur. Also, he doesn't define workstations users can log on to in the system policy file.

5. ☑ **C.** When a Windows NT user logs on to a Novell network, they can use their user logon and password in NDS if the Use NetWare credentials check box is checked. This will create an NDS user account. You can also elect to check the Volatile User box; this means the account will be removed once the user logs off the workstation.

☒ **A.** This is a user policy file on an NT workstation and is an incorrect answer. **B.** Checking the Enable Dynamic Local User box will cause the workstation to be checked for a user account. If the user account does not exist, then one is created. If the account does exist, then the user is authenticated in NDS. **D.** Checking to the Use NetWare credentials only will not remove the account after the user logs off; the account will still be present.

Managing NDS Security

1. ☑ **B.** Trustee. When an object has been granted rights to another object, the object that has been granted the rights is called the trustee. A trustee is typically a user or group that has permission to do something in the NDS tree. A user could have a special right to administer a container. The user may be able to add users and groups to this container. In order to make a user a trustee in NDS, it's necessary to right click on the User object and

then click Rights to Other Objects.

☒ **A, C, D.** are incorrect. The RIGHTS command adds and removes a trustee. A container holds other objects. The property right is what a trustee can do to an object's property values.

2. ☑ **A.** The Supervisor object right provides for complete control over an NDS object. This right includes the rights listed in the following table.

Right	Description
Supervisor (S)	Allows complete control over the objects. It also gives complete control over the object's property values. Supervisor implies the other rights.
Browse (B)	With Browse, you can only see other NDS objects.
Create (C)	With Create, you can make other objects. This is not applicable to leaf objects because leafs cannot contain other objects.
Delete (D)	Gives the right to remove an object.
Rename (R)	Gives the rights to change the name of an NDS object.
Inheritable (I)	Determines whether an NDS object's rights can be inherited by lower-level objects.

☒ **B, C, D.** are all incorrect. See the preceding table.

3. ☑ **D.** The [Public] trustee is a special-purpose object that applies to all users. So, the rights [Public] applies to all users. Be careful not to give [Public] the Supervisor right. Each user is security equivalent to [Public]. By default, [Public] trustee has Browse to the [Root]. This is why users can see objects before and after they log on to the network. By default, [Public] has the Read property right to the User's Default Server property. This is so the user can see the server for the purpose of logging on.

☒ **A, B, C.** Users are not security equivalent to these trustees or objects. So, these are incorrect answers.

4. ☑ **B.** In order to give another user the same rights you have in the NDS tree, you should make them security equivalent to your User object. Be careful giving this out arbitrarily because it gives the user the same rights another user has. User objects are security equivalent to the group objects of which they are members. There is an implied security equivalence between a leaf object and its immediate parent container object. Use caution making just any user security equivalent to ADMIN.

☒ **A.** It is not advisable to let someone have your user name and password. **C.** There is no need to disable your account. **D.** You could manually check for each and every object but it is a painstaking process and you may miss something.

5. ☑ **A, B, D.** In order to calculate effective rights, you should consider the following steps:

1. Determine what is inherited
2. Take out those rights not present (or blocked) in the IRF
3. Add the trustee and group member rights
4. Add security equivalent rights

Effective rights cannot be set, but they are the composite of rights that are in effect for a trustee at a certain point in the NDS tree.

☒ **C.** is incorrect because you need to account for group membership. If a user is a member of a group, then the user has the rights the group has and the rights he has as a User trustee.

Managing Resources in a Multicontext Environment

1. ☑ **A, C.** The major classes of NDS objects are container objects and leaf objects. Container objects are just placeholders for other object types. A Container can hold another container object. A leaf object is contained in a container object. A leaf object cannot hold another leaf object. Examples of Containers are: [Root], Organizations, Organizational Units and the Country object. Leaf objects are numerous: users, printers, volumes, servers, etc.

☒ **B.** There is only one [Root] object. You cannot create this at will. You can only create it during server installation time. **D.** The Last Name property is a property and not an object. All objects have properties. The Last Name property is a property for the User object. It has a value; for example, "Meadors" could be the value in the Last Name property for a User object.

2. ☑ **A, B, D.** When designing your NDS tree, you should consider the following questions:

- How many leaf objects will there be?
- How many Organizational Units are you going to need?
- How will you logically arrange the leaf objects into Organizational Units?
- Does your design allow for future growth?

When designing your tree, you should consider organizing your Organizational Units around divisional, departmental, and workgroup lines. For example, if you have a Finance department, then create a FINANCE Organizational Unit and place the appropriate users in that container. Keep in mind, that your organization chart for the company is the place to start when creating the NDS tree. Managers and supervisors will be just like any other User object in a container. Do not make a manager a container because you would still have to create a User object for them for logon purposes.

☒ **C.** There is no decision about how many [Root] objects you will need; there can only be one.

3. ☑ **B.** Catalog Services allows you to just go to a clieNT Workstation and simply put the user name and password in at the logon screen. The user no longer has to know the location of the object in the NDS tree. Catalog Services keeps an index of the object's location and finds it quickly at logon.

☒ **A.** A Distinguished Name is the term given to an object and is the full name as referenced from the [Root] object. **C, D.** These names do not exist, at least as far as context-less logons are concerned.

4. ☑ **C.** In NDS the leading dots are mandatory for use with distinguished names. This means they begin from [Root]. An example is .ToddMeadors.SecurityDept.MIS.Meadors-Corp. The beginning dot indicates the name is being referred to from the top-level container, or [Root]. Relative distinguished names never begin with a leading dot; however, they may have a trailing dot. An example is ToddMeadors.SecurityDept., which indicates changing the context up one level to the parent context.

☒ **A, B, C.** are all incorrect answers.

5. ☑ **A.** The User object should be located in Claxton, Georgia, which happens to be the headquarters. You should place the User object in the container where it uses the resources the most often. It is easier for managing the NDS tree if you place the user and resource objects in the same container. You could put the User object in another container representing a branch office but you would have to choose one; however, this would not make sense from an NDS organization standpoint.

☒ **B, C, D.** These are the branch offices and it would not be the best solution to place Jane's User object in one of them. She only needs access to them occasionally.

6. ☑ **B.** It does not have the distinguished name and you should refer to the distinguished name. The leading dot refers to the object by its distinguished name. The distinguished name will refer to the object in the NDS tree without question.

☒ **A, C, D.** are incorrect. You need the name of the print queue, you do need the dots between the objects, and typeful names are not required.

Performing a Simple Installation

1. ☑ **B.** If the server does have a processor with low speed (a rating of less than 1500) and there is not at least 47MB of RAM, the installation program will only run in text mode. The GUI phase will not be executed because there is not enough RAM to hold the GUI interface.

☒ **A.** is incorrect since the GUI installation program will never run on a low-speed processor and a server that has a low amount of RAM. There would not be enough memory and the processor would be too slow to handle the windows phase. **C.** There is no Custom installation on NetWare5. James must be thinking of NT. **D.** NetWare 5 has no Typical installation, the answer is incorrect.

2. ☑ **C.** The name of the default volume created during installation time is called SYS: and it is used to store the system files for NetWare files. The default volume name can be changed but it is typically left as SYS:. This volume has the folders that are in the following table.

System-created directory	Description
SYSTEM	Holds Administrator NLMs
MAIL	Exists for backward compatibility with Bindery-based services
PUBLIC	Holds user command and NWADMIN.
LOGIN	Contains logon commands
ETC	Holds TCP/IP programs and files
JAVA and JAVASAVE	Contains Java Console commands
QUEUES	Has subdirectories with a .QDR extension, each representing a NetWare Print Queue object
CDROM$$.ROM	Index files for mounted CD-ROM volumes
DELETED.SAV	Has deleted files removed from directories
LICENSE	Contains license-related files
NDPS	Holds Novell Distributed Printing Service subdirectories and files
NETBASIC	Contains NetBASIC support files
NI	Has NetWare Installation files

System-created directory	Description
PERL	Holds PERL script files
README	Has Readme text files

☒ **A, B, D.** are incorrect because the default volume name is SYS:.

3. ☑ **C.** James should load both the IPX and IP protocols for this server. In order to connect to the Internet, James must use TCP/IP. By loading the IP protocol, he will satisfy this requirement. When setting up IP for the network adapter, he will need to give the adapter an IP address and a subnet mask. The subnet mask is used to determine if the sending and destination computers are on the same local network segment. He should also set up a default gateway; this is also known as a router. If the packets of data are on a remote network, the default gateway receives the packets and forwards them on to the destination computer. Since there is another server that is running Novell's native protocol, IPX/SPX, James also should load the IPX protocol. This protocol is native for Novell and it is fast and routable; it is not used on the Internet. James will also need to bind a frame type to each protocol. By default, for NetWare 5, the default frame type for IPX/SPX is Ethernet_802.2. The default frame type for TCP/IP is Ethernet_II.

☒ **A, B, D.** are incorrect because, by loading only one of them, they won't get the connectivity to the Internet and to the Novell server.

4. ☑ **A, D.** In order for the server to become a print server in the current LAN environment, James and Todd need to have a network adapter connected via TP cable to a hub on the network. Remember in this company scenario, they have a 100BaseT network. They should also install this server in the existing NDS tree. It will be easier to manage and the main time server can propagate the time to this computer.

☒ **B.** is incorrect because this computer needs to be connected to the network for it to take some of the load off another server. **C.** is incorrect because they are not required to load IPX in NetWare 5. They could just load IP.

5. ☑ **B.** By installing this computer into the current NDS tree, it will become a secondary time server. This means its time will be synchronized from another server. By default, the very first server that is installed on a network becomes the main source of time and it is called the single reference time server. It will send, or synchronize, its time with the secondary time servers in the network. By default, other servers installed in the current NDS tree will become secondary time servers. So, by installing this computer in the current, or existing, NDS tree, the computer will be a secondary time server and receive its time from the single reference time server that already is installed.

☒ **A, C, D.** These are incorrect answer because they don't allow the new server to receive its time from a single time source, the single reference time server.

Part 2

NetWare® 5 Advanced Administration (Exam 50-640)

EXAM TOPICS

Upgrading NetWare 3.1x to NetWare 5 Server

Upgrading from Queue-Based Printing to NDPS

Performing a Custom Installation

Setting Up the Network File System

Using the Server Console

Optimizing the Network and Server

Backing Up Servers and Workstations

Using DNS/DHCP Services

Installing a Web Server

Securing the Directory Tree

Maintaining NDS™

Mobile Clients

NetWare® 5
Advanced
Administration
Questions

Q&A

T he NetWare 5 Advanced Administration exam covers a large number of topics associated with upgrading existing NetWare environments, administering larger networks, and planning and management of more complex network tasks. These tasks are often new to the network administrator, and are based on the increased functionality and new features in NetWare 5. You can expect to be tested on NetWare Distributed Print Services, NDS support for DNS and DHCP, the improved backup and restore capabilities, and the enhanced Web Server. This exam is intended for highly experienced network professionals with a solid background in personal computer technology, DOS and Windows 95/NT operating systems, and general network theory and design.

Upgrading NetWare 3.1x to NetWare 5 Server

1. What do the minimum requirements for a NetWare 5 server include?

    A. 80486 processor

    B. 64MB RAM

    C. 500MB disk space

    D. PS/2 or serial mouse

2. Which of the following items are not supported during an upgrade or migration?

    A. Third-party NLM modules

    B. The Novell₍ₑ₎ Upgrade Wizard

    C. The Novell Client for DOS/Windows 3.x

    D. Novell DSK drivers

---

exam

ⓦatch

Support for .DSK drivers has been discontinued. NetWare 5 uses NWPA (NetWare Peripheral Architecture) that requires a software driver called a HAM (Host Adapter Module) to allow communications between the computer (host) and the storage device linked to it. The storage devices will use a CDM (Custom Device Module) drive to communicate with the storage adapter.

---

3. Prior to running the Novell Upgrade Wizard, which of the following tasks need to be performed?

A. Downloading the Wizard from Novell's Web site

B. Inserting the NetWare 5 CD in the client workstation and running INSTALL.BAT

C. Running UPGRDWZD.EXE

D. Booting the client workstation from DOS and loading the DOS CD-ROM driver to access the NetWare 5 CD

QUESTIONS AND ANSWERS

Matt tested the upgrade of a NetWare 4.1 network to NetWare 5 in his lab. First, he installed NetWare 4.1 on three servers into the TEST tree. Then, he attempted to upgrade the server containing the Master replica to NetWare 5. The attempt failed. What was the problem?	Matt installed NetWare 4.1, but did not install any patches, including the patch for the DS.NLM. With the "vanilla" installation of NetWare 4.1, the DS.NLM was not a recent enough version to communicate with the NetWare 5 version of DS.NLM.

4. What does an across-the-wire migration require?

A. An existing NetWare 5 server

B. A dedicated migration workstation and a destination PC with only a 30MB or higher DOS partition

C. The source and destination servers be located on the same network segment

D. The source and destination servers bound to the same IPX frame type

exam

ⓦatch

By using the CONFIG.NLM utility, you can get your existing NetWare server's configuration information including NCF files, INETCFG configuration information, speed rating, total RAM, set parameters, modules list, disk information, volume information, name space information, LAN information, and system files. When CONFIG.NLM is loaded, it will create a file in the SYS:SYSTEM directory called CONFIG.TXT.

5. Which of the following NLM modules are required by the Novell Upgrade Wizard to be loaded on the source NetWare 3.x server?

A. UPGRADE.NLM

B. TSA312.NLM

C. INETCFG.NLM

D. LONG.NAM

exam
Ⓦatch

IPX cannot be removed with the installation program but can be removed at a later time after NetWare 5 has been installed and rebooted.

Use the Following Scenario to Answer Questions 6–7

You have been given the task of upgrading two existing NetWare 3.1x servers and a NetWare 4.1x server onto a single NetWare 5 server. Several of your users have accounts on all three of the NetWare 3.1x servers. A NetWare 3.1x print server manages all network printers. All user accounts on the existing servers will reside in the same container in NDS.

6. What is the preferred method for upgrading these servers?

A. Install a new NetWare 5 server, then use the Upgrade Wizard to migrate the 3.1x and 4.1x servers across the wire.

B. Upgrade the NetWare 4.1x server to NetWare 5 using the NetWare 5 in-place upgrade, then use the Upgrade Wizard to migrate the 3.1x servers across the wire.

C. Upgrade the NetWare 3.1x server that contains all user accounts using the in-place upgrade, then use Upgrade Wizard to migrate the other servers across the wire.

D. Remove the NetWare 4.1x server from the tree, install a new NetWare 5 server, and restore the NetWare 4.1x NDS, use, and data files from backup. Use Upgrade Wizard to migrate the 3.1x servers across the wire.

7. After completing the network upgrade, you realize that several of your users do not run the container logon script in NDS. What is the most likely reason for this?

A. These users are not members of the appropriate NetWare groups.

B. The affected users do not have sufficient rights to the container object.

C. The affected users have personal logon scripts defined.

D. The affected users require an updated client.

QUESTIONS AND ANSWERS

Cheri upgraded two NetWare 3.12 servers to NetWare 5 using the Upgrade Wizard. She knew that the user data was correctly imported with the first upgrade, but neglected to run the verification process before migrating the second server. Cheri was surprised to see that there were multiple errors on nearly every user for the second migration. What happened?	Cheri migrated the users and groups of both servers to the same context in the new NetWare 5 Novell Directory Services™ tree. Previously, the servers had duplicates of each user and group in order to facilitate access for all the users to either server. However, when migrating the second time, the user IDs already existed, so they produced an error.

Upgrading from Queue-Based Printing to NDPS

1. Which of the following features is NOT offered by Novell Distributed Print Services (NDPS)?

A. Pure TCP/IP printing

B. Automated print-driver downloads

C. Automatic detection and installation of printer devices

D. Bi-directional printer support

exam

Watch *Before an NDPS printer can be created there must be an NDPS Manager.*

2. What are the three components of the NDPS broker?

   A. SRS, ENS, and RMS

   B. Printers, queues, and agents

   C. Container, leaf, and object

   D. None of the above

QUESTIONS AND ANSWERS

Kelsey created an NDPS printing system using a new NetWare 5 server on an existing NetWare 4.11 network. When she migrated the first group of users to the new server, the workstations were able to use the file services but none could print. What was Kelsey's error?	Kelsey did not upgrade the workstations to a NetWare client that included NDPS components. The older NetWare clients are able to attach to the new file server, and use files and directories, but cannot print to NDPS printers. They would still be able to print to a legacy print queue, however.

3. When NDPS is installed for the first time in an NDS tree, it creates a broker on the server. What do subsequent NDPS installations on other servers do?

   A. They create a new broker for that server.

   B. They always use an existing broker, unless a new broker is specified.

   C. They check for the existence of a broker within three hops.

   D. They ask the installer if it should use an existing broker or create a new one.

4. In order to print to NDPS printers, what must users have?

    A. The TCP/IP protocol bound to their workstation

    B. NetWare 5 client software

    C. A licensed connection to the server supporting the NDPS manager

    D. NDS assigned rights to the public access printer

exam
ⓦatch

An NDPS gateway is a software component that allows NetWare NDPS clients to print to non-NDPS-aware printers. The Novell gateway supports legacy printers using the LPR/LPD protocol over IP and the RP protocol over IPX. The Novell gateway will allow jobs to be sent to legacy print queues.

5. Which of the following gateways are shipped with NetWare 5?

    A. Novell gateway

    B. Xerox gateway

    C. HP gateway

    D. All of the above

exam
ⓦatch

The NetWare Loadable Modules for the NDPS Manager and Print Servers—NDPSM.NLM and PSERVER.NLM—can be loaded on the same server at the same time.

6. Which of the following is not required when printing in an NDPS environment?

    A. A NetWare print queue

    B. A capture statement on the client

    C. A Novell or third-party print server on the network

    D. All of the above

QUESTIONS AND ANSWERS

Logan created a new NDPS printing environment in his lab. He used a NetWare 5 server, a locally attached HP LaserJet 6 printer, and a Windows NT 4.0 workstation. He tested all functionality of each component and then proceeded to implement NDPS in the network. When the first group was migrated, four users called Logan with problems for an application running on their Windows 98 workstations that was not able to print to a network-attached printer. What steps should Logan have taken to prevent these errors	Logan did not duplicate the enterprise network environment in his lab. He used server-attached printers when the network had network-attached printers, and he used Windows NT 4.0 when the workstations were using Windows 98. Logan should have duplicated each type of printer/workstation/server configuration, and then tested it before implementing it on the network.

exam
Ⓦatch

Do not remove print queues to which users send print jobs from DOS programs. NDPS will not allow a user to redirect printing to an LPT port, but NetWare's print-queue-based printing will. DOS programs nearly always print to LPT ports.

Performing a Custom Installation

1. What name spaces do NSS volumes automatically support?

   A. DOS, LONG

   B. DOS, MAC, OS/2

   C. DOS

   D. DOS, MAC, NFS, LONG

exam
Ⓦatch

The thing to remember is that a traditional volume can be created only on a traditional partition and an NSS volume can be created only on an NSS partition.

2. When IPX is bound to an Ethernet adapter in a NetWare 5 server, the default frame type is:

   A. 802.2

   B. 802.5

   C. 802.3

   D. Ethernet_II

3. On a NetWare 5 server, the TCP/IP subnet mask is used to:

   A. Limit the size of the network

   B. Determine which portion of an IP address identifies the network and which portion identifies host devices

   C. Limit the broadcast traffic generated by the server

   D. Determine whether client workstations can connect to the server

4. What is a necessary step in configuring the IPX internal network number for a server?

   A. Using the same internal network number on all servers

   B. Assigning a unique number

   C. Using the same internal network number on all servers connected to the same physical segment

   D. Choosing the internal network number in order of server priority on the network

Setting Up the Network File System

1. What is the primary reason for selecting a separate volume for Macintosh users?

   A. Macintosh and DOS file names are incompatible and cannot reside in the same directory.

   B. Macintosh name space and DOS name space cannot coexist on the same volume.

   C. To prevent DOS and Windows applications from accidentally attempting to access data files created with Macintosh applications

   D. To reduce the overhead associated with adding Macintosh name space to volumes that support DOS and Windows users

EXAM 50-640
QUESTIONS

2. What are the two primary drawbacks to disk mirroring?

A. The inability to mirror disks on-line and reduced disk performance

B. Additional hardware cost and reduced disk performance

C. Disk mirroring requires two identical disk drives and additional hardware overhead.

D. Disk mirroring operations are not real time and the network volume is inaccessible during the mirroring process.

3. Which of the following statements is true about the SYS:MAIL directory on a NetWare 5 server?

A. Each user has a personal directory in this folder. The folder name consists of the first eight characters of the user logon name.

B. This folder is no longer required by NetWare and can be safely deleted.

C. Novell GroupWise®, if installed, uses this directory to store mail.

D. Personal bindery logon scripts are stored in subdirectories of SYS:MAIL.

4. How is the hot fix area of a NetWare partition used?

A. To store backup copies of volume directory entry tables

B. As a temporary storage area when installing patches or hot fixes

C. To redirect data in the event of a sector write failure

D. To store memory dumps in the event of a server crash

exam
ⓦatch   *In order to repair a volume with VREPAIR, the volume must be dismounted.*

5. Which of the following volume names are invalid on a NetWare volume? Choose all that apply.

A. ACCOUNTING_APPLICATIONS

B. _PERSONNEL

C. PERSONNEL_

D. (APPLICATIONS)

E. 9&LIVES

exam
ⓦatch   *A volume name is typically represented as servername_volumename:. For example, for a server named FIVE-NW5 and a volume of SYS, the volume name is FIVE-NW5_SYS:.*

exam
ⓦatch   *An easy way to remember the important system-created directories is with the acronym SIMPLE, which stands for SYSTEM, MAIL, PUBLIC, LOGIN, and ETC.*

Using the Server Console

1. What command is used to start NetWare 5's Java-based Console One?

A. XSTART

B. STARTX

C. MONITOR

D. CONSOLE

exam
Watch *INSTALL.NLM has been replaced by NWCONFIG.NLM in NetWare 5.*

2. Which of the following key sequences can be used to navigate between screens at the server console?

A. ALT+F3 and ALT+F4

B. TAB and Shifted TAB

C. PAGEUP and PAGEDOWN

D. ALT+ESC and CTRL+ESC

exam
Watch *STARTUP.NCF can only be edited using EDIT.NLM or NWCONFIG.NLM since it resides on the DOS partition of the hard drive physically located on the server box.*

3. Which client utility can be used to remotely access a NetWare 5 server console using the TCP/IP protocol?

A. RCONSOLE

B. TELNET

C. NWADMIN NETADMIN

D. RCONJ

4. What method is used to immediately lock the server console in NetWare 5?

A. Enter SECURE CONSOLE at the server.

B. Use the console locking option in the MONITOR screen.

C. Use the console locking option in RCONSOLE or RCONJ.

D. Load the SCRSAVER ACTIVATE command.

5. Which of the following commands can be used to edit the server STARTUP.NCF control file from the server console?

A. LOAD EDIT SYS:\SYSTEM\STARTUP.NCF

B. LOAD STARTUP.NCF

C. EDIT C:STARTUP.NCF

D. EDIT C:\STARTUP.NCF

Optimizing the Network and Server

1. What is the NetWare 5 process that collects previously used memory no longer in use and returns it to the cache pool?

A. Free memory

B. Garbage collection

C. Memory alloc process

D. Virtual memory process

2. Which of the following memory statistics in the Server Memory Statistics screen on the NetWare 5 console determines if the server has sufficient RAM memory?

A. Allocated memory pool

B. Total server work memory

C. Cache movable memory

D. Cache buffer memory

exam
Watch

If a client is using packet burst and encounters a server that is not using packet burst, then the communication defaults down to normal NCP communication. So remember that both ends of the communication medium need to be using packet burst for the results to be worthy.

3. Which of the following statements about NetWare file compression is false?

   A. A volume's file compression status can be enabled and disabled using SET parameters.

   B. Files can be automatically marked for compression using FLAG.EXE.

   C. Once compressed, files must be manually uncompressed before use.

   D. NetWare will not compress files that are already compressed by some other utility, such as PKZIP, regardless of their compression flag setting.

4. In what environment is LIP (Large Internet Packet) most likely to improve performance?

   A. A switched network

   B. A routed network

   C. A bridged network

   D. All of the above

Refer to the Following Scenario in Answering Questions 5–6

You have been asked to evaluate the performance of a new NetWare 5 installation and make recommendations for improving the server performance. The NetWare 5 server is 400 MHz Pentium with 64MB of RAM, with a RAID 5 array consisting of five 4-gigabyte drives. The SYS volume is four gigabytes and the remainder of the disk space is configured as second volume. In addition to file service, the server provides DNS and DHCP service for the network.

5. What is the approximate size of the second volume on this server?

   A. 8GB

   B. 12GB

   C. 20GB

   D. 16GB

6. The number of files and the size of the second volume in this server have resulted in significant delays in mounting this volume after restarting the server. How would you resolve this?

   A. Periodically perform a purge on the volume to remove deleted files.
   B. Disable block suballocation on the volume.
   C. Delete the volume and recreate it using NSS.
   D. Increase the number of directory cache buffers using the appropriate SET statement.

Backing Up Servers and Workstations

1. What is a backup strategy that backs up only files that have been modified or created since that last backup, and that clears the archive bit on the backed up files?

   A. Full backup
   B. Incremental backup
   C. Modified backup
   D. Differential backup

exam
⚛atch
A TSA (Target Service Agent) is a program that runs on the target. It allows the SMS application to back up the data on the target.

2. What is the primary disadvantage of performing a combination of full and incremental backups?

   A. Incremental backups take longer and longer after the last full backup.
   B. Periodic differential backups have to be performed to assure a complete backup.
   C. This method takes the longest time in performing a full restoration.
   D. Possible data loss because incremental backups clear the archive bit.

Never combine differential and incremental backups. The incremental backup will not contain all of the information that has been changed since the last full backup.

3. Which of the following can be backed up using Novell's SMS suite? Choose all that apply.

A. NetWare server DOS partitions
B. The NDS tree
C. GroupWise databases
D. Windows NT and Windows 95/98 workstations

4. Which NLM module must be loaded on the server to allow communication with the WSBACK32 workstation GUI?

A. SMDR
B. QMAN
C. SBSC
D. TSADOSP

5. What is the minimum set of rights required in order to back up directories on a NetWare server?

A. Supervisor
B. Read and File Scan
C. Read , File Scan, Create, Delete
D. Read, File Scan, Create, Delete, Modify

QUESTIONS AND ANSWERS

If I have Windows 3.x workstations, can I use SMS to back them up?	No. SMS currently backs up only Windows 95 and Windows NT.
I run a 24x7 server. Which backup method is best for me?	Full with incremental. However, if you need to do a restore, it will take longer.
Can I back up my NDS and file system at the same time?	Yes. Load TSANDS and TSA500 on the server to be backed up.
I am the backup administrator and the server will not allow me to restore any data.	Make sure you have the required rights to restore data. They are different from the rights needed to back up data.
Can SMS be used in place of another nationally known backup program?	YES. SMS is fully integrated into NetWare 5. It has a re-run scheduler to allow you to set a backup schedule.

EXAM 50-640
QUESTIONS

Using DNS/DHCP Services

1. What utility is used to manage DHCP address assignments for the NetWare 5 DHCP service?

A. DNSDHCP.EXE

B. DHCPCFG.NLM

C. NAMED.NLM

D. DHCPSRVR.NLM

2. What setting can be configured to test for the presence of an IP address before providing it to a workstation through the DHCP service?

A. Configure the workstation to ping the address before accepting it.

B. Check the Ping Enabled option in the DHCP server options tab in the DNS/DHCP console.

C. Place the command SET IP PING = ON in the server AUTOEXEC.NCF.

D. Load DHCPSRVR with the command line option PING = TRUE.

3. How can DHCP address tables created by the NetWare 4.11 DHCP server be used after upgrading a server to NetWare 5?

A. DHCP tables are automatically upgraded as part of the NetWare 5 DHCP server installation.

B. By specifying the name of the NetWare 4.11 DHCP configuration file as a command line option when loading the DHCP server the first time

C. By using the DNS/DHCP Management Console to import the DHCP configuration file

D. It is not possible to import DHCP address tables created by the NetWare 4.11 DHCP server. These entries must be manually entered or a new table must be created.

Refer to the Following Scenario in Answering Questions 4–5

You have been given the task of setting up DNS and DHCP services for a small company. This company has a single NetWare 5 server connected to a 100MB switch. Two network segments, using the IP address block of 192.168.1.0 and 192.168.2.0 (subnet mask of 255.255.255.0) are each connected to the 100MB switch via an internal router. Another router connected to the 100MB switch is used to connect to the Internet. The NetWare 5 server should provide DNS, and requests for names outside of the local domain should be automatically forwarded to the ISP DNS server.

4. You decide to create a primary DNS server for this company, and have added the local hosts in the DNS table. What steps should be taken to allow local hosts to query this DNS server only, while still allowing Internet addresses to be resolved?

A. Configure DHCP services to use the NetWare 5 server IP address as the primary DNS server, and configure the NetWare 5 server to forward requests to the ISP DNS server.

B. Configure DHCP services to use the NetWare 5 server IP address as the primary DNS server, and configure DHCP services to use the ISP DNS server as a secondary DNS.

C. Configure DHCP services to use the NetWare 5 server IP address as the primary DNS server, and configure DNS on this server to use the ISP DNS as a secondary DNS.

D. Configure DHCP services to use the NetWare 5 server IP address as a secondary DNS server, and configure DHCP services to use the ISP DNS as the primary DNS.

5. During the installation, you configured the IP address of the NetWare server as 192.168.3.1 (255.255.255.0). What steps are required to allow you remote console access to this server via the Internet?

A. Load RCONJ at the server and have the local ISP add a DNS entry for your server to their DNS server with the address of 192.168.3.1.

B. Load RCONJ at the server and use a public IP address and NAT entry in the local Internet router to assign the 192.168.3.1 address to a public address.

C. Use the Telnet protocol and access the server using the IP address 192.168.3.1. No DNS is required.

D. It is not possible to perform remote console access to NetWare servers via the Internet.

Installing a Web Server

1. From where is the FastTrack Web Server installed?

   A. NWCONFIG

   B. A Windows 9x or NT Workstation

   C. Console One

   D. All of the above

---

exam
ⓦatch

The FastTrack Web Server installation must occur from a Windows 95, Windows 98, or Windows NT 4.0 workstation.

---

2. What is the TCP port for administrative access to the FastTrack server?

   A. Unless modified during setup, the administration port number is the same as the Web server.

   B. During setup, a random port number is generated. The installer can change this number.

   C. There is no TCP port for administrative access to the FastTrack server. Administration is performed at the server console.

   D. During setup, the installer must choose a TCP port for administrative access.

---

exam
ⓦatch

In order to start the Netscape FastTrack Web Server, the administrator would type NSWEB at the server's console prompt.

---

3. Which of the following databases can be used for user and group access to the FastTrack Web server? Choose all that apply.

   A. Windows NT domain accounts

   B. Local database on the Web server

   C. LDAP Directory Servers

   D. NetScape Directory Server 4.0

   E. Novell Directory Services

4. Choose the URL for connecting to the Administration page of a FastTrack server with an IP address of 192.168.1.1 and an Admin TCP port of 4500.

   A. {HYPERLINK http://192.168.1.1/4500}

   B. {HYPERLINK http://192.168.1.1} .4500

   C. {HYPERLINK http://192.168.1.1:4500}

   D. {HYPERLINK "https://192.168.1.1:4500"}

---

exam
ⓦatch   *Web services can be started and stopped from the Admin Preferences page.*

QUESTIONS AND ANSWERS

Laura has the FastTrack Web Server running on her NetWare 5 network. The CEO has mandated a new policy that only management users can have access to intranet content, which is currently being served by the FastTrack Web Server. Laura has all the management users created and grouped in NDS. What is the fastest way for Laura to implement the new policy?	Laura can go to the Global Settings page and change the user database to Novell Directory Services. Then she can apply the correct security to the users already set up in NDS.

QUESTIONS AND ANSWERS

Aaron is running the FastTrack Web Server on his NetWare 5 network. He has used the default settings during installation. Aaron has published the network standards on the server, and sent e-mail notification to all the network users that the server is available and giving its address. One user called and reported that the information was failing. Aaron discovered that the user had typed the address as http://servername:8080. What is the problem?	The user has tried to access the server content with a port number that is not being used by web services. The default port number is 80.

5. What two server commands can be used to start and stop the FastTrack server?

A. WEBSTART and WEBSTOP

B. STARTWEB and STOPWEB

C. FTSTART and FTSTOP

D. NSWEB and NSWEBDN

Securing the Directory Tree

1. In a NetWare 5 environment, where are trustee assignments stored?

A. NDS, file, and directory trustee assignments are stored in the NDS database.

B. NDS, file, and directory trustee assignments are stored in the file system access control list.

C. NDS trustee assignments are stored in the NDS database and file and directory trustee assignments are stored in the file system access control list.

D. NDS trustee assignments are stored in the NDS database and file and directory trustee assignments are stored in the bindery.

e x a m
Ⓦ a t c h   *Although the Supervisor right for objects and properties can be revoked by the IRF, file system Supervisor rights cannot be revoked by an IRF.*

2. Which of the following is true for property rights of an NDS object?

A. The Compare property allows a trustee to read the value of a property and compare it against a set value.

B. The Read property does not automatically grant the Compare property.

C. The Write property lets a trustee add, change, or delete a value of the property.

D. The Supervisor property does not grant the total of all other property rights.

EXAM 50-640
QUESTIONS

exam

Ⓦatch

The Admin object can be disabled, renamed, moved, and deleted like any NDS object. Its rights can be changed so that it no longer has administrative access. This should be done only after another Admin object has been created.

3. Which of the following is not true about the Admin object?

A. It can be renamed.

B. It cannot be deleted.

C. It can be moved.

D. Its administrative access can be removed.

QUESTIONS AND ANSWERS

Carla has just been hired as a NetWare network administrator and for her first assignment, she has been asked to make sure that no users have been granted access to the Human Resources servers, files, or NDS container. How can Carla perform this task?	Carla can implement NDS auditing and check to see if any users have accessed the objects in question.

4. Which default object property right allows users to browse the NDS tree and select an NDS context before logging onto the network?

A. The root object is a trustee of itself with Browse Object rights.

B. The [Public] trustee is a trustee of the root with the Read Property right.

C. The [Public] trustee is a trustee of the root with Browse Object rights.

D. Each container object is a trustee of the root with Browse Object rights.

5. Which statement about IRF is correct?

A. File system Supervisor rights can be blocked by an IRF but NDS object Supervisor rights cannot be blocked by an IRF.

B. An IRF can be used to block explicit trustee assignments.

C. An IRF can be used to grant additional rights.

D. NDS Object Supervisor rights can be blocked by an IRF, but file system Supervisor rights cannot be blocked by an IRF.

6. Container objects in NetWare 5 have a new object right that was not available in NetWare 4. What is it?

A. Add Self

B. Password Management

C. Inheritable

D. Inherited Rights Filter

QUESTIONS AND ANSWERS

Acme has hired a vendor to provide Help Desk services. The vendor will connect to Acme's network with a WAN link. If Acme's security policy is such that only the Global Admin group will have Supervisor rights to any container objects or the [Root], what is the highest level of services that the Help Desk can provide remotely?

The Help Desk will be able to provide server administration and user administration, since neither of these options require Supervisor rights at the container or [Root] level.

Maintaining NDS

1. What are the four types of NDS replicas?

    A. Master, slave, read, write

    B. Master, read/write, read only, and subordinate reference

    C. Root, master, parent, and child

    D. Master, primary, secondary, and subordinate reference

QUESTIONS AND ANSWERS

You are asked to create a partition.	Use NDS Manager. Select a container (a container will sometimes be specified) and use the Create Partition command.
You are asked whether it is possible to put some of the users from one organizational unit into one partition, and one into another.	Following the rule that partitions must be done along container boundaries, you know that it is not possible to put some of the users into one partition and some into another partition unless you first create a new subcontainer to put the users into.
You are shown a picture of an NDS tree and are asked what the partition root of the CA partition is. (On an exam, the partition will probably be highlighted instead of named.)	Knowing that the partition root is the container closest to the [Root] directory, you answer that the CA container is the partition root of the CA partition.
You are shown a picture of an NDS tree and are asked what the partition root of the middle partition is.	Knowing that the partition root is the container closest to the [Root] directory, you answer that the Big_Org container is the partition root of the [Root] partition.
You are shown a picture of an NDS tree and are asked which partitions are parents.	Knowing that parents are partitions with subordinate partitions below them, you select the answer that lists the [Root] and NY partitions.
You are shown a picture of an NDS tree and are asked which partitions are children.	Knowing that child partitions have partitions above them in the tree, you select the answer that lists the CA, NY, and ALB partitions.

exam
Ⓦatch

The Advanced Administration test often includes questions on the parent/child relationship of partitions as well as questions on partition roots. Be sure that you understand these concepts.

2. What server utility can be used to detect and repair NDS problems?

A. NDS Manager

B. DSREPAIR

C. NetWare Administrator

D. Console One

exam
Ⓦatch

Novell loves to test on subordinate references. You are quite likely to get a question where you have to figure out which servers in a tree hold subordinate references.

3. After loading the DSTRACE.NLM, what command can be used to log NDS synchronization activity to a file?

A. SET DSTRACE=ON

B. SET ENABLE DSTRACE=0

C. DSTRACE=ON

D. SET DS TRACE TO FILE = ON

EXAM 50-640
QUESTIONS

exam
ⓦatch

Novell tests include simulations of NetWare Administrator and NDS Manager, where you will have to perform simulated operations in each program. What's worse, you may have to take the test on a computer running Windows 3.1 in 640x480 mode. If possible, practice using both of these utilities on a computer similar to the one just described, so that you won't be thrown off by the different look of the screen at the exam.

4. Where is the actual NDS database on a server stored?

A. On a volume designated by the installer

B. On the server SYS volume

C. In a hidden partition on the server boot drive

D. In the DOS partition on the server boot drive

QUESTIONS AND ANSWERS

You are asked if a master replica is most like a read/write, read-only, or subordinate reference replica.	Choose the answer that says that a master replica is most like a read/write replica.
You are asked which replica you must have access to when changing the boundaries of a partition.	Choose the master replica of a partition. Remember that the unique thing about a master replica is that you must be able to access it when changing partition boundaries.
You are asked which types of replicas allow you to make changes to the NDS objects that they contain.	Choose the answer that lists master and read/write replicas. Remember that read-only and subordinate reference replicas are modified only by NDS, not by administrators.
You are asked which servers in a list of servers hold subordinate references.	Choose servers that hold replicas of partitions, but not replicas of the children of those partitions.

Mobile Clients

1. Which protocol is supported by NetWare 5's Remote Node Services (PPPRNS)?

   A. TCP/IP only

   B. TCP/IP and NetBEUI

   C. IPX only

   D. TCP/IP and IPX

2. What utility is used to configure remote access on a NetWare 5 server?

   A. NWCCON

   B. INETCFG

   C. PPPCON

   D. AIOCOMX

exam
Ⓦatch *Remote nodes are mobile clients that access the network using the modem as if it were a network interface card. Remote control workstations wait for a connection from a mobile client and allow it to take over its functions by sending presentation data over the wire.*

3. What does the default configuration for remote-access services include?

   A. Dial-out services only

   B. Pre-configured time limits for connections

   C. Bi-directional connections enabled on all configured ports

   D. Dial-in services only

QUESTIONS AND ANSWERS

Bruce had installed a NetWare 5 network and implemented the NetWare Connect PPPRNS service on a server with several attached modems. To test the service, Bruce used his home computer, which had Windows 95 and NetBEUI installed on it. Why would Bruce receive errors?	The PPPRNS service will allow network nodes to run over IP or IPX, but not over NetBEUI. Bruce should reconfigure the Windows 95 workstation to use IP or IPX and the NetWare client software.

EXAM 50-640 QUESTIONS

4. A Windows 95 workstation can use which of the following to dial out of the network using a NetWare Connect server's modem pool?

A. HyperTerminal

B. Dial-Up Networking

C. WIN2NCS

D. NetWare Client 32

exam
ⓦatch

When a modem is connected directly to a serial port, the correct adapter to use is Serial Adapter (COMx). If another adapter is used, such as a Digiboard multiport adapter that extends the serial ports on a server, the Serial Adapter (COMx) is not used.

NetWare® 5
Advanced
Administration
Answers

Q & A

The answers to the questions are in boldface, followed by a brief explanation. The incorrect answer choices are explained in the final paragraph following each correct answer. Some of the explanations detail the logic you should use to choose the correct answer, while others give factual reasons why the answer is correct. If you miss several questions on a similar topic, you should review the corresponding section in the Osborne/McGraw-Hill *CNE® NetWare®5 Study Guide* before taking the NetWare 5 Advanced Administration test.

Upgrading NetWare 3.1x to NetWare 5 Server

1. ☑ **B. 64MB RAM.** This is the minimum amount of RAM required for a basic NetWare 5 server. If you intend to use Java applets, such as Console One, you will need a minimum of 128MB. NetWare 5 uses free memory for caching files, so additional memory will usually result in a higher level of server performance.

   ☒ **A.** is incorrect because a Pentium-level processor is required for NetWare 5. **C.** is incorrect because the minimum amount of disk space for NetWare 5 is a 30MB DOS partition and 200MB for the SYS volume.
   D. is incorrect because NetWare 5 does not *require* a mouse. Although a mouse is recommended, NetWare allows the numeric keypad to perform mouse actions.

2. ☑ **D. Novell® DSK drivers.** These drivers were used by earlier versions of NetWare to provide disk drive and controller support. NetWare 5 discontinues support for DSK drivers and requires .CDM and .HAM drivers for disk access.

   ☒ **A.** is incorrect because many third-party NLM modules already support NetWare 5. The installer should verify that existing third-party modules have been tested. **B.** is incorrect because the Novell Upgrade Wizard is supported, and is used to perform an across-the-wire migration of a NetWare server. **C.** is incorrect because the Novell Client for DOS/Windows 3.x can be used to connect a new server to a network-mounted NetWare 5 CD, for performing the operating system installation.

3. ☑ **C.** Running UPGRDWZD.EXE. Executing the UPGRDWZD.EXE from the NetWare 5 installation CD will extract and install the Novell Upgrade Wizard application. The Upgrade Wizard is a Windows application that runs on a networked workstation. It reads data from an existing server and writes it to a target NetWare 5 server.

☒ **A.** is incorrect because it is not necessary to download the Wizard; it is located in the \PRODUCTS\UPGRDWZD directory on the NetWare 5 Operating System CD. **B.** is incorrect because the INSTALL.BAT on the NetWare 5 CD is used to install a new server or perform an in-place upgrade, not launch the Upgrade Wizard. **D.** is incorrect because the Upgrade Wizard installation can be run on a Windows 95 or NT workstation, and DOS is not required to access the CD.

4. ☑ **A.** An existing NetWare 5 server must be installed before performing an across-the-wire migration. Across-the-wire migrations use a workstation to transfer data from a source server to a destination server, and the destination server must be fully functional prior to starting the migration.

☒ **B.** is incorrect because the requirement listed for the destination PC is incorrect. The destination server must be operational and have a mounted SYS volume. **C.** is incorrect because the source and destination servers can be located anywhere on the network, provided there are no filters to prevent the migration workstation from communicating with both devices. **D.** is incorrect because the frame types have no bearing on the migration. A migration can even be performed between servers running separate protocols, such as IPX and TCP/IP, as long as the migration workstation can communicate with both servers.

5. ☑ **B.** An updated TSA312.NLM, located on the NetWare 5 CD, must be loaded on the source NetWare 3.x servers. This target service agent is used to communicate with the Upgrade Wizard workstation, and a specific version is required. This correct version, along with other updated NLM modules, is located in the PRODUCTS\NW3X directory on the NetWare 5 Operating System CD. Other NLM's that should be unloaded and updated include AFTER311 and A3112, TSA311, SMDR, SMDR31X, SPXS, TLI, CLIB, and STREAMS.

☒ **A.** is incorrect because there is no Novell module called UPGRADE. **C.** is incorrect because this NLM is used to load and configure network drivers, and is not used during a migration. **D.** is incorrect because long-name space is not a requirement for performing a migration and NetWare 3 uses a different NLM, OS2.NAM, for long-name support of NetWare 3.x servers.

6. ☑ **B.** Upgrade the NetWare 4.x server to NetWare 5 using the NetWare 5 in-place upgrade, then use the Upgrade Wizard to migrate the 3.x servers across-the-wire. Although the NetWare 4 server may require additional memory, your best option is to upgrade this server using the in-place upgrade, then use the Upgrade Wizard to migrate the users and data from the other servers. The in-place upgrade of a NetWare 4.1x server to NetWare 5 is a relatively simple procedure and eliminates the need to manually migrate data and rights from the existing 4.1x server to the new server.

☒ **A.** is incorrect because the Upgrade Wizard cannot be used to migrate NetWare 4.x servers. **C.** is incorrect for the same reason. **D.** is incorrect because it would not provide for a successful upgrade of the NetWare 4.1x server. Restoring the 4.1x NDS onto a NetWare 5 server would not allow the upgrade process to properly update the NDS schema and database structure.

7. ☑ **D.** The affected users require an updated client. NDS support is not available in the client software that shipped with NetWare 3.x. Full NDS support, as well as support for other key client changes, such as TCP/IP connections to the server, requires updating the client software.

☒ **A.** is incorrect because group membership will not affect the execution of a container logon script. **B.** is incorrect because user objects will automatically have the read attribute for their container. **C.** is incorrect because personal logon scripts will not prevent a container logon script from executing. In order of execution, container scripts will run first, followed by profile scripts, and then personal scripts.

Upgrading from Queue-Based Printing to NDPS

1. ☑ **C.** Automatic detection and installation of printer devices. NDPS does not automatically add printers to the network.

☒ **A.** is incorrect because NDPS does allow pure TCP/IP printing provided both the printer and the client workstation support the IP protocol. **B.** is incorrect because the Resource Management Service (RMS) agent in NDPS tracks printer drivers and supports automated printer downloads. **D.** is incorrect because bi-directional printer support is a supported feature of NDPS. Bi-directional printer support is currently enabled through the Event Notification Service (ENS), and allows the workstation to receive printer status messages. Future versions of NDPS will allow many of the functions to reside directly in the printer, further reducing the management requirements to the point where automatic detection and installation of printer devices can become a reality.

2. ☑ **A. SRS, ENS, and RMS.** The broker is comprised of the Service Registry Service (SRS), the Event Notification Service (ENS), and the Resource Management Service (RMS). The SRS tracks public access printer information and provides this information when queried by a client. The ENS provides event notification to clients for information such as job completion and printer status messages. The RMS maintains printer drivers, configurations, and banner pages and downloads this to clients and printers on request.

☒ **B.** is incorrect because, although printers and agents are components of NDPS, they aren't part of the broker. NDPS does not use queues. **C.** is incorrect because it lists components of the NDS tree that are not directly related to either NDPS or the broker. **D.** is incorrect because **A.** is correct.

3. ☑ **C. Check for the existence of a broker within 3 hops.** After the first installation of NDPS, subsequent NDPS installations will scan the network for brokers within three hops. The installer must have Supervisor rights to the existing broker. If a broker is found that meets these criteria, NDPS will use it. If no broker meets these criteria, NDPS will create a new broker.

☒ **A.** is incorrect since a new broker will not be created if an existing broker can be located within three hops of the server. **B.** is incorrect because the new NDPS install will not use the existing broker if it is further than three hops away. **D.** is incorrect because this is not an option during installation. After NDPS is installed on a server, you can elect to create a new broker using the NetWare Administration utility, but the NDPS installation will not ask you to use an existing broker or create a new one.

4. ☑ **B.** NetWare 5 client software. NDPS requires client software with built-in support for NDPS devices. All NetWare clients with this support will list NetWare Distributed Print Services as an option during install. This option must be checked during install. Even if your network environment does not use NDPS, it is a good idea to load the NDPS modules when updating clients. If you decide to switch to NDPS at a later date, the clients won't require another update.

☒ **A.** is incorrect because NDPS does not require TCP/IP. Either TCP/IP or IPX (or both) can be used for NDPS. **C.** is incorrect because a licensed connection to a specific server is not required. A NetWare license connection to at least one server on the network may be required, but particularly in the case of public access printers, a licensed connection to the NDPS manager's server is not a requirement. **D.** is incorrect because public access printers do not exist in the NDS tree and, by definition, can be accessed without requiring a rights assignment.

5. ☑ **A, B, C.** Novell, HP, and Xerox gateways are included with NetWare 5. The HP and Xerox gateways support their specific brands of printers. The Novell gateway is a generic gateway and can provide limited support for most printers that can be connected to a NetWare network.

6. ☑ **D.** All of the above. NDPS eliminates the need for print queues, capture statements, and print servers. In an NDPS environment, clients can communicate directly with printers.

Performing a Custom Installation

1. ☑ **D.** NSS volumes support DOS name space, Macintosh long name space, Unix Network File System name space, and Windows & OS/2 long name space. They do not require separate name space modules to be loaded, as traditional volumes require.k.

   ☒ **A, B, C.** Are all supported, so **D**, which encompasses all of them, is the only correct answer choice.

2. ☑ **A.** 802.2 is the default frame type for Ethernet adapters in both NetWare 4.1x and NetWare 5. Though 802.2 is the default, IPX can also be bound to 802.3, Ethernet_II, or Ethernet_SNAP.

   ☒ **B.** is incorrect because it does not list a valid frame type for Ethernet. **C.** is incorrect because it lists a frame type used as the default in NetWare versions prior to 3.12. **D.** is incorrect since this frame type is normally used for binding TCP/IP, not IPX. Although 802.2 is the default, IPX can be also be bound to 802.3, Ethernet_II, or Ethernet_SNAP.

3. ☑ **B.** Determine which portion of an IP address identifies the network and which portion identifies host devices. IP addresses are divided into two parts, the network portion and the host portion. The subnet mask determines how an IP address is divided. An address of 192.168.1.1 with a subnet mask of 255.255.255.0 would use the first three octets of the address to identify different networks, and the final octet to identify host devices on the network.

   ☒ **A.** is incorrect because the subnet mask itself does not limit the size of a network. Subnetting does affect the number of networks and host devices on a network, but that is not its primary purpose. **C.** is incorrect because the subnet mask does not affect network broadcast traffic. **D.** is incorrect because the subnet mask does not affect client/server connections.

4. ☑ **B.** Assign a unique number. You must always assign a unique internal IPX address. NetWare will generate a random number during the installation, but you should confirm that no other server *or network segment* is using this IPX net number. Servers connected to the same physical network segment and using the same frame type must use the same address when binding to the network adapter, but don't confuse this address with the internal net number.

☒ **A.** is incorrect since using the same internal network number on multiple servers will result in corruption of the NDS database and problems when connecting to a server. **B.** is incorrect since the same network number must be used on all servers connected to the same physical segment (bound to the same frame type), but the internal network addresses still must be unique. **D.** is incorrect because the internal network number does not affect the priority of a server on the network.

Setting Up the Network File System

1. ☑ **D.** To reduce the overhead associated with adding Macintosh name space to volumes that support DOS and Windows users. Adding name-space support to a volume will result in additional name-space directory entries for every single file and directory on the volume, regardless of the actual file type. Adding multiple name spaces that do not require support for the name space to a volume can significantly increase the DET (Directory Entry Table) requirements for the volume. In a mixed environment, it is often better to create a separate volume for Macintosh or Unix clients and add the required name space support on these volumes only.

☒ **A.** is incorrect because NetWare does allow Macintosh, DOS, Windows, and Unix files to coexist in the same directory, as long as the correct name space has been added to the volume. **B.** is incorrect for the same reason. **C.** is incorrect because DOS and Windows applications can share data files created by Macintosh applications, and vice versa.

2. ☑ **B.** Additional hardware cost and reduced disk performance. Mirroring and duplexing require a second hard disk of equal or greater size to the primary. A server with a requirement for 10GB of disk capacity would require a total of 20GB of disk capacity with mirroring enabled. Disk mirroring can also significantly reduce disk write performance, because disk writes must occur on two drives. Since both drives are connected to the same controller, the duplicate writes are sequential. In a duplexed disk environment, writes can occur simultaneously, so disk write performance is not significantly affected. Duplexing can also improve read requests, since multiple disk channels are available to service the request.

☒ **A.** is incorrect because it assumes that mirroring is an off-line process. NetWare provides mirroring on a real-time basis. A remirror process may affect overall network performance, but the volumes being remirrored are still available. **C.** is incorrect because disk mirroring does not require identical disk drives. Mirroring requires identical disk partitions on each drive, but the drive types and overall capacities do not have to match. Disk duplexing even allows different types of controllers, such as IDE and SCSI, to be used. **D.** is incorrect because it assumes that mirroring is an off-line process and that network volumes are unavailable during this process. Both of these assumptions are incorrect.

3. ☑ **D.** Personal bindery logon scripts are stored in subdirectories of SYS:MAIL. The SYS:MAIL directory is maintained by NetWare 5 primarily for backwards compatibility with earlier versions of NetWare. NDS personal logon scripts are maintained in the NDS tree, but bindery connections cannot read the NDS database. Bindery logon scripts, like previous versions of NetWare, are maintained in subdirectories under SYS:MAIL.

☒ **A.** is incorrect because it indicates that the subdirectories under SYS:MAIL contain a portion of the user logon name. Novell assigns a cryptic numeric value to these subdirectories. You can determine the owner of a particular directory in SYS:MAIL by looking at the trustee list for the directory. **B.** is incorrect because NetWare maintains the MAIL folder for compatibility. If you delete this folder, NetWare will report warning messages during DSREPAIR operations, and bindery logon scripts will be lost. **C.** is incorrect because few mail applications still use the SYS:MAIL directory. GroupWise® maintains mail in its own domain and post office directories.

4. ☑ C. To redirect data in the event of a sector write failure. NetWare offers read-after-write verification of data. In the event of a sector failure, the operating system will redirect the data to the hot fix area of the disk. A large number or redirects usually means the drive is failing. Most newer drives and controllers now support verification in hardware and the default setting in NetWare 5 disables this feature. It can be enabled using the SET ENABLE DISK READ AFTER WRITE VERIFY=ON at the server.

☒ A. is incorrect because backup copies of the DET are not stored in this area, but are stored as part of each NetWare volume. B. is incorrect because NetWare patches are loaded from a NetWare volume, and the hot fix area is specifically reserved for data redirection. D. is incorrect because server memory dumps are normally stored on the DOS partition on the server. During a new install, sufficient space should be reserved for the DOS partition to store a memory dump of the server. For example, a server with 256MB of RAM would require an additional 256MB of free space in the DOS partition to perform a memory dump.

5. ☑ A, B. ACCOUNTING_APPLICATIONS and _PERSONNEL. A volume named ACCOUNTING_APPLICATIONS exceeds NetWare's volume name limit of 15 characters. The _PERSONNEL volume begins with the underscore character. NetWare does not allow volumes to start with this character.

☒ C. is incorrect because PERSONNEL_ is a valid volume name. D. is incorrect because (APPLICATIONS) is also a valid volume name. E. is incorrect because 9&LIVES is a valid volume name. NetWare volume names can use characters in the range of a–z, A–Z, and 0–9, and the characters)(&%$#@! and _.

Using the Server Console

1. ☑ **B.** STARTX. The STARTX.NCF file, located in the SYS:JAVA\NWGFX directory, loads the server Java support modules. The GUI interface is also loaded. This interface allows the installer to run both Console One and the GUI installation program for NetWare 5.

   ☒ **A.** is incorrect because the command is STARTX, not XSTART. **B.** is incorrect because the MONITOR command loads the text-based interface, not the graphical console. **D.** is incorrect because there is no NetWare command named CONSOLE.

2. ☑ **D.** ALT-ESC and CTRL-ESC. At the server console, the ALT-ESC key sequence will jump from the current screen to the next screen. Pressing this key combination repeatedly will allow you to page through all the open screens on the server. The CTRL-ESC key sequence will present a list of active screens—pressing the number next to a screen will jump to that screen. This also provides you with a summary of the active tasks on the server.

   ☒ **A.** is incorrect because the ALT-F3 and ALT-F4 key sequence is used for remote (RCONSOLE) access only. Using RCONSOLE, these sequences allow you to page back (ALT-F3) or page forward (ALT-F4). At the console, there is no equivalent capability to page in either direction. **B.** and **C.** are incorrect because neither of these key combinations will allow you to switch between screens.

3. ☑ **D.** RCONJ. The RCONJ.EXE utility, located in the SYS:PUBLIC directory, supports both TCP/IP- and IPX-based remote console access. Although it is a GUI utility, it can only be used to access the text screens on a NetWare 5 server; remote access to the server Console One interface is not currently supported.

   ☒ **A.** is incorrect because the RCONSOLE.EXE utility only supports remote access using the IPX protocol. **B.** is incorrect because basic Telnet connections to a NetWare server are not supported; Telnet lacks support for properly displaying and switching server screens. **C.** is incorrect because the NWADMIN.EXE NETADMIN utility does not provide for remote access. This DOS utility for managing NDS is not supported in NetWare 5.

4. ☑ **D.** Load SCRSAVER ACTIVATE. The screen saver application replaces the built-in *snake* screen saver that previous versions of NetWare loaded via the MONITOR. When this application is loaded with the ACTIVATE command-line option, the screen saver will become active immediately. Pressing any key or attempting to remotely access the server will require a logon name and password. This account must be in the ACL for the server.

☒ **A.** is incorrect because the SECURE CONSOLE command does not lock the console. This command is used to prevent loading and unloading modules at the server, to enter the server debugger, and to prevent changing the server date or time. **B.** is incorrect because the MONITOR screen in NetWare 5 does not have a console lock option, unlike previous versions of NetWare. **C.** is incorrect because neither the RCONSOLE nor RCONJ utility has a console lock option.

5. ☑ **C.** EDIT C:STARTUP.NCF. The server STARTUP.NCF file resides on the DOS partition, in the same directory as SERVER.EXE (normally C:\NWSERVER). Loading the editor, followed by a drive letter and filename will cause the editor to look in the current directory on the specified drive. The autoexec.bat created by a NetWare 5 install will make the NetWare 5 install directory on the DOS partition the current directory.

☒ **A.** is incorrect because the STARTUP.NCF file is not located on the SYS volume; it must reside on the DOS partition. **B.** is incorrect because this command will attempt to load STARTUP.NCF from the SYS:SYSTEM directory as well. Loading the editor and specifying a filename without a drive letter or volume path will cause the editor to look in this directory. **D.** is incorrect because the "c:\" portion of the command will cause the editor to look in the root of the DOS drive, not the subdirectory where SERVER.EXE resides. Placing the STARTUP.NCF anywhere except in the same directory as SERVER.EXE will prevent SERVER.EXE from executing the control file.

Optimizing the Network and Server

1. ☑ **B.** Garbage collection. The garbage collection process runs periodically and scans the server for memory that was previously allocated to other processes, but is no longer in use. This memory is returned to the server memory pool for reuse.

   ☒ **A, C.** are incorrect because the process names are not valid. **D.** is incorrect because the process name is invalid and virtual memory refers to a different kind of memory not related to RAM. Only RAM memory is scanned during the garbage collection process.

2. ☑ **D.** Cache buffer memory. This memory parameter refers to the amount of unused memory in the server. Memory not in use by other processes is actually used by the server for disk caching, hence the name cache buffer memory. A low percentage of cache buffer memory is a valid indication that the server has insufficient RAM for the number and types of processes currently running. When evaluating the need for adding memory to a server, only the amount of free memory is of interest to us.

   ☒ **A.** is incorrect because the allocated memory pool refers to memory that is currently allocated to active processes. **B.** is incorrect because the total server work memory refers to the total amount of RAM in the server. This value should match the installed memory in the server. If it does not, you may have to use NetWare's REGISTER MEMORY command to recognize the additional memory. **C.** is incorrect because the cache movable memory statistic, as in **A.**, refers to memory that is in use, not free memory.

3. ☑ **A.** A volume's file compression status can be enabled and disabled using SET parameters is a false statement. Although a volume's file compression status can be enabled using a SET parameter, once enabled, you cannot disable compression on a volume without deleting and recreating it. You can, however, temporarily suspend compression across all of a server's volumes using a SET parameter.

☒ **B.** is incorrect because it is possible to mark a file for compression using the FLAG command. When a file or directory is flagged IC (immediate compression) the operating system begins compressing the files immediately, regardless of the time of day or other processes running on the server. Files that are eligible for compression based on the Days Untouched Before Compression SET parameter are only compressed during the normal file compression window (default is 12:00 am–6:00 am). **C.** is incorrect because the operating system automatically decompresses files in RAM when they are used. No manual process is required. Accessing a compressed file once will not normally result in decompressing the file on disk, but subsequent accesses will, assuming sufficient disk space is available, result in the file being rewritten to disk uncompressed. Files that are flagged IC remain compressed regardless of the number of times they are accessed. These files can be restored to uncompressed form by setting their FLAG to N (normal) or DC (don't compress). **D.** is incorrect because the operating system will evaluate the amount of space to be freed by the compression process, and will only compress files that meet the Minimum Percentage Compression Gain SET parameter. Attempting to compress an already compressed file will actually result in a larger file, due to the added compression information written to the file. Therefore, files compressed using other compression utilities will not be compressed by NetWare.

4. ☑ **B.** A routed environment. LIP is only used when a workstation must communicate with a server across a router. As part of the connection process, the workstation will negotiate the largest packet size that the server and the intermediate router(s) can support. This packet size will be used as the maximum packet size for subsequent communication. Some older versions of the NetWare client would automatically default to a maximum packet size of 576 bytes whenever a router hop was encountered.

☒ **A, C, D.** are incorrect because LIP negotiation only occurs when the source and destination are on different network segments. Both switched and bridged environments treat the network as a single physical segment.

5. ☑ **B.** 12GB. The capacity of a RAID 5 array can be determined using the formula A x (B-1) = C, where A = drive size, B = number of drives, and C = usable storage. This server has a total of 16GB usable storage, of which 4GB has been assigned to the SYS volume. The remaining 12GB was assigned to the second volume.

☒ **A, C, D.** The remaining answer choices are incorrect based on this formula for determining RAID 5 capacity.

6. ☑ **C.** Delete the volume and recreate it using NSS. Volumes created using NSS can be mounted almost instantaneously, regardless of their size. Since NSS volumes can only be set up using free disk space (not space allocated to a traditional NetWare partition), it will be necessary to resize the NetWare partition on this server. That will require removing both of the volumes on this server, resizing the NetWare partition, and then rebuilding the SYS volume. At present, the SYS volume cannot be an NSS volume.

☒ **A.** is incorrect because a purge of the volume will only reduce the mounting time of the volume IF the delay is a direct result of a large number of deleted (but not yet purged) files. **B.** is incorrect because block suballocation is not a factor in mounting a volume. **D.** is incorrect because the number of directory cache buffers simply determines how much of the directory is held in cache memory. This affects file searching after the volume is mounted, but not the actual time required to mount a NetWare volume.

Backing Up Servers and Workstations

1. ☑ **B.** Incremental backup. Incremental backups back up the files that have been created or modified since the last full or incremental backup. The archive bit is cleared so that the next incremental backup does not attempt to back up files that have not changed since the current incremental backup.

 ☒ **A.** is incorrect because full backups back up all files, regardless of their archive-bit setting. Full backups clear the archive bit so that incremental or differential backups can determine if a file needs to be backed up. **C.** is incorrect because Novell does not have a backup strategy by this name. **D.** is incorrect because differential backups do not clear the archive bit.

2. ☑ **C.** This method takes the longest time in performing a full restoration. When restoring data using a full and incremental backup, the last full backup and ALL subsequent incremental backups must be restored. The incremental backups must also be restored in the same sequence that they were created. The advantage to this method is that the incremental backups take less time than any other backup method. Only files modified since the last full or incremental backup are backed up by the next incremental backup.

 ☒ **A.** is incorrect because incremental backups do not back up files that were backed up by previous backups, so the backup time does not necessarily increase. **B.** is incorrect because differential backups should never be mixed with incremental backups. Doing so can result in lost data, since the differential backup and full backup sets would not necessarily contain modified files that exist on intervening incremental backup sets. **D.** is incorrect because, although the archive bit is set during incremental backups, this does not increase the likelihood of data loss.

3. ☑ **A, B, C, D.** SMS provides target agents that can back up the server DOS partition, the NDS tree, GroupWise e-mail databases, and Windows NT and Windows 95/98 workstations on the network.

4. ☑ **C. SBSC.** This is the SBackup Communications module and it is normally the last module loaded when configuring the server for backups. ☒ **A.** is incorrect, since this module refers to the SMS data requestor. This module is used for internal communications at the server, not for communications to the client GUI. **B.** is incorrect because QMAN is the server Queue Manager and does not communicate with the client. **D.** is incorrect because this module is a target service agent used on the server to allow an SMS host to back up the server DOS partition.
Server-based backups can be accomplished by loading (in the listed order), each of the following modules:

- Disk controller driver
- NWTAPE.CMD
- SMDR
- Server TSAs (TSA500, TSANDS, TSADOSP)
- SMSDI
- QMAN
- SBSC (if the client WSBACK32 is used)
- SBCON (if the server C-Worthy interface is used)

5. ☑ **B. Read and File Scan.** Backups can be accomplished by any account with this minimum set of rights to a directory. Subdirectories can also be backed up, provided an inherited rights filter does not block these rights. ☒ **A.** is incorrect, Supervisor rights are not required for directory and file backup. **C.** is incorrect because Create and Delete rights are not required for backups. If the same account is used to restore files, then Create and Delete rights will be required. **D.** is incorrect for the same reason.

Using DNS/DHCP Services

1. ☑ **A.** DNSDHCP.EXE. This is an executable file that runs on a network workstation. It is a Java-based application that provides management of both the DNS and DHCP modules loaded on the server.

   ☒ **B.** is incorrect because NetWare 5, unlike·NetWare 4.11, does not use the server DHCPCFG.NLM. While it is possible to load the DHCP server from NetWare 4.11 onto NetWare 5 and use this utility, it lacks integration with the NDS tree, as well as the advanced DHCP options that are available through the NetWare 5 DNS and DHCP services. **C, D.** are incorrect because these commands are used to load DNS and DHCP services at the server, but they cannot be used to manage the configuration of either service.

2. ☑ **B.** Check the Ping Enabled option in the DHCP server options tab in the DNS/DHCP console. From the workstation console utility, highlight the DHCP server icon at the bottom of the screen. This will allow you to access the DHCP server OPTIONS tab. The Ping Enabled button will instruct the server to ping an address before assigning it to a workstation. If another workstation responds to the ping, the server will skip to the next available address and send another ping. The downside to this setting is that there is additional traffic generated by this process.

   ☒ **A.** is incorrect because workstations cannot be configured to ping an address before accepting it. Windows 95/98 and NT will ping the address after receiving it, and will disable their IP assignment if another station responds, but not before. **C, D.** are incorrect because there are no SET parameters or command-line options that can enable this function; it must be configured through the workstation console.

3. ☑ C. By using the DNS/DHCP Management Console to import the DHCP configuration file. The Console includes an Import function to allow DHCP 2.0 or 3.0 format files to be imported into the NetWare 5 DHCP tables. After selecting the file to import, you can choose the subnets to import, the destination NDS container for the subnets, and the DHCP server that will manage these addresses.

☒ A. is incorrect because DHCP tables are not automatically upgraded. Before DHCP tables can be upgraded, a destination NDS location must be selected. B. is incorrect because there is no command-line option for the DHCP server that will support importing of DHCP tables. D. is incorrect because it is possible to import DHCP address tables using the DNS/DHCP Management Console.

4. ☑ A. Configure DHCP services to use the NetWare 5 server IP address as the primary DNS server, and configure the NetWare 5 server to forward requests to the ISP DNS server. After creating the DNS and DHCP servers, the DHCP subnets should be configured with at least two attributes, the default gateway and the primary DNS server. To allow all DNS queries to be resolved locally, and forwarded only as necessary, use the IP address of the NetWare 5 server as the primary and only DNS.

☒ B. is incorrect because merely adding the ISP DNS server as a secondary DNS results in failed DNS lookups. The secondary DNS server is only used if the primary is unavailable. If the primary is not configured to forward requests as necessary, then DNS queries for Internet hosts will not be resolved. C. is incorrect because this is not a valid configuration and will also result in unresolved DNS queries. D. is incorrect because this will result in the opposite problem: DNS queries for Internet hosts would be resolved, but local DNS host names would not be resolved.

5. ☑ **B.** Load RCONJ at the server and use a public IP address and NAT entry in the local Internet router to assign the 192.168.3.1 address to a public address. The address block of 192.168.0.0 is a reserved address block for local IP addressing. Because it's reserved, Internet routers are configured to ignore requests to route to these addresses. In this environment, all IP traffic is routed via the public address of the local Internet router. You can (assuming this router supports NAT (network address translation)) use NAT to map a second public address in the router to the private address of this NetWare 5 server.

☒ **A.** is incorrect because adding a DNS entry at the local ISP using a private address will not allow traffic to be routed via the Internet to this device. **C.** is incorrect for the same reason. Even if NAT is used to connect to the server via a public address, NetWare does not support Telnet access to the console. **D.** is incorrect because it is possible to access NetWare server consoles via the Internet and TCP/IP, as long as a valid IP address is used and the correct protocols and software (i.e. RCONJ) is loaded at the server.

Installing a Web Server

1. ☑ **B.** A Windows 9x or NT Workstation. The PC used to install this software must be running Novell's NetWare Client 32. This workstation must have 100MB of free disk space for temporary file storage, a CD-ROM drive, and a Web browser installed.

☒ **A, C, D.** are incorrect because the FastTrack Web server can only be installed from a client PC. The SETUP.EXE is a Windows application that runs on a client workstation.

2. ☑ **B.** During setup a random port number is generated. The installer can change this number. Administration of the Web server is performed via a browser connection to the server. An Admin connection can be made via a browser by entering the TCP/IP address of the server followed by a colon and the administrative port number in the browser URL box. Write down the random number or the number that you choose for the Admin port assignment, since you will need it to complete the FastTrack server installation.

☒ **A.** is incorrect, since setting the administrative port number to the same port as the Web server will result in administrative access to the server for any connection. **C.** is incorrect because no administrative functions can be performed at the server console. **D.** is incorrect because the installer has the option of using the randomly generated port, or selecting a new one.

3. ☑ **B, C, E.** User and group access can be configured to use one of these three options. The local database is created and maintained using the Administrative page. LDAP and NDS users and groups must be maintained using the standard administrative tools available to these directories.

☒ **A, D.** are incorrect because it is not possible to directly use either NT domain accounts or NetScape Directory Server accounts for access to the FastTrack Web server. These accounts would require an LDAP interface.

4. ☑ **C.** HYPERLINK http://192.168.1.1:4500. The syntax for connecting to the server Admin page is the IP address and the Admin port number, separated by a colon.

☒ **A, B.** are incorrect because slashes and periods cannot be used to separate the IP address and port number. **D.** is incorrect because secure hypertext transfer protocol (http) is not used to connect to the FastTrack server Administration page.

5. ☑ **D.** NSWEB and NSWEBDN. The full file names are NSWEB.NCF and NSWEBDN.NCF. These NetWare Control Files launch the NLM modules to load both the Web server and the Administrator server.
☒ **A.** is incorrect because these commands were used with the Web server that shipped with IntranetWare. **B, C.** are incorrect because there are no NCF or NLM files with these names.

Securing the Directory Tree

1. ☑ **C.** NDS trustee assignments are stored in the NDS database and file and directory trustee assignments are stored in the file system access control list. The NDS database only maintains object and property rights for NDS objects in the tree. File and directory rights are maintained as part of the file system structure itself.
☒ **A.** is incorrect because it assumes that file and directory rights are stored in the NDS database. **B.** is incorrect because NDS object rights are maintained in the NDS database and not in the file system. **D.** is incorrect because file and directory trustee assignments are not stored in a bindery file. NetWare 5 can use the NDS database to emulate a bindery, but there are no actual bindery files present on a NetWare 5 server. Bindery files in a NetWare 3.x environment are used to store user and group information, not file and directory assignments.

2. ☑ **C.** The Write property lets a trustee add, change, or delete a value of the property.
☒ **A.** is incorrect because the Compare property does not allow a trustee to read the actual value of a property. The Compare property does, however, allow the trustee to compare a property against a set value. **B.** is incorrect because the Read property does automatically grant the Compare property. **D.** is incorrect because the Supervisor property does grant the total of all other property rights.

3. ☑ **B. It cannot be deleted.** This is a false statement. The Admin account can be deleted. This should only be done after another account with administrative access has been created. Making another account the equivalent of the Admin account and then deleting the Admin account will render the equivalency invalid. You must use trustee assignments to the ROOT or appropriate container for the new account if you intend to delete the Admin account.

☒ **A, C, D.** are all incorrect because the Admin account can be treated like any other user account. It can be disabled, deleted, renamed, or moved. It can be restricted by logon time and network address. Its trustee assignments can be modified or blocked by an inherited rights filter.

4. ☑ **C. The [Public] trustee is a trustee of the root with Browse Object rights.** The [Public] object is a special object that can be used without authenticating to the NDS tree. Granting this object Browse at the root of the tree allows unauthenticated connections to browse the tree and select an NDS context before logging into the network.

☒ **A, B, D.** are incorrect because there are no default object assignments that match the listed actions.

5. ☑ **D. NDS Object Supervisor rights can be blocked by an IRF, but file system Supervisor rights cannot be blocked by an IRF.** All file system rights EXCEPT Supervisor can be blocked using an IRF. NDS object Supervisor rights, by design, can be blocked using an IRF. This allows the NDS tree to restrict Supervisor access to lower levels.

☒ **A.** is incorrect because the IRF capabilities are reversed; file system Supervisor rights cannot be blocked by an IRF, while NDS object Supervisor rights can. **B.** is incorrect because an explicit trustee assignment will ignore any IRF assignments. **C.** is incorrect because an IRF can be used to block rights from flowing down the tree, but cannot be used to grant additional rights.

6. ☑ **C.** Inheritable. This right allows or disallows the inheritance of object or property rights to a container object. It was added to allow the creation of group and password administrators. When this right is granted to a trustee, the right flows down to all containers and objects below the selected container.

☒ **A.** is incorrect because NetWare 4 does have the Add Self object right. **B.** is incorrect because there is no object right called Password Management, and the Inheritable object right allows for the creation of password managers. **D.** is incorrect because IRF is available in NetWare 4, and IRF is not an object right, but a filter to object rights.

Maintaining NDS

1. ☑ **B.** Master, read/write, read only, and subordinate reference. The master replica is used to update all other replicas of a partition and can be used for NDS™ authentication. A read/write replica can be used to update NDS objects, but its updates must be sent to the master replica for distribution to other replicas. Read/write replicas can be used to authenticate against the NDS database. Read-only replicas receive updates but cannot be used to update NDS objects. Read-only replicas cannot be used for NDS authentication. Subordinate references are created automatically when a server maintains a replica of a parent partition, but does not maintain replicas of partitions below the parent.

☒ **A.** is incorrect because there is no *slave* replica in NDS. **C.** is incorrect because the term *root* refers to the top of the NDS tree, not a type of partition. Likewise, the terms *parent* and *child* refer to the relationships between partitions in the tree, not replica types. **D.** is incorrect because there are no primary or secondary replica types in NDS. These terms are most commonly associated with NT domain controllers, not NDS.

2. ☑ **B.** DSREPAIR. The DSREPAIR.NLM can be used to check database synchronization and time synchronization, and is the primary tool for performing database repairs.

☒ **A.** is incorrect because the NDS Manager is a workstation utility, not a server utility, that provides a GUI interface to NDS management. **C.** is incorrect because the NetWare Administrator is also workstation based and cannot be used to repair NDS. **D.** is incorrect because at present, Console One does not include NDS troubleshooting capabilities.

3. ☑ **C.** DSTRACE=ON. NetWare 5 includes a new DSTRACE.NLM. After loading this module, directory synchronization traffic can be monitored and logged by entering the DSTRACE=ON command at the server console. Entering the command DSTRACE with no options provides a list of the types of traffic that can be monitored. DSTRACE <type> will enable monitoring for the specified traffic. DSTRACE – <type> will disable monitoring for the specified traffic.

☒ **A.** is incorrect because this command was used in previous versions of NetWare that did not support the DSTRACE.NLM. This command was used to enable console viewing of NDS synchronization, but did not enable file logging. **B, D.** are incorrect because they are not valid NetWare SET statements.

4. ☑ **B.** On the server SYS volume. Care should be taken to assure that the sufficient space remains available on every server to support the NDS replicas maintained by that server. During DS repair operations, additional space is usually required to allow the repair process to back up the database.

☒ **A.** is incorrect because it is not possible to designate a volume for the NDS database. **C, D.** are incorrect because neither of these locations can be used for the database.

Mobile Clients

1. ☑   **D.** TCP/IP and IPX. Both of these protocols are supported by the Point-to-Point Protocol Remote Node Service in NetWare 5.
☒   **A.** is incorrect because it does not include IPX. **B.** is incorrect because PPPRNS does not support NetBEUI. **C.** is incorrect because it does not include TCP/IP.

2. ☑   **A.** NWCCON. The first time this utility is loaded on the server, it will update the NDS schema, create the Connect object, and allow the installer to configure remote access services. The same program can be loaded later to reconfigure these services.
☒   **B.** is incorrect because the INETCFG utility can display remote-access configuration information but cannot be used to configure remote access. **C.** is incorrect because this utility is used to monitor the status of PPP connections (including remote-access sessions) but it cannot be used to configure remote access. **D.** is incorrect because AIOCOMX is the name of the device driver used for asynchronous communications (serial) ports. This driver is used by NWCCON if remote communications will be established using asynchronous ports or modems.

3. ☑   **C.** Bi-directional connections enabled on all configured ports. By default, both dial-in and dial-out connections are enabled on all ports and all ports and services are enabled for all network user accounts.
☒   **A, D.** are incorrect because both dial-in and dial-out services are enabled by default. **B.** is incorrect because the default configuration for remote access connections has no time-limit restrictions.

4. ☑ C. WIN2NCS. The WIN2NCS utility (available on the NetWare 5 CD) acts as a communications port redirector, routing local communications ports to a port on the NetWare connect server.

☒ A. is incorrect because the HyperTerminal program in Windows 95 is a communications program. Although it can be used with WIN2NCS, it does not provide native support for dial-out connectivity through NetWare Connect. B. is incorrect because Windows 95 Dial-Up Networking also requires WIN2NCS for dialing out through NetWare Connect. D. is incorrect because the NetWare Client 32 does not provide support for dial-out connections.

Part 3

Networking Technologies (Exam 50-632)

EXAM TOPICS

Network Services

Transmission Media and Connections

The OSI Model's Lower Layers

The OSI Model's Middle Layers

The OSI Model's Upper Layers

Networking
Technologies
Questions

Q & A

This section is designed to help you prepare for the Networking Technologies exam (Exam # 50-632) so you can begin to reap the career benefits of CNE® certification. The following questions are structured in a format similar to what you'll find on the exam. Read all the choices carefully, as there may be more than one correct answer. Choose all correct answers for each question.

Network Services

1. Which of the following services is provided when an end user copies the CONFIG.SYS file from a workstation hard drive to a server's drive?

   A. Print
   B. Fax
   C. Message
   D. File

2. Which type of computer does a terminal access?

   A. Server
   B. Peer
   C. Web host
   D. Mainframe

3. What are NetWare 5's NSS volumes?

   A. Online storage
   B. Nearline storage
   C. Offline storage
   D. Backup storage

4. Select an example of an offline storage service.

   A. NSS

   B. HCSS

   C. CD-ROM

   D. Tape backup system

5. Which of the following is a print service?

   A. NDPS

   B. NDS™

   C. HCSS

   D. NSS

6. Which of the following services uses a store-and-forward concept to move its data towards the destination?

   A. Storage services

   B. Print services

   C. Message services

   D. Application services

7. Select the type of service that is provided by File Transfer Protocol (FTP).

   A. Storage service

   B. Message service

   C. Database service

   D. Application service

Use the Following Scenario to Answer Questions 8–11

TDX.Com is a new Internet company with a group of NetWare® 5 servers running the FastWeb server software to provide the Web services to Internet customers. TDX.Com records the length of time that each customer uses when accessing their TDX software and manages charges based on the bytes transferred.

8. TDX.Com's network administrator has set up a firewall between the Internet Web servers and the internal TDX.Com servers. What type of network management function does a firewall provide to TDX.Com?

A. Fault management
B. Security management
C. Performance management
D. Database management

9. TDX.Com has a Web page that is dedicated to contacting various departments in the TDX.Com Corporation. Through the contacts page, a click on a department takes the user to another Web page that has the department's address in the *To:* field completed and space for the end user to write a request. When the user clicks the *Done* button, the Web server sends the Web page contents via TCP port 25. What type of service is being provided?

A. Application
B. Web
C. Message
D. Database

10. The TDX.Com network administrator uses an analysis application to watch the network traffic for SNMP messages. When certain SNMP messages are received, the application pages the administrator. What type of management feature does this represent?

A. Configuration
B. Fault
C. Security
D. Accounting

exam
Ⓦatch

Make sure you understand when network print services should be implemented. There are so many different scenarios that it is hard to tell you exact ways to do things. From the information you'll be given in the questions, come up with your own inference as to when to implement print services. If you need to share a printer, fax capabilities, or copying functions, then print services will be used.

11. TDX.Com's network administrator decides to implement the NetWare Application Launcher (NAL). The NAL configuration provides installation icons for all TDX.Com's applications. The administrator decides to secure the applications so that they cannot be launched unless using NAL. What has the administrator implemented for workstations?

    A. Configuration management

    B. Fault management

    C. Security management

    D. Performance management

Transmission Media and Connections

Use the Following Scenario to Answer Questions 1–2

George is installing a network for Private Health Care (PHC). PHC has three nursing care facilities in two states. None of the facilities has an existing network. Instead, PHC has some stand-alone PCs and Apple Macintosh computers, and a UNIX host running an accounting package with two serial terminals in a single room at one nursing facility. Data is faxed to the facility with the UNIX host and input to the accounting system.

1. When George goes to evaluate the type of cabling to put into PHC's main nursing facility, he is told that the building is old and has power problems. In fact, years ago, they had tried installing terminals to the Unix host outside its current location, but the power problems disrupted the transmission so badly

that they gave up. What consideration should George prioritize for the transmission media?

A. Attenuation

B. Cost

C. Immunity from interference

D. Capacity

2. George decides that both the Sun City and the Flagstaff sites can use Cat 5 cabling with RJ-45 connectors. What type of medium is Cat 5?

A. Copper shielded twisted-pair.

B. Copper unshielded twisted-pair.

C. Fiber optic

D. Copper coaxial

3. What type of wiring is used by cable television?

A. RG-8

B. RG-58

C. RG-59

D. RG-62

4. Why might Thin Ethernet be selected over UTP?

A. The capacity for Thin Ethernet is higher than gigabit Ethernet over UTP.

B. Thin Ethernet costs more than UTP.

C. Thin Ethernet does not require any hubs.

D. Thin Ethernet uses a wireless media connector.

5. What type of media uses the line of sight to ensure connectivity?

A. Terrestrial systems

B. Fast Ethernet

C. Radio

D. Fiber optics

6. Which connector is used with coaxial cabling?

A. T-connector

B. DB-25

C. RJ-45

D. IBM data connector

7. What equipment transforms a digital signal into an analog signal for transmission?

A. NIC

B. MODEM

C. Repeater

D. Hub

8. Which of the following performs a repeater function?

A. NIC

B. Modem

C. Active hub

D. Passive hub

9. Tim's mainframe is connected to a machine that enables multiple terminals to use the same serial connection. What type of machine is the mainframe connected to?

A. Modem

B. Bridge

C. MUX

D. Hub

10. Which of the following pieces of equipment can forward data based on a network address, or forward it based on the MAC address if the data meets configuration criteria?

A. Brouter

B. Bridge

C. Router

D. Switch

11. What does a CSU/DSU convert?

A. Analog signals to digital signals

B. Analog signals to analog signals

C. Digital signals to analog signals

D. Digital signals to digital signals

The OSI Model's Lower Layers

1. Which of the following OSI layers defines bitstream signaling?

A. Physical

B. Data link

C. Network

D. Transport

2. What physical topology consists of several point-to-point links connected to a single central station?

A. Ring

B. Star

C. Bus

D. Mesh

3. What best describes TCP/IP?

A. Protocol

B. Protocol stack

C. Layer

D. Network

4. What type of connection is made between a computer and a locally attached printer?

A. Point to point

B. Multipoint

C. Single

D. Multiple

5. What physical topology offers the highest level of redundancy?

A. Ring

B. Mesh

C. Bus

D. Star

exam
Ⓦatch   *Ethernet MAC addresses are six bytes in length. The first three bytes are the manufacturer's assigned number, and the remaining three bytes are allocated serially to ensure that there are no duplicate Ethernet MAC addresses.*

6. Which of the following physical topologies uses wireless media?

A. Cellular

B. Star

C. Mesh

D. Ring

7. Which of the following physical topologies can be implemented with a logical ring topology?

A. Cellular

B. Star

C. Bus

D. Mesh

8. What type of signal does encoding create?

A. Digital

B. Frequency

C. Amplitude

D. Analog

9. Which of the following encoding techniques does not use a transition between a positive or negative voltage and a zero voltage to represent data?

A. Polar encoding

B. RZ

C. NRZ

D. Biphase encoding

10. What type of modulation technique will increase the voltage for a one-bit value, but not for a zero-bit value?

A. Amplitude shift keying

B. Frequency shift keying

C. Phase shift keying

D. Biphase encoding

11. Which transmissions use the entire bandwidth of the media?

A. Baseband

B. Ring

C. Broadband

D. Contention

12. Which of the following media access methods uses a special frame to grant media access to each network computer?

   A. Contention

   B. Token passing

   C. Polling

   D. Media access control

13. What method does the Data Link Layer use to check for errors in transmissions?

   A. Parity

   B. Clocking

   C. Contention

   D. Bit synchronization

exam
ⓦatch

The two sublayers of the Data Link Layer are the Media Access Control, which controls how multiple network devices share the same media channel, and Logical Link Control, which controls the establishment and maintenance of links between communicating devices.

The OSI Model's Middle Layers

Use the Following Scenario to Answer Questions 1–9

JNS is an enterprise with four sites. The JNS internetwork will be implemented as shown in the following illustration. This configuration is a hub and spoke network, where the HQ site is the hub and all other networks are the spokes with direct point-to-point links to the HQ site. RTR1 will have an IP address of 199.5.5.52 on one interface and 199.5.6.81 on the other interface. The subnet masks for all IP addresses at JNS is 255.255.255.0.

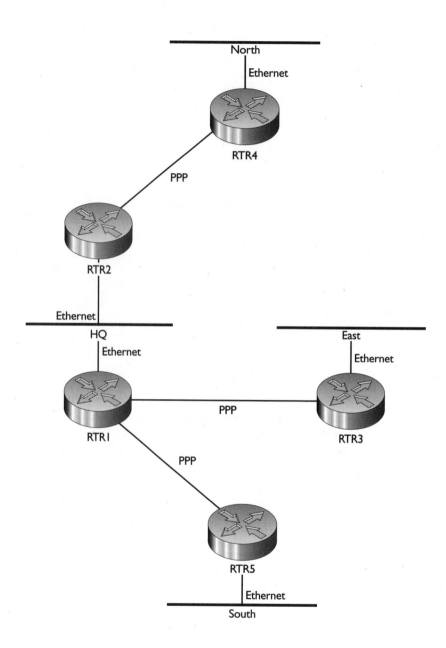

1. Pat, JNS's administrator, wants to apply the addresses of 199.5.5.1 and 199.5.5.2 to each of the interfaces on RTR2 as the first part of standardizing the addressing scheme on all routers. What will prevent this scheme from working?

A. The node addresses must be the same for each interface.

B. The network segments must have unique addresses.

C. The network addresses cannot have the same first three bits.

D. The network segments must not have unique addresses.

2. Pat runs a sniffer on the network and asks a consultant what the numbered output of one line means. The line was 1a03.0000.0000.0001.0452. The consultant replied that this was the internal IPX network address (1a03), the internal node address (0000.0000.0001) and the service address (0452). What does a service address represent?

A. Workstation

B. Server

C. Segment

D. Process

exam
ⓦatch *It is sometimes useful to think of Network Layer addresses in the way a letter is addressed through the U.S. Post Office. The network address is like a street, since many nodes (like houses) can exist on it. The node address is the house number and the service address is the person in the house who can receive the letter.*

3. Pat is thinking of replacing the JNS point-to-point links with ATM switches. What type of switching does ATM perform?

A. Packet switching

B. Circuit switching

C. Message switching

D. Cell switching

4. Pat asks a consultant what mechanism the routing protocol will use to build the routing table. What is the consultant's answer?

A. Route selection

B. Static routes

C. Route discovery

D. Packet switching

5. Pat is considering using a distance vector routing protocol for IPX routing. What is the IPX distance vector routing protocol?

A. NLSP

B. OSPF

C. RIP

D. RTMP

6. Pat wants to know what the hops metric is from the East network to the South network. How many hops are there?

A. Two

B. Three

C. Four

D. Five

7. Pat knows that TCP is considered a reliable transport layer protocol. He was surprised to see that some packets were dropped and errors occurred on his network. What does reliability guarantee?

A. Data receipt

B. Data transmission

C. Acknowledgment of receipt

D. Error-free data

8. Pat is concerned that his protocol analyzer output does not have any server names identified. The consultant tells him not to worry, that the address is mapped to a name. What is the mechanism used to map names to addresses?

A. Address/name resolution

B. Connection identifier

C. Port

D. Aggregation

9. If a host is not listed in JNS's DNS server, Pat believes that ARP can be used to update hosts files with an address-to-name mapping. What type of packet does ARP use to resolve names and addresses?

A. Token

B. Broadcast

C. Port

D. Multicast

10. How does a workstation identify which packets are meant for which data conversations if they are all multiplexed into a single datastream?

A. Error control

B. CRC

C. Windowing

D. Connection identifier

11. What is the application that NetWare uses to manage address/name resolution for the TCP/IP protocol suite?

A. NetWare administrator

B. NDS manager

C. DNSDHCP

D. Address manager

12. What other mechanism is used to determine whether errors have occurred?

A. DNS

B. Parity

C. Segmentation

D. Multiplexing

13. What can determine whether duplicate packets have been received?

A. Connection identifier

B. Sequence number

C. Acknowledgment

D. Window

The OSI Model's Upper Layers

1. Which of the upper layers handles bitstream formatting?

A. Session

B. Presentation

C. Application

D. None of the above

2. What layer handles data translation and formatting?

   A. Session

   B. Presentation

   C. Application

   D. None

3. What lower level mechanism does the session layer depend upon to notify it of interruptions in service?

   A. Multiplexing

   B. Sequence number

   C. Port

   D. ACK

4. What type of dialog provides simultaneous, bidirectional communication?

   A. Simplex

   B. Half duplex

   C. Full duplex

   D. Multiplexing

5. What type of dialog is a commercial radio broadcast?

   A. Simplex

   B. Half duplex

   C. Full duplex

   D. Triplex

6. Which of the following is NOT handled at the presentation layer?

   A. Encryption

   B. Compression

   C. Sequencing

   D. Expansion

7. Which method is used to read data from the first byte received?

A. Big endian

B. Little endian

C. Bit-order translation

D. Compression

8. Which two methods are examples of character translation?

A. ASCII

B. EBCDIC

C. NDS

D. ANSI

9. What mechanism sometimes uses a public and private key?

A. Encryption

B. Compression

C. Expansion

D. Bit-order translation

exam
ⓦatch   *The Session Layer is usually considered to be the source location of remote procedure calls (RPCs). RPCs transmit data over the internetwork in a manner that is transparent to the end user.*

10. What layer specifies the user's interface to the network?

A. Application

B. Session

C. Presentation

D. Network

11. Which of the following transport layer services advertises applications?

    A. NDS

    B. SAP

    C. DNS

    D. RIP

12. At what layer does an RPC work?

    A. Application

    B. Presentation

    C. Session

    D. Transport

exam
ⓦatch

Decryption is the process of deciphering the code in an encrypted file.

13. Which application layer service provides a remote terminal of a NetWare server?

    A. FTP

    B. NDIR

    C. RCONSOLE

    D. REMOTE.EXE

Networking Technologies Answers

Q & A

The answers to the questions are in boldface, followed by a brief explanation. The incorrect answer choices are explained in the final paragraph following each correct answer. Some of the explanations detail the logic you should use to choose the correct answer, while others give factual reasons why the answer is correct. If you miss several questions on a similar topic, you should review the corresponding section in the *CNE® NetWare®5 Study Guide* before taking the Networking Technologies test.

Network Services

1. ☑ **D. File services are provided when an end user copies the CONFIG.SYS file from a workstation hard drive to a server drive.** File transfer is the actual function performed. File transfer can be as simple as a drag-and-drop function from a GUI (graphical user interface), or as complex as a command typed on the command line with multiple arguments to manipulate the properties of the transferred file. File services incorporate more than transfer to a server. Files can also be transferred from a server. The server provides a form of storage for the end user. File services on a central server can provide a level of security that may not be available on a workstation.

    ☒ **A.** Print services is incorrect because it refers to printers, not files. **B.** Fax services is incorrect because it is a subset of print services. **C.** Message services is incorrect because it refers to electronic messaging, or e-mail.

2. ☑ **D. A terminal accesses a mainframe computer.** Mainframes perform centralized computing. Mainframes were the precursors to networks, but are still used today. Mainframes provide the total processing power, data storage, and security of their applications. Terminals are considered "dumb" because they have no processing power of their own. A terminal consists of a monitor and keyboard, but little else. Terminals present a window into the mainframe, so that each terminal acts as a separate console. Most terminals tend to be text only.

    ☒ **A.** Server is incorrect because it does not support terminals. **B.** Peer is incorrect because terminals do not have peer computers. **C.** Web host is incorrect because it supports Web browser clients, not terminals.

3. ☑ **A.** NSS volumes on NetWare® 5 are an example of online storage. NSS can be installed through NWCONFIG to replace the NetWare File System. NSS is a new storage architecture for providing file services to end users. It is installed on a server and is provided transparently as a service to NetWare clients. Clients can transfer files to and from an NSS volume as easily as to and from a legacy NetWare file system volume. NSS improves on several areas:

—It can support larger files—up to 8 terabytes in size for a single file. The old NetWare system could only support a 4 gigabyte size for a single file.

—It can load volumes faster, including CD-ROMs.

—It can load a DOS FAT partition as a volume, so the administrator can manage the DOS partitions without having to take the server down.

—It can logically pool storage space on several devices to provide a device-independent volume.

—NSS provides a 64-bit file system. The legacy NetWare File System is a 32-bit system.

☒ **B.** Nearline storage is not correct because it is a form of removable media. **C.** Offline storage is not correct because it is a backup system. **D.** Backup storage is not correct because it is not a term commonly used.

4. ☑ **D.** A tape backup system is an example of an offline storage service. Offline storage services are not intended to be part of the files served to end users. Instead, offline storage is meant to be taken away from the network. Tape backup systems are used to copy all or some of the files on NetWare file server volumes. Once a file has been copied to the tape backup file system for a full or incremental backup, the archive property of the file is removed. If the file is changed, the archive property is set again. The server knows which files have changed since the last backup due to this archive property. A differential backup does not change the archive property. Full backups copy all files on a NetWare volume. Incremental backups copy all files changed since the last backup. Differential backups copy all the files that have changed since the last full backup.

☒ **A.** NSS is not correct because it is a new 64-bit online storage service. **B.** HCSS is not correct because it is a nearline storage service. **C.** CD-ROM is a nearline storage device.

5. ☑ **A.** Novell Distributed Print Services (NDPS) is a NetWare print service. NDPS is a newer print service in comparison to the legacy print-queue-based services. NDPS was created in partnership by Xerox, Hewlett-Packard, and Novell₀. It takes advantage of 32-bit Windows operating systems' printing abilities and new print technologies to provide a point-and-print function on the network. NDPS does require workstations to be 32-bit Windows operating systems.

☒ **B.** NDS™ is a directory service. **C.** HCSS is a nearline storage service. **D.** NSS is an online storage service.

6. ☑ **C.** Message services use the store and forward concept to move data through the internetwork to its destination. A message service consists of electronic post offices and gateways, or connectors, that interconnect them. When a message is sent from a client, it is stored on the client's post office and put into an outbox. The outbox is periodically checked for stored contents, or initiates transfer upon receipt of contents, depending on the post office configuration. The address of each recipient for each message is checked against the address book and address type to determine the final destination post office. The message is then forwarded on to the next post office in the path to the final destination post office. At the next post office, the message is again stored until it can be forwarded further on.

☒ **A.** Storage services does not forward data. **B.** Print sevices does not use a storage and forward concept. **D.** Application services does not store and forward data.

7. ☑ **A.** Storage service is provided by FTP. A server must be equipped with the TCP/IP protocol stack in order to provide FTP because it is part of the TCP/IP protocol stack.

Storage services include the provision of files for download by client workstations. This is a form of online storage, because the files are stored on the hard drive of the server and are available for immediate use.

☒ **B.** Message service uses SMTP in the TCP/IP stack. **C.** Database service does not use FTP. **D.** Application service also does not use FTP.

8. ☑ **B.** A firewall provides security management to the TDX.Com network, as shown in the following illustration. Firewalls are computers with two or more network interface cards in them. One network interface card connects to one segment and the other connects to another segment. The firewall performs routing of data between the segments, but with a twist. Instead of simply forwarding the data from one segment to another, the firewall looks at each packet of data and forwards it if it meets certain criteria. These criteria are designed to prevent unauthorized access to the network. The result is that the firewall filters data.

☒ **A.** Fault management is incorrect because a firewall does not watch network faults. **C.** Performance management is incorrect because a firewall does not watch network performance. **D.** Database management is incorrect because a firewall does not require a database to run.

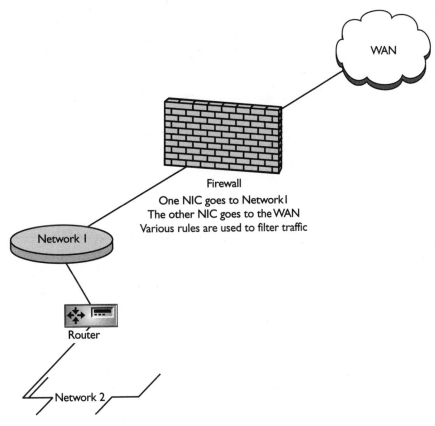

Firewall
One NIC goes to Network1
The other NIC goes to the WAN
Various rules are used to filter traffic

9. ☑ **C.** The server is providing a message service to Internet users. SMTP uses TCP port 25, and SMTP is a message service. It is a common practice to integrate a message service with a Web page. This enables a person with a Web browser to send e-mail without requiring that person to have an e-mail account or e-mail application.

☒ **A.** Application services does not use TCP port 25. **B.** Web service is incorrect because the Web uses TCP port 80. **D.** Database service does not use port 25.

10. ☑ **B.** The TDX.Com administrator is using fault management. This is the detection, prevention, diagnosis, and reparation of network problems. SNMP is a protocol in the TCP/IP protocol stack that creates messages on a network device and sends them to a designated IP address. The messages are received by the SNMP management console and given a value based on the criteria configured by the network administrator. Many SNMP applications will send out alerts via fax or pager, based on whether a message meets certain conditions.

☒ **A.** Configuration management is not normally transmitted over the wire. **C.** Security management is incorrect because it refers to management of passwords and access. **D.** Accounting management refers to the utilization of a resource.

11. ☑ **A.** The TDX.Com administrator has implemented configuration management for workstations. NAL includes many features that can be used to distribute software in a managed fashion. It is typically used for securing applications so that only certain end users are able to use the applications. Applications do not appear in the NAL window unless the user has been granted access to the application.

☒ **B.** Fault management is incorrect because NAL does not manage faults. **C.** Security management is incorrect because NAL does not manage network security. **D.** Performance management is incorrect because NAL does not monitor performance.

Transmission Media and Connections

1. ☑ **C.** George should prioritize interference immunity when selecting a transmission media. The problems that PHC described are typical of electromagnetic interference, or EMI. Serial terminals are typically installed on unshielded, low-category copper twisted-pair cabling. This type of cabling is very susceptible to EMI. When George selects transmission media for the PHC main facility, he should automatically eliminate any cabling that is susceptible to EMI. George will probably find that the cost will increase for this requirement. Fiber cabling is not susceptible to EMI and will probably prove to be the best option for PHC's main facility.

☒ **A.** Attenuation is not related to power problems, but to cable length. **B.** Cost is incorrect because budgeting is not mentioned. **D.** Capacity is not correct because speed or amount of transmission is not mentioned.

2. ☑ **B.** Cat 5 cabling is a copper, unshielded, twisted-pair wiring. Unshielded twisted-pair is commonly known as UTP. It is capable of high-speed throughput of up to 100 Megabits per second. The Cat 5 cabling is commonly installed in new networks. It is a flexible transmission medium because it supports Token Ring, Ethernet 10BaseT and Ethernet 100BaseT, as well as some less common protocols.

☒ **A.** Copper-shielded twisted-pair is not correct because it does not use RJ-45 connectors. **C.** Fiber optic is incorrect because it also does not use RJ-45 connectors. **D.** Copper coaxial is incorrect because it, too, does not use RJ-45 connectors.

3. ☑ **C.** Cable television uses RG-59 cabling. The RG-59 cabling is similar in appearance to Thin Ethernet, which uses RG-58 coaxial cabling. The OHM rating for cable television is 75 ohms.

Cable television has begun to offer "cable modems" for Internet access. This is actually a network connection to the cable network. Cable television has also implemented a fiber backbone in many locations. Although a cable modem uses the modem name, it is not a modulator/demodulator device but a digital service unit. It accesses and transmits digital data, not analog.

☒ **A.** RG-8 is incorrect because it is Thicknet. **B.** RG-58 is incorrect because it is Thinnet **D.** RG-62 is incorrect because it is used for ArcNet.

4. ☑ **C.** One reason that Thin Ethernet might be selected over UTP (unshielded twisted-pair) is that Thin Ethernet does not require any hubs. Thin Ethernet is implemented in a true physical bus, connecting each node directly into the cable. Thin Ethernet is the RG-58 coaxial cabling with a 50-ohm rating.

    ☒ **A.** Thin Ethernet has a lower capacity than UTP, so this answer is incorrect. **B.** Thin Ethernet actually costs less than UTP. **D.** Thin Ethernet does not use any wireless connectors, so this answer is also invalid.

5. ☑ **A.** Terrestrial systems using microwaves use line of sight to ensure connectivity. The terrestrial systems use directional parabolic antennae, which are similar in appearance to satellite TV dishes that are pointed at each other. Terrestrial systems antennae must be within a certain distance of each other, so that the curvature of the earth does not prevent connectivity. There cannot be any interfering physical structures between the antennae.

    ☒ **B.** Fast Ethernet is incorrect because it uses cable media. **C.** Radio is incorrect because it does not require line of sight. **D.** Fiber optics is incorrect because it uses fiber media.

6. ☑ **A.** Coaxial cables commonly use T-connectors. The T-connector is an improvement over the older vampire clamps, which literally bite into the coaxial cabling in order to create the connection.

    ☒ **B.** DB-25 connector is not correct because it is more commonly used for serial connections. **C.** RJ-45 connector is incorrect because it is typically used for unshielded twisted-pair cabling. **D.** IBM data connector is incorrect because it is used with STP.

7. ☑ **B.** A modem transforms a digital signal received from the computer into an analog signal and transmits it across the wire. A modem also receives analog signals from the wire and transforms them into digital signals that the computer will understand. When a digital signal is changed into an analog signal, the process is called modulation. The opposite process is called demodulation.

The modem gets its name from modulator/demodulator, which is its function. A similar piece of equipment is called a CODEC, which stands for coder/decoder. A CODEC, acting much like a digital cellular phone, takes an analog signal and transforms (codes) it into a digital signal for transmission, then performs the opposite action (decodes) for received signals.

☒ **A.** NIC is incorrect because it does not transform a digital signal to analog. **C.** Repeater does not use analog signals. **D.** Hub is incorrect because it does not use analog signals at all.

8. ☑ **C.** An active hub performs a repeater function for all the segments connected to it. This is not the same as a passive hub, which simply sends the signal on without repeating it. The difference of using an active hub instead of a passive hub is that the active hub allows the maximum segment length of cable to be connected to each port. However, because a passive hub does not perform repeating, the maximum length of all cables connected to the hub must be less than the maximum length. Because an active hub enables much more cable length to be used to reach each workstation, active hubs are more common than passive hubs.

☒ **A.** NIC is wrong because it does not repeat signals. **B.** Modem is incorrect because it modulates digital signals to analog. **D.** Passive hub is incorrect because it does not have the power to copy and retransmit a signal.

9. ☑ **C.** A multiplexer (MUX) is a type of equipment that enables multiple terminals to use the same connection. The MUX can use different types of multiplexing techniques.

A time division multiplexer takes each transmission and slices it into time slots, then interleaves the time slots of each signal onto the single connection. A frequency division multiplexer uses different frequencies for each transmission and sends them simultaneously across the same connection.

☒ **A.** Modem is incorrect because it does not multiplex connections. **B.** Bridge is incorrect because it does not handle a serial connection. **D.** Hub is incorrect because it does not handle a serial connection.

10. ☑ **A.** A brouter can forward data based on either the MAC address or the network layer address. The word *brouter* is a contraction of the words "bridge" and "router." The brouter performs the functions of a bridge for any data that is configured to be bridged, making forwarding decisions based on a MAC address. The brouter can also perform the functions of a router for any data that is configured to be routed, making a forwarding decision based on the network layer address.

☒ **B.** Bridge is incorrect because it does not use the network address. **C.** Router is incorrect because it does not use the MAC address. **D.** Switch is incorrect because it does not forward data based on either a MAC or network address.

11. ☑ **D.** A Channel Service Unit/Digital Service Unit (CSU/DSU) converts digital signals to digital signals. The CSU/DSU transfers data in a format that can be transmitted across a WAN. It also receives data from the WAN and transfers it in a format that can be transmitted on a LAN.

☒ **A.** Analog to digital is incorrect because it would be converted by a modem or CODEC. **B.** Analog to analog is incorrect because it does not involve digital signals at all. **C.** Digital to analog is incorrect because it would be converted by a modem or CODEC.

The OSI Model's Lower Layers

1. ☑ **A.** The Physical layer of the OSI reference model defines bitstream signaling, which is the actual format of the data signals that are interpreted as ones and zeroes. The data must be received by a node that uses the same signal format in order for the data to be understood. The physical layer is also responsible for specifying the transmission media, which is usually a form of cabling. Transmission media can take the form of wireless transmissions, such as radio, microwave, or infrared.
☒ **B.** Data link is incorrect because it handles hardware addressing.
C. Network is wrong because it handles logical addressing and data routing.
D. Transport is wrong because it handles datastream connection services.

2. ☑ **B.** The star topology consists of several point-to-point links connected to a single central station. A physical topology is the layout of the network. It creates a shape. The types of shapes that a topology can take are ring, star, mesh, bus, and cellular.
☒ **A.** Ring is not correct because it is several links connected in a circle.
C. Bus is not correct because it is a multipoint connection on a single cable.
D. Mesh is not correct because it is a collection of point-to-point links between every node.

3. ☑ **B.** Transmission Control Protocol/Internet Protocol (TCP/IP) is the common name for a nonproprietary protocol stack. It is a nonproprietary protocol stack developed by the Advanced Research Projects Agency (ARPA), for use in sharing data between heterogeneous computers.
☒ **A.** Protocol is incorrect because a protocol represents a single element within a protocol stack. **C.** Layer is incorrect because a layer is only a single element's place within a protocol stack. **D.** Network is incorrect because a network represents a group of computers that communicate with each other.

4. ☑ **A.** The type of connection made between a computer and its locally attached printer is a point-to-point connection. Two devices share a point-to-point connection. No more than two can access the point-to-point connection. A multipoint connection is the type of connection that allows more than two devices to access the link.

☒ **B.** Multipoint is incorrect since the link is shared between only two nodes. **C.** Single and **D.** multiple are invalid answers.

5. ☑ **B.** The mesh topology offers the highest level of redundancy. A mesh topology has a link from each node to each other node in the network. The multiple links provide redundant paths to the same destination in the network, as shown in the following illustration.

☒ **A.** Ring is incorrect because the ring has no redundancy. **C.** Bus is incorrect because the bus has no redundant links. **D.** Star is wrong because the star has no redundancy.

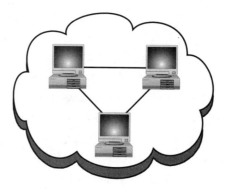

6. ☑ **A.** The cellular topology uses wireless media. Cellular topology is composed of multiple areas that are called cells. Each is serviced by a wireless hub. The network devices are contained within the cells and then gain access to the network through the wireless hub.

☒ **B.** Star is incorrect because it typically uses copper UTP cabling. **C.** Mesh is incorrect because it tends to be a WAN technology and always uses cables. **D.** Ring is incorrect because it requires either copper or fiber-optic cabling between each station in the ring.

7. ☑ **B.** The physical star topology can be implemented with a logical ring topology. Token ring is an example where the physical star topology can be implemented with a logical ring topology. In this configuration, the signal travels around the network in a ring, even though the physical topology is a star. This is shown in the following illustration.

☒ **A.** Cellular is a wireless physical topology that can only be implemented with a cellular logical topology. **C.** Bus is a physical topology that can only be implemented with a logical bus topology. **D.** Mesh is a physical topology that can only be implemented with a logical mesh topology.

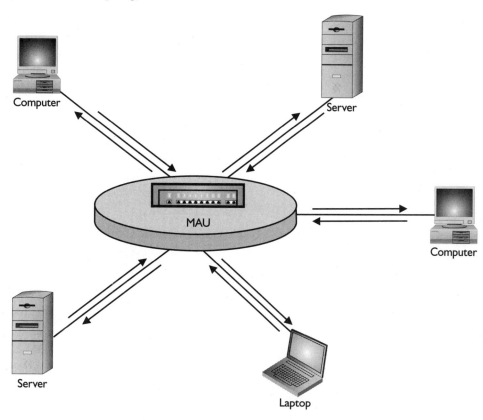

8. ☑ **A.** Encoding creates a digital signal. A digital signal is encoded when it is created. The techniques for encoding a digital signal use different voltages and voltage changes to specify a one bit or a zero bit. Equipment that is used to create digital signals is called a coder/decoder (CODEC).
☒ **B.** Frequency is incorrect because it represents an analog modulation technique. **C.** Amplitude is incorrect because it represents an analog modulation technique. **D.** Analog is incorrect because it is created through modulation.

9. ☑ **A.** Polar encoding does not use a transition to represent data.
☒ **B.** Return to Zero (RZ) is incorrect since it determines all data from the transitions. **C.** Non Return to Zero (NRZ) is incorrect since it determines all one bits of data from transitions. **D.** Biphase encoding is incorrect since it requires a transition for each bit.

10. ☑ **A.** Amplitude shift keying (ASK) increases the voltage for one-bit values and not for zero-bit values. Amplitude shift keying modulates the amplitude of the carrier between two levels. If the analog wave were drawn out on paper, it would show that this technique increases the heights of the waves so that they are more easily discernible from the other bit values.
☒ **B.** Frequency shift keying is incorrect because it assigns a different frequency to each of the bit values. **C.** Phase shift keying is incorrect because it shifts the phase of the signal to show that the value of the bit has changed. **D.** Biphase encoding is incorrect because it is a digital encoding technique and not a modulation technique.

11. ☑ **A.** A baseband transmission uses the entire bandwidth of the media. Baseband transmissions are typically used for LAN data transmissions. The opposite of a baseband transmission is a broadband transmission. Broadband transmissions are similar to a cable television transmission, which sends several signals across the same cable simultaneously.
☒ **B.** Ring is incorrect because it is a physical topology. **C.** Broadband is incorrect because it is a transmission type that divides the bandwidth into channels. **D.** Contention is incorrect because it is a media access method.

12. ☑ **B.** Token passing is a media access method that uses a special frame, called a token, to grant media access to each network computer. Token passing uses a token frame that is passed from computer to computer on the network. When a computer has data to transmit, it can only begin to send after it receives the token. Once it has completed the transmission, it passes the token to the next computer on the segment.

   ☒ **A.** Contention is incorrect since it allows all network computers to access the network at any time. **C.** Polling is incorrect because a central polling device polls each computer in order to grant media access. **D.** Media access control is incorrect because it is a data-link sublayer.

13. ☑ **A.** The data-link layer uses parity to check for transmission errors. Parity is only one type of error checking. It is a bit that is added as either a zero or a one value to ensure that the data is always an even number (even parity) or odd number (odd parity). If a frame is received that is not the expected parity, then the frame is discarded. Another error-checking method that the data-link layer employs is the cyclic redundancy check (CRC). The CRC is an algorithm that is executed before the data is sent and the result is sent along with the data frame. The receiving node executes the same algorithm, and if the result does not match, the frame is discarded as having been in error.

   ☒ **B.** Clocking is incorrect because that is a physical layer mechanism. **C.** Contention is incorrect because it is a media access method. **D.** Bit synchronization is incorrect because it is a physical layer clocking mechanism.

The OSI Model's Middle Layers

1. ☑ **B.** The network segments must have unique addresses. Pat's IP address scheme will not work because it attempts to give the HQ segment and the point-to-point WAN segment the same network address of 199.5.5.0. IP addresses are network layer addresses. The network layer requires that network segments have unique network addresses.

   ☒ **A.** This option is incorrect because the node addresses must not be the same. **C.** This option is incorrect because there is no such requirement. **D.** This option is incorrect because the network segments must have unique addresses.

2. ☑ **D.** A service address represents a process. IPX uses a service address to represent the applications that run on a computer. This is known as a Source Service Access Point (SSAP) or Destination Service Access Point (DSAP).

☒ **A.** Workstation is incorrect because it is represented by a node address. **B.** Server is incorrect because it is represented by a node address. **C.** Segment is incorrect because it is represented by a network address.

3. ☑ **D.** Asynchronous Transfer Mode (ATM) performs cell switching. It uses a 53-byte cell, which is shorter than a packet. A 53-byte cell is so small that it can be switched without storing it on an ATM router before forwarding it. This enables ATM to be extremely fast.

☒ **A.** Packet switching is incorrect because ATM uses cells. **B.** Circuit switching is incorrect because ATM does not create a circuit for the entire data transmission. **C.** Message switching is incorrect because ATM uses cells.

4. ☑ **C.** The consultant answers that the routing protocol uses the route discovery mechanism to build the routing table. Route discovery is the mechanism that a routing protocol uses to find out how to reach destination networks. There are two types of route discovery, and a routing protocol is classified as either one type or the other. The two types of route discovery are distance vector and link state.

☒ **A.** Route selection is wrong because it is the mechanism that determines which is the best route when there are multiple routes. **B.** Static routes is incorrect because they are not built by dynamic routing protocols. **D.** Packet switching is incorrect because it is not a routing protocol mechanism.

5. ☑ **C.** Routing Information Protocol (RIP) is a distance vector routing protocol that works over IPX. IPX has a version of RIP for its protocol stack. TCP/IP has two versions of RIP for its protocol stack, namely, RIP I and RIP II. All versions of RIP are distance vector protocols that use a hops metric (distance) and a direction to the next router (vector).

☒ **A.** NLSP is wrong because it is a link-state protocol that works over IPX. **B.** OSPF is wrong because it is a link-state protocol that works over TCP/IP. **D.** RTMP is wrong because it is a distance vector protocol that works over AppleTalk.

6. ☑ **B.** There are three hops between the East network segment and the South network segment. The number of hops is determined by the number of routers that must be passed between the source and destination. The route between the East segment starts with RTR3, goes through RTR1, and then through RTR5 until it reaches the destination South network segment. On RTR3, the hops would number only two because RTR3 would not include itself as a router in the path.

☒ **A.** Two is wrong because there are more routers than two between the segments. **C.** Four is wrong because there are only three routers. **D.** Five is also wrong because there are only three routers.

7. ☑ **C.** Reliability guarantees that an acknowledgment will be sent when data is received. Reliability refers to the use of acknowledgment (ACK) packets. An ACK will convey to the sending node that the data was received. ACKs are not sent when the data is not received and they are not sent when the data received has errors. The sending node will wait for the ACK packet. If an ACK is not received, the sending node will either notify upper layers or it will resend the data.

☒ **A.** Data receipt is wrong because there is no guarantee that the data will be received. **B.** Data transmission is wrong because there is no guarantee that the data will be transmitted. **D.** Error-free data is wrong because there is no guarantee that an error will not occur.

8. ☑   **A.** Address/name resolution, or simply, name resolution, is the mechanism used to map names to addresses. Since computer devices communicate and transmit data using numeric addresses and their operators use alphanumeric names, there has to be some resolution between the name and the address of the same device.

☒   **B.** Connection identifier is incorrect because it is a port or socket used to specify the data conversation. **C.** Port is incorrect because it is used to specify the data conversation. **D.** Aggregation is incorrect because it is the reassembly of packets into a message.

9. ☑   **B.** The Address Resolution Protocol (ARP) uses broadcasts to resolve names and addresses. It uses a broadcast to all addresses, but lists the name in the broadcast packet of the device that it is trying to reach. A broadcast is a packet that is sent to all nodes on a network. A receiving computer looks at the ARP broadcast and, if the name listed in it matches its own, responds directly to the ARP sender. Otherwise, the ARP broadcast packet is discarded.

☒   **A.** Token is incorrect because a token is a frame used for media access. **C.** Port is incorrect because a port is the identification of a service. **D.** Multicast is incorrect because a multicast does not participate in address resolution.

10. ☑   **D.** The workstation identifies which packets are meant for which data conversations by the connection identifier in each packet. At the sending node, multiple messages are split up into multiple packets. The packets for each application are given a connection identifier number, or port, for that application. When the packets are again assembled into messages at the peer transport layer, the ports are used to determine which packets go to which application.

☒   **A.** Error control is incorrect because it is used to determine errors. **B.** CRC is incorrect because it is one mechanism of error control. **C.** Windowing is incorrect because it is used to manage the flow of data.

11. ☑ **C.** DNSDHCP is the application used by NetWare to manage address/name resolution. Domain Name Service (DNS) is the address/name resolution service for TCP/IP. NetWare 5 manages DNS along with Dynamic Host Control Protocol (DHCP) from the DNSDHCP utility that can be launched from within NetWare administrator.

☒ **A.** NetWare administrator is incorrect because it does not directly manage DNS. **B.** NDS manager is incorrect because it manages the distribution of the NDS database over multiple servers. **D.** Address manager is incorrect because it does not exist.

12. ☑ **B.** Parity is a mechanism used to determine whether errors have occurred. Bits are added to a packet to ensure that the value of the packet is either even or odd. It would be an even value if the parity were even and odd value if the parity was odd. When the packet is received, the parity value is determined and if not the expected value, it is considered to be in error and dropped.

☒ **A.** DNS is incorrect because it is an address/name resolution service. **C.** Segmentation is incorrect because it is used to split messages into packets. **D.** Multiplexing is incorrect because it is used to interweave multiple messages into a single datastream.

13. ☑ **B.** A sequence number can determine whether duplicate packets have been received. When redundant paths exist in the internetwork, there is a possibility that duplicate packets can result. The receiving transport layer looks at the sequence number, and discards any packets with duplicate sequence numbers.

☒ **A.** Connection identifier is incorrect because it represents the data conversation. **C.** Acknowledgment is incorrect because it ensures transmission reliability. **D.** Window is incorrect because it is a mechanism for flow control.

The OSI Model's Upper Layers

1. ☑ **D.** None of the upper layers handles bitstream formatting. The bitstream is the electronic or optical signaling that transmits across the wire. The physical layer specifies the bitstream format for signaling.

   ☒ **A.** Session is incorrect because it handles establishing a virtual connection between two nodes. **B.** Presentation is incorrect because it handles data formatting. **C.** Application is incorrect because it handles the services that access the network.

2. ☑ **B.** The presentation layer handles data translation and formatting. The presentation layer at a sending node will receive the data from the application layer and then translate it into an agreed upon format with the destination node.

   ☒ **A.** Session is incorrect because it handles the establishment and release of a dialog between two nodes. **C.** Application is incorrect because it specifies applications for the network. **D.** None is incorrect because the presentation layer handles this function.

3. ☑ **D.** The session layer depends on ACKs at lower layers to determine if there has been an interruption in service and to notify it. ACKs are acknowledgment packets that are used during reliable transport. When an ACK is not received as expected, the transport layer can attempt resending the data or can notify the session layer of the service interruption.

   ☒ **A.** Multiplexing is incorrect because it enables multiple applications to use the same datastream connection. **B.** Sequence number is incorrect because it is used to reassemble packets into messages. **C.** Port is incorrect because it is used to identify the service.

4. ☑   **C.** Full-duplex dialogs provide simultaneous, bidirectional communications. Each device in a full-duplex dialog acts as a transmitter and a receiver. The data flows in both directions and a device both receives and sends data at the same time.

☒   **A.** Simplex is incorrect because it is a one-way communication method. **B.** Half duplex is incorrect because it is not simultaneous data transmission. **D.** Multiplexing is incorrect because it is a transport layer mechanism.

5. ☑   **A.** A commercial radio broadcast transmission is a simplex communication. Simplex communication is one way, and only one device can be a transmitter. The other device in a simplex transmission cannot respond. This is typical of a radio transmission–the radio does not send any information back to the radio station.

☒   **B.** Half duplex is incorrect because it enables a response from the receiver. **C.** Full duplex is incorrect because it also enables a response from the receiver. **D.** Triplex does not exist.

6. ☑   **C.** Sequencing, which is the ordering of packets to create messages, is not handled at the presentation layer, but at the transport layer.

☒   **A.** Encryption is incorrect because it is handled at the presentation layer. **B.** Compression is incorrect because it is handled at the presentation layer. **D.** Expansion is incorrect because it is handled at the presentation layer.

7. ☑   **A.** Big endian is the method used to read data from the first byte received. The big endian method is used by Motorola processors. The processor will begin reading data from the first byte, or "big end," of the transmission.

☒   **B.** Little endian is incorrect because it reads data from the last byte. **C.** Bit-order translation is incorrect because it reads bits, not bytes. **D.** Compression is incorrect because it is dependent upon the bit- or byte-order translation method.

8. ☑   **A, B.** Both the American Standard Code for Information Interchange (ASCII) and Extended Binary Coded Decimal Interchange Code (EBCDIC) are examples of character translation. ASCII is commonly used by Intel workstations. EBCDIC is used by IBM mainframes.
☒   **C.** NDS is incorrect because that is a directory service. **D.** ANSI is incorrect because it is an acronym for the American National Standards Institute.

9. ☑   **A.** Encryption is a mechanism that uses a public and private key in some implementations. In this method, a public key for a user is used to encrypt a file. The public key is published so that anyone can use it. The private key is used to decrypt the file. The private key is not published.
☒   **B.** Compression is incorrect because it does not use keys. **C.** Expansion is incorrect because it does not use keys. **D.** Bit-order translation is incorrect because it does not use keys.

10. ☑   **A.** The application layer specifies the user's interface to the network. Applications and services are provided at the application layer. They are the main access that end users will have to the network and its resources.
☒   **B.** Session is incorrect because it specifies the dialog establishment, management, and release. **C.** Presentation is incorrect because it specifies the data translation method. **D.** Network is incorrect because it specifies logical addressing and routing.

11. ☑   **B.** Service Advertising Protocol (SAP) is a transport layer service that advertises applications. It is used to resolve addresses to names for services on the internetwork, so that accessing a service is transparent to end users.
☒   **A.** NDS is incorrect because it is a directory service. **C.** DNS is incorrect because it is a non-advertising method of resolving names to addresses. **D.** RIP is incorrect because it is a routing protocol.

12. ☑ **C.** A remote-procedure call (RPC) works at the session layer. This is a mechanism for making remote applications appear to be working locally.
☒ **A.** Application is incorrect because RPC is not a network application. **B.** Presentation is incorrect because RPC does not handle data translation or format. **D.** Transport is incorrect because RPCs work independently of the datastream.

13. ☑ **C.** RCONSOLE is the application layer service that provides a remote terminal to a NetWare server.
☒ **A.** FTP is incorrect because it provides file services. **B.** NDIR is incorrect because it provides a directory listing. **D.** REMOTE.EXE is incorrect because it is not an application for NetWare.

Part 4

Novell Directory Services® (NDS) Design and Implementation (Exam 50-634)

EXAM TOPICS

Assessing the Network

Defining and Justifying the Network Solution

Designing the Directory Tree

Implementing Time-Synchronization Strategies

Creating an Accessibility Plan

Conducting a NetWare Implementation

NDS™ Design and Implementation Questions

Q & A

This section is designed to help you prepare for the NDS™ Design and Implementation exam (Exam # 50-634) so you can begin to reap the career benefits of CNE® certification. The following questions are structured in a format similar to what you'll find on the exam. Read all the choices carefully, as there may be more than one correct answer. Choose all correct answers for each question.

Assessing the Network

1. On what model is the Novell®-recommended design and implementation process based?

   A. DLC

   B. NDS

   C. SDLC

   D. HCSS

2. Which SDLC model requires each phase to be completed before beginning the next?

   A. Linear

   B. Structured

   C. Incremental

   D. Modified spiral

3. Which phase of the SDLC model includes creating a project schedule?

   A. Implementation

   B. Maintenance

   C. Design

   D. Analysis and specification

4. What is the initial set of system installations in the implementation phase?

   A. Installation

   B. Implementation

   C. Pilot

   D. Analysis

5. The NetWare NDS design cycle is a subset for the linear SDLC model. What is the NetWare name for the first phase, if the SDLC's first phase is analysis and specification?

A. Analysis and specification

B. Design

C. Project schedule

D. Project approach

6. Which phase of the NetWare NDS design cycle determines a partition and replication scheme?

A. Project approach

B. Design

C. Implementation

D. Manage and monitor

7. Which phase of the NetWare NDS design cycle includes the pilot?

A. Project approach

B. Design

C. Implementation

D. Manage and monitor

Refer to the Following Scenario to Answer Questions 8–13

Justine is rolling out a NetWare network and she is trying to decide which of four candidates to place on the NDS design team. George is the receptionist and uses a computer simply to access the company's intranet phone list. Chris is the mainframe backup operator and handles tape changes and backup problems on the mainframe from a dumb terminal. Yvette is a network specialist and originally contracted the network cabling. Julie is the company trainer and holds classes and develops training materials, as well as publishes them on her own intranet server.

8. Which person(s) may Justine wish to add to the NDS design team? (Choose all that apply.)

A. George

B. Chris

C. Yvette

D. Julie

9. Justine has to decide which person will fill the education and training coordinator position. Both network specialist Yvette and corporate trainer Julie have asked for this job. Justine is also considering Frank and Erin for the position. Frank is a consultant whose specialty is NetWare installation and NDS design. Erin is also a consultant whose specialty is workstation deployments. Which person is best suited for the education and training coordinator role?

A. Yvette

B. Julie

C. Frank

D. Erin

10. Justine decides that Erin will be the server specialist since she has more experience with NetWare servers than the other candidates for the position. For which of the following tasks will Erin be responsible?

A. Acting as a liaison to upper management

B. Recording IP and IPX addresses and frame types

C. Automating workstation updates

D. Creating or designing menu programs

11. Justine makes the decision to place Vesna in the application specialist role. For which of the following tasks will Vesna be responsible?

A. Ensuring disk space requirements on the server are met

B. Making the network accessible for traveling users

C. Setting up a lab

D. Making sure that future planned applications are compatible

12. Justine assigns Yvette as the connectivity specialist because of her experience in the infrastructure. What is a task for Yvette?

    A. Gathering network information to simulate it in the lab

    B. Designing the directory tree

    C. Maintaining consistent workstation configuration files

    D. Maintaining WAN links

13. George, who is the printing specialist, is given the task of looking for information for his role. Which of the following will George look for?

    A. LAN topology map

    B. WAN topology map

    C. Resource list

    D. Organization chart

Defining and Justifying the Network Solution

1. What is the first of the four steps to gain acceptance of a network solution?

    A. Defining the solution

    B. Creating the schedule

    C. Calculating the solution results

    D. Selling the solution

exam
ⓦatch

The process for designing and implementing NetWare® 5 includes organizing and educating the project team, understanding NDS and creating a naming standard for it, designing the NDS tree, creating the implementation approach, establishing a lab and pilot, migrating clients and servers, and maintaining daily operations.

2. What is a design decision for servers?

A. Time synchronization

B. Use of NDPS

C. Tree structure

D. Use of Z.E.N.works

Refer to the Following Scenario
When Answering Questions 3–5

Accessus.com is a new company on the Internet. It currently rents a service that provides its Internet Web site. It plans on installing a NetWare network of its own, both for its Web site and for the employees. The owner, Jill, wants all end users to use network printers to realize the savings from sharing those resources.

3. Jill wants to be able to set up a network operations center that is not required to physically visit a workstation unless the hardware has broken. Jill believes that this will reduce support expenses. What solution design component does this affect?

A. NDS tree design

B. Server design

C. Workstation design

D. Printer design

4. Accessus.com administrator Taylor has gathered all the requirements and resources and has designed an initial solution. She is ready to take on the next step in the solution definition. What is it?

A. Creating a schedule

B. Selling the solution

C. Determining the costs of the solution

D. Designating a project administrator

5. When Taylor creates the schedule, she realizes that some tasks can be executed concurrently. Which task can be executed concurrently with the task of creating a naming standard?

A. Designing NDS tree

B. Gathering resources for the lab

C. Designing servers

D. Testing the NDS design

6. Why should creating the naming standard be scheduled before other design tasks?

A. To increase productivity

B. To reduce expenses

C. To add complexity

D. To ensure consistency

7. Grace already has a NetWare 4.11 network that she is hoping to upgrade to NetWare 5. Grace defines an initial solution, puts together the budget and schedule, and presents it to management. Management asks why, if Grace already has the solution, she has included a design phase in the schedule. What is her reply?

A. The initial solution is too detailed.

B. The design phase adds errors to the solution.

C. The designed solution should have more detail and specification.

D. The design phase can be ignored.

8. What type of document can show the value of a network solution?

A. Cost-benefit analysis

B. Risk assessment

C. Contingency plan

D. Implementation schedule

9. What type of document identifies the concerns with implementing a network solution?

   A. Business requirements definition

   B. Cost-benefit analysis

   C. Risk assessment

   D. Initial solution design

10. Once a solution has been approved by management, what is the administrator's next step?

   A. Assigning a project manager for the IS manager role

   B. Installing servers

   C. Installing workstations

   D. Creating user accounts

11. What additional cost should a cost-benefit analysis include to cover changes during the project?

   A. Hardware cost

   B. Software cost

   C. Percentage for variance

   D. Salary or hourly cost for project team members

Designing the Directory Tree

1. When should an NDS tree design be reviewed?

   A. The first time the first server is installed

   B. Never. It will grow of its own accord.

   C. Only when upgrading NetWare

   D. Periodically

2. Tim is a network consultant hired to review the NDS tree design for Acme Co. He discovers a problem with the names of the servers and immediately decides to change them in a naming standards document. Of the following options, what were the names?

A. PHXSVR01, PHXSVR02, NYCSVR01

B. Data_slc_01, Apps_nyc_01, Web_la_01

C. Spinach, Okra, Broccoli

D. WEB_BLDG1_FL2, PTR_BLDG2_FL1, FTP_BLDG3_FL4

QUESTIONS AND ANSWERS

Jolene is a new network administrator given the task of redesigning the NDS Tree in preparation for upgrading to NetWare 5. In reviewing the network, Jolene finds that the servers have names of cartoon characters. Is this a standard that Jolene should maintain after the upgrade?

Unless the network is for a cartoon creator and each server holds the work done for that character, this naming standard is not easy for new users to understand. Jolene should probably evaluate a naming standard that will better describe the server's function and/or location within the enterprise, and then implement that naming standard during the migration to NetWare 5.

3. Tim finds out that there are two NDS trees at Acme. One is used for lab testing and the other is the production NDS tree. The servers on the lab tree use a naming standard that Tim would like to use on the production tree. If the lab tree has three servers named phx-apps-01, phx-apps-02, and phx-data-01, which of the following sets of names can be used on the production tree?

A. Phx-apps-01, lax-data-01, slc-data-01

B. Phx-data-01, nyc-apps-01, nyc-apps-02

C. Phx-apps-03, phx-data-01, lax-data-01

D. Phx-apps-03, phx-data-02, phx-data-03

4. Tim's user naming standard specifies that within each container object a user account will be the first name's initial, the last name's first five characters, and a two-digit serial number. The first account in each container object will have no serial number. As shown in the following illustration, Tim's tree has two container units with a user account for Jack Jones in Paris and a user account for Janet Jones in Phoenix. What mechanism does NDS employ so that Tim can use jjones as the user account name for both Jack and Janet?

NDS Top Level Design : Meshed Network

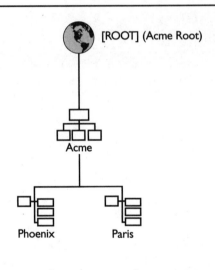

A. Distinguished name

B. Common name

C. Fully qualified domain name

D. DNS

5. Acme's owner has a new initiative that uses the equal sign (=) in a marketing campaign. He has asked Tim to use the equal sign in the user-account naming standard to keep that campaign fresh in the minds of the staff. What does Tim say to the owner?

    A. Cannot use the = sign because it is a bindery object symbol

    B. Cannot use the = sign because it will place an alias for the account in every container

    C. Cannot use the = sign because it is reserved for typeful names

    D. Can use the = sign

6. Tim has decided to name both the NDS trees. He is planning on naming the production tree ACME. Which of the following names is appropriate for the lab tree?

    A. Acme

    B. ACME=LAB

    C. Acme Lab

    D. AcmeLab

7. The Acme company has four physical sites and four divisions, as shown in the following illustration. Tim is now ready to design the first layer of Organizational Units. What Organizational Units should be in the first layer?

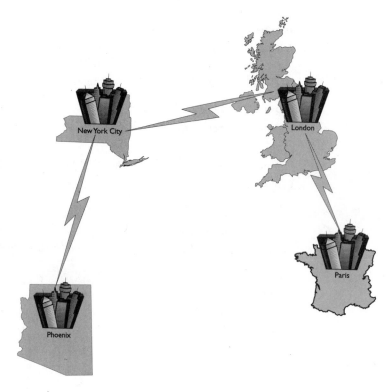

| Phoenix
Engineering
Sales | New York
HeadQuarters
Operations
Administration
Engineering
Sales | Paris
Administration
Engineering
Sales | London
Engineering
Sales |

A. Headquarters

B. HQ, SALES, ENG, ADMIN, OPS

C. Phoenix, New York, Paris, London

D. Admin, ops, sales

8. Which of the following naming standards provides both the function and the location of a server?

A. FS01

B. DATA-01

C. CITY-APPS-01

D. CITY01

9. Which of the following naming standards, based on the name Terence Edwin Jackson, will enable 99 accounts to have users with the same or similar names?

A. TERENCE

B. TERENCEEJ

C. TEJACK01

D. TJACKS1

10. Which of the following NDS objects should NOT be given a naming standard?

A. Workstation

B. Printers

C. Servers

D. None of the above

exam
Watch

The uniqueness of object Distinguished Names is not limited to the type of object. If a printer is named DELT and a server is also named DELT, they cannot exist in the same context.

11. Which Z.E.N.works workstation name option represents the IPX or IP address of the workstation?

A. Container

B. Network address

C. OS

D. DNS

12. What is always located at the very top of the NDS tree?

A. Organization

B. Country

C. Organizational Unit

D. [Root]

13. When designing the upper layers of the NDS tree for a global company, which of the following methods is recommended?

A. The top-layer OUs should mirror WAN locations.

B. The top-layer OUs should mirror business units.

C. The top-layer OUs should span WAN links.

D. The top-layer OUs should represent logical workgroups.

exam
Watch
The exam typically includes one or more questions about NDS design at the upper layers. The questions usually contain exhibits or diagrams of the physical network and corporate structure at a high level. Then you are asked to select an appropriate NDS design for this network.

Implementing Time-Synchronization Strategies

1. What is Novell Directory Services?

    A. A file

    B. A directory or folder

    C. A database

    D. A Novell Server

2. What is a result when an NDS tree is partitioned?

    A. Server duplication

    B. Increase volume size

    C. Load balancing across servers

    D. None of the above

exam
    ⓦatch   *It might be a good idea to get a piece of paper and practice turning a vertical "NetWare Administrator" view of an NDS tree into a horizontal "design" view, and vice versa. Novell's exams may have you create objects in NetWare Administrator based on a design, or may have you select a design based on a NetWare Administrator view.*

3. Why should a partition not span a WAN link?

    A. To avoid increased network traffic on the WAN

    B. To increase network traffic on the WAN

    C. To synchronize time across the WAN

    D. To centralize administration

4. How many replicas should a partition have before the administrator splits it into two or more partitions?

A. 3

B. 10

C. 25

D. 50

5. Which of the following tools will allow an administrator to determine the point when NDS synchronization is allowed across WAN links?

A. NDIR

B. NDS Manager

C. DNSDHCP

D. WAN Traffic Manager

6. How does a NetWare server coordinate file and NDS updates with other servers?

A. Time synchronization

B. WAN Traffic Management

C. Using LAN Area objects

D. SAP

7. To what type of server does a single-reference time server provide updates?

A. Primary

B. Reference

C. Secondary

D. All of the above

8. What protocol provides time services to non-NetWare systems?

A. SAP

B. RIP

C. NTP

D. NNTP

QUESTIONS AND ANSWERS

An exam question shows you a diagram of an NDS tree and asks you where partitioning is appropriate.	Look for containers separated by WAN links, containers with over 3,500 objects, a container that must be locally administered, or a partition with more than 10 to 15 replicas.
The question asks for ways that WAN traffic can be minimized.	Look for answers that mention partitioning along container boundaries and/or WAN traffic manager.
The question shows you an NDS tree and asks you to point out an object that could be used to manage WAN traffic between servers.	Select the LAN Area object.
The question shows several servers and the protocols they communicate with, and asks which server is a source.	Select the server that uses both IP and IPX protocols.

9. What is the threshold number of servers on the network before the single-reference server setup is no longer viable?

A. 8

B. 16

C. 30

D. 64

10. AllTek is designing a new NetWare network. The server expert has decided that all servers will use the IPX protocol. The NDS expert wants to implement NTP for time synchronization. What else must be decided before using NTP?

A. All servers must use SAP.

B. All servers must use IP.

C. At least one server must use IP.

D. At least one server must use SAP.

11. When the AllTek administrator is ready to configure time synchronization on the NetWare 5 servers, which utility should be used?

A. TIMESYNC

B. SERVMAN

C. CONFIG

D. MONITOR

12. One of AllTek's sites is in Arizona, which uses mountain time without any daylight savings time changes. The rest of the servers are located in the eastern daylight savings time zone. The NetWare 5 servers are installed back East with EDT time, and shipped to Arizona. Which utility will AllTek's Arizona administrator use to reset the time to mountain time?

A. MONITOR

B. TIMESYNC

C. CONFIG

D. SERVMAN

QUESTIONS AND ANSWERS

You are asked if you should use NTP in a network that uses only IPX.	No, NTP requires at least one server to use the IP protocol.
You are asked whether a custom setup is needed for a network in a single location with 31 servers.	Yes, because Novell recommends a custom setup whenever the number of servers exceeds 30, even if all of the servers are at a single location.
You are asked which utility should be used to customize time settings: TIMESYNC, SERVMAN, or MONITOR.	NetWare 5 uses the MONITOR utility to configure time settings.
You are asked which type of NTP server can synchronize with other servers.	Peer servers can synchronize with other peer servers.
You are asked which time source would be better overall: a reference server set maintained by the network administrator, or an external trusted time source such as the U.S. Naval Observatory.	As reliable as the network administrator may be, they can't match the accuracy of a trusted time source with an atomic clock. Choose the external trusted time source.

Creating an Accessibility Plan

1. Galax Industries is installing a NetWare network. The administrator, Hallie, is creating the accessibility plan for end users. What three items should she review for this plan?

   A. Application needs

   B. Physical network needs

   C. Legacy services needs

   D. FAX needs

2. Which of the following questions will affect how Hallie's connectivity expert handles WAN traffic design?

A. Are there groups that need access to applications?

B. Are any applications used across the WAN?

C. Are users dependent on applications running at specific times?

D. Do all the users in the same container have the same access needs?

3. Galax Industries has a legacy NetWare 2.15 network for its accounting group. What should Hallie review for them?

A. Application needs

B. Networked resources

C. Network storage devices

D. Legacy application needs

4. The Galax Industries end users will be placed in the Admin, Sales, Service, HQ, and Manufacturing containers depicted in the following illustration. Which OUs should contain the user policy packages?

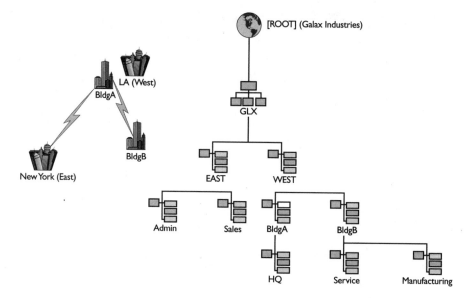

A. Admin, Sales, Service, HQ, Manufacturing
B. East, West
C. GLX
D. BldgA, BldgB, East

5. Hallie has two network administrators. John is in New York and administers the single building there. Lucy is in Los Angeles and administers the two buildings there. Which OUs should hold the Organizational Role objects that John and Lucy will be using for administration?

A. GLX
B. BLDGA and BLDGB
C. ADMIN and SALES
D. EAST and WEST

6. The accounting group's NetWare 2.15 server login script creates a drive G mapped to a group directory, and drive H, mapped to a home directory for each user. However, each user's remaining drive mappings are not consistent with each other. When Hallie creates the login scripts for the new NetWare 5 servers, what would enable a consistent drive mapping system?

A. Alias objects
B. User login scripts
C. Standard directory structure
D. IRF

7. What type of login script is best for creating a common environment for all users in the same Organizational Unit?

A. Container login script
B. Profile login script
C. User login script
D. Organization login script

8. Which of the following type of administrator roles has access to the NDS tree [Root]?

A. Enterprise administrator

B. Container administrator

C. Backup administrator

D. Password administrator

9. Which command can add a user's container to a server so that the user log is in a bindery mode?

A. ADD CONTEXT

B. SET BINDERY CONTEXT

C. SET BINDERY MODE

D. ADD BINDERY CONTEXT

10. Which of the following decisions will affect the configuration of Client 32?

A. Storage limits for each user

B. Creation of aliases for file access

C. Applications that will be stored on the workstation

D. The name of the NDS tree

11. Gerald travels frequently from branch to branch to train salespeople. Gerald hooks up to the internetwork in each branch so that he can access files, share e-mail, and print. What type of user is Gerald?

A. remote user

B. mobile user

C. local user

D. system administrator

12. Frank has a NetWare 5 network with five sites around the world. Each site has at least one or more NetWare 5 servers and seven or more printers. The NDS tree has been designed and partitioned around the WAN links, so bandwidth consumption is low. Frank's standard configuration for workstations is to load most applications from the network servers. Frank has been asked to add three users, the first remote users via modem, to the network. What design consideration should Frank revisit for the new remote users?

A. The number of sites

B. The number of servers

C. The NDS tree design

D. The configuration of the workstations

Conducting a NetWare Implementation

1. Warren is implementing a NetWare network for TFX, Inc. He is planning on installing a single NDS tree with servers at each site. When Warren conducts visits to each of TFX's three sites, he discovers that none of the sites has WAN connections to the others. How does this affect the implementation?

A. It will not affect it.

B. Warren will be limited to a single NetWare server.

C. Warren must create a unique NDS tree for each site.

D. Warren cannot install NetWare 5 without the WAN, so the project will be stopped.

2. Warren persuades TFX, Inc.'s management to install WAN links before NetWare 5 is implemented. Not only will TFX have three sites with NetWare servers and interconnecting WAN links, it will have a single NetWare administrator. Which implementation type did Warren pursue when he convinced TFX, Inc. to connect the WAN links prior to NetWare 5 and a single NDS tree installation?

   A. Departmental implementation

   B. Divisional implementation

   C. Organizational implementation

   D. None of the above

3. Warren tests the installation of NetWare 5 without installing NDS on a server. What utility can he use to install NDS after the server installation is complete?

   A. INSTALL

   B. NWCONFIG

   C. SERVMAN

   D. MONITOR

4. Warren has moved the servers around the NDS tree so that they are in the containers shown in the following illustration. Master1 contains the master partition of [Root], while Master2 and Master3 each have a read/write copy of it. No other servers have partitions on them. Warren wants to make sure that the users will authenticate locally, and not across the WAN. Which container units should Warren make into partitions?

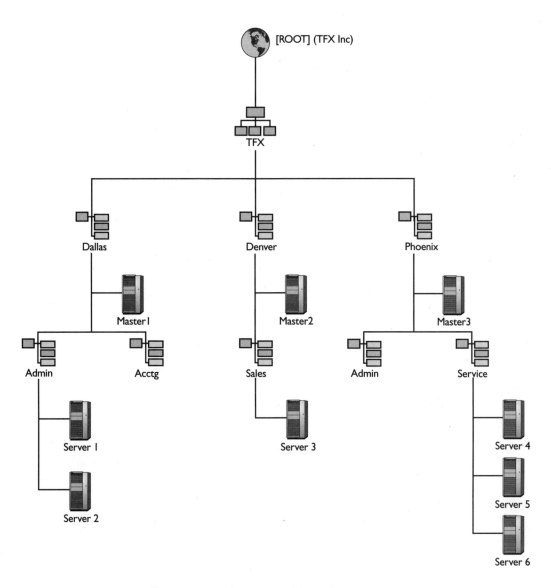

A. Dallas, Denver, Phoenix, and [Root]

B. Sales, Admin, Service

C. TFX

D. Dallas, Sales, Admin

5. Warren has a bindery application running on the Server6. It has a bindery context set for the Service.Phoenix.TFX context. What should Warren ensure in the replication scheme?

A. All servers have subordinate references to the Phoenix partition.

B. All servers have read-only replicas of the Denver partition.

C. All servers have read/write or master replicas of the Phoenix partition.

D. All servers have master replicas of the Denver partition.

6. Warren then prepares to implement time synchronization on the TFX network. Warren originally installed the Master1 server as a reference server using an external time reference service. Since TFX pays for the external time service, Warren wants all servers to use the Master1 as the reference server. All other servers are secondary servers. In order to decrease bandwidth utilization between the three sites, what type of servers should Warren implement in Denver and Phoenix?

A. Single-reference servers

B. Reference servers

C. Primary servers

D. Secondary servers

7. Warren learns that TFX is acquiring another company, Sandscapes. Warren speaks with the Sandscapes administrator and discovers that they have a NetWare 5 network. What must Warren do to ensure that TFX has a single tree after the acquisition with the least amount of effort?

A. Reinstall all the TFX servers as part of the Sandscapes tree.

B. Reinstall all of the Sandscapes servers as part of the TFX tree.

C. Merge the two trees into a single NDS tree.

D. Reinstall all of the TFX and Sandscapes servers as part of a new NDS tree.

8. The following illustrations depict the TFX tree and the Sandscapes NDS tree, respectively. After Warren merges the TFX tree and the Sandscapes tree, what will the layer under the [Root] be?

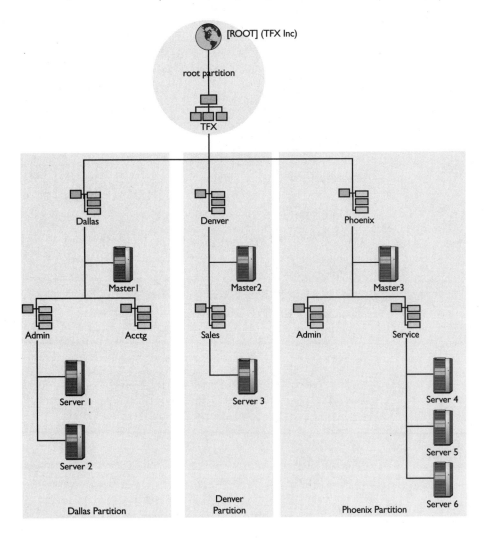

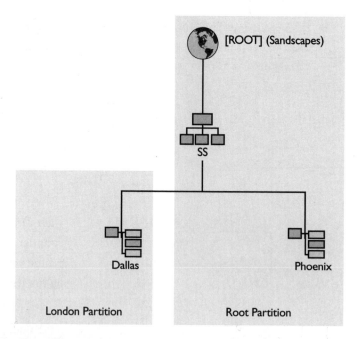

A. London, New York

B. Dallas, Denver, Phoenix

C. Dallas, Denver, Phoenix, London, New York

D. SS, TFX

9. Warren designates the TFX tree as the target tree, which means that the Sandscapes tree is the source whose [Root] disappears. How will this affect the partitions in the Sandscapes NDS tree?

A. The partitions will not be affected.

B. Both partitions, London and Root, will be merged as a single partition under the [Root] of the new tree.

C. The Root partition of the Sandscapes tree will be created as a partition under the root of the new tree and will not include the new tree's [Root].

D. The London partition of the Sandscapes tree will be merged into the Phoenix partition from the TFX tree.

10. Warren must ensure that the schema of both trees is the same before merging them. Which utility will he use to import the schema of one tree into another, if they are different?

A. DSMERGE

B. DSREPAIR

C. DSIMPORT

D. DSUPDATE

11. Which of the following criteria must be met before merging two NDS trees?

A. Both trees must have the same name for their Organization.

B. At least one tree must have an Alias object under the [Root].

C. Servers in both trees must be running the same version of NDS.

D. All servers must be "down" before merging the trees.

12. Before running DSMERGE, what utility should Warren run?

A. DSREPAIR

B. MONITOR

C. NWCONFIG

D. RCONSOLE

13. What option in DSMERGE can ensure that servers are up and running?

A. Check the servers in this tree.

B. Check the time synchronization.

C. Merge the two trees.

D. Rename this tree.

14. Once two NDS trees are merged, Warren must then establish network access. At first, both companies will act much the same as they had prior to the acquisition. However, the TFX owner wants his executive team, including members of both the TFX and the Sandscapes management, to have access to both companies' network resources. What should Warren use for this?

A. Group object

B. Profile object

C. Alias object

D. IRF

15. Which type(s) of rights will the executive group need if the team will be looking at the user accounts, password policies, files, workstation objects, server objects, and printers?

A. File rights

B. NDS rights to printers, servers, and containers

C. NDS rights to users and workstation objects

D. All of the above

NDS™ Design and Implementation Answers

The answers to the questions are in boldface, followed by a brief explanation. The incorrect answer choices are explained in the final paragraph following each correct answer. Some of the explanations detail the logic you should use to choose the correct answer, while others give factual reasons why the answer is correct. If you miss several questions on a similar topic, you should review the corresponding section in the *CNE®* *NetWare® 5 Study Guide* before taking the NDS™ Design and Implementation test.

Assessing the Network

1. ☑ **C.** Novell's recommended design and implementation process is based on a linear System Design Life Cycle (SDLC) model. Its stages are: systems analysis, general systems design, systems evaluation, detailed systems design, systems implementation, systems acceptance, systems operation, with a final stage to begin further major system changes.
☒ **A.** DLC is incorrect because it is a protocol. **B.** NDS is incorrect because it is the Novell Directory Service. **D.** HCSS is incorrect because it is a near-line storage service.

2. ☑ **A.** The linear model of SDLC requires each phase to be completed before moving on to the next. Systems Design Life Cycle (SDLC) provides a consistent, methodical approach to designing a network.
☒ **B.** Structured is incorrect because it contains overlapping phases. **C.** Incremental is incorrect because it has concurrent phases. **D.** Modified spiral is incorrect because it has overlapping phases.

3. ☑ **D.** The analysis and specification phase includes the creation of a project schedule. The schedule describes the tasks, milestones, beginning of and end of each phase, and the dates for each task. The schedule may also include an assigned person to perform each of the tasks.
☒ **A.** Implementation is incorrect because it occurs after the schedule has been determined. **B.** Maintenance is incorrect because it occurs at the last step in an ongoing mode. **C.** Design is incorrect because it is a phase described in the schedule.

4. ☑ **C.** Pilot is the initial set of installations in the implementation phase of the systems design life cycle. The pilot is the first deployment of systems to be used in the production environment of a network. Before the pilot, the only systems that were installed were test systems.

☒ **A.** Installation is incorrect because that is the actual procedure to implement a system. **B.** Implementation is incorrect because that is the name applied to the entire phase. **D.** Analysis is incorrect because it is part of the initial phase of analysis and specification.

5. ☑ **D.** The first phase of the NetWare NDS design cycle is project approach. This phase is equivalent to the analysis and specification phase of the SDLC. The NetWare NDS design cycle has four phases, as shown in the following illustration.

☒ **A.** Analysis and specification is incorrect because that is the first phase of the SDLC model. **B.** Design is incorrect because that is the second phase of the NetWare NDS design cycle. **C.** Project schedule is incorrect because that is a task that happens during the first phase.

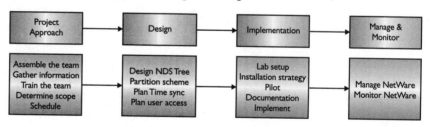

6. ☑ **B.** The NetWare NDS design cycle's design phase determines a partition and replication scheme. Partitioning and replication are the methods involved with distributing the NDS database across multiple servers. The design of the NDS partition and replication scheme can influence how quickly and easily an end user can authenticate and access network resources on the NetWare network.

☒ **A.** Project approach is incorrect because it occurs prior to any construction of the NDS tree. **C.** Implementation is incorrect because it occurs after all decisions have been made about how the NDS tree will work. **D.** Manage and monitor is incorrect because it is the final phase and does not include changing or deciding how things will work.

7. ☑ **C.** The implementation phase of the NetWare NDS design cycle includes the pilot. The pilot is the first implementation of NetWare in the production environment. It is a test of the design to ensure that it meets the original design goals and can be used in production. The pilot usually affects a small group of end users so that its impact on the environment is small. In the case where a pilot is unsuccessful, it can be reversed and a second pilot implemented later after the team revisits the design phase.
☒ **A.** Project approach is incorrect because it is the initial definition of the project. **B.** Design is incorrect because it designs the NDS solution. **D.** Manage and monitor is incorrect because all implementations should be completed before it starts.

8. ☑ **C, D.** Justine should add both Yvette and Julie to the NDS design team. The NDS design team should have IS staff and/or consultants with different knowledge areas of the network and production environment. Yvette and Julie have knowledge of the infrastructure and network training, respectively.
☒ **A.** George is incorrect because as the receptionist, he has little experience with the detailed workings of the network. **B.** Chris, the backup operator for the mainframe, is incorrect because he has no experience with the distributed computing network, but only with the mainframe environment.

9. ☑ **B.** Julie is best suited for the education and training coordinator role. Julie's current function in the company is to train end users on network software. Her experience will be especially valuable in this new role. The question and answer illustrate how the CNE test is structured and seem fairly cut and dry. However, no person's experience will be perfectly suited for a role. Sometimes a very experienced person does not want to fill a role he or she has been selected for, because it is not an opportunity for growth in skills. The IS manager role must consider these factors when deciding who will perform which function or role. The IS manager may ask a more experienced person to review a design created by a less experienced person as a quality assurance check. Often a consultant is retained for this function.
☒ **A.** Yvette is not a correct answer because she has no training experience. **C.** Frank is not a correct response because his experience is in design. **D.** Erin is an incorrect response because her experience is in workstation implementation.

10. ☑ **B.** As the server specialist, Erin will be responsible for recording IP and IPX addresses and frame types. The server specialist position is responsible for the success of the pilot, providing server information to the team, disk-space requirements, backup processes, and the protocol specifications.

☒ **A.** Acting as a liaison to upper management is incorrect because that is the IS manager function. **C.** Automating workstation updates is incorrect because that is a workstation specialist's task. **D.** Creating or designing menu programs is incorrect because that is an application specialist's task.

11. ☑ **D.** Vesna will be responsible for ensuring that future planned applications are compatible with the NDS environment. The application specialist has a focus on applications and must design the login scripts, the menu programs, and the compatibility for each of them.

☒ **A.** Ensuring disk space requirements on the server are met is incorrect because it is a server specialist's responsibility. **B.** Making the network accessible for traveling users is incorrect because it is a workstation specialist's responsibility. **C.** Setting up a lab is incorrect because it is a testing-lab coordinator's responsibility.

12. ☑ **D.** Yvette will maintain WAN links as the connectivity specialist. A connectivity specialist must be knowledgeable about the existing infrastructure and about the bridges, routers, switches, and other infrastructure equipment, and be able to make recommendations based on that knowledge.

☒ **A.** Gather network information to simulate it in the lab is incorrect because that is a testing-lab coordinator task. **B.** Design the directory tree is incorrect because it is an NDS expert's task. **C.** Maintain consistent workstation configuration files is incorrect because it is a workstation specialist's task.

13. ☑ **C.** George will look for a resource list. The resource list that George will need is of the printers, their types, locations, drivers, and user accessibility. George may need more information than the single resource, but it will typically be supplied by his team members, primarily, the IS manager and the NDS expert. All team members work together, but with a focus on their own responsibilities. Information that is gathered, then, must be directly required to be the responsibility of a particular member. A resource list of workstations is required by the workstation specialist and a resource list of servers is required by the server specialist.

☒ **A.** LAN topology map is incorrect because it is used by the NDS expert for the NDS design and the server specialist for the server design. **B.** WAN topology map is incorrect because it is used by the NDS expert and server specialist for the NDS and server designs. **D.** Organization chart is incorrect because it is used by the IS manager and the NDS expert.

Defining and Justifying the Network Solution

1. ☑ **A.** The first step in gaining acceptance for a network solution is to define the solution. This step involves discovering requirements, gathering data, designing NetWare 5 components and documenting an initial solution.

☒ **B.** Create the schedule is incorrect because a schedule cannot be created until an idea of the solution is specified. **C.** Calculate the solution results is incorrect because it cannot be done until after a solution is defined. **D.** Sell the solution is incorrect because a solution must be defined first.

2. ☑ **A.** Time synchronization is a design decision for servers in the network solution definition. Time synchronization strategy directly affects the server installation and configuration.

☒ **B.** NDPS is incorrect because it affects printers. **C.** Tree structure is incorrect because it affects the NDS design. **D.** Use of Z.E.N.works is incorrect because it affects workstations.

3. ☑   C. Jill's business affects the workstation design component. The capability of managing a workstation so that it does not need to be physically visited is offered through remote control and help desk request solutions. These capabilities are offered through NetWare add-on components of ManageWise® or Z.E.N.works.

☒   A. NDS tree design is incorrect because the tree design is unaffected by this requirement. **B.** Server design is incorrect because the server is not directly affected by this requirement. **D.** Printer design is also incorrect because printers are not affected by the business requirement.

4. ☑   A. Taylor's next step is to create a schedule for the design and implementation. The schedule is a list of the tasks and resource requirements and milestones expected for an actual implementation. This is required for the selling of the solution in order to give an estimate of the duration of the project.

☒   B. Sell the solution is incorrect because Taylor had not created a schedule yet. **C.** Determine the costs of the solution is incorrect because it is dependent on the time spent in implementing the solution. **D.** Designate a project administrator is incorrect because it is unnecessary before the solution is sold.

5. ☑   B. The task of gathering resources for the lab can be executed concurrently with the task of creating a naming standard. The task of gathering lab resources is not dependent on any tasks and can be started at any point before the lab testing commences.

☒   A. Designing the NDS tree is incorrect because the NDS tree design is dependent on the naming standard. **C.** Designing the servers is incorrect because the server design is dependent on the naming standard. **D.** Testing the NDS design is incorrect because it is dependent on the NDS tree design, which is then dependent on the naming standard.

6. ☑ **D.** Creating the naming standard should be scheduled before other design tasks to ensure consistency during the subsequent design tasks. Names are used for user accounts, drive mappings, network resources, NDS containers, servers, volumes, workstations, and so on. Using standard rules to create the names makes it easier and faster to implement them.

   ☒ **A.** To increase productivity is incorrect because the names do not affect productivity. **B.** To reduce expenses is incorrect because names do not affect expenses. **C.** To add complexity is incorrect because a naming standard will simplify network usage, not make it more difficult.

7. ☑ **C.** Grace should reply that the designed solution should have more detail and specification than the initial solution. This requires that the design phase be included. Designing a network is somewhat like preventative dentistry, where the more you floss and brush, the better your teeth. In networking, the better the network design, the more likely the network will stay online.

   ☒ **A.** The initial solution is too detailed is incorrect because it is a general proposal. **B.** The design phase adds errors to the solution is incorrect because it reduces errors in the solution. **D.** The design phase can be ignored is incorrect because ignoring the design phase and moving directly into implementation will cause problems on the network.

8. ☑ **A.** The cost-benefit analysis document can demonstrate the value of a network solution. It lists the expected costs involved with implementing a network solution. At the same time, the cost-benefit analysis lists the benefits, then compares the value of those benefits to the costs. The analysis must compare "apples to apples" by amortizing the costs and benefits over the same period of time.

   ☒ **B.** Risk assessment is incorrect because it does not present a network solution's value. **C.** Contingency plan is incorrect because it is a backout option for a problem pilot implementation. **D.** Implementation schedule is incorrect because it does not demonstrate any value for the network solution.

9. ☑   **C.** A risk assessment document identifies the concerns with implementing a network solution. It also identifies any concerns with not implementing a network solution. This document will provide guidance for a contingency plan.

☒   **A.** Business requirements definition is incorrect because it will identify the needs of the business that may be answered by a network solution. **B.** Cost-benefit analysis is incorrect because it will identify the costs and the benefits to implementing the network solution. **D.** Initial solution design is incorrect because it documents the proposed generic solution.

10. ☑   **A.** The administrator's next step is to assign a project manager for the IS manager role, which initiates the first phase of the design project.

☒   **B.** Install servers is incorrect because they should not be installed until after they have been designed in a detailed design that begins with the assignment of a project manager. **C.** Install workstations is incorrect because workstations should not be installed until after they have been designed in a detailed design that begins with the assignment of a project manager. **D.** Create user accounts is incorrect because they follow the server installation.

11. ☑   **C.** The percentage for variance is an additional estimated cost that covers changes during the project. The reason that a variance is added is because the cost-benefit analysis is completed before a final detailed solution is reached. The final detailed solution may have additional components of hardware or software or may have a longer duration than originally estimated.

☒   **A.** Hardware cost is incorrect because that is a cost already determined to be part of the solution. **B.** Software cost is also a cost already specified as part of the solution. **D.** Salary or hourly cost for project team members is incorrect because it is assigned to a team already specified.

Designing the Directory Tree

1. ☑ **D.** An NDS tree design should be reviewed periodically. This review will ensure that the NDS tree meets the business requirements of the enterprise. The frequency with which the NDS tree design should be reviewed depends on the growth of the enterprise. At the very least, the NDS design should be looked at prior to making large changes to the enterprise such as a merger or migration, or large technology change on the network.

    ☒ **A.** The first time that the first server is installed is incorrect because it will not keep pace with enterprise changes. **B.** Never. It will grow of its own accord is incorrect because it will most likely result in a poor design that causes problems with network access for end users. **C.** Only when upgrading NetWare is incorrect because it will not keep pace with enterprise changes.

2. ☑ **C.** Tim discovered that the servers were named after vegetables. These names did not give any indication of the location or use of the server on the internetwork.

    ☒ **A.** PHXSVR01, PHXSVR02, NYCSVR01, is incorrect because the names indicate the city location of each server in a consistent way and are useful as a naming standard. **B.** Data_slc_01, Apps_nyc_01, Web_la_01, is incorrect because the names indicate the usage and the city location of the servers in a consistent way and are useful as a naming standard. **D.** WEB_BLDG1_FL2, PTR_BLDG2_FL1, FTP_BLDG3_FL4 is incorrect because the names indicate the usage of the server, the building, and the floor location of the server in a consistent way and are useful as a naming standard.

3. ☑ **D.** The names that could be used on the production tree are phx-apps-03, phx-data-02, and phx-data-03. These names use the same naming standard of city-server type-##. Additionally, these servers do not use names that are already used by the lab servers on the other NDS tree. Server names, regardless of their tree, must be unique on the internetwork.

☒ For answers **A**, **B**, and **C**, the naming standard is used, but each one has a server name that duplicates one of the names of the lab servers.

4. ☑ **A.** NDS employs a distinguished name to make names unique, even when their common names are identical. Jack Jones, under the naming convention, has a user account jjones. The jjones account is in the Paris Organizational Unit, which is in the Acme Organization. Janet Jones also has a user account jjones. Her jjones account is in the Phoenix Organizational Unit, which is in the Acme Organization. A distinguished name concatenates the user account with the container objects that can be followed to the NDS tree root. For example, the distinguished name for Jack is jjones.paris.acme, while the distinguished name for Janet is jjones.phoenix.acme. Their common names are each jjones, but because NDS has the distinguished name, the context makes them unique.

☒ **B.** Common name is incorrect because both of the accounts have identical common names. **C.** Fully qualified domain name (FQDN) is incorrect because it is a mechanism used for TCP/IP hosts that specifies the hostname and domain name together. For example, host.domain.com. **D.** DNS is incorrect because it is the Domain Name Service in the TCP/IP suite that handles hostname-to-IP address resolution from a centralized server.

5. ☑ **C.** Tim tells the owner that NDS cannot use the = sign in the user account name because the = sign is reserved for typeful names. Typeful names are those that indicate the type of object by an abbreviation and an = sign before each of the words in the distinguished name. For example, the user account jjones.phoenix.acme is .cn=jjones.ou=phoenix.o=acme when translated to a typeful name. The cn abbreviation stands for common name. The ou abbreviation stands for Organizational Unit. The o abbreviation stands for Organization.

   ☒ **A.** Cannot use the = sign because it is a bindery object symbol is incorrect. The bindery object symbol is a plus (+) sign. **B.** Cannot use the = sign because it will place an alias for the account in every container is incorrect because no mechanism will create aliases automatically. That would require someone to create the alias or some type of program to populate the tree with aliases. **D.** Can use the = sign is incorrect because the = sign is reserved by NDS for typeful names.

6. ☑ **D.** The name AcmeLab is appropriate for the lab's NDS tree. This name indicates the name of the Organization and the use of the tree. When there are multiple trees in a network, the tree name is clearest if it indicates for what the tree is used.

   ☒ **A.** Acme is incorrect because it is interpreted as an identical name to the production tree ACME. **B.** ACME=LAB is incorrect because the equal sign (=) is reserved for use with typeful names and cannot be used in a tree name. **C.** Acme Lab is incorrect because the NDS tree cannot be named with spaces present.

7. ☑ **C.** The first layer of Organizational Units in the new NDS tree should represent Phoenix, New York, Paris, and London. The first layer of Organizational Units should mirror the WAN. This method will facilitate the partition and replication scheme for the NDS database. It will also make access to resources easier for end users. The names of the Organizational Units do not need to be spelled exactly the same as the cities themselves. This can be too lengthy and complex for ease of use, especially when city names can include difficult-to-spell names like Bahrain and Tallahassee. Instead, a naming standard that uses a short abbreviation, or even the closest airport abbreviation, can simplify the Organizational Unit names.
☒ Answers **A, B,** and **D.** are incorrect because they do not mirror the WAN and will cause problems with being able to partition the NDS database, as well as cause problems with end-user authentication and access to resources.

8. ☑ **C.** The naming standard CITY-APPS-01 provides both a function and a location of a server. It also provides for multiple servers in the same location and with the same function because of the serialized number at the end of the name. This naming standard concatenates the city location of the server with the function (this server provides applications) and a serial number.
☒ **A.** FS01 is incorrect because it provides a function and a serial number. The function in this case is FS, which is a typical abbreviation for *file server.* **B.** DATA-01 is incorrect because it provides a function and a serial number. In this case, the server is used to store information, or data. **D.** CITY01 is incorrect because it provides the location and a serial number.

9. ☑   **C.** The naming standard represented by TEJACK01 will enable 99 accounts to have users with the same or similar names. TEJACK01 represents a naming standard of the first initial, the middle initial, and the first four letters of the last name, concatenated with a serial number of 01. The serial number will allow up to 99 people to have the same first two initials and first four letters of the last name.

☒   **A.** TERENCE is incorrect because it represents the first name as the naming standard and there can be many people with the same first name. **B.** TERENCEEJ is incorrect because it represents the first name, middle, and last initials as the naming standard and there can be many repetitions of this name. **D.** TJACKS1 is incorrect because it represents the first initial and the first five letters of the last name concatenated with a single serial digit. The single, serial digit will enable up to nine persons with the same first initial and first five letters of the last name to have accounts.

10. ☑   **D.** All of the NDS objects that are commonly used in a network should be given a naming standard. This is not only good practice, but facilitates network administration later on.

☒   **A.** Workstation is incorrect because they should be given a naming standard to help their administration. **B.** Printers is incorrect because printers should be named for easy access. **C.** Servers is incorrect because servers should have a naming standard defined before installing the first one on the network.

11. ☑   **B.** The network address of Z.E.N.works workstation name options represents the IPX or the IP address of the workstation. This is the logical node address assigned to the PC.

☒   **A.** Container is incorrect because it represents the container that the workstation exists in. **C.** OS is incorrect because it represents the type of operating system running on the PC. **D.** DNS is incorrect because it represents the IP domain name assigned to the workstation.

12. ☑ **D.** The [Root] object is always located at the very top of the NDS tree. The [Root] object is the basis of the NDS tree and all objects are located within it.

☒ **A.** Organization is incorrect because the Organization object can be located directly beneath the [Root] or beneath a Country object. **B.** Country is incorrect because the Country object is located directly beneath the [Root], or is an option in the NDS tree. **C.** Organizational Unit is incorrect because an Organizational Unit is located beneath the Organization object.

13. ☑ **A.** The recommended design is that the top-layer OUs should mirror the WAN. This design recommendation means that each site separated by a WAN link should be represented by a separate Organizational Unit. This design will facilitate NDS partitioning and replication.

☒ **B.** The top-layer OUs should mirror business units is incorrect because this will not facilitate NDS partitioning. **C.** The top-layer OUs should span WAN links is incorrect because spanning WAN links is a rule that should be avoided. **D.** The top-layer OUs should represent logical workgroups is incorrect because this will not facilitate NDS partitioning. All of these answers will affect the partitioning scheme negatively. An OU should be wholly contained within a partition.

Implementing Time-Synchronization Strategies

1. ☑ **C.** Novell Directory Services® (NDS) is a database. NDS can be distributed across multiple servers so that it is easily accessible by local users. To provide redundancy, multiple copies or replicas of the NDS database can be placed throughout the network. This will prevent a failure of NDS if one of the partitions becomes corrupted and is irretrievably damaged.

☒ **A.** A file is incorrect because multiple database files are part of NDS and they are then replicated and distributed across multiple servers. **B.** A directory or folder is incorrect because NDS is not a directory or folder. **D.** A Novell® server is incorrect because NDS is a directory service contained within a database.

2. ☑ **C.** One of the results when an NDS tree is partitioned is load balancing across servers. A partition separates the NDS database into two or more parts. Each partition is placed on different servers. This means that no single server is dedicated to the NDS authentication processes, and it reduces the load.

☒ **A.** Server duplication is incorrect because partitioning does not affect the server itself, just the NDS database. **B.** Increase volume size is incorrect because the volume size is not affected by partitioning. **D.** None of the above is incorrect because partitioning does result in load balancing across servers.

3. ☑ **A.** The reason that a partition should not span a WAN link is to avoid the increased network traffic on the WAN. A partition creates a significant amount of network traffic to synchronize itself. When a WAN link is spanned by a partition, synchronization can be interrupted if the WAN link goes down, which can corrupt the partition. In general, the rule "don't span the WAN" should always be followed.

☒ **B.** To increase network traffic on the WAN is incorrect because the opposite happens when a WAN link is not spanned by a partition. **C.** To synchronize time across the WAN is incorrect because this will not affect the process of time synchronization. **D.** To distribute administration by sites is incorrect because this will not affect central administration.

4. ☑ **B.** There should be no more than 10–15 replicas of a partition. When there are more, the network will see a performance problem. The administrator can create another partition and reduce the number of replicas for each partition.

☒ Answers **A, C,** and **D.** are all incorrect because the number of replicas should be between 10 and 15 when an administrator makes the decision to add another partition.

5. ☑ **D.** WAN Traffic Manager (WTM) enables an administrator to control when NDS synchronization traffic is allowed across WAN links. Normally, NDS synchronization traffic is transmitted immediately upon any update. WTM must be added to a server by loading the WTM.NLM. The WTM.NLM will extend the NDS schema so that a new object, the LAN Area Object is added to the NDS tree.

☒ **A.** NDIR is incorrect because NDIR will create a directory listing of the files and directories on the NDS tree. **B.** NDS Manager is incorrect because the NDS Manager manages the NDS partitions and replicas. **C.** DNSDHCP is incorrect because this utility manages DNS domain name resolution and DHCP address distribution.

6. ☑ **A.** A NetWare server coordinates file and NDS updates with other servers through time synchronization. Time synchronization lets the server know whether its NDS database and files are the most current versions, or whether they have been updated by a user. This system relies on time stamps to determine which file or NDS update is the latest.

☒ **B.** WAN Traffic Management is incorrect because it only controls the amount of traffic, not whether or not files and NDS objects are updated. **C.** Using LAN Area objects is incorrect because they only enable WAN Traffic Management. **D.** SAP is incorrect, because it is a protocol used to advertise services.

7. ☑ **C.** A single-reference time server provides time updates only to secondary servers. The single-reference time server provides updates to all other NetWare servers. They do not check time on other servers. However, the single-reference time server can be connected to an external time provider.

☒ **A.** Primary is incorrect because a single-reference time server is the sole time provider. **B.** Reference is incorrect because the single-reference time server is the sole time provider. **D.** All of the above is incorrect because a secondary time server works with single-reference time servers.

8. ☑ **C.** Network Time Protocol (NTP) is an open standard that can provide time services to non-NetWare servers. NTP works with the TCP/IP protocol stack and allows an IP server to receive time from a trusted time source. To load NTP on a NetWare server, the administrator would use the NTP.NLM.

☒ **A.** Service Advertising Protocol (SAP) provides service updates to the network. **B.** Route Information Protocol (RIP) is incorrect because it provides route updates to the network. **D.** Network News Transfer Protocol (NNTP) is incorrect because it is used in the TCP/IP protocol stack to provide newsgroup information.

9. ☑ **C.** When the number of servers on the network exceeds the threshold number of 30, the single-reference-server time provider with secondary-server time consumers configuration is no longer viable. When the network contains WAN links, this configuration is not viable, either. After the network has more than 30 servers or if it includes WAN links, the network should have a time provider group (the reference, primary, and secondary server configuration) or NTP (an NTP server, or peer, to provide time updates) configured to handle time synchronization.

☒ Answers **A, B,** and **D.** are incorrect because the threshold number is 30.

10. ☑ **C.** Before AllTek decides to use NTP, it must decide that at least one server will use IP. NTP requires IP to provide time synchronization services. The NTP server can implement transitive synchronization with both IP and IPX protocols to provide time synchronization services to IPX-only servers.

☒ **A.** All servers must use SAP is incorrect, because they will already use SAP as IPX servers. **B.** All servers must use IP is incorrect because only a single server is required to run IP. **D.** At least one server must use SAP is incorrect because all servers already use SAP as part of the IPX protocol stack.

11. ☑ **D.** MONITOR on the NetWare server is used to configure time
synchronization on a NetWare 5 server. This utility is a NetWare Loadable
Module (NLM) and is executed on the server console with the MONITOR
command.

☒ **A.** TIMESYNC is incorrect because this utility does not configure time
synchronization. **B.** SERVMAN is incorrect because the SERVMAN utility
options were merged into the MONITOR utility and SERVMAN is not
available under NetWare 5. **C.** CONFIG is incorrect because this utility
simply displays the server's current configuration.

12. ☑ **B.** The Arizona AllTek administrator will use the TIMESYNC
NetWare Loadable Module to reset the servers' time to mountain time.
TIMESYNC will let the administrator configure the time source, hardware
clock, polling mode, et cetera.

☒ **A.** MONITOR is incorrect because it is used to configure the type of
time server, not the time settings. **C.** CONFIG is incorrect because it
simply displays the server's configuration. **D.** SERVMAN is incorrect
because it is not a NetWare 5 utility.

Creating an Accessibility Plan

1. ☑ **A, B, C.** Hallie should review the application needs of the end users,
physical network needs, and legacy services needs for the accessibility plan.
These encompass the different types of resource access that an end user
may require.

☒ **D.** FAX needs is incorrect because it is a subset of the application
needs. FAX needs provides a much smaller scope for the accessibility plan,
and is not always applicable to some networks because they do not use
FAX services.

2. ☑ **B.** Are any applications used across the WAN? This question will affect the traffic on the WAN and that will affect how the connectivity expert makes other design decisions, such as adjusting the frequency of sending time synchronization updates.

☒ **A.** This option is incorrect because the answer will not affect WAN traffic. **C.** This option is incorrect because the answer will not affect WAN traffic. **D.** This option is incorrect because it will not affect WAN traffic.

3. ☑ **D.** Hallie should review the legacy application needs for the accounting group. NetWare 2.15 is a bindery-based network operating system. That network may have bindery-based applications that the accounting group will need to access after the upgrade to NetWare 5. Although Hallie may be able to upgrade the bindery-based applications to NDS-aware applications, she will need to review the legacy needs first. Because a NetWare 5 server can support up to 16 bindery contexts, Hallie will be able to place users in different containers, but the server expert will need to include the bindery context requirements for the new servers.

☒ Although answers **A, B,** and **C.** will need to be reviewed for the accounting group, their specific needs center on the legacy NetWare server.

4. ☑ **A.** The user policy packages should be contained in the Admin, Sales, Service, HQ and Manufacturing OUs. User policy packages are a different type of object than container policy packages. A user policy package governs user information and should therefore be placed in the same OUs as the user objects are located.

☒ **B.** East and West is incorrect because there are no user objects in these containers. **C.** GLX is incorrect because it is not an Organizational Unit and because there are no users in GLX. **D.** BldgA, BldgB, and East is not correct because there are no user objects in these containers.

5. ☑ **D.** The Organizational Units that should hold the Organizational role objects for the administrators are East and West. East would contain the Organizational role for John, while West would contain the Organizational role for Lucy. By setting up the roles in these OUs, both John and Lucy can administer their respective buildings and any containers below them.

☒ **A.** GLX is incorrect because that would give John access to Lucy's containers and Lucy would have access to John's containers. **B.** BLDGA and BLDGB are incorrect because neither one has access to the East. **C.** Admin and sales are incorrect because some of the other containers are not included, which excludes some of the end users.

6. ☑ **C.** A standard directory structure used on the NetWare 5 servers would enable a consistent drive mapping system. This also eases administration. If the administrator always finds the files where they are expected on each server, the administrator can quickly handle file and directory issues. End users also benefit because they can refer to a drive by its drive letter and be able to communicate effectively with each other and the network administrators because those drive letters represent the same data, even if it is on different servers.

☒ **A.** Alias objects is incorrect because they do not enable consistent drive mappings. **B.** User login scripts is incorrect because their use tends to result in inconsistent drive mappings. **D.** IRF is incorrect because it will not enable consistent drive mappings.

7. ☑ **A.** A container login script is best for creating a common environment for all users that are located in the same Organizational Unit. The container login script is the login script property associated with an Organization or an Organizational Unit NDS object.

☒ **B.** Profile login script is incorrect because a profile login script is more applicable to groups of users, not an entire container of users. **C.** User login script is incorrect because it is applicable to a single user. **D.** Organization login script is incorrect because it is really a container script for the Organization object, and that would not be applicable to the Organizational Unit described in the question.

8. ☑ **A.** As the name implies, the enterprise administrator has administrative access to the entire NDS tree. Because rights are inherited from the NDS tree [Root], the Enterprise administrator must have full rights from the [Root] object.

   ☒ **B.** Container administrator is incorrect because this administrator has access to a single container or section of the NDS tree. **C.** Backup administrator is incorrect because this administrator only has the rights necessary to back up the servers. **D.** Password administrator is incorrect because this role is capable of resetting passwords, and has limited NDS rights to manage user and group objects.

9. ☑ **B.** The NetWare 5 server console command SET BINDERY CONTEXT can add a user's container to the server so that the user can log on in bindery mode. An administrator executes this command to enable legacy bindery services, too.

   ☒ Answers **A, C,** and **D.** are all incorrect because they are not valid NetWare console commands.

10. ☑ **D.** The name of the NDS tree will affect the configuration of Client 32. A standard Client 32 configuration will ensure that users will first log in to the correct environment. One of the parameters for Client 32 is the preferred NDS tree. The name of the NDS tree is placed in this field. Other parameters that will affect the Client 32 configuration are the name context for the user at that workstation, the preferred server, and the first network drive letter.

    ☒ **A.** Storage limits for each user is incorrect because they do not affect Client 32. **B.** Creation of aliases for file access is incorrect because aliases do not affect Client 32. **C.** Applications stored on the workstation is incorrect because those applications should not affect the Client 32 configuration.

11. ☑ **B.** Gerald is a mobile user. He needs access to information in the container wherever he happens to be logging in. The needs of mobile users are unique because they are rarely in the same place using the same resources for extended periods of time. Defining locations in Client 32 is one of the methods used to manage mobile users, so that they have instant access to their environment.

☒ **A.** Remote user is incorrect because a remote user is one that is not connected to the internetwork. **C.** Local user is incorrect because Gerald is not local. **D.** System administrator is incorrect because Gerald has not been granted extended access.

12. ☑ **D.** Frank should revisit the configuration of the workstations for the new remote users. While local users have local servers, the remote users do not. When they attempt to load the applications from the servers using Frank's default workstation configuration, the limited bandwidth of the modems will cause a tremendous delay in the applications' performance.

☒ **A.** The number of sites is incorrect because the remote users will not be located at a site. **B.** The number of servers is incorrect because the remote users will not be affected by them. **C.** The NDS tree design is incorrect because the remote users will have no need for changes to it.

Conducting a NetWare Implementation

1. ☑ **C.** If the WAN links cannot be added, the NetWare 5 implementation must be changed so that there are three NDS trees, one for each of the sites. If WAN links are installed after the NDS trees are created, they can be merged. Even if WAN links are not planned, the NDS trees should be designed with a future merger in mind. Technology changes quickly, and decisions regarding technology within companies change just as quickly. It is always best to prepare for some decisions, especially when the preparation will not adversely affect the network's performance.

   ☒ **A.** This option is incorrect because a single NDS tree cannot be installed across multiple, non-connected sites. **B.** Warren will be limited to a single NetWare server is incorrect because a single NetWare server will not be accessible by any users at either of the other two sites. **D.** Warren cannot install NetWare 5 without the WAN, so the project will be stopped is incorrect because Warren can install NetWare 5 using multiple unique NDS trees.

2. ☑ **C.** Warren was pursuing an Organizational implementation. This approach means designing the tree completely prior to installing it across the entire enterprise.

   ☒ **A.** Departmental implementation is incorrect because it implements multiple NDS trees. **B.** Divisional implementation is incorrect because it implements multiple divisional NDS trees. **D.** None of the above is incorrect because the Organizational implementation is Warren's plan for NDS.

3. ☑ **B.** NetWare 5 servers use the NWCONFIG utility for further NDS installation on a NetWare server. In order for NetWare servers to participate in NDS they must each have NDS installed on them. The NWCONFIG utility is used during the installation process and is available to further configure the server after installation.

   ☒ **A.** INSTALL is incorrect because INSTALL is a NetWare 4 utility not NetWare 5. **C.** SERVMAN is incorrect because it no longer exists on NetWare 5 servers. **D.** MONITOR is incorrect because the MONITOR utility is used to manage the server and watch its performance.

4. ☑   **A.** Warren can partition the NDS tree to make authentication easier for end users by partitioning the containers for Dallas, Denver, Phoenix, and the [Root]. The [Root] partition would also contain the Organization container, TFX. Each of the Dallas, Phoenix, and Denver partitions would include the lower-level OUs. This partition scheme ensures that there is at least one partition for each physical location.

   ☒   **B.** Sales, Admin, and Service is incorrect because they are not containers that hold all the end users. **C.** TFX is incorrect because it spans the WAN. **D.** Dallas, Sales, and Admin is incorrect because they do not contain all the end users.

5. ☑   **C.** Warren should ensure that all servers have read/write or master replicas of the Phoenix partition. The Phoenix partition contains the bindery context for Service.Phoenix.TFX. Replicas of this partition make it more easily accessible by end users.

   ☒   **A.** All servers have subordinate references to the Phoenix partition is incorrect because a subordinate reference is automatically created when a server has a replica of the parent, but not the child. **B.** All servers have read-only replicas of the Denver partition is incorrect because the Denver partition does not contain the bindery context. **D.** All servers have master replicas of the Denver partition is incorrect because there can only be a single master replica and because the Denver partition does not contain the bindery context.

6. ☑   **C.** Warren should implement a primary server in Denver and a primary server in Phoenix. This scheme will ensure that Master1 is the reference server, and the primary servers will provide time to the servers in Denver and Phoenix so that WAN bandwidth is not used.

   ☒   **A.** Single reference servers is incorrect because a single reference server cannot be used with reference servers. **B.** Reference servers is incorrect because Warren's requirement was to have only Master1 as the reference server. **D.** Secondary servers is incorrect because the secondary servers are time consumers and all servers would contact the Dallas Master1 server via the WAN link for time updates. This would overuse bandwidth.

7. ☑ **C.** The least amount of effort for Warren is to merge the two NDS trees into a single NDS tree. Merging is the process of adding two NDS trees together so that there results a single tree with both structures under a merged [Root].

☒ **A.** Reinstall all the TFX servers as part of the Sandscapes tree is incorrect because that is more effort than merging and includes adding back in all the TFX user accounts and NDS objects. **B.** Reinstall all of the Sandscapes servers as part of the TFX tree is incorrect because that is more effort than merging and includes adding back in all the Sandscapes user accounts and NDS objects. **D.** Reinstall all of the TFX and Sandscapes servers as part of a new NDS tree is incorrect because this will be more effort than any of the other options and requires all objects to be created anew.

8. ☑ **D.** The first layer under the [Root] of the merged tree will consist of two Organizations, SS and TFX. When two NDS trees are merged, they are merged at the [Root]. The remainder of the newly merged NDS tree will be the same as the two separate trees.

☒ Answers **A, B** and **C.** are incorrect because none of these container objects exists directly beneath the [Root] of the merged NDS tree.

9. ☑ **C.** The Root partition of the Sandscapes tree will be created as a partition under the [Root] of the new NDS tree. It will not include the new NDS tree's [Root]. The Sandscapes tree is the source tree in the merge. As the source tree, the Sandscape's [Root] disappears. The partition that includes the [Root] simply becomes a new partition below the [Root] of the new NDS tree.

☒ **A.** The partitions will not be affected is incorrect because the root partition will be affected. **B.** Both partitions, London and Root, will be merged as a single partition under the [Root] of the new tree, is incorrect because partitions are not merged during an NDS tree merger. **D.** The London partition of the Sandscapes tree will be merged into the Phoenix partition from the TFX tree is incorrect because source partitions are not merged into partitions of the target NDS tree during a merger.

10. ☑ **B.** Warren will use the DSREPAIR utility to import the schema of one tree into the other tree. DSREPAIR is used to repair NDS databases, but is also useful for ensuring that the schema is synchronized between two different NDS trees. The schemas must be synchronized in order for objects to be recognized for what they are under the newly merged tree.

☒ **A.** DSMERGE is incorrect because DSMERGE performs the merger of the trees. **C.** DSIMPORT is incorrect because it is not a utility under NetWare 5. **D.** DSUPDATE is incorrect because it is not a utility under NetWare 5.

11. ☑ **C.** A prerequisite for merging two NDS trees is that the NetWare servers in both of the trees must run the same version of NDS. NDS is updated for each version of NetWare. Additionally, Novell releases updates to NDS via service packs. The result is that NetWare servers are often not running the same version of NDS. It's a good practice to obtain the latest NDS update from Novell on their Web site, http://support.novell.com, test it, and then update all servers to the same version. If some servers are not NetWare 5, but are NetWare 4.x, it's best to obtain the latest versions of NDS for both NetWare 4 and NetWare 5, test them, and update the servers appropriately.

☒ **A.** Both trees must have the same Organization name is incorrect because the Organization object names must be unique prior to merging the trees. **B.** At least one tree must have an Alias object under the [Root] is incorrect because no Alias objects should be under either tree's [Root] at the time of merging. **D.** All servers must be "down" before merging the trees is incorrect because the servers should be up and running in order to update their NDS database partitions and replicas appropriately.

12. ☑ **A.** Warren should run DSREPAIR before running DSMERGE. DSREPAIR stabilizes both trees by:

   - Reporting synchronization status
   - Time synchronization
   - Rebuilding the operational schema

   ☒ **B.** MONITOR is incorrect because that utility views the performance of the server. **C.** NWCONFIG is incorrect because that utility is involved in installation and configuration of the server. **D.** RCONSOLE is incorrect because that is a workstation utility that is used to view the server console.

13. ☑ **A.** The option to check servers in this tree ensures that NetWare servers are up and running on the NDS tree.
   ☒ **B.** Check time synchronization is incorrect because this option ensures that both the trees are synchronized for time. **C.** Merge two trees is incorrect because this option will perform the merger. **D.** Rename this tree is incorrect because this option is used to rename an NDS tree. Renaming a tree may be necessary when merging two trees that are not yet connected via a network link. The tree names must be unique prior to merger.

14. ☑ **A.** Warren should use a Group object. The designated executive team should be added as members of the Group. After that, the Group can be granted access to the network resources.
   ☒ **B.** Profile object is incorrect because it cannot be used for common rights to resources. **C.** Alias object is incorrect because it is not used to grant rights to resources. **D.** Inherited Rights Filter (IRF) is incorrect because it removes inherited rights to resources.

15. ☑ **D.** The executive group will need file rights, NDS rights to printers, servers, containers, users, and workstation objects. The file rights will enable the group to look at files and data on the network. The rights to containers and users will allow the group to look at password policies. The rights to users will enable them to look at user accounts. The other rights will let them review, access, and utilize printers, servers and workstations.
   ☒ Answers **A, B,** and **C.** are all incorrect because the executive group will need more rights than any of these choices provides.

Part 5

NetWare Service
and Support
(Exam 50-635)

EXAM TOPICS

Network Troubleshooting

Installing and Troubleshooting Network Interface
Cards and Cables

Installing and Troubleshooting Network Storage
Devices

Troubleshooting the DOS Workstation

Troubleshooting Network Printing

Troubleshooting and Optimizing the Network

NetWare Service and Support Questions

This section is designed to help you prepare for the NetWare Service and Support exam (Exam # 50-635) so you can begin to reap the career benefits of CNE certification. The following questions are structured in a format similar to what you'll find on the exam. Read all the choices carefully, as there may be more than one correct answer. Choose all correct answers for each question.

Network Troubleshooting

Use the Following Scenario for Questions 1–3
Joe has been asked by his company to design a new server room that will be an ideal environment for the company's servers.

1. What is the best type of floor for the server room?

   A. A carpeted floor, for the comfort of the technicians

   B. A solid concrete slab for stability

   C. An inlaid hardwood floor

   D. A raised floor of ESD-inhibiting tiles, with space beneath to run cabling

2. What should Joe do when designing the electrical system?

   A. Make sure all electrical wires are orange and easily visible.

   B. Use fuses rather than circuit breakers.

   C. Plan for an Uninterruptible Power Supply (UPS).

   D. Make sure that the outlets in the server room are not grounded.

3. In deciding where to place network cabling, what would Joe *not* consider to be too close?

   A. Air vents

   B. Microwave ovens

   C. Fluorescent lights

   D. The building's main air-conditioning unit

The exam will most likely have a question or two concerning which Web site you should visit to retrieve a patch or get product information.

4. The company wants to make sure that the important data on the servers is not destroyed by viruses and asks Joe how to keep viruses from infecting the files on the server. How should the files be scanned when Joe configures the virus scanning software?

   A. Program files (.EXE, .COM, .DLL) only

   B. Program files and document files (.DOC, .WPD, .XLS, etc.)

   C. All files

   D. Image files (.BMP, .GIF, .TIF, etc.)

5. Joe's company needs to keep proprietary files and information on the servers, and wants to ensure that the information can be accessed only by authorized employees of the company. What should Joe do to prepare, since network security also means being able to retrieve files in the event of a catastrophic hard-drive failure?

   A. Use a third-party backup program to schedule backups of NDS™ and the files on the servers, which would run during non-business hours.

   B. Instruct his customers to back up all essential files to floppy disks.

   C. Manually back up the server using Novell's SBACKUP utility.

   D. Copy all files from each server to another server at the end of each day.

6. Joe uses Novell's recommended method of troubleshooting when solving network problems. He takes the following steps to do so:

1. Tries a quick fix/gathers basic information
2. Develops a plan to isolate the problem
3. Executes the plan
4. Ensures user satisfaction
5. Documents the solution and takes steps to avoid a recurrence

After going through the troubleshooting process, Joe determines that there was a problem with the login script. Now that he has solved the problem, Joe should:

A. Move on to the next problem

B. Log his time spent working on the problem and move on to the next problem

C. Document the problem and its solution so that other network administrators will know how to solve the problem in the future

D. Make some more changes to the login script to see what effect the changes have

Use the Following Scenario for Questions 7–8

Joe's company wants to make sure that he has access to all of the information and tools that he needs to be effective as a network administrator. To that end, it purchases a monthly subscription to the CD-based *Novell's Support Connection* (formerly known as *Novell Support Encyclopedia Professional/NSEPro*), then purchases a copy of *Microhouse's Support Source* (formerly known as *Microhouse Technical Library*) on CD, and makes sure that Joe has a reliable connection to the Internet from which he can access Novell's support web site, http://support.novell.com where he will find the online content, files, and forums that were once found on NetWire on CompuServe.

7. While updating the workstations with the new client software, Joe notices that the network card on one of the workstations is sharing an IRQ with the interrupt used by the printer port on that workstation. Joe would like to change the IRQ setting of the network card, but cannot find the documentation that specifies the jumper settings for the network card. What should Joe do to get information about the jumper settings?

A. Search Novell's Web site.
B. Search the Support Connection CD.
C. Call Novell's technical support line.
D. Search the Support Source CD.

8. The next day, Joe notices that another CNE has experienced the same problem, and has fixed the problem by specifying the 802.2 protocol rather than the 802.3 protocol in the NET.CFG file. Joe wants to modify the login script to copy a NET.CFG file with the appropriate settings to each workstation, but needs to review login script syntax. Joe should look for login script documentation:

A. On the Support Source CD
B. On the Support Connection CD
C. On Novell's Web site
D. On NetWire on CompuServe

Installing and Troubleshooting Network Interface Cards and Cables

1. Gary knows that networks following the Ethernet standards are the most prevalent types of networks installed and wants to consider whether or not to design the network around Ethernet standards. If a workstation begins showing "Server not found" errors, what should Gary check?

A. An outdated NetWare client

B. Whether the customer's password has expired

C. Invalid frame types

D. Interference from a network printer

Use the Following Scenario for Questions 2–3

Although Gary has noted that the 100Mbps speed of Ethernet's 100baseTX meets his requirements, he wonders if a Token Ring-based network would offer any compelling advantages over 100baseTX.

2. Token Ring networks do offer a few more cabling options than Ethernet networks. Which of the following is *not* a type of cabling that is primarily designed to be compatible with Token Ring?

A. IBM Type 5 fiber-optic cable

B. IBM Type 8 shielded twisted-pair, designed to be run under carpet

C. IBM Type 9, designed to be fire resistant

D. IBM Type 12, designed to be run under water

---

exam
ⓦatch *PCMCIA (Personal Memory Card International Association) standard is also covered in the course, although mentioned only briefly, and Novell® omits the fact that everyone else now calls it PC-Card, because people can't memorize computer industry acronyms.*

3. Each MSAU has a Ring-In and Ring-Out port, used for expanding the network by attaching together MSAUs. Does this offer any advantage over Ethernet hubs?

A. Yes, Ethernet hubs may not be linked together.

B. No, all Ethernet hubs may be linked together.

C. Perhaps. Most, but not all, Ethernet hubs are designed to link to other hubs.

D. No, Ethernet hubs may only be linked to routers.

Use the Following Scenario for Questions 4–5

Gary knows that Fiber Distributed Data Interface (FDDI) fiber-optic networks are relatively expensive, but wonders if there are any advantages to FDDI that would justify spending the extra money necessary to implement an FDDI network.

4. Which of the following are disadvantages of FDDI?

A. Documentation for most FDDI network components is available only in German.

B. FDDI network components are very expensive compared to other types.

C. FDDI network components are only made by one company, so you must rely on that company for continued support.

D. FDDI network components burn out after approximately 10,000 hours of continuous use and must be replaced.

5. Which of the following is *not* a disadvantage of FDDI cabling?

A. FDDI cabling is more susceptible to a break than other types of cabling.

B. Terminating an FDDI cable is more difficult than terminating other types of cabling.

C. FDDI cabling is more expensive than other types of cabling.

D. FDDI cabling is subject to interference from microwave ovens.

QUESTIONS AND ANSWERS

My customer wants to upgrade his Arcnet network to Ethernet 10Base2. Can I just change the cards in the clients and re-use the old coax cable?	No, Arcnet used a RG-62/U cable and 93-ohm terminators. 10Base2 uses RG-58A/U or RG-58C/U coax cable with 50-ohm terminators.
I need to run Ethernet 802.2 , Ethernet 802.3, and Ethernet II on my network. Do I have to have three NICs in my server to support these different frame types?	No, you can bind up to four protocols or frame types to one NIC.
Can I connect my company's art department that uses Apple computers on a Token Ring network to the rest of my company's Ethernet network?	Yes. The cheapest way to accomplish this is to add a Token Ring card to a server that already has an Ethernet card installed and configure it to act as a router. There are also more expensive solutions out in the market that can provide higher throughput.
Our company just bought 100 10Mbps NICs that support Full Duplex. However, when I configure the NICs for Full Duplex, the network does not seem any faster. Why is that?	You are most likely still using shared media hubs and concentrators and your NICs have switched themselves back to Half Duplex operation. To take advantage of Full Duplex operation on your network, you have to use switches instead of hubs.
My EISA NIC in my server just stopped working. The only spare NIC I have is a 16-bit ISA NIC card. Will this NIC work in place of my EISA NIC?	Yes, 8- and 16-bit ISA cards will work in EISA slots. This is one of the advantages of the EISA slot design.
My NetWare console screen keeps displaying messages about a "router configuration error." What does this mean?	You most likely have a second server on the same network segment that has a different network address bound to the frame type used by the first server. All servers on the same segment must have the same network address.
I just set up a new server on my network, and whenever I use the Display Servers command from this server, no other servers are found. Why is this?	The most likely cause is that the wrong frame type is being used on this server. Make sure that the correct frame type is being used and that the correct protocols are bound to the NIC.

Installing and Troubleshooting Network Storage Devices

Use the Following Scenario for Questions 1–2

Jim has been asked to build a new server that will host the company's e-mail. Although he has decided on the other specifications of the server, he is not quite sure what type of hard-drive setup would be the best given the heavy demands that he expects will be made on the server. Jim first reviews the basics about hard drives, as a starting point in the decision-making process.

1. Having looked at other types of storage media, Jim notes that hard drives, rather than tape drives or CD drives, are used as storage devices in servers because, compared to other media types, hard drives:

   A. Offer faster read/write capability

   B. Are the most durable form of storage

   C. Are the cheapest storage in cost-per-megabyte of information stored

   D. Are a removable medium

2. What does a sector on a typical hard drive hold?

   A. 256 bytes of data

   B. 256 megs of data

   C. 512 bytes of data

   D. 512 megs of data

Use the Following Scenario for Questions 3–6

Having reviewed the characteristics of hard disks versus other types of storage media, Jim has determined that a hard disk or array of hard disks will be the best form of data storage for the server. Now he must consider which type of hard drive interface would be the best.

3. Jim would also like to minimize the chance of lost data. What advantage would SCSI drives/controllers offer over IDE?

A. SCSI drives can be set up in a Redundant Array of Inexpensive Disks (RAID) configuration where the loss of any one drive will not mean a loss of data.

B. SCSI drives are designed to function for at least ten years.

C. SCSI drive platters can easily be removed and placed into a new drive case and put back into the server.

D. The warranty on SCSI drives includes data recovery by the manufacturer if the drive ever fails.

4. As Jim begins putting together the hardware specifications proposal for the purchasing department, the IDE hard drive on his computer runs out of space. Jim decides to add a second IDE drive to his workstation to hold additional files. If he plans to continue booting from his existing hard drive, to what configuration should the hard drives be set?

A. Original = Master, New = Master

B. Original = Master, New = Slave

C. New = Master, Original = Slave

D. New = Slave, Original = Slave

5. Jim's hard drives are not being recognized by the system and he suspects that a cabling problem may be to blame. What is the first thing that he should check?

A. The cable is neatly folded with sharp creases where the cable folds over.

B. The red stripe on one side of the cable lines up with the highest-numbered pin on the controller and drives.

C. Only Novell-brand cables are used.

D. The red stripe on one side of the cable lines up with *pin 1* on the controller and drives.

6. Jim has used the manufacturer's program to low-level format the hard drive. However, DOS will not format the drive. What must Jim do next?

A. Jim must first install NetWare.

B. Jim must use the /S (for SCSI) switch with the FORMAT command.

C. Jim must first use FDISK to create the DOS partition.

D. Jim must use the manufacturer's program to high-level format the drive.

Use the Following Scenario for Questions 7–11

Jim's supervisor is concerned by the cost of the server and wonders if perhaps the company could save some money by not using RAIDs on the server. He knows that with RAID, data is written onto two or more disks in such a way that the data can be recovered from the good disks if any one disk fails. However, the supervisor asks Jim to explain why the server should not have only one hard drive and depend on the tape backup for recovery.

7. Jim's supervisor asks him whether RAID is built into NetWare, or if it requires a special SCSI controller. Which of the following levels of RAID should Jim explain is built into NetWare?

A. Level 0

B. Level 1

C. Level 5

D. None of the above

8. Although they will be using SCSI drives for this server, Jim's supervisor wonders if RAID is available for IDE drives. What is Jim's response?

A. Yes, it is available, and there is no difference other than the drives themselves.

B. Yes, it is available using the disk mirroring/duplexing feature built into NetWare, or by buying dedicated IDE RAID controllers.

C. No, RAID is only available for SCSI drives.

QUESTIONS AND ANSWERS

I have a tall computer case and I need an IDE cable that is 26 inches in length to reach from the controller to the disks. Can't I just buy a length of cable and snap the ends on it and use it?	No, IDE cables cannot be longer than 18 inches.
I just replaced my SCSI controller in my server. Now when I boot the server, the following message appears: "No SCSI Boot Device Found" and the server just hangs there. What's wrong?	The SCSI controller's BIOS needs to be enabled to allow it to boot from the SCSI drive.
I just replaced my IDE drive in my server and now when I boot it, I get a "Controller Failure" message. Is my disk too large for my controller?	Most likely not. You probably forgot to jumper the drive as a Master or Single Drive in a one-drive system.
After installing a new RAID subsystem, NetWare does not see it in NWCONFIG. What is going on here?	The RAID system you installed most likely requires special HAM and CDM drivers. Check with the vendor for the correct drivers to use with the RAID system.
Whenever I use the command CDROM to mount my CD, NetWare loads the CDHFS.NSS module. The CD is in ISO9660 format. Why does NetWare load the Apple support module?	In NetWare® 5, the command to mount a CD-ROM volume is CD9660.NSS. To mount an Apple format CD-ROM, use CDHFS.NSS. The command CDROM will load both modules by default.
Can I use my old SCSI I-type drives on my Fast Wide SCSI controller?	Yes, you can with the proper SCSI cable adapter(s). However your controller will use the slower transfer speed for all devices on the cable.
Someone told me that you can use a floppy drive cable for an IDE hard drive in an emergency. Is this true?	Absolutely not. While the 34-pin floppy cable will plug into an IDE drive and controller, you will be short 6 wires and the drive will not work.

9. Jim's company has placed the employee handbook on a CD-ROM and would like the CD to be shared from the CD-ROM drive on the server as a NetWare volume. Is it possible to do this?

   A. No, a dedicated CD-ROM server is required.
   B. Yes, but the drive must be mounted as a DOS device.
   C. Yes, a CD-ROM may be mounted as a NetWare volume without loading DOS drivers.
   D. Yes, but only with a SCSI CD-ROM drive.

10. Jim's supervisor wonders whether the company should consider using Magneto-Optical (MO) drives for backups or other data storage and asks Jim to explain the basic method by which MO drives store data. Jim explains that MO drives:

    A. Write data optically and read data magnetically
    B. Write data magnetically and read data optically
    C. Can read or write by magnetic or optical means
    D. Write using a laser beam and magnetism and read optically

11. Given the fact that MO disks are very durable, Jim's boss asks why MO disks should not be used as a backup platform instead of tape drives. What does Jim tell him?

    A. MO disks read and write more slowly than tape drives.
    B. MO disks and drives are more expensive than tape drives.
    C. MO backup solutions are expensive because each disk may only be used once.
    D. MO drives are more likely to have a media error than tape drives.

Troubleshooting the DOS Workstation

Use the Following Scenario for Questions 1–11

Dave has been asked to set up Novell's DOS client on some older PCs with limited memory. The PCs will be used for collecting data from some manufacturing machinery designed to be monitored by a DOS program.

1. If Dave allows the DOS client installation program to modify the CONFIG.SYS and AUTOEXEC.BAT files, then the DOS client:

   A. Will be ready to load at the DOS prompt when the computer finishes the boot process

   B. Will ask if the client should be loaded each time the computer boots

   C. Will load automatically each time the computer boots

   D. Will be combined into a file called STARTNET.BAT

2. Dave also knows that network drivers must be loaded in a specific order, or the DOS client will not load properly. Which of the following describes the correct load order for the network drivers?

   A. IPXODI.COM, LSL.COM, NIC driver, VLM.EXE

   B. VLM.EXE, NIC driver, LSL.COM, IPXODI.COM

   C. IPXODI.COM, LSL.COM, VLM.EXE, NIC driver

   D. LSL.COM, NIC driver, IPXODI.COM, VLM.EXE

3. Dave notices that he can also use MSD to determine the I/O settings that are already in use and sets the card to an address that is not being used by another device. However, the NIC driver is not loading properly. Which file should Dave edit to tell the NIC driver which IRQ and I/O settings should be used?

   A. NIC.CFG

   B. NET.CFG

   C. IO.CFG

   D. NICIO.CFG

Watchdog parameters are SET at the NetWare server console.

4. Other than letting the network administrator know when a workstation stops communicating with the server, why is it important for the server to keep track of workstation connections via the watchdog feature?

   A. If not for the watchdog feature, the server would assume that a workstation was connected until LOGOUT was run at the workstation, even if the link between server and workstation were broken.

   B. If each user is limited to a single login, the server needs to know whether each connection is truly active, or users might be prevented from logging in.

   C. Because NetWare servers are licensed based on the number of concurrent connections, it is important that the server have a reliable way of knowing exactly how many connections are truly active, and which ones should be dropped.

   D. All of the above

5. In addition to configuring the diskless workstation with a boot PROM, Dave must run the following NLM at the server:

   A. REMOTE.NLM

   B. RPL.NLM

   C. RPX.NLM

   D. RPROM.NLM

The NetWare Workstation INSTALL process will prompt you to update AUTOEXEC.BAT and CONFIG.SYS. It will then back up the old files and generate a .BNW extension of each.

6. Dave observes the packets being sent out over the network and notes that several packets include [00002345:FFFFFFFFFFFF]. What does the sequence of 12 Fs following the colon in the packet address indicate?

A. That there is a problem with the workstation or server sending the packet

B. That the packet is being addressed to everything on the network

C. That the packet size is too large for the hub

D. That the packet is being sent to a router

exam
Watch

The NIC software device driver must match the type of NIC installed on the client PC.

7. Dave wants to minimize the chance of running into IRQ problems in the future. When buying new computers, which bus/NIC type would be the least likely to be susceptible to IRQ conflicts?

A. PCI

B. ISA

C. EISA

D. VESA Local

exam
Watch

A workstation can access at most 26 drive letters from A: to Z: by setting LASTDRIVE=Z in CONFIG.SYS.

8. Since Dave needs the PCs to address at least four megabytes of RAM, what would be the least powerful CPU that he could use in each workstation?

A. 8088

B. 286

C. 386

D. 486

*The NetWare network connection files must be executed in this order:
LSL, NIC driver, IPXODI, and VLM.*

9. What specification allows most modern programs to use memory above the
first megabyte?

A. Extended memory (EMS)

B. Expanded Memory (XMS)

C. High Memory Area (HMA)

D. Upper memory blocks (UMB)

Watchdog parameters are SET at the NetWare server console.

10. Dave decides that the best course of action would be to run a memory
optimization program to configure the network drivers to load into upper
memory, freeing base memory for the monitoring program. Although he
knows Quarterdeck's QEMM would be the best program to accomplish
this, which program that is included with DOS could Dave try first?

A. Defrag

B. Scandisk

C. MSD

D. Memmaker

*Get Nearest Server is requested by a workstation when the
workstation needs to attach to a NetWare server.*

11. Dave has heard of other versions of DOS, namely DR DOS and Novell DOS. He learns that DR DOS was made by Digital Research, and that Novell bought DR DOS, enhanced it, and released it as Novell DOS. Should Dave consider getting Novell DOS for his workstations?

   A. Yes, because Novell DOS is optimized for networking

   B. Yes, because Novell DOS is free to use on workstations that have a licensed connection to a Novell server

   C. No, because Novell DOS is incompatible with some software

   D. No, because Dave would have to learn command syntax that is different from the MS-DOS that he already knows

exam
ⓦatch   *Give Nearest Server is sent by the closest NetWare server. The server is then saying it will be used to authenticate the workstation.*

Troubleshooting Network Printing

Use the Following Scenario for Questions 1–9

Leslee is responsible for setting up and maintaining network printers for several hundred users that work at one of her company's larger sites. These responsibilities include physically setting up the printers, as well as setting up the NDS objects that make up network printing in NetWare 5. Finally, Leslee is responsible for troubleshooting the NetWare 5 print process when there is a problem with printing.

1. A user named Tim is reporting that he is suddenly unable to print to the printer that is shared by the members of his workgroup. What should Leslee do first to troubleshoot the problem?

   A. Determine if there is a paper jam

   B. Determine if the problem is hardware related or software related

   C. Determine if the other members of the workgroup can print to the printer

   D. Determine if the print queue is locked up

A local printer is attached to a standalone PC or workstation and cannot be accessed through the network.

2. A user named Mike has a workstation attached to a laser printer by a parallel printer cable. Recently Mike attached a longer cable to the printer so that he could move it across the room. Since the move, Mike has been experiencing intermittent printing problems. Which of the following is the most likely cause of the problems?

A. The new cable is defective.

B. The new cable is too long.

C. The printer must be set up again with the new cable in place.

D. Electromagnetic interference from something near the printer is causing problems.

3. A laser printer that Leslee supports is ejecting blank pages, but seems to be going through the mechanical process of printing when a print job is sent from a workstation. She suspects that the toner cartridge may be empty. What would be one of the fastest ways for Leslee to determine if the toner needs to be changed?

A. Open the printer, take out the toner cartridge, and see if it feels empty.

B. Print a self-test page.

C. Send a print job from each workstation.

D. Change to another network port on the hub, and resend the print job.

4. When troubleshooting problems with dot-matrix printers, what must you be careful to avoid?

A. Touching the ink on the ribbon

B. Tilting one side of the printer more than three degrees higher than the other side

C. Moving the print head or platen knob when the printer is on

D. Forgetting to apply WD-40 to all of the gears

Manual load is used when the printer is physically attached to a workstation. That workstation must be running NPRINTER.EXE or NPTWIN95.exe. Auto load is used when the printer is physically attached to a server. That server must be running PSERVER.NLM and PSERVER.NLM will automatically load NPRINTER.EXE. In either case, NPRINTER.EXE must be loaded.

5. When opening a laser printer to replace a toner cartridge, you must take care not to expose the drum inside the printer to what effect?

A. Light

B. Cold air

C. Static electricity

D. Hot air

A networked printer can be attached to either a server, a workstation, or directly to the network.

6. What does it signal when spots and/or lines appear on pages printed on a laser printer?

A. The roller is damaged.

B. The drum is damaged.

C. The toner cartridge needs to be replaced.

D. The corona wires need to be cleaned.

A printer attached to a workstation is called a remote printer or network printer.

Assign print queues to printers and assign printers to print servers.

7. In checking the print queue, Leslee notes that there are no jobs listed in the queue. Which of the following should she check?

A. The space available on the volume where the print queue is stored

B. Whether a job created using the INSERT key in PCONSOLE will enter the queue and be printed

C. Whether the people trying to print to the queue are correctly designated as users in the print queue object in NetWare Administrator

D. All of the above

To redirect a print job to a printer attached to a workstation or print server, the workstation's local printer port must be CAPTUREd.

8. In setting up a new printer, Leslee has created a Printer object, Print Server object, and Print Queue object in NetWare Administrator. She has linked the printer to the print server, and the print queue to the printer. Finally, she has run PSERVER.NLM at the server and selected the correct print server object. However, jobs sent to the print queue are not being printed. Leslee suspects that the server may not have enough free RAM to run PSERVER.NLM properly. How can Leslee check to make sure that PSERVER is actually running?

A. Check the PSERVER screen from the server console.

B. Check the Print Server Information and Status from PCONSOLE.

C. Check the LCD display on the printer.

D. Both A and B

9. Leslee remembers that a local printer is generally one that is physically connected to a NetWare server's parallel or serial port, while a remote printer is connected to a network card or workstation with which the server communicates over the network. Through which protocol does the server communicate?

A. SPX

B. IPX

C. RAW

D. EMF

Troubleshooting and Optimizing the Network

Use the Following Scenario for Questions 1–9

Mark has been put in charge of coming up with a disaster recovery strategy for his company. The company wants to ensure that there is minimal down time under several different scenarios.

1. A user has accidentally deleted a file from a network directory and wishes to recover the file. What would be the first step Mark should take in attempting to recover the file?

A. Restore the file from a backup.

B. Use the DOS UNDELETE command.

C. Use the NetWare SALVAGE utility.

D. Use a third-party data recovery tool.

2. Mark considers backing up the server volumes to a tape drive attached to his workstation. What is the main reason that this would not be a good idea?

A. Backup to a workstation tape drive would be slow.

B. Backup to a workstation tape drive would not back up NDS or hidden NetWare system files.

C. Backup to a workstation tape drive would increase network traffic.

D. Backup to a workstation tape drive would be compromised if Mark's workstation crashed.

3. Although it is not necessary to use a brand-new tape every time, it is important to rotate tape sets so that you can recover old files if necessary. If you create one-week sets of tapes, how many sets of tapes might it be prudent to use in rotation?

A. Two sets, rotated every other week

B. One set, overwriting each day's tape once a week

C. Three sets, rotating every 21 days

D. Four sets, rotating once a month

4. Mark wants to recover a database file for a customer, but the SALVAGE utility is unable to restore it. He runs VREPAIR, but finds that the file still is not recoverable. What third-party utility does Novell recommend for recovering the file?

A. Norton Utilities for NetWare

B. Ontrack Data Recovery for NetWare

C. PowerQuest Partition Magic

D. Nuts&bolts NetWare Utilities

5. Mark wants to make sure that he loads and keeps track of the latest patches to the NetWare OS. What is the name of the utility that Mark should use?

A. PATCHMGR.NLM

B. PATCHMAN.NLM

C. PATCH.NLM

D. PATCH5.NLM

6. Mark runs the MONITOR utility by typing MONITOR at the server console prompt. He notes that the Long Term Cache Hits statistic reads 93 percent. Mark should consider upgrading the RAM in the server when the Long Term Cache Hits statistic consistently reads below:

A. 60 percent

B. 70 percent

C. 80 percent

D. 90 percent

7. Mark notices that VIRSIG.NLM, used to check for virus signature updates on the Internet, is using up a lot of CPU time. Since he knows that it is not necessary to let the NLM have that much CPU time, what command should Mark type at the system console to tell NetWare to give lower priority to VIRSIG.NLM?

A. SET PRIORITY VIRSIG.NLM = 0

B. SET PRIORITY VIRSIG.NLM = 10000

C. LOAD SCHDELAY VIRSIG = 0

D. LOAD SCHDELAY VIRSIG = 10000

8. Mark wants to improve network communications. One of the quickest ways to do this is to read the documentation that came with the network boards in the server. Which of the following parameters needs to be increased to the maximum that the network card can handle?

A. Maximum data buffers

B. Maximum physical receive packet size

C. Maximum megabits per second

D. Maximum packets per second

9. Why should Mark also monitor LANalyzer's Errors's gauge?

A. More than 100 errors per second is cause for concern.

B. More than 64 errors per second is cause for concern.

C. More than 32 errors per second is cause for concern.

D. Any number of errors per second on an ongoing basis means that there is a problem somewhere on the network that should be fixed.

NetWare Service and Support Answers

Q & A

The answers to the questions are in boldface, followed by a brief explanation. The incorrect answer choices are explained in the final paragraph following each correct answer. Some of the explanations detail the logic you should use to choose the correct answer, while others give factual reasons why the answer is correct. If you miss several questions on a similar topic, you should review the corresponding section in the *CNE® NetWare® 5 Study Guide* before taking the NetWare Service and Support test.

Network Troubleshooting

1. ☑ **D. A raised floor of Electro-Static Discharge (ESD)-inhibiting tiles, with space beneath to run cabling.** Several companies manufacture and install flooring of this type for server rooms.
   ☒ **A.** is incorrect because carpeting tends to generate static electricity as people walk across it and carpet fibers can clog ventilation systems. **B, C.** are incorrect because although concrete and wood do not promote the generation of static electricity, they do not give you the advantages that a raised floor offers.

2. ☑ **C. Plan for an Uninterruptible Power Supply (UPS).** A UPS that can provide power to the servers during an outage will allow the servers to shut down gracefully, if the outage is extensive, and will allow the servers to continue running through short outages without shutting down at all. Modern UPSs also offer surge protection.
   ☒ **A.** is incorrect because the color of the wiring will not have any effect on server performance. **B.** is incorrect because there is no advantage to the use of fuses over circuit breakers. **D.** is incorrect because the outlets in the server room should be grounded.

3. ☑ **A. Air vents.** Air vents should not generate any electrical interference that would cause a problem with network transmission.
   ☒ **B, C, and D.** are incorrect because microwave ovens, fluorescent lights, and air-conditioning units do generate electromagnetic radiation that can interfere with network transmissions.

4. ☑ C. All files. These days, a virus can infect program *and* document files, and a virus may be hidden in a file that does not have a standard extension, such as .DLL or .DOC.

☒ A. and B. are incorrect because, as stated, a virus can hide in a file that does not have a standard program or document extension. D. is incorrect because, as of this writing, viruses do not infect image files, so you would not configure the virus scanning software to scan them exclusively.

5. ☑ A. Use a third-party backup program to schedule backups of NDS™ and the files on the servers, which would run during non-business hours. Scheduling the backup to run during non-business hours means that the server will not be slowed down with the backup process while most people are logged into it.

☒ B. is incorrect because it would be impractical for people to back up to floppy disk since it would take far too much time. C. is incorrect because Novell's SBACKUP utility does not allow you to schedule backups in advance and it needs to be monitored as it progresses. D. is incorrect because it would take far too much time to copy all files from one server to another, and NDS would not be backed up using this method.

6. ☑ C. Document the problem and its solution so that other network administrators will know how to solve the problem in the future. Maintaining a problem/solution database will benefit all of the network administrators.

☒ A. is incorrect because Joe should take the time to document the solution to the problem before moving on to the next problem. B. is incorrect because merely logging the time spent on a problem does nothing to help document the solution to the problem. D. is incorrect because after solving a problem, you should never make changes that could cause further problems.

7. ☑ **D.** Search the Support Source CD. The Support Source CD has documentation and jumper-setting information for most of the network cards that have ever been manufactured.

☒ **A.** is incorrect because Novell's Web site has very little information about jumper settings on network cards. **B.** is incorrect because the Support Connection CD has little information about network card jumper settings. **C.** is incorrect because Novell's technical support line may not have information about network card jumper settings, particularly if the network card in question is not a Novell₍ₑ₎ network card.

8. ☑ **B.** On the Support Connection CD. The Support Connection CD contains the latest product documentation for NetWare, including documentation on login scripts.

☒ **A.** is incorrect because the Support Source CD does not contain Novell product documentation **C.** is incorrect because Novell does not maintain complete product documentation on the web site as of the time of this writing. **D.** is incorrect because NetWire on CompuServe does not maintain complete Novell product documentation.

Installing and Troubleshooting Network Interface Cards and Cables

1. ☑ **C.** Invalid frame types. For example, the workstation may be trying to communicate using the 802.3 frame type, and the server may only be using 802.2.

☒ **A.** is incorrect because an outdated NetWare client should generate a "Server not found" error. **B.** is incorrect because an expired password would prompt the customer to change the password rather than state that the server could not be found. **D.** is incorrect because a network printer would not generate interference that would result in a "server not found" error.

2. ☑ **D.** IBM Type 12, designed to be run under water. This type does not exist, according to currently available information.

   ☒ **A, B,** and **C.** are not correct because they are actual types of cabling that are designed to be compatible with Token Ring networks.

3. ☑ **C.** Perhaps. Most, but not all, Ethernet hubs are designed to link to other hubs.

   ☒ **A, B, D.** The other choices are all incorrect because they do not adequately answer the question.

4. ☑ **B.** FDDI network components are very expensive compared to other types.

   ☒ **A.** is incorrect because documentation is available in English. **C.** is incorrect because FDDI network components are made by multiple vendors. **D.** is incorrect because FDDI network components, unlike light bulbs, do not fail after a specified number of hours.

5. ☑ **D.** FDDI cabling is subject to interference from microwave ovens. This is the correct answer, as microwave ovens do not interfere with FDDI cabling.

   ☒ **A, B, C.** are incorrect responses, as they are all legitimate disadvantages to FDDI cabling.

Installing and Troubleshooting Network Storage Devices

1. ☑ **A.** Offer faster read/write capability. Although great strides have been made in the speed at which other media can read and write information, no other type of storage is currently faster except for RAM, which requires constant electrical power to retain the information that it stores.

   ☒ **B.** is incorrect because CDs and other optical media are generally more durable. **C.** is incorrect because DVD and tape media are generally cheaper in cost per megabyte of information stored. **D.** is incorrect because, although "hot-swappable" hard-drive arrays exist, a hard drive is not a removable medium in the traditional sense.

2. ☑ **C.** 512 bytes of data. Using the formula (Cylinders) x (Heads) x (Sectors) x (512) = Bytes of Data Stored, you can determine the storage capacity of a hard drive.

☒ **A.** is incorrect because a typical sector holds 512 bytes, not 256 bytes of data. **B, D.** are incorrect because current technology would not allow multiple megabytes of data to be stored in one sector on a hard-disk platter.

3. ☑ **A.** SCSI drives can be set up in a Redundant Array of Inexpensive Disks (RAID) configuration where the loss of any one drive will not mean a loss of data. Enough data is written on the other disks in the array that the system can rebuild the missing data lost by any other single disk.

☒ **B.** is incorrect because the drive mechanism in IDE drives is often identical to that in SCSI drives. **C.** is incorrect because SCSI drive platters are not designed to be easily removable or replaceable. **D.** is incorrect because SCSI drives do not come with a data recovery warranty.

4. ☑ **B.** Original = Master, New = Slave. IDE systems boot from the drive jumpered as Master. Both drives are also controlled by the circuitry on the Master drive.

☒ **A.** is incorrect because an IDE system will not function with two drives on the same bus configured as Master. **C.** is incorrect because Jim wants to boot from the original drive and an IDE system will boot from the Master drive only. **D.** is incorrect because at least one drive must be jumpered as master for the system to boot.

5. ☑ **D.** The red stripe on one side of the cable lines up with *pin 1* on the controller and drives. In fact, many cables are keyed with a notch that prevents a cable from being improperly connected.

☒ **A.** is incorrect because computer cables should not be folded so that they are sharply creased. **B.** is incorrect because *pin 1*, not the highest-numbered pin, should line up with the red stripe on the cable. **C.** is incorrect because Novell does not manufacture hard-drive ribbon cables.

6. ☑ **C.** Jim must first use FDISK to create the DOS partition. A NetWare installation still requires a small DOS partition from which the hard drive first boots. After using FDISK to create a small DOS partition, Jim can format that partition using the FORMAT command that comes with DOS. ☒ **A.** is incorrect because the DOS partition must be created and formatted prior to the installation of NetWare. **B.** is incorrect because the /S switch (system) puts boot files on a drive, and does not pertain to SCSI. **D.** is incorrect because DOS utilities are generally used to high-level format hard drives.

7. ☑ **B.** Level 1 RAID is built into NetWare and does not require that the SCSI controller be specifically designed for RAID. NetWare refers to its implementation of Level 1 RAID as mirroring, or duplexing. ☒ **A, C.** are incorrect because RAID Levels 0 and 5 are not built into NetWare—they are special SCSI controllers. **D.** is incorrect because there is a level (Level 1) that is built into NetWare.

8. ☑ **B.** Yes, it is available using the disk mirroring/duplexing feature built into NetWare or by buying dedicated IDE RAID controllers. However, since the IDE bus is limited to two drives per controller, the number of disks and capacity will be limited. In practice, IDE RAID controllers are also extremely rare, due to the performance advantages of SCSI. ☒ **A.** is incorrect because IDE is limited to two disks per controller and SCSI may have up to seven per controller. **C.** is incorrect because IDE RAID controllers are available, and NetWare allows for mirroring/duplexing, equivalent to Level 1 RAID.

9. ☑ **C.** Yes, a CD-ROM may be mounted as a NetWare volume without loading DOS drivers. ☒ **A.** is incorrect—it is not necessary to get a dedicated CD-ROM server to share CDs. **B.** is incorrect because the drive need not be mounted as a DOS device. **D.** is incorrect because either an IDE or SCSI drive may be used.

10. ☑ **D.** Write using a laser beam and magnetism and read optically. The laser beam is used to heat a 1-bit area on the surface of the disk and a magnet then polarizes the heated material to a north-south or south-north alignment. The 1-bit area then cools in a polarized state and is stored as a 1 or 0, depending on the polarization of the bit. Stored information is read by directing an optical beam at the polarized area; the plane of the optical beam's reflection is then rotated clockwise or counter-clockwise, depending on the polarization of the bit on the surface of the disk.
    ☒ **A.** is incorrect because data is not written optically. **B.** is incorrect because writing requires both the laser beam and the magnetic head. **C.** is incorrect because MO drives cannot read and write by both magnetic and optical means.

11. ☑ **B.** MO disks and drives are more expensive than tape drives. Although the price of MO drives continues to fall, MO drives still tend to be more expensive than other backup solutions.
    ☒ **A.** is incorrect because most MO drives can read and write faster than most tape drives. **C.** is incorrect because MO disks are reusable many, many times. **D.** is incorrect because the magnetic coating on the tapes used by tape drives tends to wear down and be more susceptible to media errors.

Troubleshooting the DOS Workstation

1. ☑ **C.** Will load automatically each time the computer boots.
    ☒ **A.** is incorrect because the client will load without the need for typing any further commands at the DOS prompt. **B.** is incorrect because the computer will merely load the client without asking each time the computer boots. **D.** is incorrect because the computer will still have CONFIG.SYS and AUTOEXEC.BAT files and will call STARTNET.BAT from AUTOEXEC.BAT.

2. ☑ **D.** LSL.COM, NIC driver, IPXODI.COM, VLM.EXE is the correct load order.

☒ **A, B, C.** are incorrect because they describe load orders that will not result in successful loading of the client. Although Novell wants you to know the order by memory, in the real world, each driver will tell you if it requires that another driver be loaded first.

3. ☑ **B.** NET.CFG should be edited to specify I/O and IRQ settings if the driver cannot automatically determine which addresses the card is set to.

☒ **A, C, D.** are incorrect as the NIC driver would not look for .CFG files with these names.

4. ☑ **D.** All of the above are valid reasons why the watchdog feature is important.

5. ☑ **B.** Remote Program Load (RPL.NLM) will allow the workstation to boot from an image stored on the server.

☒ **A.** is incorrect because REMOTE.NLM is used to allow RCONSOLE sessions from a workstation to the server. **C, D.** are incorrect, because they are not NLMs that would allow a diskless workstation to boot from an image stored on the server.

6. ☑ **B.** That the packet is being addressed to everything on the network. This is also referred to as a broadcast packet.

☒ **A, C, D.** are incorrect because they do not correctly describe what a packet with FFFFFFFFFFFF indicates.

7. ☑ **A.** PCI. NICs are the least likely to conflict with another device.

☒ **B.** is incorrect because ISA bus NICs are much more likely to conflict with another device. **C, D.** are incorrect because they are extensions of the ISA bus and therefore more likely to conflict with other devices.

8. ☑ **B.** 286 CPUs could address up to 16 megabytes of RAM. Therefore, a 286 would be the least powerful CPU that Dave could use in the workstation.
☒ **A.** is incorrect because an 8088 (found in IBM XTs and clones) could only address one megabyte of RAM. **C, D.** are incorrect because they are more powerful than the 286 chip.

9. ☑ **A.** Extended memory (EMS) is the most-used specification with modern software.
☒ **B.** Expanded memory is incorrect because, although it did allow programs to use memory above the first megabyte, it fell out of favor by using a memory-swapping method that would only allow a program to access a 64K block of memory at a time. **C.** is incorrect because the high-memory area is only a 64K area immediately above the first megabyte of RAM. **D.** is incorrect because the upper-memory blocks are the region from 641K–1024K in the first megabyte of system RAM.

10. ☑ **D.** Memmaker does a fairly good job of optimizing memory, though QEMM generally does the very best job of memory optimization.
☒ **A.** is incorrect because Defrag is designed to defragment the data on the hard disk, not optimize memory. **B.** is incorrect because Scandisk is designed to find and fix file errors on the hard disk. **C.** MSD is incorrect because it does not include a memory optimization feature.

11. ☑ **C.** No, since Novell DOS is incompatible with some software. Unfortunately for Novell, few programmers tested their products with Novell DOS. Although Novell put a lot of effort into making Novell DOS fully compatible with MS-DOS, some programs would simply not run properly on Novell DOS. (Also, Novell dropped out of the DOS market, and Novell DOS is no longer sold.)
☒ **A.** is incorrect because although Novell DOS was optimized for networking, its incompatibility with some programs outweighs its networking benefits. **B.** is incorrect because Novell DOS was not free for licensed workstations. **D.** is incorrect because learning new syntax should not prevent you from purchasing a product if it has no other significant drawbacks.

Troubleshooting Network Printing

1. ☑   **C.** Determine if the other members of the workgroup can print to the printer. This will tell Leslee whether to look for a network-related problem or a problem with Tim's individual workstation.

   ☒   **A.** is incorrect because looking for a paper jam would come later in the troubleshooting process. **B.** is incorrect because determining whether the problem is hardware related or software related would come after checking to see if the other members of the workgroup can print to the printer. **D.** is incorrect because in determining whether or not the other members of the workgroup can print, Leslee will find out whether or not the print queue is locked up.

2. ☑   **B.** The new cable is too long. The parallel printer cable specification only officially supports cables that are 15 feet in length or shorter. In practice, high-quality cables that are longer than 15 feet will sometimes work, but it is best to use the shortest possible cable when printing through a parallel connection.

   ☒   **A.** is incorrect because although the cable could be defective, a defective cable is not the most likely cause of the problem, given the other facts. **C.** is incorrect because a printer does not have to be set up again unless you switch to another type of cable (from parallel to serial, for example). **D.** is incorrect because electromagnetic interference is not a likely cause of printing problems through a parallel connection.

3. ☑   **B.** Print a self-test page. Printing a self-test page is usually the fastest way to determine if a printer is mechanically sound and has enough ink or toner.

   ☒   **A.** is incorrect because taking out the toner cartridge takes longer than printing a self-test page. **C.** is incorrect because printing from each workstation would not be a practical way to find out if the toner cartridge is empty. **D.** is incorrect because changing the network port would not be a practical way to see if the toner cartridge is empty.

4. ☑ **C.** Moving the print head or platen knob when the printer is on. The movements of both the print head and platen knob are controlled by motors that move in very precise increments, called *stepper motors.* The stepper motor mechanism can be damaged if it is moved while the power is on.

☒ **A.** is incorrect because the ink on the ribbon is not toxic enough that it is dangerous to the touch. **B.** is incorrect because dot-matrix printers are not affected by one side of the printer being slightly higher than another. **D.** is incorrect because you should never apply oil to the gears of a dot-matrix printer. Only a trained technician will know what type of oil to use, and how and where to apply it.

5. ☑ **A.** Light can damage the drum so you should be very careful not to expose the drum to light, particularly sunlight.

☒ **B, C, D.** are incorrect because the drum is more susceptible to light than to cold air, static electricity, or hot air.

6. ☑ **A.** The roller is damaged. A certified technician will probably need to replace the roller before calling a technician; however, it wouldn't hurt to put a new toner cartridge in the printer and see if there is any difference in printed pages.

☒ **B.** is incorrect because a damaged drum will more often result in faded or missing areas on the printout, rather than spots or lines. **C.** is incorrect because it is more likely that lines or spots will be caused by a damaged roller, though, from time to time, a bad toner cartridge could cause spots or streaks on the printed page. **D.** is incorrect because dirty corona wires are more likely to produce blurred printouts than spots or lines.

7. ☑ **D.** All of the above is correct and should probably be done in the following order: C, A, B. If users are not properly designated, then assign them to the queue in NetWare administrator. If there is little space available on the volume which hosts the print queue, then delete or purge enough files to allow new print jobs to be created in the queue. If jobs created in PCONSOLE do not enter the queue and print, PSERVER.NLM or NPRINTER.EXE program may have to be stopped and reloaded, or the print setup deleted and recreated.

8. ☑ **D.** Both A. and B. are correct ways to check that PSERVER is loaded properly. Look for a status of RUNNING to indicate that PSERVER is loaded properly.

☒ **C.** is incorrect because the LCD display will not give information about PSERVER's status.

9. ☑ **A.** SPX. The NPRINTER.EXE or NPTWIN95.EXE program running on the workstation communicates with the NetWare server.

☒ **B.** is incorrect because it is not the protocol used for communicating between NetWare servers and remote printer hosts. **C, D.** are incorrect because they are Windows print formats, not NetWare protocols.

Troubleshooting and Optimizing the Network

1. ☑ **C.** Use the NetWare SALVAGE utility. NetWare always writes to empty space on a volume if available and if it must overwrite files, overwrites the oldest files it can find. The SALVAGE utility makes it easy to recover files, particularly if you know the directory that the file was in before being erased.

☒ **A.** is incorrect because it would take much longer than using the SALVAGE utility and would be no more effective. **B.** is incorrect because the DOS UNDELETE command cannot restore files on NetWare volumes. **D.** is incorrect because a third-party recovery tool is generally no more likely to recover the file than SALVAGE is, unless there are file system errors on the volume where the deleted file resides.

2. ☑ **B.** Backup to a workstation tape drive would not back up NDS or hidden NetWare system files. It would probably be impossible to restore a server to its former configuration without being able to restore NDS.

☒ **A, C, D.** are incorrect because they do not describe the main reason not to back up to a workstation tape drive. Apart from that, they are additional excellent reasons not to back up to a workstation tape drive.

3. ☑   **D.** Four sets, rotating once a month. Although expensive, this makes for the most complete and easy-to-recover backup scheme. If you buy 31 tapes, one for each day of the month, and rotate monthly, you'll know at a glance which tape contains the backup for each day of the previous month.

☒   **A, B, C.** are not truly incorrect, but are less complete and less easy to administer.

4. ☑   **B.** Ontrack Data Recovery for NetWare.

☒   **A, C, D.** are incorrect as they describe products that do not exist, according to current information.

5. ☑   **B.** PATCHMAN.NLM is the correct name for the utility.

☒   **A, C, D.** are incorrect because they are not correct names for the utility, according to current information.

6. ☑   **D.** 90 percent. When Long Term Cache Hits fall below 90 percent, it means that there is not enough free RAM to cache the files most needed by users. At that point the server RAM should be upgraded.

☒   **A, B, C.** are incorrect, as they are well below the 90 percent cutoff.

7. ☑   **D.** LOAD SCHDELAY VIRSIG = 10000 would set the VIRSIG process to the lowest possible priority by telling the CPU to only execute the process every 10000 cycles instead of every cycle. Delay values may be set between 2 and 10000.

☒   **A, B.** are incorrect because they do not describe valid commands given current information. **C.** is incorrect because it would tell the CPU to run the VIRSIG process with zero delay, which is already the default.

8. ☑   **B.** Maximum physical receive packet size. By increasing this parameter, you keep the server from having to break large packets down into smaller packets of the NetWare default packet size of 512 bytes.

☒   **A, C, D.** are incorrect since they are not valid NetWare parameters according to current information.

9. ☑   **D.** Any number of errors per second on an ongoing basis means that there is a problem somewhere on the network that should be fixed. You can trace the source of the error by noting the MAC address of packets with errors in the lower portion of the LANalyzer screen.

☒   **A, B, C.** are incorrect because there is no defined number of acceptable errors per second. Any indication of ongoing error, particularly if traceable to a single MAC address, should be investigated and corrected.

Part 6

NetWare: Integrating Windows NT (Exam 50-644)

EXAM TOPICS

Introduction to Windows NT

Introduction to Windows NT Networking

Windows NT Domain Networking

Managing Windows NT Security

Integrating Windows NT Workstations

Multiple Domain Windows NT Networking

Integrating NetWare and Windows NT Domains

Designing, Implementing, and Maintaining an Integrated Network

Implementing and Maintaining Accessibility in an Integrated Network

NetWare:
Integrating
Windows NT
Questions

Q & A

This section tests your knowledge of how to integrate Windows NT into a NetWare network and examines the different facets of the Windows NT operating system. In this section, you will draw on your experience with Windows NT, from the Registry to configuration of network components, and will need to be familiar with the differences between Windows NT and Windows 95, since this is covered on the exam. In this vein, we will look at the different file systems, protocols, and types of NT servers.

Introduction to Windows NT

1. What type of multitasking allows the operating system to determine who gets processing time?

A. Preemptive

B. Cognitive

C. Cooperative

D. Simulated

QUESTIONS AND ANSWERS

Is local file system security an issue?	If it is, then you will need to look at Windows NT Workstation.
Which platform best matches the existing hardware and software?	Unless your company has a big upgrade project, because of legacy MS-DOS applications or devices that utilize only MS-DOS drivers, you may want to deploy Windows 95.
Do you need to run processor-intensive applications?	Windows 95 loses some of its performance with mathematically intensive applications, such as certain graphics and drawing packages, whereas Windows NT was optimized for processor-intensive applications.
Does your environment use plug-and-play hardware that does not require legacy device drivers?	Plug-and-play is not available in Windows NT, making Windows 95 the choice in this scenario.

exam
ⓌatCh

While the certification exam focuses on Windows NT, you are required to know the basics of Windows 95. Know when Windows 95 is appropriate and when Windows NT Workstation is required.

2. In order for a user to access and use an object, such as a file, an application, or a printer, what is needed?

   A. Proper rights
   B. Proper permissions
   C. Administration equivalency
   D. A guest account

3. Which Registry subtree stores all software configuration information for the computer?

   A. HKEY_LOCAL_MACHINE
   B. HKEY_USERS
   C. HKEY_CLASSES_ROOT
   D. HKEY_CURRENT_CONFIG

4. With the Windows NT files system what three object items are there?

   A. Folder
   B. File
   C. Shortcut
   D. Directory

exam
ⓌatCh

Do not get confused by the terminology. Novell® uses the term Log In when you authenticate to the network, while Microsoft uses the term Log On. If you get a question on the certification exam regarding this process, read through it very carefully.

5. What three logs exist in the Event Viewer?

   A. System

   B. Application

   C. Error

   D. Security

6. Which of the following is NOT a box you can check within the properties of a user account in User Manager?

   A. User Must Change Password at next Logon

   B. User Can Change Password

   C. Account Disabled

   D. Password Never Expires

7. What is the filename for the 32-bit Registry Editor specific to Windows NT and not available in Windows 95?

   A. Regedit

   B. REGEDT32

   C. Regeditor

   D. RGeditor

exam
ⓦatch

You need to remember the purpose of each Registry key in order to pass the Novell certification exam.

Introduction to Windows NT Networking

1. Which account is used to provide limited access to the resources on a Windows NT computer?

A. Administrator

B. Admin

C. Guest

D. New

2. Which network model requires a Windows NT server to provide access to network resources?

A. Workgroup

B. Server group

C. Domain

D. Peer to peer

---

exam

ⓦatch

Remember that you cannot switch a Windows NT server between a domain controller and a member server without a full reinstallation of the Windows NT server operating system.

---

3. If two domains are to share resources, what has to be established?

A. Junior domain

B. Workgroup

C. Trust relationship

D. Master domain

4. If you have a small-to-medium-sized network that does not span WAN links, what protocol option is recommended for easiest configuration?

A. IPX/SPX compatible protocol

B. TCP/IP

C. DLC

D. NetBEUI

5. If you are not using the NT File System (NTFS) what file system would you use?

    A. FAT

    B. HPFS

    C. TNFS

    D. OSFS

6. What does DLC in the DLC protocol stand for?

    A. Data-link control

    B. Dual-link channel

    C. Dual-link control

    D. Data-link channel

7. What is the maximum storage available with NTFS?

    A. 2MB

    B. 40GB

    C. 400TB

    D. 16EB

exam

ⓦatch

Note that Novell documentation incorrectly lists the Domain Admins group as Domain Administrators. While this may seem a minor point, you will see several questions regarding global groups on the certification exam.

8. What are the types of servers in a Windows NT domain environment? (Choose all that apply.)

A. Primary domain controller

B. Member computer

C. Member server

D. Backup domain controller

QUESTIONS AND ANSWERS

What size is the volume?	If it is over 400MB, you should consider using NTFS.
Will you need to access the volume from MS-DOS or OS/2?	If so, you should consider using FAT.
Will you require file-level security?	Since FAT has no file-level security, you will need to use NTFS.
Is file compression required?	If so, you will need to use NTFS unless you have a third-party utility that can handle compression.

9. What is a volume set?

A. A collection of hard drives in a server

B. Areas of free space resident in a partition

C. A collection of servers with the same-sized volumes

D. Space taken up on the hard drive(s) in a server

---

exam
Ⓦatch

When you are presented with questions on the Novell certification exam that list both local and global groups, remember that global groups are always prefixed by the word "Domain." When you create a global group, you are creating a group that is to be used on the domain level, as opposed to the client. The Domain Users group encompasses all user accounts on the domain level. Therefore, you must use the User Manager for Domains utility to create, delete, or modify global groups.

Windows NT Domain Networking

1. If you wanted to make sure a user does not have access to a particular file, what permission would you assign the file?

A. Read

B. Write

C. No Access

D. Simply do not assign a permission.

2. How is Windows NT directory services different than Novell Directory Services® regarding backup copies of the user and security database?

A. Novell does not have directory services.

B. Novell's directory is copied completely throughout the network, while Windows NT is partitioned into pieces and then copied out in those partitioned pieces.

C. Microsoft's directory is copied completely throughout the network, while Novell's is partitioned into pieces and then copied out in those partitioned pieces.

D. Novell does not have a backup of their directory. They store the directory in one location only.

exam
ⓦatch

Remember that an object is associated with a resource, and that a process is associated with an activity. These terms will be used on the Novell certification exam.

3. How many primary domain controllers can exist in a Windows NT domain?

A. One

B. Two

C. Three

D. Four

4. What are the two primary functions of BDCs?

A. Provide logon authentication

B. Provide the main account database on the network

C. Provide redundancy for the account database

D. Provide users with a map to network resources

5. What key sequence is necessary in order to log on to a Windows NT workstation or server?

   A. CTRL+ALT+L

   B. CTRL+ALT+DEL

   C. CTRL+DEL

   D. ALT+DEL

6. What is used to determine who has rights to the resource when permissions are assigned to a resource?

   A. An access control list containing the security IDs of the users granted access

   B. A list of shares on the server

   C. A random list of users generated by User Manager For Domains

   D. A list of users from the NT workstation that is the domain controller

exam
ⓦatch
Remember the different file and directory permissions, and their associated individual permissions. Also keep in mind that you cannot secure local files that reside on a FAT volume. These issues come up rather frequently in the Novell certification exam.

7. You are on a Windows NT machine trying to add a local group to another local group for redundancy, but you keep getting errors. Why?

   A. Local groups allow only users to be added and no other kind of groups.

   B. Local groups cannot be added until the machine is rebooted.

   C. Local groups cannot be added to local groups.

   D. The local group must have the same name as the one you are adding.

8. Which of the following is NOT a default global group with Windows NT?

A. Domain Users

B. Domain Guests

C. Domain Operators

D. Domain Administrators

exam
Ⓦatch

Study local and global groups and understand them thoroughly. You must be able to differentiate between the two and know the default groups in order to pass the certification exam.

9. In order to add a workstation to the domain with Windows NT what must you have?

A. Administrative rights in the domain

B. A valid SID to enter in the domain dialog box

C. Guest equivalency in the domain

D. You cannot do this from a workstation. It must be done at the server.

10. In Windows NT what does the acronym SAM mean?

A. Security Administration Management

B. Security Accounts Minimums

C. Security Accounts Manager

D. Synchronized Account Management

Managing Windows NT Security

1. Which default local group grants create, delete, install, share, and modification access rights to printers on the server?

A. Server Operators

B. Print Operators

C. Backup Operators

D. Account Operators

2. Which of the following is a security model used with Windows NT?

A. FAT file system

B. Optional logon

C. Workgroup model

D. Mandatory logon

3. In order to protect files on the server by requiring users to access files based on their logon username, what network implementation model should be used?

A. Workgroup

B. Domain

C. Peer to peer

D. Workstation

4. What types of policies are used to set domain-level user account security options?

A. System

B. Account

C. Audit

D. User rights

5. What types of policies are used in conjunction with user accounts to monitor user activities on the network?

A. System

B. Account

C. Audit

D. User Rights

6. What would you implement if you wanted to control things such as the user's desktop configuration, startup applications, and automatic network connections?

A. System policies

B. User profiles

C. Group membership

D. Account policies

7. In what file is the user profile information stored for Windows NT?

A. USER.DAT

B. NT.DAT

C. SYSTEM.DAT

D. NTUSER.DAT

8. If an administrator wants to makes sure a user gets the same profile every time he or she logs on to the network, what would the administrator have to do?

A. Implement roaming profiles

B. Use local profiles

C. Use absolute profiles

D. Use mandatory profiles

9. What utility is used to configure system policies?

   A. User Manager

   B. User Manager for Domains

   C. System Policy Editor

   D. System Policy Configurator

10. What two categories are there for system policies?

   A. User

   B. Workstation

   C. Computer

   D. If...Then

Integrating Windows NT Workstations

1. Where are profiles stored on a Windows NT workstation?

   A. C:\WINNT\SYSTEM32\PROFILES

   B. C:\WINNT\PROFILES

   C. C:\PROFILES

   D. C:\WINNT\SYSTEM32\ETC

2. What is the term for a domain requesting resources from another domain?

   A. Trusted

   B. Trusting

   C. Master

   D. Secondary

3. What utility is used to set up trust relationships?

    A. Server Manager

    B. User Manager

    C. User Manager for Domains

    D. Network Monitor

4. Which domain model is the most difficult to install, manage, and maintain?

    A. Single domain model

    B. Single master domain model

    C. Multiple master domain model

    D. Complete trust model

---

exam
Ⓦatch
While the workgroup model and the domain model are very similar, know the differences between them. You may be asked questions on the certification exam that requires you to know when you would prefer one model over the other.

---

5. What is another term for the trusting domain?

    A. Account domain

    B. Resource domain

    C. Trusted domain

    D. Trustee domain

---

exam
Ⓦatch
Do not confuse the trusted domain with the trusting domain. The Novell certification exam will require you to know that the domain containing user accounts (account domain) is the Trust-Ed domain and that the domain containing resources (resource domain) is the Trust-ing domain. This is one of the concepts that most people have the hardest time remembering.

---

6. What is the main requirement in a single domain model when setting up the server?

   A. The server should be a member server.

   B. The server should be a backup domain controller.

   C. The server should be a primary domain controller.

   D. The installation should be done to the C: drive.

7. If Domain A and Domain B have a two-way trust relationship set up, which domain is the trusting domain?

   A. Domain A

   B. Domain B

   C. Both Domain A and B

   D. Neither Domain A nor B

exam
Ⓦatch

You may be required to demonstrate knowledge that trust relationships are not transferable. Be careful when analyzing trust relationship questions.

8. What do you use to assign permissions across domains?

   A. Local groups

   B. Global groups

   C. Users

   D. Folders

9. If a user is part of the Dallas domain and logs on at the New York location and domain, what happens if there is a two-way trust relationship between the domains?

   A. The user cannot log on since he/she is not in their home domain.

   B. The user can log on but must have a user account in the New York domain.

   C. When the user logs on, his/her authentication request is passed to the Dallas domain and then back to the New York domain.

   D. As long as the domain is changed to the Dallas domain in the WIN.INI, logon will work fine.

exam
ⓦatch   *Know the formula n(n-1), as you may be tested on trust relationship calculations.*

Multiple Domain Windows NT Networking

1. What is the limit on the number of inbound trusts for Windows NT Server?

A. 64

B. 100

C. 128

D. 12

2. What standards does Windows NT support to allow for multiple protocols to be bound to a network card? (Choose all that apply.)

A. ODI

B. NDIS

C. DNIS

D. DOI

3. What allows the workstation to take full advantage of the file and print services provided by the NetWare server through NDS™?

A. NetWare Client for Windows NT

B. Workstation Manager

C. Z.E.N.works

D. NWLINK

4. What is the name of the configuration file that is used during an unattended installation?

A. UNATTEND.INI

B. UNATTENDED.INF

C. UNATTEND.CNF

D. UNATTEND.TXT

5. What component must be enabled if you have various versions of the client software on your workstations and want to make sure everyone is at the same version?

A. Workstation Manager

B. Z.E.N.works

C. ACU

D. NDS

6. What is needed on the NetWare client for Windows NT workstation so that policies work within Z.E.N.works? (Choose one.)

A. NetWare Client version 7.0 or higher

B. Workstation Manager

C. User Manager

D. Unique SID

7. What utility is used to configure the snap-in component for Windows NT Configuration objects?

A. NWGINA

B. NWADMIN

C. ADMSETUP

D. SETUP

exam
ⓦatch

Be sure to know that the NWGINA component handles the synchronization and management of local NT Workstation accounts and the User account/object in NDS.
    The NT Configuration object can be created and then associated with a user, group, or container.

8. In what file is the policy information stored when Z.E.N.works is installed on the server?

    A. CONFIG.POL

    B. NTCONFIG.POL

    C. POLICY.INF

    D. The information is stored in NDS, not in a file

9. What can a Windows NT User Policy Package be associated with? (Choose all that apply.)

    A. User Objects

    B. User Group Objects

    C. Domain Objects

    D. Windows NT Configuration Objects

10. What is the recommended location of Application objects by Novell?

    A. Under the Organization Container

    B. Under the Organizational Unit Container

    C. Under a container called Application

    D. In the container with the users

11. Which of the following actions cannot be administered once the NT Configuration object is created?

A. Administer Windows 95 user accounts

B. Configure components of the workstation configuration from NDS

C. Work with the client piece to create local NT workstation accounts when the user logs on

D. Manage items such as policies, profile information, and logon screen banner

Integrating NetWare and Windows NT Domains

1. What service allows an administrator to use NWADMIN to administer Windows NT configuration information?

A. Snap-in

B. Schema

C. Extension

D. Trust

2. Where does the NDS Object Replication Service reside on the network? (Choose all that apply.)

A. Runs as an NLM on the NetWare Server

B. Runs as a service on the Backup Domain Controller

C. Runs as a service on the Primary Domain Controller

D. On a Workstation that is permanently logged in

---

exam
ⓦatch

Remember that the IGRATE.EXE application is used during the initial integration process. Become familiar with the IGRATE.EXE integration utility and know how to perform the three integration tasks.

---

3. How is the communication between the NT and NetWare kept secure?

A. There is no security in the communication between the two.

B. They use a private authenticated NDS connection.

C. They use a bindery type of connection.

D. They use scripts that encrypt the data.

4. How is synchronization kept current once the users in Windows NT and NetWare are integrated?

A. With the IGRATE utility

B. With the Event Monitor service itself

C. With the Event Monitor and the NDS Object Replication Service

D. With NWADMIN

exam
ⓦatch   **Become familiar with the dialog boxes presented during the installation of Novell Administrator for Windows NT.**

5. If users already exist in both Windows NT and NetWare how are objects merged?

A. The NT user attributes take precedence and overwrite the NetWare attributes.

B. The NetWare user attributes take precedence and overwrite the NT attributes.

C. The attributes are lost and go to all default values.

D. Duplicate objects cannot be integrated.

6. What utility should not be used if your Windows NT users are integrated into NDS?

A. Server Manager

B. User Manager for Domains

C. Disk Administrator

D. NWADMIN

---

e x a m
Ⓦatch *Know the different options available under the Passwords and Other Properties tabs, as the exam will most likely have a question or two on them.*

---

7. What is the purpose of the application server object?

   A. To manage communications between the Event Monitor that resides on the NetWare server and the ORS that resides on the Windows NT server

   B. To manage communications between the Event Monitor that resides on the Windows NT server and the ORS that resides on the NetWare server

   C. To provide Application to Windows NT computers

   D. To provide Application Program Interface services to Windows NT computers

8. What does LSA stand for?

   A. Legal Service Agreement

   B. License Service Action

   C. Local Service Authority

   D. Loopback Service Address

9. You have a network that is using NetBEUI for its protocol. You are having problems with computers accessing each other on the WAN. Why?

   A. NetBEUI is not a valid protocol for any type of networking.

   B. NetBEUI is not a routable protocol and cannot be used in a WAN environment.

   C. NetBEUI takes up too much memory.

   D. None of the above.

---

e x a m
Ⓦatch *Become familiar with the Network Settings page for the Novell Certification exam, as the NDS Event Monitor and ORS are important features of Directory database synchronization.*

Designing, Implementing, and Maintaining an Integrated Network

1. When installing NDS for NT, what DLL is renamed in order to redirect domain access calls to NDS?

   A. SAMLIB.DLL

   B. SAMS.DLL

   C. SAMSSRV.DLL

   D. SAMSRV.DLL

2. What allows for migrating Windows NT objects into more than one container?

   A. Multi-Pass Migration

   B. Multi-Pass Integration

   C. SAMSSRV.DLL

   D. This is not possible.

3. Which property page in NWADMIN allows for controlling of settings that only apply to the Windows NT platform?

   A. Domain Access

   B. Members of the Domain Object

   C. Domain User Settings

   D. Replica Advisor

Implementing and Maintaining Accessibility in an Integrated Network

1. Which of the following are the correct requirements for the Novell Client for Windows NT?

    A. Intel-Based Workstation running NT 3.51, 10MB of disk space, 16MB of additional disk space for administrator utilities

    B. Intel-Based Workstation running NT 4.0, 10MB of disk space, 16MB of additional disk space for administrator utilities

    C. Intel-Based Workstation running NT 4.0, 16MB of disk space, 10MB of additional disk space for administrator utilities

    D. Intel-Based Workstation running NT 4.0, 20MB of disk space, 16MB of additional disk space for administrator utilities

2. You need to remove the Novell Client for Windows NT, but you cannot logon to the local workstation. Your workstation is using the NTFS file system. What can you do?

    A. Login from a remote workstation and rename the NWGINA.DLL to NWGINA.SAV and then copy the MSGINA.DLL to NWGINA.DLL

    B. Boot to a DOS diskette and rename the NWGINA.DLL to NWGINA.SAV and then copy the MSGINA.DLL to NWGINA.DLL

    C. Boot to a FAT32 diskette and rename the NWGINA.DLL to NWGINA.SAV and then copy the MSGINA.DLL to NWGINA.DLL

    D. It cannot be done unless the operating system is reinstalled.

CERTIFIED NOVELL ENGINEER℠

NetWare: Integrating Windows NT Answers

Q & A

The answers to the questions are in boldface, followed by a brief explanation. Some of the explanations detail the logic you should use to choose the correct answer, while others give factual reasons why the answer is correct. If you miss several questions on a similar topic, you should review the corresponding section in the *CNE® NetWare® 5 Study Guide* before taking the Integrating Windows NT test.

Introduction to Windows NT

1. ☑ **A.** Windows 95 introduced the concept of preemptive multitasking, which lets the operating system determine when an application has to relinquish system time to another process. This prevents applications from monopolizing the processor's time.

   Each application is given its own memory address space to prevent processes from bumping into each other. This results in a much more stable operating system. Preemptive multitasking is provided for Win32 applications and some MS-DOS applications.

   ☒ **B, C.** Cognitive and simulated multitasking do not exist in Windows 95. **D.** Cooperative multitasking controls the relinquishing of the processor and, in some cases, monopolizes the processor.

2. ☑ **B.** Proper permissions. Windows NT comes with several default accounts that allow for different levels of access through rights and permissions. Permissions authorize a user to access and use an object, such as a file, an application, or a printer.

   ☒ **A.** A right allows the user to perform some form of activity on the machine, such as logging on locally, shutting down the server, or backing up files and directories. **C.** Administration equivalency gives too much access and therefore is not a good choice here. **D.** The guest account by default in Windows NT machines is disabled and doesn't permit access to anything.

3. ☑ **C.** The HKEY_CLASSES_ROOT subtree stores all software configuration information for the computer. This includes such items as screen location and colors, recently accessed files, executable location and name, and any other information the vendor has defined.

☒ **A.** The first subtree, HKEY_LOCAL_MACHINE, contains all of the computer's hardware information. Applications, device drivers, and the operating system use this information when they need to access data on a particular device. When a Windows NT machine boots, the boot process determines which device drivers to load by referencing this subtree. **B.** The HKEY_USERS subtree contains the system default settings and the security settings for each user. This information is used by the operating system to determine what each user is allowed to view and access on the computer. Examples of the data stored in this subtree are default user settings, network settings, and control panel settings. When a user logs onto a Windows NT machine, this data is copied into the HKEY_CURRENT_USER subtree. As we have mentioned, the HKEY_CURRENT_USER subtree obtains its information from the HKEY_USERS subtree. This data is kept for each user that has logged into the machine, and includes such items as keyboard layout, software used, desktop settings, and remote access definitions. **D.** The HKEY_CURRENT_CONFIG subtree stores the active hardware profile. This subtree obtains its initial data from the HKEY_LOCAL_MACHINE subtree when the user logs on and maintains it for the active hardware profile.

4. ☑ **A, B, D.** Three objects are used with the Windows NT file system: folders, files, and shortcuts. Folders are used to hold directory information, other folders (subdirectories), and files. When you use My Computer to look at the properties of a folder or file, you will notice that you have a General tab and a Sharing tab. The General Tab contains information about that object, such as: name, location, creation date, and local security attributes. The Sharing Tab allows you to grant or deny access to an object on the network. The My Computer utility lets you delete, rename, or modify security attributes to both files and folders. However, while you can create folders, you must create files using other applications. Directories exist in a DOS environment but the terminology is not used with Windows NT much anymore.

☒ **C.** Shortcuts are pointers to another object. For example, if you wanted to create an icon on the desktop that will start a particular application, you would create a shortcut. When you examine a shortcut's properties through the My Computer utility, you will notice that there is a General tab and a Shortcut tab. The General tab contains the same type of information that a file or folder would have. The Shortcut tab contains the exact name and location of another object, such as an executable program or a batch file. Some shortcuts have other tabs that allow you to modify the appearance and memory usage of the target when it runs. With the My Computer utility, you can create, delete, rename, or modify shortcuts.

5. ☑ **A, B, D.** The Event Viewer is used to view Windows NT system logs. These logs contain useful information about system events. There are three types of logs used by Windows NT:

- ■ **Application** Contains information on application-related events, such as application failures

- ■ **Security** Contains security-related events, such as logon failures or file access events

- ■ **System** Contains information on hardware events, such as component failure

☒ **C.** is incorrect because the Error log on Event Viewer does not exist.

6. ☑ **B.** User Can Change Password. There are five fields to complete for each account:

■ **Username** Required. A unique name used to log on to a Windows NT computer.

■ **Full Name** The user's full name. This option is highly useful for large companies that may have more than one individual with the same first and last name, or when there are several individuals who have the same initials.

■ **Description** Any type of descriptive information about the user, such as the user's location or their phone number.

■ **Password** Required, although a blank password is considered a valid entry. This field is limited to a maximum of 14 characters, and displays asterisks (*) instead of the characters typed.

■ **Confirm Password** Required, although a blank password is considered a valid entry. This field must exactly match the Password field, and is used to ensure that what you thought you typed is what you really typed.

☒ **A, C, D.** Along with these five fields, User Manager also permits you to select one of several options on the user account:

■ **User Must Change Password at Next Logon** This option is set by default, and requires the user to change their password the next time they log on.

■ **User Cannot Change Password** Normally used when you have several users sharing an account, such as the guest account. This option ensures that the password will remain unchanged unless modified by an account with Administrator privileges.

■ **Password Never Expires** This option allows an account to retain the same password even if a maximum password age is set in the system policy. As this can pose a potential security threat, this option is seldom used.

■ **Account Disabled** Normally used to temporarily disable an account prior to its deletion such as after an employee is terminated, but it is also useful if you have a traveling user who will not need local access to a Windows NT machine for a long period of time.

7. ☑ **B.** REGEDT32. One thing to be aware of is that Microsoft's Registry Editor program, REGEDT32.EXE, is not the method you should use to modify Registry settings. Since the Registry is the most critical component in the Windows operating system, be very careful whenever you make changes to it. It is important to maintain current backups of the Registry, especially when you need to make a change to the system, when installing or removing system components, for instance.

☒ **A.** Regedit is available in Windows NT but is also available in Windows 95. **C.** Regeditor, and **D.** RGeditor, do not exist in any Windows operating system.

Introduction to Windows NT Networking

1. ☑ **C.** The guest account is used to provide limited access to the resources on a Windows NT computer. This allows the occasional user, such as a company employee visiting from another location, to access network resources without a permanent account. Because of the restrictions placed on this account, any changes to desktop settings or additional network connections are discarded once the user logs off. This provides a consistent environment for traveling users. When you install Windows NT, the guest account is created with a blank password. On Windows NT Workstation, this poses a security threat by allowing anyone on the network access to the machine. To remedy this problem, it is recommended that you either put a strong password on the account or that you disable it. With Windows NT Server, the guest account is disabled by default. While you may disable this account, you may not delete or rename it.

☒ **A.** Administrator is incorrect because the Administrator account has full rights. There is no Admin account so **B.** is also incorrect. There is also no account called New, so **D.** is not correct.

2. ☑ **C.** The domain model takes the workgroup model and upgrades it for the enterprise. A Windows NT domain is composed of network servers and computers that have been logically grouped together for the purpose of sharing resources. Unlike the workgroup model, a Windows NT domain requires a Windows NT server to provide access to network resources. The server, known as a primary domain controller (PDC), is responsible for maintaining the master database, or directory, that contains user and resource accounts for all workstations in the domain. This provides centralized administration of user accounts and security settings.

☒ **A.** Workgroup and **D.** Peer to peer are not correct, but represent the same model. The workgroup model is a peer-to-peer network where each node has its own SAM. **B.** Server group is not correct because it is a made-up term.

3. ☑ **C.** You can establish multiple domains in a Windows NT network, but in order for them to communicate you will need to implement a trust. Trusts in Windows NT are built to allow one domain to access resources located on another domain. When you establish a trust relationship, you can set up a one-way trust, a two-way trust, or a complete trust. Because of the complexity of the domain model, it is much more difficult to plan and implement than the workgroup model, but because the domain model can support a larger number of users, it is usually the model of choice.

☒ **A.** is not correct because there is no such thing as a junior domain. **B.** is not correct because there would be no domains in a workgroup. **D.** Master domain, does not exist under Windows NT.

4. ☑ **D.** NetBEUI. Of all the protocols used in Windows NT, Microsoft's NetBIOS Extended User Interface (NetBEUI) is the easiest one to implement because it is not only self-configuring, but self tuning as well. In Windows 95 and NT Workstation it is one of the protocols selected by default. For smaller networks, such as workgroups or networks that do not use WAN links, it is a fast protocol that has very low memory requirements. However, there are several major disadvantages to using NetBEUI that have led Microsoft to recommend its use only on small to medium-sized networks.

☒ **B, C.** TCP/IP and DLC require more configuration than NetBEUI. **A.** IPX/SPX doesn't take a lot of configuration, but may require setting the frame type, which you do not have to do with NetBEUI.

5. ☑ **A.** Making its debut with MS-DOS, the File Allocation Table (FAT) is one of the oldest file systems in use today and is supported by MS-DOS, Windows, and OS/2. This support is primarily provided for backward compatibility with older software applications that have been written around the FAT file system. Although it has been revised several times to upgrade its capabilities, all versions of FAT utilize the same basic underlying methods to store and manage data.

The FAT file system uses the file allocation table as an index to translate a file or directory name into its physical location on the disk. However, the index is maintained in a first-come, first-served manner in which each new entry is placed in the next available spot. There is no sorting mechanism available for FAT, resulting in longer disk access times as the number of files increase. If a volume on a Windows NT computer exceeds 400MB, you might consider using NTFS for that volume's format.

☒ **B.** HPFS is the high-performance file system from the days of OS/2. **C.** TNFS, and **D.** OSFS, are made-up terms for this exam and do not exist in the Windows NT environment.

6. ☑ **A.** The data-link control (DLC) protocol is used primarily to connect to IBM mainframes and AS/400 systems. While the main reason this protocol is supported is because of the number of IBM and AS/400 systems currently in use today, HP JetDirect printers also use this protocol to enable network printing capability.

☒ **B.** Dual-link channel may exist but is not a protocol. **C, D.** are not correct either because dual-link control does not exist in the protocol world. Data-link channel is not a protocol, either.

7. ☑ **D.** 16EB. The Windows NT File System (NTFS) makes up for the restrictions imposed by the FAT file system. First, the size restriction of 400MB is increased to 16 exabytes (EB). To put this into its proper context, an exabyte is equal to 1,024 terabytes, which is in turn equal to about 1,024 gigabytes. Since it is rare to find an exabyte hard disk, this gives you a virtually unlimited amount of disk storage capacity. However, this does come with a price in that NTFS does not work well with volumes smaller than 400MB and cannot be used to format floppy disks.

NTFS has file compression built-in to the file system structure, whereas you must use a third-party utility with FAT. However, this compression is on an individual file basis rather than on a volume basis. This makes up in part for the overhead associated with NTFS, as you are given the capability to set file-level security. Since NTFS allows for a range of permissions associated with files and directories, which will be discussed in the next section, there is more storage used per file. There is also the capability of tracking access events and file modifications through NTFS, and there is no equivalent when using FAT.

☒ **A.** 2MB, **B.** 40GB, and **C.** 400TB are all incorrect because they are values that are
way too small. Windows NT supports much larger storage than these answers present.

8. ☑ **A, C, D.** Primary domain controller, backup domain controller, and member server. When dealing with domains, it helps to understand the terminology that is used. For example, any workstation running a version of Windows that has networking capability (Windows for Workgroups, Windows 95, Windows 98, Windows NT Workstation) is capable of joining a domain. These computers are then called member computers. Also, any computer running Windows NT as its operating system (except those configured as domain controllers) must also have a computer account in the domain in order for a user to log on to that computer. A Windows NT server is slightly different from the desktop operating systems because it can play multiple roles in a domain: primary domain controller (PDC), backup domain controller (BDC), and member server. When a Windows NT server stores the original or copies of the directory database, it is a domain controller. If it contains the master copy of the directory database, it is a primary domain controller. With domains there can be only one primary domain controller at any given time on the network. Hence, all other controllers are backup domain controllers.If a Windows NT server machine does not store a copy of the directory database, it is called a member server.

☒ **B.** Member computer is incorrect because it is not a type of Windows NT Server, as explained above.

9. ☑ **B.** A volume set is made up of areas of free space resident in a partition. When you gather up the free space, you assign a drive letter to it so that the operating system can reference it. However, before you can actually use the new volume set, you must first format it with a file system, such as FAT or NTFS.

☒ **A.** A collection of hard drives in a server is usually referred to as a Redundant Array of Inexpensive Disks (RAID) if a volume is spanned across them. **C.** A collection of servers is more of a server farm than a volume set. **D.** Space taken up on the hard drive(s) in a server is simply that.

Windows NT Domain Networking

1. ☑ **C.** No Access. When you assign this to a file, no access is permitted to the file, even if they have been given other access rights through use of a group or explicitly set permissions.

   ☒ **A, B.** Read and Write are not correct because they permit access to the file in question. **D.** This answer is not right because there must be a permission of some sort assigned to a file or folder.

2. ☑ **C.** Microsoft's directory is copied completely throughout the network, while Novell's directory is partitioned into pieces and then copied out in those partitioned pieces. Formerly known as Microsoft Domain Service, NT directory services (NTDS) is based on the concept of domains and is a replicated database system. The master directory database resides on the primary domain controller (PDC) and is replicated to the backup domain controllers (BDC). While it is a replicated database system, it is not a distributed database system as is Novell Directory Services® (NDS). In a distributed database system, the database is partitioned and stored in parts. In contrast, a replicated database system copies and stores the entire database.

   ☒ **A.** is not correct because Novell does have a Directory Service, **B.** is backwards and therefore incorrect, and **D.** is incorrect because there is fault tolerance with Novell and the Directory is stored in more than one location.

3. ☑ **A.** One. The most important server in a domain environment is the primary domain controller (PDC). The PDC is responsible for storing the master copy of the directory database, which contains all user account information for the entire domain. When a modification to the directory database is required, such as adding a workstation to the domain, the PDC must be online and accessible from the network in order to complete any administrative changes. This is because you can have only one PDC operating in the domain at any given time.

   ☒ **B, C, D.** are incorrect because only one PDC can exist in a domain.

4. ☑ **A, C.** BDCs provide logon authentication and redundancy for the account database. Periodically, the PDC will replicate copies of the master directory database to BDCs to ensure that the BDCs have an updated copy. The BDC uses its copy of the directory database to unload some of the logon authentication responsibilities from the PDC. Imagine if you worked on a medium-to-large network and everyone attempted to log on at the same time in the morning. If everyone tried to authenticate to the same domain controller, there would be a severe drain on system resources that would result in a bottleneck and some very upset users. However, because BDCs have a copy of the directory database, they can take some of the burden off the PDC and allow for faster logon times.

Another reason to have at least one backup domain controller is for fault tolerance. If you manage to lose the primary domain controller, such as with a hard disk failure or a corrupted directory database, you can recover through the BDC. In this case, you would promote a BDC to a PDC and allow it to remain the PDC until you could get the original PDC back online. By performing this step you are allowing administrative changes to the network, since only a PDC can perform those types of modifications. However, the BDCs can continue to perform logon authentication services to the network, even though a PDC is not available.

☒ **B, D.** are incorrect: to provide the main account database on the network and to provide users with a map to network resources are not primary functions of BDCs.

5. ☑ **B.** CTRL+ALT+DEL. This process, known as the WinLogon process, is initiated every time the computer is restarted and displays a logon dialog box that requires a CTRL+ALT+DEL keystroke sequence. This keystroke sequence brings up the logon information dialog box that allows you to supply your access credentials in the form of a username and password. From there, your access credentials are passed to the local-security authority (LSA) for routing to the security accounts manager (SAM) for verification. The results are then passed back to the LSA for routing to the WinLogon process. If you have been validated, you are then allowed access to local resources. However, if you are not validated, the WinLogon process will deny access until valid credentials are presented.

☒ **A, C, D.** These are all incorrect or invalid key sequences for the Windows NT Logon process.

6. ☑ **A.** An access control list (ACL) containing the security IDs to the users with access. The SID is also used to assign security access rights to resources. Each resource has an access control list that contains a list of SIDs that are permitted to access the resource. When a user successfully logs on to a domain, an access token is generated and attached to the user's workstation. The access token contains the account's SID and every activity performed by the user is associated with the SID. When a user attempts to access a resource, the user's account SID is compared against the resource's ACL. If a match is found, the user can then access the resource.

☒ **B.** is incorrect because Share permissions are different than resource permissions. **C.** is incorrect because there is no such thing as a random list. **D.** is incorrect because an NT Workstation cannot be a domain controller.

7. ☑   **C.** Local groups cannot be added to local groups. Since local groups permit access only to local resources, the group's information is stored in the local machine's account database. This has the advantage of offloading some of the burden from the domain's directory database. However, local groups can assign rights and permissions only to resources that reside on that particular machine. It cannot grant rights or permissions to global resources. In addition, you are limited to assigning only users and global groups to a local group; that is, you cannot assign a local group to another local group. However, you can include users and global groups from any domain in the network in which a trust relationship has been established.

☒   **A, B, D.** are false statements.

8. ☑   **C.** Domain Operators. Windows NT provides for three built-in, or default, global groups: Domain Administrators, Domain Guests, and Domain Users. Since these are global groups, they are used to grant access rights across the domain. Each global group is used for a different purpose:

■ Domain Administrators (**D.**), known as Domain Admins, is used to perform administrative functions, such as adding new workstations and granting/revoking access rights on domain accounts. When the Domain Admins global group is created, it is automatically added to the local Administrators group on every Windows NT machine in the domain. By doing so, it allows the domain administrator to remotely manage workstations and servers in the domain.

■ Domain Guests (**B.**) is used to provide guest-level accounts across the domain, just as the local Guests group is used to provide guest-level access on the local machine. When Domain Guests is created, it is automatically added to each Windows NT machine's local Guests group. You would use this group if you wished to provide limited network access to roaming users.

■ Domain Users (**A.**) encompasses all user accounts on the domain. When a new domain account is added to the network, it is automatically added to this group. This allows users to log on from different workstations on the domain. However, since this global group contains all users on the network including the Administrator account, care must be taken to which privileges are granted or denied to this group. For example, if you give the Domain Users group No Access rights to log on locally to the domain controller, you have effectively blocked out everyone from managing that domain controller.

9. ☑   **A.** Administrative rights in the domain. This is part of the Windows NT security system that stops unknown workstations from accessing any part of the domain. There are actually two methods that are used to allow a workstation to join the domain:

■ Log onto the domain as Administrator and start the Server Manager utility. This is performed by choosing Start | Administrative Tools (Common) | Server Manager.

■ Select Add to Domain from the Computer menu item. The Add Computer to Domain dialog box will appear.

The first method does not require the administrator to go to the workstation to add it to the domain as long as you provide the user with the appropriate steps to complete the process.

☒   **B.** A valid SID to enter in the domain dialog box is wrong because you do not enter the SID number. **C.** Guest equivalency in the domain is wrong because Guest equivalency will not get you anything. **D.** is a false statement because you can add a workstation to the domain from a workstation if you have administrative rights in the domain.

10. ☑   **C.** Security Accounts Manager. Your access credentials are passed to the Local Security Authority (LSA) for routing to the Security Accounts Manager (SAM) for verification. The results are then passed back to the LSA for routing to the WinLogon process. If you have been validated, you are then allowed access to local resources. However, if you are not validated, the WinLogon process will deny access until valid credentials are presented.

☒   **A, B, D.** These are all incorrect definitions of SAM.

Managing Windows NT Security

1. ☑ **B.** Print Operators. Windows NT comes with several default groups that can aid the network administrator in assigning rights and permissions. These groups, which cannot be deleted or renamed, are listed in the following table.
☒ **A, C, D.** The other options—Server Operators, Backup Operators, and Account Operators—are incorrect. They have other functions that are detailed in the table.

Group Name	NT Workstation	NT Server	Description
Administrators	X	X	Full access to the local computer
Account Operators		X	Used to manage and maintain user and group accounts
Backup Operators	X	X	Allows backup and restore operations to files regardless of the user's permissions
Guests	X	X	Allows access permissions for users who do not use the system often, such as traveling users
Power Users	X		Permits members to set networking options and share files
Print Operators		X	Grants create, delete, install, share, and modification access rights to printers on the server
Replicator	X	X	Used by the replicator server to manage and maintain security during the file replication process
Server Operators		X	Grants the appropriate rights and permissions to perform administrative duties on the server such as backup and restore operations, server shutdown, change the server time, lock the server, and share resources
Users	X	X	Allows members to perform normal, day-to-day operations such as managing files and running applications

2. ☑ **D.** Mandatory logon. The mandatory logon process requires a user to press the CTRL+ALT+DEL keystroke sequence prior to logging onto a Windows NT machine. Until this keystroke sequence has been completed, all other processes are suspended. This ensures that password-capture programs cannot steal your access credentials as you log on. By requiring a username and password to access a Windows NT machine's resources, you are also ensuring that the security system can successfully track the user's activities through auditing policies.

☒ **A.** FAT file system is wrong since the FAT file system has no security. **B.** Optional logon is incorrect because it is fictitious. **C.** Workgroup model is a peer to peer setup, so there would be no logon.

3. ☑ **B.** The domain security model is yet another implementation of the Windows NT security system. Just as you must initiate the WinLogon process to gain access to a Windows NT machine's resources, you must first initiate the NetLogon process to gain access to network resources. Authentication procedures in a domain are regulated by the PDCs and BDCs because they contain a copy of the directory database. However, only the PDC can make administrative modifications to the network. This is because the master copy of the directory database resides only on the PDC. The directory database also contains security information, such as rights and permissions, which grant or deny access to network resources.

☒ **A.** Workgroup and **C.** peer to peer are incorrect since there are no accounts in these configurations. **D.** There is no such thing has Workstation network implementation model.

4. ☑ **B.** Account policies are used to set domain-level user account security options. This means that one account policy is used throughout the domain, rather than configured for each account. To access the Account Policy dialog box, you would select the Account option from the Policies menu in User Manager for Domains.

☒ **A.** System Policies and **C.** Audit Policies are incorrect because they do not set domain-level user account security options. **D.** is incorrect because user rights are different than policies.

5. ☑ **C.** Audit policies are used in conjunction with user accounts to monitor user activities on the network, such as file access or account modifications. However, since Windows NT defaults to no auditing, audit policies cannot be used unless you have enabled the auditing feature. This is due to the additional amount of overhead in processor time and disk space that the auditing feature uses. Use caution when selecting the events to audit.

   ☒ **A.** System and **B.** Account policies are incorrect because they have different functions than what the question calls for. **D.** User Rights is incorrect because they are separate from policies.

6. ☑ **B.** User profiles allow the administrator to control a user's environmental settings from the network. Environmental settings include items such as the user's desktop configuration, startup applications, and automatic network connections. These types of configuration settings are typically set by the user according to personal preferences and are retained in configuration files known as user profiles. By storing the environmental settings in user profiles, the operating system can automatically load the user's configuration from the previous logon session. This is obviously a benefit to the user, who does not have to take the time to reconfigure the workstation.

   ☒ **A.** System policies and **D.** Account policies do not allow control over a user's environmental settings. **C.** Group membership will not determine a user's environmental settings.

7. ☑ **D.** NTUSER.DAT. The local user profile is initially created the first time the user logs onto the workstation and is based on the default user profile. As modifications are made, the system stores this information in a file, called NTUSER.DAT, which is located in the user's profile directory. The next time the user logs onto the workstation, the NTUSER.DAT file is merged with the Registry information to recreate the same environment the user had when they logged off the workstation.

   ☒ **A.** User.DAT and **B.** NT.DAT do not exist in Windows NT. **C.** System.DAT has nothing to do with user oriented information.

8. ☑ **D.** Use mandatory profiles. When the administrator needs to ensure that the user obtains the same workstation configuration every time he logs onto the network, he would use mandatory profiles. This is similar to the roaming profile in that it is stored on the network and is copied from the network to the local user profile. However, there are several differences: First, the mandatory profile is stored in a file called NTUSER.MAN rather than the usual NTUSER.DAT file used for roaming and local user profiles. Second, each time the user logs onto the network the mandatory profile is copied over the user's local profile without comparing timestamps or allowing the user to specify which profile to use. Third, if the user should make any changes to the workstation's configuration, the modifications are discarded at the time the user logs off.

☒ **A.** Roaming profiles is wrong because the profile can be modified by the user. **B.** Local profiles take away the ability to administer the profile information. **C.** Use absolute profiles is a fictitious term.

9. ☑ **C.** System Policy Editor. System policies enable the administrator to control user activities on the workstation at various levels. In order to create or modify a system policy, you will need to use System Policy Editor rather than User Manager for Domains, which you use to manage and maintain other types of policies. The network operating system is responsible for ensuring the enforcement of the other policies (account, audit, and user-rights). However, system policies are used and enforced on the workstation level through the Registry.

☒ **A.** User manager and **B.** User manager for domains have nothing to do with user policies. **D.** System Policy Configurator is a fictitious term.

10. ☑ **A, C.** User and computer. Because system policies directly affect the Registry, you need to understand how the Registry is modified before establishing one. System policies are broken down into two categories, system policies for users and system policies for computers. System policies for users will allow you to manage user-desktop settings, such as disabling the RUN command from the Start menu or locking down program groups. This type of policy modifies the HKEY_CURRENT_USER section of the Registry. System policies for computers will allow you to manage logon and network settings, such as requiring a user to wait for the logon script to process and to set up which applications process during startup. System policies for computers also modify the HKEY_LOCAL_MACHINE portion of the Registry.

☒ **B.** Workstation policies do not exist in system policies. **D.** If...Then is not a policy type.

Integrating Windows NT Workstations

1. ☑ **B.** C:\WINNT\PROFILES. The individual user profiles are originally loaded from the default user profile. This file is located in the Profiles directory of the system root directory, which is typically C:\WINNT\PROFILES. When the user logs onto a workstation for the first time, the system creates a subdirectory in the Profiles directory that has the same name as the user's username. Several other subdirectories are created that contain specific desktop settings. The default user profile is then copied to this directory and used for the remainder of the user's session. When the user logs back onto the workstation, or the network, as in the case of a roaming profile, the settings are restored.

☒ **A, C, D.** The other paths shown are incorrect; they do not have profiles information.

2. ☑ **A.** Trusted. When implementing a trust relationship, one domain contains user accounts that require access to resources located in the second domain. The domain containing the user accounts is called the account domain and the domain containing the resources is called the resource domain. In order for the account domain to access resources in the resource domain, the resource domain must trust the account domain. Since the resource domain trusts the account domain, the resource domain is said to be the trusting domain. The account domain then becomes the trusted domain. This point can cause some confusion, and it helps to have a mnemonic to remember it by. The easiest method to remember which is the trusting domain and which is the trusted domain is to remember that the account domain contains user accounts, such as Ed. The resource domain must Trust-Ed.

☒ **B.** Trusting is opposite of the correct answer. **C.** The Master and **D.** Secondary domains are incorrect because they do not exist in Windows NT.

3. ☑ **C.** User Manager for Domains. Trust relationships are set up using the User Manager for Domains utility from the Trust Relationships dialog box. Trust relationships cannot be implemented until you log onto the PDC with administrative rights, such as using the administrator account. If you are initiating a trust relationship with a domain in which you do not have administrative rights, you must coordinate with that domain's administrator.

☒ **A.** Server manager, **B.** User Manager (without Domains) and **C.** Network monitor are all incorrect because they do not allow for shares to be set up.

4. ☑ D. Complete trust model. Of all the domain models that Windows NT can implement, the complete trust is the most difficult to install, manage, and maintain. In this model, each domain trusts every other domain with a two-way trust. In order to calculate the number of trusts needed for each domain, you can use the formula $n(n-1)$, where n represents the number of domains. By looking at the formula, you can tell that the number of trust relationships can get enormous after a period of time.
☒ A. is not correct since the single domain is the easiest to install, manage, and maintain. **B, C.** The single master and the multiple master become more difficult to install, manage, and maintain, but are much easier to manage than the complete trust model.

5. ☑ B. Resource domain. The account domain is considered the trusted domain and all resource domains are considered the trusting domains.
☒ A, C. The term *account domain* refers to the trusted domain, not to the trusting domain. **D.** Trustee domain does not exist.

6. ☑ C. The only requirement is to install the first server as the PDC.
☒ A, B, and D. are all incorrect because they are not requirements in a single domain model when setting up a server.

7. ☑ C. Both Domain A and B. A two-way trust occurs when both domains trust each other equally; that is, both domains become the trusted and trusting domains at the same time. This permits users in both domains to access resources located in both domains and allows for pass-through authentication.
☒ A, B, D. are incorrect because they rule out at least one domain.

8. ☑ **B. Global groups.** Windows NT uses global groups to assign permissions across the domain. When you are dealing with groups across domain boundaries, you place global groups from the trusted (account) domain into local groups in the trusting (resource) domain, just as you would in a single domain situation. The trusting domain would then assign the necessary permissions to access its resources in the local group.
☒ **A.** Windows NT uses local groups to assign permissions to local resources. **C, D.** Assigning users and folders would make administration burdensome.

9. ☑ **C.** When the user logs on his/her authentication request is passed to the Dallas domain and then back to the New York domain. Since two-way trust relationships are established between the domains, users can still use one account to gain access to all authorized network resources. When a user logs on from a domain other than the one to which he/she is assigned, the domain that they log onto passes the logon request to the appropriate domain.
☒ **A, B,** and **D.** are incorrect because they do not acknowledge the fact that there is pass-through authentication.

Multiple Domain Windows NT Networking

1. ☑ **C. 128.** Windows NT Server is limited to 128 inbound trusts. You can see that if you use the complete trust model you will be limited to only 11 domains. For this reason, Novell and Microsoft agree that you should use the complete trust model only when the number of domains in the network is relatively small.
☒ **A. 64, B. 100, D. 12** are incorrect because these numbers would limit the number of inbound trusts more than necessary.

2. ☑ **A, B.** ODI, NDIS. The NetWare client for Windows NT supports both ODI and NDIS standards. ODI and NDIS standards allow a network adapter to have multiple protocols bound to network board drivers. Thus, both IPX and IP can be bound to the same network adapter.

☒ **C.** DNIS, **D**, DOI are incorrect because these acronyms don't represent any standards in Windows NT networking.

3. ☑ **A.** The NetWare Client for Windows NT allows the workstation to take full advantage of the file and print services provided by the NetWare server through NDS™. The client allows Windows NT workstations to access bindery print services and bindery file services on previous versions of NetWare.

☒ **B.** Workstation Manager is a component of the client that interacts with Z.E.N.works. **C.** Z.E.N.works is an add-on component with NetWare 5. **D.** NWLINK is not correct since it is a protocol only.

4. ☑ **D.** UNATTEND.TXT. There are three ways to install the client software. The first is the basic local installation at the workstation. The second is a network installation from a shared directory on the network. With this method you must have some client on the system to access the information. This is usually the method chosen for an upgrade. The third method is the unattended installation. There are two ways to do an unattended installation. One is to use a basic configuration file, UNATTEND.TXT, to address most of the questions during the installation. The other method, also unattended, but more of an upgrade, is the Automatic Client Update.

☒ **A, B, C.** The other choices are not correct because they are made-up file names.

5. ☑   **C.** ACU. If there are users with different versions of the client software, you can update everyone to the same basic network installation. First, you must enable the ACU component. To do this you have to copy the NetWare Client I386 directory to the server so workstations can get to the object. Next, you must grant users read and file-scan rights to the directory. Once you have these two steps completed, add a line to the logon script to run the update component.

☒   **A.** Workstation Manager, **B.** Z.E.N.works, and **D.** NDS are all incorrect because they have nothing to do with client upgrades. They are pieces of the tree or client that do other things.

6. ☑   **B.** Workstation Manager is a component of the client that runs and interacts with the NDS workstation and policy packages. Workstation Manager makes it possible to administer both the local Windows NT user accounts and the NetWare objects in NDS. Tying these two items together makes for simpler and more efficient administration. The Workstation Manager also lets us centrally administer from NDS user profiles and policy information, as well as computer/workstation profiles and policy information.

☒   **A.** NetWare Client version 7.0 or higher does not exist. **C.** User Manager does not allow for anything to happen at the workstation for Z.E.N.works. **D.** A unique SID is needed in general terms, but for this question it doesn't fit as the most correct answer.

7. ☑   **C.** The snap-in is configured using the ADMSETUP utility. It is important to the centralized administration of NT configurations. The one thing to remember here is that the snap-in can be used only by the user who installed it.

☒   **A.** The NWGINA module is what handles making workstations for Windows NT. **B.** NWADMN is the administrator utility. **D.** The SETUP utility is not correct because it is a generic utility, and ADMSETUP is the specific utility for configuring snap-in components.

8. ☑ **D.** The information is stored in NDS, not in a file. Along with the association is the basic configuration of the object. The main configuration is the policy information and profile. The policy information replaces the old NTCONFIG.POL that would be used in previous versions of NetWare before Z.E.N.works came about.

The profile information extant with Windows NT makes up the user portion of the policy configuration as well as the Desktop and Start menu icons and layout. This can be centrally managed within NDS, making an administrator's job much easier.

☒ **A, B, C.** The other answers are files and the information is stored in NDS, so therefore they are incorrect.

9. ☑ **A, B.** User Objects and User Group Objects. A Windows NT User Policy Package can also be associated with Containers. In order for the policy to be used, it must be associated with a User Object, a User Group Object or a Container.

☒ **C. and D.** are wrong because a Windows NT User Policy Package cannot be associated with Domain Objects of Windows NT Configuration Objects.

10. ☑ **C.** Under a container called Application. Novell recommends having an Application container that holds the Application objects and then you can create application groups that are associated with the application. The group can be assigned rights and the appropriate will be members of the group.

☒ **A, B, D.** The other answers are not correct since Novell recommends having a unique container for the Application objects.

11. ☑ **A.** Administer Windows 95 user accounts. Once the object is imported, you can do the following:

- Administer NT Workstation user accounts

- Configure components of the workstation configuration from NDS (**B.**)

- Work with the client piece to create local NT workstation accounts when the user logs on (**C.**)

- Manage items such as policies, profile information, and logon screen banner (**D.**)

☒ **B, C, D.** are incorrect, since they are actions that can be done, as shown in the preceeding list.

Integrating NetWare and Windows NT Domains

1. ☑ **A.** The Novell Administrator snap-in service allows the network administrator to centrally manage Windows NT domains through the NetWare administrator as Windows NT server objects. Synchronization between NDS and Windows NT is transparent to the administrator and makes the routine administration tasks easier because you will not have to manually migrate users from Windows NT to NDS. Through the snap-in service, Windows NT users and groups are stored in NDS as native NDS objects and are referenced to the Windows NT server object that stores the Windows NT domain account.

☒ **C.** Extensions do not exist in NDS. **B.** The schema is what tells NDS what an object is. **D.** A trust relationship, or simply trust, is a communications and administrative link between two domains that permits the sharing of resources and account information.

2. ☑ **B, C.** The NDS Object Replication Service resides on the Windows NT primary domain controller and any backup domain controllers that are administered using NDS. When a change occurs to certain objects in NDS, the NDS Event Monitor passes those changes to the NDS Object Replication Service. When the NDS Object Replication Service receives the changes, it first formats the modifications to fit the Windows NT SAM database. Once reformatting is complete, it makes the changes in the SAM database. Since the PDC contains the master copy of the domain's SAM database, changes are not made on the BDCs. Should the PDC fail, NDS information is synchronized with a BDC only if it has been promoted to a PDC. If there is no PDC on-line during a synchronization, NDS will hold onto (queue) the appropriate modifications until a PDC is available.

☒ **A.** Runs as an NLM on the NetWare Server, and **D.** On a Workstation that is permanently logged in, are incorrect—these mention NetWare and a Workstation, which cannot be domain controllers. The key here is domain controller.

3. ☑ **B.** They use a private authenticated NDS connection. Network security is important to every administrator and hackers use any method they can to gain entry to your network. The Novell Administrator for Windows NT provides for a secure communications channel between a Windows NT network and a NetWare network by establishing a private, authenticated NDS connection. The connection is not shared by any other process nor is it viewable when browsing the network. If a hostile entity attempts to locate your secure connection, it is much more difficult for them to find you if that connection is not advertised over the network.

☒ **A.** is incorrect because there is security in the communication between NT and NetWare. **C.** is incorrect because Windows NT and NetWare don't use a bindery type of connection to keep communication secure. **D.** is incorrect because Windows NT and NetWare do not use scripts which encrypt the data.

4. ☑ **C.** With the Event Monitor and the NDS Object Replication Service. The IGRATE.EXE integration utility is a component of the Novell Administrator for Windows NT. Its function is to synchronize existing Windows NT users and groups with NDS during the initial integration process. Since the NDS Event Monitor and NDS Object Replication Service maintains Directory database synchronization once the two platforms have been integrated, you will not need to run IGRATE.EXE more than once.
☒ **A, B, D.** IGRATE, NWADMN, and the Event Monitor itself do not keep synchronization current and are incorrect.

5. ☑ **B.** The NetWare user attributes take precedence and overwrite the NT attributes. During the synchronization process, you will encounter situations in which there is a Windows NT User object and an NDS User object for the same individual. When you encounter this type of situation, you can merge the attributes of both User objects by designating the Windows NT User object as a Common User object. However, when duplicate information exists between these two objects, the NetWare attributes will be retained and the Windows NT attributes will be overwritten.
☒ **A.** is incorrect since the reverse is true. **C.** The attributes are not lost. **D.** Duplicate objects don't exist and cannot be integrated.

6. ☑ **B.** User Manager for Domains. Once you have integrated your Windows NT users into NDS, you should not use User Manager for Domains to manage Windows NT users. If you do, any changes that you make will not be replicated to NDS and will be overwritten by NDS parameters during the next synchronization. Instead, you would use the NetWare Administrator to manage and maintain both Windows NT and NetWare accounts through NDS. When you receive a new user who requires access to the Windows NT network, you will need to replicate their NDS User object to Windows NT. While you can perform the replication process from the integration utility, it is highly recommended (and assumed on the Novell examination) that you will use the NetWare Administrator.
☒ **A, C, D.** Server Manager and Disk Administrator are Windows NT utilities but are available for different functions. NWADMN handles the NetWare side of things.

7. ☑ **A.** Because everything is an object to NDS, you can manage application server objects as easily as you can manage other objects. The purpose of the application server object is to manage communications between the Event Monitor that resides on the NetWare server and the ORS that resides on the Windows NT server. The NDS Event Monitor tracks modifications made to objects that will require synchronization with a Windows NT network. When it finds that a change has been made, it alerts its counterpart on the Windows NT server, the NDS Object Replication Service (ORS), and passes those changes to it. The ORS then validates the data it has received by formatting it for the SAM database and makes the modifications required. Through the network settings page of the application server object, you can configure the protocol settings and the synchronization interval to Windows NT.

   ☒ **B.** is wrong since it the opposite of **A**, the correct answer. **C.** and **D.** are incorrect because they focus on application objects in the tree versus application server objects.

8. ☑ **C.** Local Service Authority. When you supply your credentials to the operating system, the WinLogon process will pass that information to the LSA process, which then queries the SAM for verification. If your username and password are invalid, you are denied access to the machine. However, if the SAM validates your credentials, the LSA will generate an access token with your rights and pass it back to the WinLogon process. At this point, you will be allowed to access any of the computer's resources that your logon ID grants you.

   ☒ **A.** and **D.** are incorrect because Legal Service Agreement and Loopback Service Address do not exist. **B.** License Service Action is not known by this acronym.

9. ☑ **B.** NetBEUI is not a routable protocol and cannot be used in a WAN environment. This means that a second protocol that is routable (such as IPX or IP) will become necessary to encapsulate NetBEUI packets if your network traffic has to cross a router. Another problem with NetBEUI is that there are few platforms, primarily Windows and OS/2, that support it. This limits your connectivity options for current and future network growth.

   ☒ **A.** is incorrect because NetBEUI is a valid protocol. **C.** NetBEUI is small so it does not take up much memory. **B.** None of the above, is incorrect.

Designing, Implementing, and Maintaining an Integrated Network

1. ☑ **D.** SAMSRV.DLL. The original SAMSRV.DLL is renamed to MSSAMSRV.DLL and the new Novell version is installed. This new DLL allows for NDS to fulfill requests to Windows NT Servers.
   ☒ **A.** is not correct since SAMLIB.DLL serves another function on a Windows NT machine. **B.** SAMS.DLL, and **C.** SAMSSRV.DLL, do not exist in regards to NDS for NT.

2. ☑ **A.** Multi-Pass Migration. Using the Domain Object Wizard you can migrate into multiple containers by making multiple passes through the migration process.
   ☒ **B.** is not correct because Multi-Pass Integration is a made-up term. SAMSSRV.DLL has nothing to do with this process, so **C.** is wrong. **D** is wrong since it is possible to do this.

3. ☑ **C.** Domain User Settings. The Domain User Settings is the same as the User Environment Profile and Logon Workstations screens from User Manager for Domains. This allows for centralization of NT configuration information.
   ☒ **A.** is not correct since the Domain Access property page controls access to the domains and groups a user belongs. **B.** is wrong since this deals with single domain membership. **D.** is incorrect because the Replica Advisor allows for management of replicas and partitions within NDS.

Implementing and Maintaining Accessibility in an Integrated Network

1. ☑ **B.** Intel-Based Workstation running NT 4.0, 10MB of disk space, 16MB of additional disk space for administrator utilities. In order to install the client there must be a minimum of 10MB of disk space and also an additional 16MB for administration utilities.

   ☒ **A, C,** and **D.** are incorrect because they have either the wrong operating systems or the wrong number of MB of disk space.

2. ☑ **A.** Login from a remote workstation and rename the NWGINA.DLL to NWGINA.SAV and then copy the MSGINA.DLL to NWGINA.DLL. Since the workstation is using the NTFS file system you have to access the files remotely.

   ☒ **B** and **C.** are incorrect since FAT32 and DOS cannot access the NTFS volume. **D.** is wrong since it can be done, as stated in answer A.

Part 7

Test Yourself:
Practice Exam 1:
NetWare®5
Administration
(Exam 50-639)

Test Yourself:
Practice Exam 1
Questions

Q&A

Before you call to register for the actual NetWare 5₍ₐ₎ Administration exam (Exam # 50-639), take the following test and see how you make out. Set a timer for 90 minutes—the same time you'll have to take the live exam—and answer the following 69 questions in the time alloted. Once you've finished, turn to the Practice Exam I Answers section and check your score to see if you passed! Good luck!

Practice Exam I Questions

1. In NDS™, objects are said to exist in a context. What is meant by the context of an object?

   A. The context is the child of the actual object.

   B. The context is the location in the DOS file system where the object resides.

   C. The context is the location in the NDS tree where the object resides.

   D. The context is always set to [Root].

Use the Following Scenario for Questions 2–4

Jessie is a network engineer and she works for a medium-sized firm, Short Stuff Enterprises, outside of Atlanta, GA. The company is organized with various users in the following departments: Accounting, Engineering, Information Technology and Human Resources. The organization of the NDS for SSE is displayed in the following illustration.

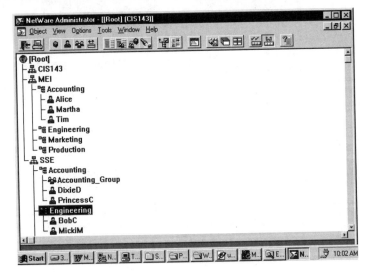

2. Which of the following are considered leaf objects in the NDS tree for SSE? Choose all that apply.

A. [Root]

B. Jessie

C. Accounting

D. SYS

3. Jessie needs to create a User object for Todd M. What property is she required to enter in order to create the User object? Choose all that apply.

A. Login name

B. Given name

C. Last name

D. Title

4. Jessie is on vacation and another person is helping out. Why can't this inexperienced new administrator create an Organizational Unit under the MickiM object? Choose all that apply.

A. MickM is a User object.

B. A container must be created within another container.

C. MickM is a leaf object.

D. Leaf objects can only contain other leaf objects.

5. What services are used by Workstation Manager? Choose all that apply.

A. Workstation Inventory

B. Printer Management

C. User Account Management

D. Password Synchronization

E. Activity Scheduling

6. What types of NDS right enables a trustee to perform an action on an NDS object?

A. Property
B. Object
C. Inherited Rights Filter (IRF)
D. Effective rights

Use the Following Scenario for Questions 7–11

Zac Meadors is a Network Administrator who works for a small firm. The firm is concerned about security and Zac has the job of implementing security for the departments.

7. Given the following file system structure and rights output for a user named Ralph, what are his Effective rights to the folder Shift1?

```
\  (DOS root)
|____ Production  Inherited from above:  [                    ]
      |           Inherited Rights Filter:[SRWCEMFA]
      |           Effective rights:      [                    ]
      |
      |__Shift1   Inherited from above:  [                    ]
                  Inherited Rights Filter: [SRWCEMFA]
                  Ralph                  [   R        F   ]
                  Effective rights:      [        ?       ]
```

A. SRWCEMFA
B. RF
C. Nothing
D. SWCEMA

8. Zac supports a user named Mike. Mike is the Manager of the sales team for the firm. Given the following file system structure and rights output for Mike, what are his Effective rights to the folder NewLeads?

```
\  (DOS root)
|____ Sales     Inherited from above:  [                    ]
      |         IRF:                    [SRWCEMFA]
      |         Mike:                   [   RWCEMF   ]
      |         Effective rights:       [   RWCEMF   ]
      |
      |__NewLeads Inherited from above: [   RWCEMF   ]
```

```
IRF:                          [ SRWCE   F ]
Effective rights:             [        ?    ]
```

A. RWCEMF

B. SRWCEF

C. RWCEF

D. Supervisory only

9. In the following file-system structure, Zac set Bob's user name as a member of the production group and engineering group. What are his Effective rights to the folder ProdLine?

```
\ (DOS root)
|____ Supervisor  Inherited from above:   [              ]
     |              IRF:                   [SRWCEMFA ]
     |              Bob:                   [ RWC     F ]
     |              Effective rights:      [ RWC     F ]
     |__ProdLine    Inherited from above: [ RWC     F ]
                    IRF:                   [SRWCEMFA ]
                    Bob:                   [ R       F ]
                    Production:            [    WCE    ]
                    Engineering:           [    C   M  ]
                    Effective rights:      [      ?    ]
```

A. SRWCEMFA

B. WCEMA

C. WCE

D. RWCEMFA

10. Zac's company is planning to purchase a smaller company. He needs to plan for the new company's file-system structure on the current server. What rules should Zac follow? Choose all that apply.

A. Grant greater access at higher levels using trustee assignments and an IRF that allows everything.

B. Don't grant unnecessary rights at any level.

C. Consider the effect of Security Equivalence.

D. Grant greater access at lower levels using trustee assignments.

11. What command will allow Jack to make trustee assignments?

    A. FLAG

    B. RIGHTS

    C. CX

    D. LOGIN

    E. WHOAMI

12. What command registers a Windows 95/98 workstation?

    A. WSRIGHTS.EXE

    B. WSREG32.EXE

    C. WSREG16.EXE

    D. NWADMIN.EXE

13. What can be modified in Windows NT to look for a system policy file that has a name other than the default? Choose the best option.

    A. You should change Accessibility options for Windows NT.

    B. You should edit the Registry and manually change the name for NTCONFIG.POL.

    C. You should enable a workstation system policy where the Remote Update is changed to account for the new file name.

    D. You should enable a workstation roaming policy where the Console options reflect the new file name.

14. What is the best method for placing an object's context in a login script?

    A. Trailing dots

    B. The Relative Distinguished name

    C. The DOS Full-Path name

    D. The Distinguished name

15. You want to give another employee the same rights you have. What must you do?

A. Set the Compare property for the User object

B. Change the IRF to block out Supervisory NDS rights

C. Set Security Equivalence on the User object to be the same as your User object

D. Change the Effective rights variable to be the same as your User object

16. What is the object that represents the actual disk-storage area for the print jobs?

A. The Print Server object

B. The Print Queue object

C. The Printer object

D. The Server object

17. What would the logic look like for a user on a Windows 95 computer if their login script had the statements to register their workstation?

A. IF " PLATFORM" = " WNT" THEN BEGIN
#F:\PUBLIC\WSREG32.EXE

B. IF " PLATFORM" = " W95" THEN BEGIN
#F:\PUBLIC\WSREG16.EXE

C. IF " PLATFORM" = " W95" THEN BEGIN
#F:\PUBLIC\WSREG32.EXE

D. IF " PLATFORM" = " WIN" THEN BEGIN
#F:\PUBLIC\WSREG32.EXE

18. What is true of an NT user printer and an NT Workstation printer? Choose all that apply.

A. An NT user printer will be available at certain workstations regardless of who logs in at the workstation.

B. An NT Workstation printer will be available at certain workstations regardless of who logs in at the workstation.

C. An NT user printer will be available to a certain user regardless of the workstation they log into.

D. An NT Workstation printer will be available to a certain user regardless of the workstation they login to.

Use the Following Scenario for Questions 19–24

Todd is a LAN Manager whose job is to install NetWare 5 on computers. His company receives the computers, his department loads NetWare 5 on them, and they ship them out to remote sites for the company. They also have an internal LAN that must be supported. The internal LAN has a 100BaseT network connected with 100 MBps hubs. The cabling is Category 5.

19. Todd hired a new employee who is used to installing NT Server and Workstation. James, the new hire, needs to understand the options that exist to install NetWare 5. What are the available options James has for installing NetWare 5? Choose all that apply.

    A. GUI

    B. Text

    C. WUSER.EXE

    D. Remote Control Agent

20. James needs to gather information about the server. What type of information is needed during the GUI phase of the NetWare 5 server installation? Choose all that apply.

    A. Country setting

    B. Mouse type

    C. Protocol selection

    D. Server name

    E. Time zone information

21. Todd and James are installing a server for one of the company's departments. They are discussing block size. They have a server volume that is 1GB. What is the default block size for this volume?

    A. 4KB

    B. 8KB

    C. 16KB

    D. 32KB

    E. 64KB

22. The company just acquired some computers at a low price per unit at an auction. Most of the computers are Intel 386-class computers with 100MB–300MB of disk space. Most have about 16MB of RAM. Todd knows these cannot be installed as servers because they don't meet the requirements, so they'll have to be upgraded. What are the minimum requirements for installing a server? Choose all that apply.

A. The computers will need at least a 486 but a Pentium-class computer is better.

B. The computers will need at least 110MB of hard disk space.

C. The computers must have at least a Pentium III-class CPU.

D. The computers will need at least 250MB of hard disk space.

23. James and Todd are discussing whether to use block suballocation on a server or not. They know block suballocation is enabled by default but are considering disabling it. What is true about block suballocation? Choose all that apply.

A. Block suballocation stores data more efficiently than without block suballocation enabled.

B. Block suballocation is stored in units of 4KB.

C. Block suballocation wastes more disk space than if it were not used.

D. Block suballocation is stored in units of 512 bytes.

24. James has a network adapter that is not being automatically detected by the server installation process. He ran the setup program that came with the adapter and it tests out fine. What should he do?

A. James should change the interrupt on the network adapter to IRQ 0.

B. James should install the drivers from the disk that came with the network adapter.

C. James should remove this network adapter and install a Token Ring network adapter.

D. James is probably not running the IP protocol.

Use the Following Scenario for Questions 25–29

Zac works as a network administrator for a large international firm. He is installing the client software for NetWare 5 on various computers in his organization. Logon security will be an issue for the users logging in. Zac also needs to automate the login process for the computers so the users are able to access applications and printers.

25. Micki, Zac's manager, gave Zac the job of installing the vice president's computer, which has never connected to an Internet server. The vice president's computer is currently running Windows 3.1, on an Intel 80286 CPU with 2MB of RAM. What must Zac do to get this computer connected to the server? Choose all that apply.

   A. Upgrade the computer to a Pentium class CPU with 16MB of RAM and install Windows 95/98
   B. Install a printer to the computer
   C. Install a PCI network interface card
   D. Install Client 32 for Windows 95/98
   E. Install the IPX/SPX protocol for the client

26. Zac needs to make sure he knows the load order for NetWare clients running to ODI specifications. What is the correct load order for the ODI-compliant clients?

   A. MLID, LSLC32.NLM, IPX.NLM/IPHLPR.NLM, CLIENT32.NLM.
   B. LSLC32.NLM, MLID, IPX.NLM/IPHLPR.NLM, CLIENT32.NLM.
   C. CLIENT32.NLM, LSLC32.NLM, IPX.NLM/IPHLPR.NLM.
   D. MLID, LSLC32.NLM, CLIENT32.NLM, IPX.NLM/IPHLPRNLM.

27. Zac wants to install the Novell Client for Windows NT on one of the Manager's Windows NT computer. Assuming the CD-ROM is drive D:, what is the full path name of the Client for Windows NT software that he must type in at the Start | Run box?

A. D:\PRODUCTS\WINNT\I386\SETUPNW

B. D:\PRODUCTS\WIN95\IBM_ENU\SETUP

C. D:/PRODUCTS/WINNT/I386/SETUPNW

D. D:/PRODUCTS/WIN95/IBM_ENU/SETUP

28. A user called Zac and is having trouble logging in. Zac pulls up the Login Restrictions page for the user and finds the restrictions as shown in the following illustration. Based on this figure, when can the user log in to the system? Choose all that apply.

A. The user can log in Sunday all day.

B. The user can log in all day Saturday.

C. The user can log in Monday at 8 am.

D. The user can log in Tuesday at 8 am.

E. The user can log in Thursday at 2 pm.

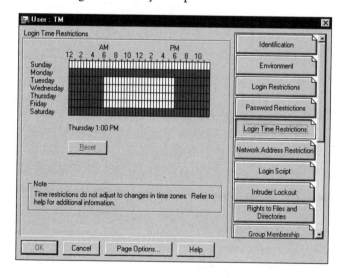

29. One of the users whom Zac supports is concerned about his password being sent out over the network. What can Zac tell the user regarding this issue?

A. The password is sent over the wire but there should be no cause for concern.

B. The password is sent in a separate packet from the username so there would be no way a hacker could put them together.

C. The password is not sent across the network.

D. The password is sent only when login scripts are in use.

30. What is the name of the program that must be run on a Windows 95 Client computer with a network printer physically attached to it?

A. NPRINTER.EXE

B. NPTWIN95.EXE

C. PSERVER.NLM

D. PCONSOLE.NLM

31. What are the methods you could use to run the Windows 95/98 Remote Control Agents? Choose all that apply.

A. NAL

B. Login script

C. Execute NTSTACFG.EXE manually

D. Execute WUSER.EXE manually

32. What are the object types in NDS that can be affected by security? Choose all that apply.

A. [Root]

B. Container objects

C. Leaf objects

D. Hardware addresses

Use the Following Scenario for Questions 33–38

Todd is a LAN manager for a small firm. He must set up users for all the employees in Meadors Enterprises Incorporated. There are 125 users who work in Production, Accounting, Sales, and Engineering. The User objects must reside in the correct container in the NDS tree.

33. If Todd creates a user called Mel in the Production container, what is the Typeful Distinguished Name for Mel?

    A. .CN=Mel.OU=Production.O=MEI

    B. .O=MEI.OU=Production.CN=Mel

    C. Mel.Production.MEI

    D. CN=Mel.OU=Production.O=MEI

34. Todd is creating a new User object. What are valid properties for a User object? Choose all that apply.

    A. Home Directory

    B. Title

    C. Last Login

    D. Print Server Name

35. Todd wants to create a User object. What methods can he employ? Choose all that apply.

    A. NetAdmin

    B. NWADMIN

    C. ConsoleOne

    D. UIMPORT

    E. CX

36. Todd created a User object. What are the default rights for this user at creation time? Choose all that apply.

    A. Browse object rights to the user object itself

    B. Supervisory rights to the [Root] object

    C. Read property rights to all its own Property rights

    D. Read and Write property rights to the user's own login script so he can write his own login scripts

    E. All file system rights to the user's own home directory

37. Todd is overworked and needs some assistance. MEI hires a junior network administrator to assist in the workload. Todd wants to give this new user, Dixie, the same rights, his own User object has. What is the best way to implement this?

    A. Create a login script for Dixie that copies all of the rights and has the same drive mappings that Todd has

    B. Manually assign all of Todd's NDS object and property rights to Dixie

    C. Use a user template for creating the new user, Dixie

    D. Set Dixie to be security equivalent to Todd

38. Todd gets a call from a distressed user. The user has logged in one workstation and is trying to log in to the server from another workstation. The server is running TCP/IP and has a printer attached to it. What is the most likely reason for the user's inability to log in from another workstation? Choose all that apply.

    A. The user has a network address restriction set.

    B. The user is limited to the number of concurrent connections.

    C. The user has forgotten his password.

    D. The user account is disabled.

39. Which Novell® command line utility will allow you to sort files and folders by owner, creation date, and access date?

    A. NLIST

    B. CX

    C. NDIR

    D. NWADMIN

40. What NDS rights are needed to install Z.E.N.works?

A. Delete

B. Rename

C. Supervisor

D. Browse

41. What guidelines would you suggest for implementing NDS security? Choose all that apply.

A. Grant Supervisor rights to [Public]

B. Avoid using Security Equivalence

C. Create multiple administrator objects

D. Always assign explicit rights to individual user trustees

42. What NDS right will only allow you to see other NDS objects?

A. Supervisor

B. Rename

C. Create

D. Browse

43. What are the components of NDPS? Choose all that apply.

A. Printer Agent

B. Print Server

C. Printer Gateways

D. Print Client

E. NDPS Manager

44. What are the buttons available to users within the Help Request application? Choose all that apply.

A. Mail

B. Call

C. Info

D. Help

E. Enabler

45. What are the two types of printer gateways in NDPS? Choose all that apply.

    A. Hewlett-Packard gateways

    B. Xerox gateways

    C. Novell gateways

    D. Microsoft gateways

46. Which of the following are features of NAL? Choose all that apply.

    A. Software distribution

    B. Application management

    C. Print Server management

    D. Secured applications

47. What NDS property right gives the user the ability to only look at the contents of an object's property value?

    A. Supervisor

    B. Compare

    C. Browse

    D. Read

48. What utility can end users use from their workstation to install printers and manage their print jobs?

    A. NWCONFIG.NLM

    B. NWPMW32.EXE

    C. RCONSOLE.EXE

    D. INSTALL.NLM

49. What type of login script will execute for all users in a certain Organizational Unit?

    A. Container

    B. Organization

    C. User

    D. Profile

50. What is the NAL launched executable for Windows NT Workstation?

    A. NALW31.EXE

    B. NALW95.EXE

    C. NALWIN32.EXE

    D. NALWINNT.EXE

51. What describes the process of rights flowing downward from one object to another?

    A. NDS object rights

    B. Inheritance

    C. NDS Property rights

    D. Trustee rights

52. What is the execution order of login scripts?

    A. Container, default, user, profile

    B. Default, user, profile, container

    C. Container, profile, user, default

    D. User, profile, container, default

53. What types of partitions are created for a NetWare server when installing a server? Choose all that apply.

    A. DOS partition

    B. Macintosh partition

    C. NetWare partition

    D. OS2 partition

54. What type of information is stored in the .AOT file? Choose all that apply.

    A. .INI file changes

    B. Registry changes

    C. Text file changes

    D. List of files copied during installation

    E. NDS changes

55. What is the term for blocking inheritance?

    A. Effective rights (ER)

    B. Attributes

    C. Files system rights

    D. Inherited Rights Filter (IRF)

56. After inserting the Novell Client Software into the drive, what is the correct path name of the Z.E.N.works installation program?

    A. PRODUCTS\WIN32\NWADMIN32

    B. PRODUCTS\WIN16\SETUP.COM

    C. SYSTEM\NWCONFIG.NLM

    D. PRODUCTS\ZENWORKS\SETUP.EXE

57. What type of property information can be seen for a Workstation object? Choose all that apply.

    A. Drives available on the workstation

    B. Devices on the workstation

    C. IRQ, I/O Port, and DMA settings

    D. Video adapter settings

    E. Printers captured

58. What object in NetWare Administrator would give you information about files and folders?

    A. Server

    B. User

    C. Group

    D. Volume

Use the Following Scenario for Questions 59–61

Mack is a network administrator with several users who need access to an application called TOUR on a Novell server named BOSS. The TOUR.EXE program is stored on a folder called SOUTH on a volume called APPS.

59. Mack wants to remove the drive mapping G: to SOUTH for a user who is leaving the company. What command will accomplish this for Mack?

A. MAP NEXT G:

B. MAP INS S16: G:

C. MAP REMOVE G:

D. MAP DEL G:

60. Mack has a temporary worker helping out by adding users and groups. The contractor needs to know the location of NetWare Administrator so he can create a drive mapping to it. What directory contains NetWare Administrator?

A. PUBLIC\NETADMIN.NLM

B. PUBLIC\WIN32\NWADMIN32.EXE

C. SYS\WIN16\NWADMIN32.EXE

D. PUBLIC\WIN32\NWCONFIG.NLM

61. A few of Mack's users are so computer knowledgeable that they like to roam around to other folders above their main home directory; and like to snoop around the file system structure to see what files are out there. What type of mapping could Mack use to prevent the users from looking at a level higher than their current one?

A. MAP DEL

B. MAP INS

C. MAP NEXT

D. MAP ROOT

E. MAP /VER

62. What is the default polling interval for a Windows NT Workstation to check NDS for any change that should be made to the NT Workstation?

A. 1 minute

B. 10 minutes

C. 60,000 minutes

D. 1 second

63. What is the difference between Typeful name and Typeless names?

A. Typeful names always begin at [Root] while Typeless names never begin at [Root].

B. Typeless names always begin at [Root] while Typeful names never begin at [Root].

C. Typeful names use abbreviation codes such as CN, OU, and O when referring to the object; Typeless names don't use the abbreviation codes.

D. Typeless names use abbreviation codes such as CN, OU, and O when referring to the object Typeful names don't use the abbreviation codes.

Use the Following Scenario for Questions 64–67

Scott is on a team of network engineers that is building login scripts for a set of users. They will create container, profile, and user login scripts. They have an Organization called Meadors-Corp and several Organizational Units called Accounting, IT (Information Technology), Sales, and Engineering.

64. Scott wants to have the user's name appear when they log in. He wants all users in the Sales Organizational Unit to see their login name. What is his best option?

A. He should use the %LOGIN_CONTEXT and add it to each user's login script.

B. He should use the %LOGIN_NAME and add it to each user's login script.

C. He should use the %LOGIN_NAME and add it to the Sales container.

D. He should modify the default login script.

65. A programmer in the IT department wrote a Visual BASIC program for the accounting department that needs to be executed each time an accounting user logs in. The full name of the program is: SERVER_A\SYS:APPS\ACCT.EXE. What should Scott do in the Accounting container's login script to execute this program?

A. Scott should use the REM statement.

B. Scott should use the # symbol.

C. Scott should use the semicolon (;) symbol.

D. Scott should use the FDISPLAY statement.

66. Scott is attempting to document his login scripts. What can he use for a comment in a login script? Choose all that apply.

A. REM

B. Semicolon (;)

C. Asterick ()

D. Pound sign (#)

67. Scott wants a login script to display the hardware address of the user's machine for a particular user. What variable should he place in a login script in order to see the hardware address of the computer?

A. %HW_ADDRESS

B. %MACHINE

C. %P_STATION

D. %STATION

68. What is the purpose of the Enable Load Balancing property for an Application object?

A. It enables a user to confirm a reboot.

B. It enables the execution load of an application to be distributed across multiple application servers.

C. It enables one application server to take over in the event of another application server crash.

D. It allows editing of Registry settings and .INI files.

69. Let's say you were an employee of a large international firm. The firm had offices in the US, Canada, Mexico and Australia. What is the best approach for initially setting up the NDS tree?

A. Create a leaf object for each of the countries

B. Create a Server object for each of the countries because they will have servers

C. Create a Country object for each of the countries

D. Create a [Public] trustee for each of the countries

Test Yourself: Practice Exam 1 Answers

Q&A

The answers to the questions are in boldface, followed by a brief explanation. The incorrect answer choices are explained in the final paragraph following each correct answer. Some of the explanations detail the logic you should use to choose the correct answer, while others give factual reasons why the answer is correct. If you miss several questions on a similar topic, you should review the corresponding section in the *CNE® NetWare® 5 Study Guide* before taking the NetWare® 5 Administration test.

Practice Exam I Answers

1. ☑ **C.** In NDS™, an object has a place. The place is where it resides in the NDS tree. If an object is located in a container called PRODUCTION, the object's current context is PRODUCTION. If the User object name Todd exists in PRODUCTION and another person named Todd works in PAYROLL, they have different contexts. All objects, whether they are container or leaf objects, have a context, which is their position in the NDS tree from [Root].

   ☒ **A.** The context is not the child of an object. If the object in question is a leaf object, it will have no child object. **B.** An object does not reside in a folder and is thus not part of the DOS file system. **D.** The context of an object is not always [Root].

2. ☑ **B, D.** The User object, Jessie, and the Volume object, SYS. NDS is a database that allows you to organize network resources into objects. Examples of objects are User, Volume, Server and Printer. NDS also provides for organization through the use of container objects. These are much like Windows folders in that folders store files and other folders; containers store leafs and other containers. Leaf objects cannot contain any other object. However, they do have properties and values associated with them. An example of a property for a User object would be Name, Title, Phone Number. An object's property can contain data and this is called the object's value. An example of a value is "Todd Meadors" for the Name property of the User object.

   ☒ **A.** [Root] is not right due to the fact that [Root] is a container object and not a leaf object. **C.** Accounting is incorrect because Accounting is an Organizational unit and it is also called a container object, not a leaf object.

3. ☑ **A, C.** In order to create a User object, you must enter a value for the login name and a last name property for the user. Both are required. NDS allows you to create objects that have properties associated with them. In NDS, there are three components that make up a resource, namely, objects, properties, and values. Each object in NDS has a different set of properties. Each of these properties has a value associated with it. A property is like a field in traditional file designs and a value is the data that goes in the field (property). Some of the other properties that are applicable to a User object are: given name, full name, generational qualifier (like Sr., Jr., II, III, IV, etc.), middle initial, other name, title, description, location, department, telephone, and fax number. These properties are not required. Since everyone in an organization has a title, let's take a look at the title property for the User object. A value could be senior vice president, network engineer, or short-order cook.

☒ **B.** Given name is incorrect because you don't have to put a value in the given name property. **D.** Title is incorrect because you don't have to put a value in the title property either.

4. ☑ **A, B, C.** The reason the new administrator cannot create an Organizational Unit under the MickiM object is because MickiM is a User object, which happens to be a leaf object. Also, a container must be created within another container. Therefore, NDS simply won't allow it, and all three statements are correct. In fact, if you click on a User object in NetWare Administrator and attempt to use the Create option, it will be dimmed or grayed, implying Create is disabled and cannot be executed. If you were to click on an Organizational Unit object and then Create, the Create option will be in bold or black, implying the Create activity is a valid operation.

☒ **D.** Leaf objects can only contain other leaf objects, is incorrect since leaf objects cannot contain any other objects at all. NDS allows you to create container objects to hold other container objects and leaf objects but a leaf object cannot contain any other leaf objects. A leaf object will have properties and values.

5. ☑ **A, C, D, E.** Workstation Manager allows you to manage your Windows 95 and NT Workstations from within NDS. The services provided by Workstation Manager are listed in the following table.

☒ **B.** is incorrect because there is no Printer Management service.

Service	Operating System	Purpose
Workstation Inventory	Windows NT and 95	Maintains an inventory of workstation hardware and applications in NDS
System Policy Management	Windows NT and 95	Allows centralized control over system policies
Password Synchronization	Windows NT	Synchronizes passwords between NT and NetWare for a user
User Account Manager	Windows NT	Removes the need for users to be in a local or domain directory database on NT
Activity Scheduling	Windows NT and 95	Allows scheduling of programs to execute
Desktop Management	Windows NT and 95	Allows you to manage the user's desktop appearance

6. ☑ **B.** NDS object rights allow a person trustee access to the object in some form. The object rights are: Supervisor, Browse, Create, Delete, and Rename. The Supervisor right gives complete control over the object. Browse only allows the trustee to look at an NDS object. The Create NDS right allows the trustee to create an object within a particular container NDS object. Delete permits the dispensing of the object, and Rename changes the name of an NDS object. Note that NDS rights have nothing to do with file-system rights. File-system rights are at the file and directory level within the DOS/Windows file system. NDS rights deal with the NDS directory tree. They are two different tree structures.

☒ **A.** Property is incorrect because Property rights allow a trustee to access the values in a property. **C.** Inherited Rights Filter (IRF) is not correct because the IRF is used to filter out unwanted rights from flowing down in the NDS directory tree. **D.** Effective rights is not correct because they are the true rights a trustee can use. Effective rights are exercised after your NDS rights have been passed through the IRF and are explicitly granted.

7. ☑ **B.** RF. Ralph will have Effective rights of Read and File Scan to the Production folder. Effective overrides any rights that are inherited from above and it overrides the Inherited Rights Filter (IRF). By having the entry of Ralph for the folder Shift1, it is implied that a trustee assignment was made. Ralph's trustee assignment is Read and File Scan. Remember, if a trustee assignment is made, these become the Effective rights. You must also include group trustee assignments. If a user is a member of a group and that group has a trustee assignment, then the user's Effective rights are a combination of all the rights as a user and as a member of the group.
☒ **A.** is incorrect, since Ralph would not get all of these rights. The IRF allows all of the rights if they are inherited from above. Nothing was inherited from Production. **C.** is incorrect, since Ralph does get some rights. **D.** is incorrect because it is nowhere in the structure in the question.

8. ☑ **C.** Although Mike is a trustee in the Sales folder, he does not have a trustee assignment in the NewLeads folder. Therefore, the Effective rights of sales flow down as the inherited from above entry in the folder NewLeads. Then, the inherited from above entry must pass through the IRF. Only when the right is in both places will it become an effective right. So, RWCEMF are the rights inherited from sales and the IRF allows SRWCEF, so Mike's Effective rights are RWCEF.
☒ **A.** This is an incorrect answer because it is just the inherited from above entry. The inherited rights must first get through the filter (IRF) in order for the right to be effective. **B.** is incorrect because it is the filter. The rights in the filter do not equate to the Effective rights. First, you must have rights inherited before they can pass through the IRF. **D.** The Supervisory right is not an effective right to either sales or NewLeads, therefore it is an incorrect answer.

9. ☑ **D.** As a trustee, Bob gets his User Trustee rights, R and F. Because he is a group member of production and engineering and because group trustee assignments have been made to those groups, he also gets WCE (from production) and CMA (from engineering). So, his Effective rights are RWCEMFA. Note that the Create right is listed in both of groups, but he still only gets Create once. You either have the rights or you don't—the Create right applies to both production and engineering and is not two different rights. Trustee assignments override the inheritance and IRF concept. When calculating Effective rights for a trustee, the trustee gets both user assignments and all group assignments as long as the user is a member of the group.

   ☒ **A.** This is incorrect because this is the IRF and his Effective rights are not what is in the IRF. **B, C.** are both incorrect because they have to list just what is in the groups. Neither of these includes the user trustee assignment.

10. ☑ **B, C, D.** When planning for file-system security, Zac should not grant unnecessary rights at any level. If the IRF on a given level allows everything, then from that point downward, the Effective rights will be affected. Rights flow down and once they get through the IRF, become the Effective rights for that level. Giving someone Security Equivalence means that user has the same rights as another user throughout the entire file system. Zac should grant access at lower levels because this minimizes the number of rights that get inherited (or flow down) in the DOS tree. Lower levels means fewer folders than if the rights were granted at higher levels.

    ☒ **A.** is incorrect because if Zac grants greater access at a higher level, these get passed through the IRF and become Effective rights at a certain level. Since rights flow down, by granting greater access on higher-level directories, you are affecting what gets inherited from that point downward in the DOS tree.

11. ☑ **B.** The RIGHTS command can be used at the DOS command line to make trustee assignments. This command will allow you to set rights to a particular folder or file. It takes the form:

```
RIGHTS path +rights_list /NAME=trustee's_NDS_context
```

Note in this sample code, that the plus symbol (+) is used to add rights to the current list of rights. A minus sign (–) could be used to take the rights away. The rights that would go in the list are: Supervisory (S), Read (R), Write (W), Create (C), Erase (E), File scan (F), Modify (M), and Access Control (A).

☒ **A.** The FLAG command is used to set attributes, not rights, and is incorrect. **C.** The CX command is used to show or set your NDS context and is therefore incorrect. **D.** The LOGIN command is used to actually log into a Novell₀ server **E.** The WHOAMI command is used to identify your login name.

12. ☑ **B.** The WSREG32.EXE is a program that is run on the workstation to register the workstation. Workstations are registered with NDS and this can be executed in a login script. WSREG32.EXE is located in SYS\PUBLIC on a server. You could also register your workstation in the NetWare Application Launcher (NAL.EXE).

☒ **A.** The WSRIGHTS.EXE command is located in SYS\PUBLIC\WIN32 and it is used to grant the appropriate rights for NEBO. Therefore, it is an incorrect answer. **C.** WSREG16.EXE is used to register Windows 3.1x workstations to NEBO and it is an incorrect answer, too. **D.** NWADMIN.EXE is used to manage NDS and is incorrect.

13. ☑ C. Windows NT and Windows 95 allow creation of a system policy. A system policy governs what users can do and what appears on the desktop. The default name of the Windows NT system policy file is called NTCONFIG.POL. The default name of a Windows 95 system policy file is CONFIG.POL. You could change the name of either of them by enabling the Remote Update option and changing the name of the path to reflect the new name of the system policy file.

☒ A. The Accessibility Options allows you to configure options that assist disabled users, and is an incorrect answer. B. It is not advised to alter the Registry on any computer unless you need to. Most things can be done with Windows utilities. This happens to be one option that can be changed with Windows. D. is incorrect because this cannot be done through Console options. Console options modify the way the DOS prompt appears.

14. ☑ D. When referring to an object in a login script, make sure you refer to the object by its Distinguished name. Remember the object name is the location in the NDS tree based on [Root]. If you refer to the object based on the Relative Distinguished name, the resource may not be found. For example, when capturing a printer, refer to it in a login script as:

```
#CAPTURE S=.Print_Server.Payroll.Meadors-Corp
Q=.Print_que.Payroll.Meadors-Corp
```

☒ A, B, C. are incorrect because they do not fully qualify the name of the NDS object.

15. ☑ C. Set Security Equivalence on the User object to be the same as your User object. Security Equivalence allows you to grant an object the same rights another object has. This is typically used for making one User object resemble another User object in terms of rights. Use caution when giving out Security Equivalence since one object will now have the same rights. If you grant an object to be Security Equivalent to the [Root] of the NDS tree, you effectively give that object all Supervisory rights to every object in the NDS tree.

☒ A. Set the Compare property for the User object is incorrect because you cannot set the Compare property for the User object. You would set the Compare property for a *property* for a User object. B. Change the IRF to block out Supervisory NDS rights is incorrect since blocking Supervisory NDS rights has nothing to do with one object having the same rights as another. D. Change the Effective rights variable to be the same as your User object is incorrect because there is no Effective rights variable. Effective rights are not set per se. They are the actual rights an object has which include the rights inherited, rights masked with the IRF, and trustee rights.

16. ☑ **B.** The Print Queue object represents a folder on a NetWare volume that holds the print jobs prior to actually being printed. A print job is a print request initiated by a user. When creating a Print Queue object, you must assign it to a NetWare volume. The volume is an area of disk and the disk is on a NetWare server. You can only create a queue on a Novell server. As jobs are printed to a single printer, the print jobs are placed in a folder. If the printer is available, the jobs in the print queue will be sent to the physical print device on a first-come-first-served basis. Of course, the priority of the print job can be changed in case a vice president wants that special report *now*. If the printer is unavailable, or offline due to being turned off or out of paper, the print jobs will wait in the print queue until the printer is online again.

 ☒ **A.** The Print Server object is the program that is running at a NetWare server that manages the network printing process. The print server will send the jobs from the print queue to the Printer object. The Printer object is logical representation of the physical print device. The Print Server object does not represent the disk location. **C.** The Printer object represents the physical print device. The print device may be attached to a NetWare Server or to a workstation. The Printer object points to the physical print device attached to that server or workstation. The Printer object does not represent the disk-storage area, so this answer is incorrect. **D.** Although the server maintains the volume where the Print Queue is assigned, the Server object itself does not store the object that represents the disk storage area.

17. ☑ **C.** You can have your workstation automatically registered via a login script as long as you have the PLATFORM variable checking for "W95". If it's there, execute the PUBLIC\WSREG32.EXE program.

 ☒ **A.** is incorrect because it assumes the workstation's platform is Windows NT. For a Windows NT Workstation, you should run the WSREG32.EXE, too. **B.** is incorrect because it is set to run WSREG16.EXE instead of WSREG32.EXE. WSREG16.EXE is the registration program for a Windows 3.1 workstation. **D.** is incorrect because it assumes the workstation is Windows 3.1x and it runs the WSREG16.EXE program.

18. ☑ **B, C.** You can manage printers as part of Z.E.N.works Workstation Manager. Printers can be set up for Windows 95 workstations, Windows NT Workstations and Windows NT users. Right now, there is no Windows 95 user printer option. A user printer will be available for a user no matter what workstation they log into. This is like a roaming user profile in that respect. A workstation printer will be available for the workstation no matter what user logs in to the workstation.

    ☒ **A, D.** These are incorrect statements. An NT user printer follows the user, not the workstation. An NT Workstation printer stays with the workstation and not the user.

19. ☑ **A, B.** There are at least two methods of installing a NetWare 5 server. The Graphical User Interface (GUI) issues text screens to gather information such as type of installation, regional settings, and mouse and video settings. Then if there is enough RAM, the installation program will execute the GUI phase. Here, the server name is created, the protocol is chosen, and the time zone and license information is loaded. You can also create the server in a new tree or insert the server in an existing tree. If there is not enough available memory on the server, the installation stays in the text-mode phase.

    ☒ **C.** The WUSER.EXE program is the Remote Control Agent software for a workstation. **D.** The Remote Control Agent is software that allows you to connect to a workstation.

20. ☑ **C, D, E.** The type of information that is gathered during the GUI phase of the server installation is:

1. Server name
2. Protocol selection, such as IP, IPX, and IP only
3. Time zone
4. Whether the installation of the server is in a new or existing tree
5. License
6. Whether to install additional products such as online documentation

☒ **A, B.** The type of information that is needed during the text-based installation is as follows:

- Whether this is an upgrade or a new installation
- Regional settings such as country name, code page, and keyboard type
- Whether or not the installation finds the disk drives and network adapter. If so, it will automatically load the drivers for them. Otherwise, you must select a driver for them.
- Whether or not the NetWare partition is created

21. ☑ E. The block size depends on the size of the volume. The following table summarizes Novell's recommended default block size for a volume:

Size of Volume	Default Block Size
0–31MB	4KB or 8KB
31–149MB	16KB
150–499MB	32KB
500+MB	64KB

By using the default block size you are minimizing memory and disk space. The larger block sizes use less server memory but they use more disk space. However, using block suballocation will minimize the amount of disk space used. Block suballocation is a term applied to NetWare's ability to optimize disk space by storing data in small 512KB-sized suballocated blocks. The smaller block size requires more server memory to keep track of the File Allocation Table (FAT) and Directory Entry Table (DET) files; this is because each volume has a separate FAT and DET.

☒ A, B, C, D. These are all incorrect default block sizes for the default volume of 1GB.

22. ☑ A, D. In order to install a computer as a server, the computer will need to have at least 64MB of RAM, be a 486-or-better CPU, have about 250MB of hard disk space, and have a VGA or SVGA monitor. The computers will also need a network adapter in order to connect to the network. The computers should also have a PS/2 or serial mouse and an ISO9660-compatible CD-ROM.

☒ B. has too little hard-disk space. C. would be great for a server, but a Pentium III-class processor is not required.

23. ☑ **A, D.** The minimum default block size is 4KB, so this is the minimum amount of disk space that will be used to store a file. If the file is 6KB, it will take up two blocks of 4KB each for a total of 8KB. In effect, 2KB is wasted (8KB–6KB) and cannot be used by another file or folder. Novell introduced block suballocation to optimize this disk space. With block suballocation, the storage is in units of 512 bytes (or half of 1KB). If the same 6KB file is stored using block suballocation, it would take up one 4KB block and then four 512-byte suballocated blocks. Here, there is no waste; the 2KB that was wasted, without block suballocation, can be used to store other files.

    ☒ **B.** Blocks are not suballocated in 4-KB chunks but 512-byte chunks, so this is incorrect. **C.** Block suballocation does not waste any disk space, and this is an incorrect response.

24. ☑ **B.** The server installation process will attempt to automatically detect the disk drives, tape drives, and CD-ROM drives. It will also try to detect the network adapters. However, if it fails to detect one, it could be a network adapter configuration problem or it could be that the adapter is too new to be on the server installation program. In the latter case, James should take the disk that came with the network adapter and install it from there. The installation program will allow you to install the driver from floppy.

    ☒ **A.** James should not arbitrarily change the interrupt to IRQ 0. This is already being used. IRQs are unique numbers that are used by the CPU and a device to signal each other. IRQs need to be unique so the CPU knows which device is talking to it. **C.** James should not install a Token Ring network adapter. Remember, from the company scenario, they are using 100 BASE T. These two network types are incompatible without a bridge or router. **D.** James is not required to run the IP protocol, so this is incorrect.

25. ☑ **A, C, D.** Zac needs to immediately upgrade this computer's CPU, RAM, and operating system. By installing a Pentium CPU with 16MB of RAM and Windows 95/98, he meets the hardware minimum. The minimum hardware requirements are as follows:

- DOS 5 or greater

- Windows 3.1, Windows 95/98, or Windows NT 4

- Network interface card (NIC)

- Minimum RAM (DOS/Windows 3.1 is 5MB and Windows 95/95/NT is 8MB)

In order to access the server, Zac will need to physically install a network interface card (NIC) on the computer. Since the machine is being upgraded to a Pentium, he might as well get a fast NIC. Most Pentium-class motherboards come with a PCI slot; these are typically 32-bit or 64-bit; faster than ISA/EISA NICs. Since the machine needs access to the Internet server, Zac needs to install the Client 32 for Windows 95. The fact that this is an Internet server means it is running TCP/IP. So, Zac must install TCP/IP.

☒ **B.** is incorrect since installing a printer to the computer is not a necessary requirement. E. Install the IPX/SPX protocol for this client does not meet the need of accessing an Internet server. An Internet server will be running TCP/IP. TCP/IP is the protocol that runs the Internet. All workstations and servers that are connected to the Internet must have TCP/IP loaded.

26. ☑ **A.** MLID, LSLC32.NLM, IPX.NLM/IPHLPR.NLM, CLIENT32.NLM. Novell's Client 32 software supports the open data-link (ODI) specification. ODI is software written to be modular and allows a NIC to support multiple protocols concurrently. Microsoft's competitive standard is NDIS. The Client 32 includes several software programs called NetWare Loadable Modules (files ending in .NLM). One of them is the the multiple-link interface driver (MLID) that allows the transmission of data through the NIC. This component is different for each NIC. An Ethernet NIC will not use the same MLID as a Token Ring NIC. Think of the MLID as analogous to a printer driver. Not all printer drivers support the same printer. The MLID will have a .LAN extension instead of a .NLM extension. The next software is called LSLC32.NLM. It handles communication at Layer 2, the data-link layer, of the OSI model and provides for communication for the protocol and the NIC. The third piece of software is either IPX.NLM (for the IPX protocol) or IPXHLPR.NLM (for the IP protocol) Depending on which protocol you want to run, you would pick either IPX.NLM or IPXHLPR.NLM. This is your protocol software. The last piece of software is called CLIENT32.NLM. This software provides for the client's connection to the network. The CLIENT32.NLM allows for drive mappings and capturing of printers. The software components must be loaded in this order: MLID, LSLC32.NLM, IPX.NLM/IPHLPR.NLM, and finally CLIENT32.NLM.

☒ **B, C, D.** are all incorrect because they have the load order out of sequence.

27. ☑ **A.** D:\PRODUCTS\WINNT\I386\SETUPNW. Zac can install the Client 32-bit software on a Windows NT computer. Assuming his CD-ROM is the D: drive and that he wants to install at the Start|Run box, Zac would have to type in the full path to the installation program, SETUPNW.EXE. For Windows NT, the full path to the program is \PRODUCTS\WINNT\I386\SETUPNW. The WINNT\I386 folder is a standard Microsoft folder on an NT computer that holds a 32-bit Intel-platform, hence the I386 program code. So, Novell kept that part of the path name consistent. Remember that a full-path name begins at the drive letter, D:, followed by the root symbol, the "\". The full path name to the Windows 95 installation program, SETUP.EXE, is \PRODUCTS\WIN95\IBM_ENU\SETUP.

☒ **B.** D\PRODUCTS\WIN95\IBM_ENU\SETUP is incorrect because it is the full path name to the Windows 95 Client software. **C.** D:/PRODUCTS/WINNT/I386/SETUPNW is incorrect because the separator between the folder names is the incorrect symbol. The correct symbol for the separator is the backslash, "\", instead of the forward slash, "/". **D.** D:/PRODUCTS/WIN95/IBM_ENU/SETUP is incorrect because it uses the incorrect separator symbol and it gives the complete full path name to the Windows 95 Client software.

28. ☑ **A, D, E.** Login time restrictions limit a user's login access to a certain time. You have the ability to control this by blocking out the times when you don't want the user logging in. By default, a user can log in any time of the day and any day of the week. However, if you want to restrict the time, then you could click in the appropriate time box as shown in the following illustration. The cells that are gray colored are the times when the user cannot log in. The light colored cells are when the user can log in. So, the user can log in Sunday at any time. The user can log in Tuesday at 8 am, but not at 8 pm. The user can also log in Thursday at 2 pm.

☒ **B.** The user cannot log in at all on Saturday since all time slots are blocked in gray. When you click the time cell block, it turns gray indicating the user cannot log in at that time. **C.** The user cannot log in at all on Monday.

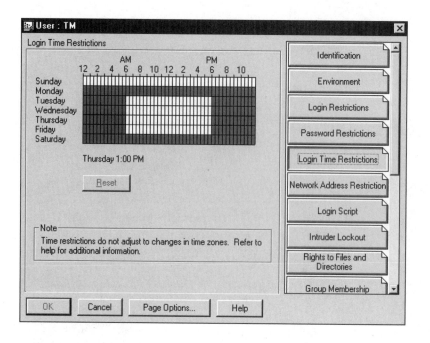

29. ☑   **C.** During the login process, a NetWare server will authenticate a user. A user needs only a single login name because any server in the NDS tree can authenticate the user. The password is not sent across the network. Instead, the workstation creates an encrypted code that represents the user name, password, workstation address and other login properties. This encrypted code is created only for the login process. The server then uses the same algorithm to create an encrypted code for the workstation and, if the two match, network access is granted.

   ☒   **A.** is incorrect. The password is not sent over the wire. **B.** The password is sent in a separate packet from the username so there would be no way a hacker could put them together. **D.** The password is sent only when login scripts are in use. This is a false statement and is therefore incorrect.

30. ☑ **B.** You must run NPTWIN95.EXE at the workstation that has the printer physically attached to it. PSERVER.NLM running on the server will forward the print job from the print queue to the computer in the network that has NPTWIN95.EXE loaded for that printer. The general name for the program that runs NPTWIN95.EXE is called NPRINTER.EXE. NPRINTER.EXE is run on a DOS or Windows 3.1 client computer with a network printer attached. If the printer is attached to a server, a similar program is loaded on the server automatically. It is called NPRINTER.NLM.

☒ **A.** NPRINTER.EXE is the generic name for the program that runs on a workstation with a network printer attached, but this program is loaded on DOS and Windows 3.1 Client computer, not on Windows 95 clients. **C.** PSERVER.NLM runs on the NetWare server and makes the NetWare server a Print Server. It is not loaded on a client. **D.** PCONSOLE.NLM creates the network printing objects. It is not loaded on a client.

31. ☑ **A, B, D.** You can execute the Windows 3.1, Windows 95, and Windows 98 Remote Control Agent software using any of these methods:

- Run NetWare Application Launcher (NAL.EXE) from the PUBLIC folder.

- Have a login script command execute WUSER as in the following syntax: #F:\PUBLIC\WUSER.EXE.

- Run WUSER.EXE manually by clicking on it in the PUBLIC folder.

☒ **C.** The utility NTASCFG.EXE is the Windows NT service that executes the Remote Control Agent. It can be automatically started as a Service in Control Panel on an NT Workstation computer. NTASCFG.EXE is not used to run the Remote Control Agent for a Windows 95/98 computer workstation.

32. ☑   **A, B, C.** In NDS, we deal with security of the [Root] object, container objects and leaf objects. The [Root] object is the top of the NDS tree. If a user had complete rights to the [Root] object they have those rights throughout the NDS tree. So, be careful with the [Root] object. Container objects represent that class of objects that hold other containers or leaf objects. Leaf objects are the objects that represent users, printers, servers, and volumes. You can apply security to both container and leaf objects.
    ☒   **D.** is an incorrect answer because a hardware address is not an NDS object type.

33. ☑   **A.** The Typeful Distinguished Name always begins with a period, or dot. The dot indicates that the user is referenced from the [Root] and the User object is fully distinguished from any other name in the NDS tree. If another user named Mel existed in the Accounting container, the Typeful Distinguished Name for that user would be .CN=Mel.OU=Accounting.O=MEI. Notice the first period, or dot. The Mel in Accounting is a different user, with different properties, values, and possibly rights, than the Mel in Production. The distinguished name starts at the top container, or [Root], to distinguish one user from another. By having the object-type abbreviations in front of each object, it is clarifying to NDS what object type is in use. The common codes are shown in the following table.

Abbreviation	Description	Object class
CN	Common Name	Leaf
OU	Organizational Unit	Container
O	Organization	Container

☒   **B.** O=MEI.OU=Production.CN=Mel is incorrect because the object names are backwards. In NDS, you always refer to the object by first specifying the inner-most object in the NDS tree, continuing upwards in the tree, until you get to the top. **C.** Mel.Production.MEI is incorrect because the object does not include the initial period, implying Distinguished, and it does not use the abbreviation codes, implying Typeful. Actually, this is a Typeless Relative Distinguished name. Relative means you are referring to the object based on your current context and not from the [Root].
D. CN=Mel.OU=Production.O=MEI is incorrect because it is not a Distinguished Name. It is, however, a Typeful Relative Distinguished name.

34. ☑ **A, B, C**. The Home Directory, Title, and Last Login properties are all valid properties for a User object. The Home Directory is a property that identifies a default location for the user's file to be stored. A Home Directory will have a volume that the files are stored on and then a path to the folder on that volume. A volume exists on a server and can be created either at install time or at a later date using NWCONFIG at the server console. The Title is a property that can identify what position the user holds within the company. For example, if a user named Micki was a vice president in an organization, you could use *vice president* as a value for the Title property of the user. The Last Login property is not a property where you can put values. It just identifies the date and time the user logged in. It is blank if the user has not logged in at all. Note this is a good place to look if a security breach occurs. The Last Login is proof that a user did log in at a certain time.

☒ **D**. Print Server Name. This is an incorrect property for a User object, but it is a valid property for a Printer object.

35. ☑ **A, B, C, D**. Todd can create a User object using either NetAdmin, NWADMIN, ConsoleOne, or UIMPORT. NetAdmin is a menu-based tool that can be used to create User objects as well as other objects. NetAdmin cannot be used to set up printers. NWADMIN is the Windows-based tool for setting up User objects along with other objects. NWADMIN can be used to set up printing. Don't discount the use of NetAdmin. Sometimes NWADMIN has problems that NetAdmin does not, and it's a good backup tool. ConsoleOne is the server-console tool that is used to create User objects. UIMPORT is used to import a lot of users that may be in a database file from another application. You would run the UIMPORT utility to add a large number of users to NDS.

☒ **E**. The CX command is not used to create User objects. It is used to change or view your current context in NDS when at the DOS prompt.

36. ☑ **A, C, D, E.** The user object will receive the following default rights at User object creation:

- Browse object rights to the User object itself
- Read Property rights to all the user's own property rights
- Read and Write property rights to the user's login script. This enables the user to create his own login script
- Read and Write property rights to the Print Job Configuration property. This allows users to manage their own print jobs.
- All file system rights to the user's own home directory if one is created

☒ **B.** The user does not get the Supervisory right to the [Root] object. That would give him Supervisory access to all the objects in the NDS tree.

37. ☑ **D.** The Dixie User object should be set security equivalent to Todd. By setting Security Equal To, Dixie will have rights identical to Todd's.
☒ **A.** Creating a login script is used to customize the login process. It is not used for managing security, so this is an incorrect answer. **B.** Manually assigning all the same rights to Dixie that Todd has would be too impractical. That would mean you would have to check all NDS objects and properties in the NDS tree to see Todd's NDS rights. You would also have to check all the files and folders to see what files and folders Todd could access. **C.** Using a user template when creating the Dixie object would not give Dixie the same security rights that Todd had.

38. ☑ **A, B.** The user could have a network address restriction. This could prevent logging in from certain workstations. The user could be limited in terms of the number of concurrent connections he could have. This would limit the number of login sessions he could have open at one time. If set to *one*, then the user could only log in once.
☒ **C.** The user has probably not forgotten their password. They just logged into another computer. **D.** The user account is most likely not disabled since the user just logged in.

39. ☑ **C.** The NDIR command is similar to the DOS DIR command except the NDIR command shows more network related information, such as rights and ownership. The DOS DIR does not show ownership and rights information. The following illustration shows a sample screenshot of the NDIR command.

☒ **A.** NLIST is used to search for NDS objects and not for files and folders. **B.** The CX command is used to set and change your NDS context. **D.** NWADMIN is used to administer the Novell NDS database.

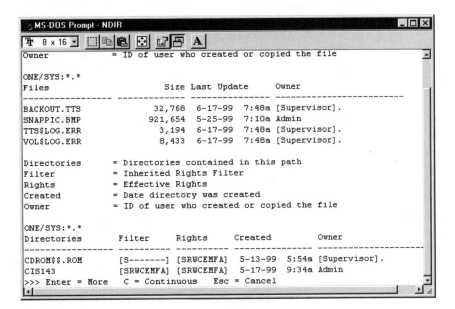

40. ☑ **C.** When installing Z.E.N.works to manage your clients, the NDS object right that is needed is Supervisor. This is because Z.E.N.works will modify the NDS schema. The NDS schema has a list of all object types and the type of properties that are required or optional. An administrator can extend the schema by changing it. Since Z.E.N.works extends the schema, the Supervisor right is needed.

☒ **A, B, D.** are incorrect because they don't give enough permission.

41. ☑   **C.** Create multiple administrator objects. The NDS security guidelines are:

   - Use multiple administrators that are security equivalent to ADMIN, then disable ADMIN so hackers won't have a login name to try.

   - Use Group trustee assignments to assign trustees. Adding a user to a group that has a trustee assignment is easier than making individual user trustee assignments.

   - Do not use Security Equivalence, because it is difficult to track those users.

   - Don't grant more rights than are needed.

   - Grant the rights appropriate to a trustee's function.

   - Be careful assigning rights to [Root] or [Public].

   ☒   **A, B, D.** These are all incorrect because they don't follow the guidelines.

42. ☑   **D.** The Browse rights is the trustee right that will only allow you to see other NDS objects in the NDS tree. You cannot create, delete, rename or modify the properties of an object with merely the Browse right. By default, all users are granted the Browse right to the [Root] object. This allows users to see other objects in the NDS tree before and after they log into a server.
   ☒   **A.** The Supervisor right gives a user complete control over an NDS object. This would not only allow a user to see but also to create, delete, and rename other objects. Supervisor rights include: Browse, Create, Delete, Rename, and Inheritable objects rights. **B, C.** These are incorrect because they give too much permission over the object. Rename allows you to change an object's name property. The Create right allows you to create an NDS object. We only need Browse in this case.

43. ☑ **A, C, D, E.** The following components make up NDPS:

- Printer Agent
- Printer Gateways
- NDPS Manager
- NDPS Broker
- Print Client

The Printer Agent is the focal point of NDPS. It combines the same functions as the traditional (non-NDPS) NetWare Printer, Print Queue, and Print Server objects. The Printer Agent is software that runs on a server or firmware embedded in a network printing device. Printer Gateways provide for communication between non-NDPS printers and NDPS clients so NDPS clients can put jobs in non-NDPS print queues. The NDPS Manager is where NDPS Printer Agents are created as well as managed. The NDPS Broker provides a list of NDPS printers to an NDPS client, provides for event notification, and provides for a central location for printer drivers, banners, and print fonts. The NDPS Print Client is software integrated with NetWare 5 Client software that transmits the print jobs to the Printer Agent.

☒ **B.** The Print Server object, used for non-NDPS printing, is not part of the NDPS subsystem.

44. ☑ **A, B, C, D.** The Help Request application allows users to use the Mail, Call, Info, and Help buttons. The Mail button allows users to send e-mail messages via the network's messaging service. The user's e-mail address is used automatically. The user can enter a subject and a line of text for the message. The user can view sent messages. The messages will include the workstation's name and user's context that used the Help Request application to send the message. The Call button will allow a user to see the name and phone number of a contact person if mail is not used. The name and phone number are retrieved from the Help Desk policy. The Info button has two tabs, User and Help Desk. The User tab includes user-specific information and the Help Desk tab provides information such as an e-mail address of someone to contact. The Help button allows users to review Help Requestor functions.

☒ **E.** There is no such button as the Enabler button, so it is incorrect.

45. ☑ **A, B, C.** The Printer Gateway enables communication between non-NDPS printers so NDPS clients can place jobs in the print queues. Novell provides for the following types of gateways:

   ■ Novell gateways

   ■ Third-party gateways

   Novell gateway will support a printer that does not have a Printer Agent connected to a NetWare client or server. Third-party agents are developed by other vendors and are available to support network attached printers in order to provide access to non-NDPS-aware printers. Currently, NetWare 5 contains the Hewlett-Packard and Xerox gateways to provide for this support. The Novell gateway uses a Print Device Subsystem (PDS) to store information in a database that is used for the Printer Agents. There is also a port handler to ensure there is communication between the PDS and the physical-print device.

   ☒ **D.** There is no such entity as a Microsoft gateway related to Novell NetWare NDPS printing.

46. ☑ **A, B, D.** NetWare Application Launcher will allow you to push or pull applications to the desktop. NAL can also be used to manage applications. It allows you to modify the Registry and .INI files. You can also create drive mappings and capture printers. Another benefit not listed in the answers is single seat administration. Applications are built as objects in NDS, just like other resources. You also get security with NAL because users have to be granted rights to the Application object before they can use it.

   ☒ **C.** is incorrect because NAL does not provide Print Server management.

47. ☑   D. The Read property right only gives the user the ability to look at the contents of a property. For example, if one had the Read right to a user's Last Name property, they could see what someone's last name was. The Read property right does not give the user the ability to modify the value stored in a property.

☒   A. This incorrect because is gives someone too much capability. With Supervisor rights, a user has complete control over an object's properties. He can modify or delete a value. **B.** With the Compare right, you cannot see the contents of a property. Compare compares a property value with a given value to determine if they are equal or not; either True or False is returned. **C.** There is no Browse property right. Browse is an object right. A list of the Property rights appears in the following table.

Right	Description
Supervisor (S)	Gives all other Property rights to that property
Compare (C)	Gives the ability to compare a value to another value. Only returns True or False. With Compare, a user cannot see the contents of a property.
Read (R)	With Read, you can only see the contents of a property. This implies the Compare right.
Write (W)	With the Write property right, you can modify, add, or delete a property value
Add-Self (A)	With Add-Self, the trustee can add or remove itself from a value in a property. Add-Self implies the Write right.

48. ☑ **B.** In order for an end user to install their own printer, they would use the NWPMW32.EXE located in SYS:PUBLIC\WIN32. They would follow these steps to install their printer:

1. At the printer menu select New.
2. Select Add.
3. Select Browse and locate the NDPS printer in the correct context.
4. Select Ok.
5. Select Install.
6. The installed printers will show up in the Novell Printer Manager window.

☒ **A.** The NWCONFIG.NLM is not used on a workstation. It is the installation utility on NetWare 5. No NLMs can run on a workstation. **C.** The RCONSOLE command is run on a workstation to connect to a NetWare server. **D.** The INSTALL.NLM is equivalent to NWCONFIG.NLM; however, INSTALL does not run on NetWare 5, but on pre-5 NetWare.

49. ☑ **A.** A container login script will be executed for all users that are in a certain container. By clicking on the details page of an Organizational Unit, you can created the login script. There are several types of login scripts. They are executed in the following order:

1. Container (if present)
2. Profile (if present)
3. User (if present)
4. Default (if there is no User login script)

☒ **B.** There is no such login script called an Organization login script. Even if there were one, we are discussing an Organizational Unit, not an Organization. However, you can assign an Organizational Unit a login script. In that case, the login script would execute for all users in a particular Organizational Unit. **C.** The User login script will only execute for a single user. **D.** The profile login script is executed for a group of users. Think of a profile login script as a group type of login script. But it won't be executed for all users in a container, so the answer is incorrect.

50. ☑ **C.** NAL implements a wrapper technology whereby NAL.EXE is executed, but it will call or launch another program depending upon the operating system of the workstation. The following table lists operating systems and their NAL-launched executable name. NAL selects the application icons to display for the user, which is dependent upon the user's operating system. NAL updates the workstation files from the SYS:PUBLIC\NALLIB folder. Local workstation files will only be modified if the files in NALLIB are newer than the local workstation files.

☒ **A, B, D.** The other answer choices are incorrect because they are the NAL-launched programs for operating systems other than Windows NT Workstation, as shown in the following table.

Operating System	NAL Launched Program
Windows 3.1	NALW31.EXE
Windows 95	NALW95.EXE
Windows NT Workstation	NALWIN32.EXE
Windows 98	NALWIN32.EXE

51. ☑ **B.** Inheritance. NDS rights will flow down from one level to another level in the NDS tree. This is called inheritance. Both Object and Property rights can be inherited. An explicit trustee assignment is used to give a user certain rights to an NDS object. Inheritance can be altered by using an IRF. It masks rights and keeps them from flowing down.

☒ **A.** NDS object rights are a class of rights that a trustee can be assigned. This is an incorrect answer. **C.** NDS property rights are also just a class of rights that a trustee can be assigned. **D.** Trustee rights are those object and property rights that have been assigned.

52. ☑ **C.** The execution order of login scripts is as follows: container, profile, user, default. If a container login script is created, it will execute first. Then, if there is a profile login script, it will execute next. A user login script is executed next if it exists. Finally, the default login script is executed if there is not a user login script. It is easier to manage the login scripts at the container or profile login script level. All user objects in a container that has a login script will execute the container's login script. So it affects a large number of users. If there is no user login script, the default login script will be executed. This ensures basic drive mappings to PUBLIC.

☒ **A, B, D.** are all incorrect because they are in incorrect order.

53. ☑ **A, C.** In order to install a NetWare server, you must create a DOS partition on the hard disk of the chosen computer. The steps are as follows:

1. Use FDISK to create a DOS partition of at least 50MB.
2. Use FORMAT C: /S to transfer the system files to the hard disk.
3. Load your CD-ROM drivers so you can use the NetWare 5 installation CD.
4. During the installation process, a NetWare partition is created. This is used to store the system files such as the NLMs.

☒ **B.** There is no Macintosh partition created on a NetWare5 server. Macintosh files can be stored on a NetWare volume as long as you load the MAC name space. **D.** There is no OS/2 partition created on a NetWare server, so this is incorrect.

54. ☑ **A, B, C, D.** The .AOT file is composed of the following:

1. .INI file changes
2. Registry changes
3. Text file changes
4. Lists of files that are copied during application installation
5. Macros defined during the installation
6. Application object name

☒ **E.** NDS changes are not recorded in the .AOT file.

55. ☑ **D.** Inheritance flows from one object in the NDS tree to another on a lower level. For example, if a user is located in a container and the container has the Read right, then inheritance will cause the user to have the Read right. However, if we no longer wanted this user to have the Read right, we could use IRF to block the Read right.

☒ **A.** Effective rights are calculated by what is inherited that passes through the filter. Effective rights can be set by trustee and group membership assignments too. **B.** Attributes do not apply to NDS objects. Attributes apply to file systems rights. **C.** File system rights are the set of rights that will apply to files and folders in the NDS tree. This is incorrect.

56. ☑ **D.** The correct location of the Z.E.N.works setup program is PRODUCTS\ZENWORKS. The name of the setup utility is SETUP.EXE, not SETUP.COM. It offers three types of installations and they are:

- ■ Typical   is recommended for most users
- ■ Compact   will install with minimum options
- ■ Custom   is suggested for advanced users and allows the users to change settings

☒ **A.** is NetWare Administrator and is used to handle NDS object management. **B.** is nonexistent software therefore it is incorrect. **C.** is the installation utility that you run on a NetWare server and is an incorrect answer.

57. ☑ **A, B, C, D.** Workstation Manager will allow you to manage a workstation's inventory. In order to do so, you will need to view Advanced Information on the Workstation object. You will see tabs that allow you to view the following type of information: Drives, Buses, Services, Resources, Display Adapters.

☒ **E.** You will not see the printers being captured, so this is an incorrect answer.

58. ☑   **D.** The Volume object in NetWare Administrator will give you information about the files and folders stored on it. By clicking on the Volume object, you can create folders and also delete the folders. You can administer file-system security here too by clicking on the object and then on Details. This is just another interface that allows you to create files and folders. You can still do it in Windows and DOS. The following illustration shows a screenshot of NetWare Administrator displaying folders on a volume.

☒   **A.** The Server object does not allow you to create files and folders on it. Although the files and folders are stored on a volume and the volume is stored on the server, this object will not allow you to manage files and folders. **B.** The User object is used for logging into a NetWare server. It has nothing to do with files and folders and is incorrect. **C.** The Group object is used to combine users that have like security characteristics and is an incorrect answer.

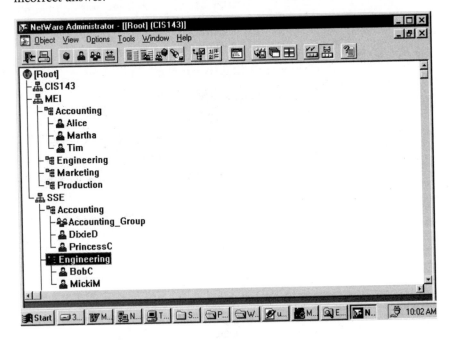

59. ☑ **D.** Mack would use the MAP command with the DEL option to delete a drive mapping. Up to 26 drive mappings are possible and these are logical pointers to physical devices; they are either on the local computer or on a network server.

☒ **A.** is incorrect because you use MAP with the NEXT option to actually create a regular drive mapping. **B.** The MAP command with the INS S16: option is used to create a search drive mapping. **C.** There is no such option as REMOVE on the MAP command, so this is incorrect.

60. ☑ **B.** The 32-bit version of NetWare Administrator is located on the PUBLIC folder, in the WIN32 folder as the program name NWADMIN32.EXE. This tool will allow the new contractor to fully administer NDS objects, security, and even partitioning and replication.

☒ **A, C.** are incorrect because they don't exist. **D.** NWCONFIG.NLM is not located in PUBLIC. It is located in the SYSTEM folder. It is not used to manage NDS objects, but is used to add licenses, create volumes and mirrors, create NetWare partitions, modify the server's configuration files (AUTOEXEC.NCF and STARTUP.NCF), and install other products. It is not the correct answer.

61. ☑ **D.** MAP ROOT. Mack should create a virtual ceiling (or fake root) at the users home-directory level. Mack would accomplish this by issuing a MAP ROOT command. For example, say a user named Tom had a home directory called HOME\TOM on the volume APPS on the server named BOSS. To set a fake root, then Mack would issue the following command:

```
F:\SYSTEM> MAP ROOT H:=BOSS\APPS\HOME\BOB
```

When Tom tried to change to the root directory or go above his current directory level, all he would see as his top-level directory would be \HOME\BOB.

☒ **A.** The MAP DEL command will remove a drive mapping so it is incorrect. **B.** The MAP INS command will create a search drive mapping and would do nothing to limit what a user would see. **C.** The MAP NEXT command creates a regular/standard drive mapping and would not limit what a user could see. **E.** The MAP /VER command will display version information and it will not limit what a user sees.

62. ☑ **B.** Workstation Manager is installed under Windows NT as a service. You would check Control Panel on the NT system for this. Once Windows NT Workstation Manager authenticates to Novell's NDS, it will check NDS periodically for any updates that need to occur on the NT Workstation. This checking is called polling and the default time is 10 minutes.

☒ **A, C, D.** are all incorrect answers.

63. ☑ **C.** With NDS, you can use Typeful or Typeless names when referring to an object. A Typeful name will use one of the abbreviation codes, such as CN, OU, or O, when referring to an NDS object. When referring to the NDS object with the Typeful name, you do not use the abbreviation codes. The abbreviation codes help NDS identify the type of object when retrieving object information. An example of a Typeful NDS name is .CN=TMeadors.OU=CIS.O=Meadors-Corp. Using the same example, the Typeless name would be .TMeadors.CIS.Meadors-Corp.

☒ **A, B.** are both incorrect because both Typeless and Typeful names can begin at the [Root]; neither are required to begin at [Root]. **D.** This answer is incorrect because Typeless names do not use the abbreviation codes while Typeless do.

64. ☑ **C.** Because he wants each user in the SALES container to have their login name appear during login, he should place an entry such as the one below in the login script for the container:

```
WRITE "Hello, %LOGIN_NAME"
```

By placing the login script in the container, Scott minimizes the effort of placing the statement in the user's login script.

☒ **A.** The variable he needs is %LOGIN_NAME, not %LOGIN_CONTEXT. The %LOGIN_CONTEXT variable will display the context in which the user is located. **B.** He could place the statement in each user's login script, but it would be more difficult to maintain. **D.** Scott cannot modify the default login script. He can only stop it from being executed by placing the NO_DEFAULT statement in a container or profile login script.

65. ☑ **B.** Scott must use the # symbol in front of the command in order for it to be executed. This is an external command and all external commands require the # symbol in front of them. Consider the sample code:

```
MAP F:= SERVER_A\SYS:APPS

#F:\ACCT.EXE
```

Note the first statement, the MAP command, will set a drive mapping to the server, volume, and folder that holds the program. The next statement refers to drive F:, followed by the program's name.

☒ **A.** is incorrect because it is reserved as a comment. **C.** The semicolon is also used as a comment. **D.** The FDISPLAY statement does not cause an external program to be executed. It will just display a text file.

66. ☑ **A, B, C.** Scott can use any of the following as a comment in a login script:

- REM
- REMARK
- Semicolon (;)
- Asterisk ()

Comments are useful because they provide documentation about what the login script does. An example of using all three symbols is:

```
REM This login script was created by Todd Meadors, MS, MBA, MCSE, CNE.

; It was created on May 23, 1999 at 11:48 /aN

It will execute for all users of the SALES department.
```

☒ **D.** The pound sign (#) is used to execute an external program. It is not used as a comment.

67. ☑ **C.** In order to see a user's hardware address, Scott will need to place the %P_STATION entry in the user's login script. If he wants the hardware address to appear for all users in a container, he should place the entry in a container login script. He should place an entry that looks like the following:

```
WRITE "Your Hardware Address is %P_STATION"
```

The hardware address is also known as the MAC address. It is hard-coded in the firmware of a network adapter. Here is a sample: 00-EE-E1-A1-FA-35.

☒ **A.** This is not a valid variable for a login script and is therefore incorrect. **B.** The %MACHINE variable represents the class of workstation such as IBM_PC and does not represent the hardware address. It is an incorrect answer. **D.** The %STATION variable represents the workstation's connection number for the server.

68. ☑ **B.** If you have multiple application servers when the Enable Load Balancing property is selected, the processing load will be distributed evenly. This is optimal for overall performance, because one server does not become a bottleneck. Enable Load Balancing is on the Fault Tolerance property page of an Application object.

☒ **A.** There is a Prompt user for Reboot property on the Distribution property page, which is not used for load balancing. This allows or disallows a user to confirm a computer reboot. **C.** Enabling one server to take over in the event another server crashes, occurs by selecting the Enable Fault Tolerance property on the Fault Tolerance property page. But this has nothing to do with balancing application load. **D.** There are two properties that allow you to modify Registry entries and change .INI files. They are Registry Settings and .INI Settings, respectively.

69. ☑   C. NDS allows you to create a Country object to represent the various countries in which your organization may have users. The Country object can store an Organizational Unit that can be used to represent divisions or departments that reside in that country. You would then place your User objects in the Organizational Unit of which she is a member.

☒   A. You should not create a leaf object for each of the countries. B. You should not create a Server object to represent the countries. Server objects are considered leaf objects and leaf objects cannot hold other objects. You would not have a place to put your User and Printer objects. D. You cannot create a [Public] trustee; it is not considered an object in NDS.

Part 8

Test Yourself:
Practice Exam 2:
NetWare®5
Advanced
Administration
(Exam 50-640)

Test Yourself:
Practice Exam 2
Questions

Q & A

Before you call to register for the actual NetWare 5 Advanced Administration exam (Exam # 50-640), take the following test and see how you make out. Set a timer for 105 minutes—the same time you'll have to take the live exam—and answer the following 73 questions in the time alloted. Once you've finished, turn to the Practice Exam 2 Answers section and check your score to see if you passed! Good luck!

Practice Exam 2 Questions

1. What task is required when upgrading a NetWare 3.1x server into an existing NDS™ tree with NetWare 4.1x servers?

   A. Updating the DS.NLM on all 4.1x servers to version 5.99 or higher

   B. Creating a new tree for the upgraded server, and then merging the trees together

   C. Defining a context for the new NetWare₀5 server

   D. Changing the name of the server to allow the NetWare 4.1x servers to recognize the new server

2. Which of these methods should be used to reverse the SECURE CONSOLE command?

   A. Execute the command UNSECURE CONSOLE and enter the Admin username and password when prompted.

   B. Shut down and restart the server.

   C. Select the UNSECURE CONSOLE option in Console One.

   D. Execute the command SECURE CONSOLE, UNLOAD.

3. Under what conditions is it advantageous to create a subnet pool on the DHCP server?

   A. When several physical network segments that use the same IP subnet will access the DHCP server via a router

   B. When several physical network segments that use the same IP subnet will access the DHCP server via a bridge or switch

   C. When a large number of devices will share a small number of IP addresses

   D. When a single physical network segment is supporting multiple virtual IP networks

4. Which of the following statements about security equivalence are true? Choose all that apply.

A. Security equivalencies can be filtered using an inherited rights filter (IRF).

B. Leaf objects are security equivalent to all container objects that lead from the Leaf to the [Root] object, and are security equivalent to the [Root] object as well.

C. All objects are security equivalent to the [Public] trustee.

D. Objects are security equivalent to all objects listed in their Security Equals property page.

5. A NetWare Connect server configuration can be easily reviewed by what means?

A. Using the Generate Configuration Report option in NWCCON

B. Choosing Details on the CONNECT_<server name> object in Network Administrator

C. Opening the SYS:\ETC\NETINFO.CFG file in a text editor

D. In Network Administrator, choosing Details on the server where NetWare Connect was installed

6. After completing an upgrade, what must be confirmed? (Choose all that apply.)

A. Drive mappings and logon scripts

B. Third-party server applications

C. The TCP/IP protocol is loaded and an IP address is bound on the NetWare 5 server

D. Network printer functionality

7. Enabling suballocation when creating a traditional NetWare volume will allow the operating system to:

A. Compress unused files, freeing up disk space on the volume

B. Allow multiple volumes to reside on the same NetWare partition

C. Define volumes with block sizes up to 64K

D. Place multiple files in a volume block

8. Console One is a Java utility that executes in the NetWare 5 graphical interface. The GUI itself is called:

A. X-Console

B. ServerTop

C. WinShell

D. JavaCon

9. What is the purpose of zone transfers?

A. To convert a secondary DNS server to a primary DNS server

B. To send DNS updates from a master DNS server to replica DNS servers

C. To forward DNS queries for unknown DNS objects to other DNS servers

D. To convert DHCP host entries into DNS resource record (RR) entries

10. What determines effective rights?

A. Adding the explicit trustee assignments of an object to the rights of its higher-level containers (minus any IRF blocks) and adding this to the rights granted through security equivalencies, group memberships, and the [Public] trustee

B. Adding the explicit trustee assignments of an object to the rights granted through security equivalencies, group memberships, and the [Public] trustee

C. Adding the explicit trustee assignments of an object to the rights granted through security equivalencies, group memberships, and the [[Root]] trustee

D. Adding the explicit trustee assignments of an object to the rights granted through security equivalencies, group memberships and the [Public] and [[Root]] trustees

11. Remote-control network access suffers from which of the following drawbacks?

A. Multiple workstations are required for connectivity.

B. Network node security

C. Additional remote-control software must be loaded on both the network and remote client.

D. All of the above

12. To be upgraded, what must the CONFIG.SYS file on a server include?

A. device=HIMEM.SYS

B. device=<CDROM driver>

C. files=40 and buffers=30 statements

D. lastdrive=z

13. What does dynamic Network Address Translation (NAT) allow?

A. IPX workstations to communicate with a server running only TCP/IP

B. Internal IP hosts to communicate with other IP networks using the public address of the NetWare server

C. External host access to hosts on your internal network

D. None of the above

14. NetWare 5 supports virtual memory. Which of the following statements is true about virtual memory and NetWare 5?

A. A virtual memory swap file is created on every NetWare volume automatically.

B. The network administrator can modify the swap files using the SWAP MODIFY command.

C. Swap files are deleted when a volume is dismounted.

D. Swap file changes can only be made when the associated volume is mounted.

Refer to the Following Scenario in Answering Questions 15–17

You have been given the task of setting up DNS and DHCP services for a small company. This company has a single NetWare 5 server connected to a 100MB switch. Two network segments, using the IP address block of 192.168.1.0 and 192.168.2.0 (subnet mask of 255.255.255.0) are each connected to the 100MB switch via an internal router. Another router connected to the 100MB switch is used to connect to the Internet. The NetWare 5 server should provide DNS, and requests for names outside of the local domain should be automatically forwarded to the ISP DNS server.

15. After defining the 192.168.1.0 network segment for DHCP, what address should be used as the default gateway for hosts on this segment?

A. The NetWare 5 server's IP address

B. The address of the ISP router

C. The address of the interface in the local router connected to the 192.168.1.0 segment

D. The address of the router connected to the Internet

16. After creating a resource record (RR) for a local host in the DNS, you determine that the IP address is incorrect. What is the best way to fix this problem?

A. In the Management Console, you click on the (+) sign next to the RR, highlight the IP address for the host, and reenter the IP address in the IP address fields.

B. You modify the DHCP address table to assign the address in DNS to the host, and reboot the host to get the new DHCP assigned address.

C. You delete the RR and recreate it.

D. You create an ALIAS for the RR, and assign it the correct address.

17. For the 192.168.2.0 subnet, what is the name of the corresponding IN-ADDR.ARPA zone?

A. 0.2.168.192.IN-ADDR.ARPA

B. 192.168.2.IN-ADDR.ARPA

C. 192.168.2.0.IN-ADDR.ARPA

D. 2.168.192.IN-ADDR.ARPA

18. Which of the following statements is true regarding NDS auditing?

A. Auditing can prevent unauthorized access to network resources.

B. Audit log files appear as NDS objects in the directory tree.

C. Access to audit logs is independent of NDS security.

D. Auditing is automatically enabled when the NDS tree is created.

19. The modem selection screen in NWCCON includes certain modem types followed by a superscripted "n", i.e., ^{n}. This character indicates that:

A. The modem has not been certified for use with NetWare Connect, but a modem script has been provided.

B. The modem has been certified for use with NetWare Connect.

C. The modem script for this modem uses the generic modem script settings.

D. Novell$_®$ and not the modem manufacturer provides the modem script.

20. An existing NetWare 4.1x server in a tree with a new NetWare 5 server should have:

A. Novell Licensing Services installed

B. The master replica of the root partition

C. Either the master or a read-write replica of the root partition

D. A separate context for its server and volume objects

21. What is contained in the network file system?

A. Partitions, directories, and folders

B. Partitions, volumes, and directories

C. Volumes, folders, and files

D. Servers, partitions, and volumes

22. Which of the following statements is true regarding packet receive buffers?

A. One buffer should be allocated for each workstation connected to the server.

B. Packet receive buffers are used to store outgoing packets until a workstation can accept them.

C. The server will automatically allocate the maximum number of packet receive buffers on startup.

D. Insufficient number of packet receive buffers will result in dropped connections and network performance degradation.

23. What is the default TCP port number used by the FastTrack Web server?

    A. 8000

    B. 8080

    C. 80

    D. No default is assigned. The port number must be entered during setup.

24. Partitions can be created at what levels in the NDS tree?

    A. Root, Organization, Organizational Unit, and User Object

    B. Root, Organizational, Organizational Unit, and Volume Object

    C. Root, Organizational, Organizational Unit, and Server Object

    D. Root, Country, Organizational, Organizational Unit, and Locality

25. Which of the following NetWare versions cannot be upgraded by the in-place upgrade option for NetWare 5?

    A. NetWare 2.x

    B. NetWare 3.1x

    C. IntranetWare for Small Businesses

    D. IntranetWare (NetWare 4.11)

26. In what way does disk mirroring differ from disk duplexing?

    A. Disk mirroring uses multiple disk controllers to mirror both the drive and the disk channel.

    B. Disk mirroring uses a single disk controller while disk duplexing uses multiple controllers.

    C. Disk duplexing uses RAID 5 technology to stripe data across multiple disk drives.

    D. Disk mirroring provides for fault tolerance in the event of a disk failure.

27. During a packet burst transaction, what action will be taken if a single packet is lost?

A. The receiver will not transmit an acknowledgment packet and the sender will retransmit the packet burst.

B. The receiver will transmit a request only for the missing packet.

C. The receiver will transmit an acknowledgment for each packet in the packet burst stream, so the missing packet will not be acknowledged and will be resent.

D. It is not possible to lose a single packet, since the burst transaction transmits all the data as a single frame.

28. Which of these functions can be performed using a Web browser connected to the Administration page of the FastTrack server? Choose all that apply.

A. Start and stop the Web server.

B. Change the TCP port for administrative access.

C. Review access and error logs.

D. Configure Secure Sockets Layer (SSL) options.

E. Configure User and Group access to the Web Server.

29. On what must servers participating in NDS synchronization agree?

A. Network frame types

B. The NDS database version

C. The time

D. The update sequence number

Refer to the Following Scenario to Answer Questions 30–31

You have been given the task of upgrading two existing NetWare 3.1x servers and a NetWare 4.1x server onto a single NetWare 5 server. Several of your users have accounts on all three of the NetWare 3.1x servers. A NetWare 3.1x print server manages all network printers. All user accounts on the existing servers will reside in the same container in NDS.

30. As users are migrated from the NetWare 3.x servers, how does the Upgrade Wizard handle duplicate user accounts on the servers?

A. Ignoring the duplicate users and generating an error during the migration

B. Generating multiple, identical user names in the context

C. Assigning subsequent users with a numeric ID after the name

D. Leaving the existing user name intact, and adding the trustee assignments of the matching user name to the rights of the existing object

31. As part of this upgrade, you have decided to convert all the network clients and the NetWare 5 server to utilize TCP/IP exclusively. At what point in the migration process can IPX protocol support be removed?

A. Continued support for the IPX based network print services precludes switching to a TCP/IP only environment.

B. Only after all servers are migrated and client software has been updated

C. The workstation used to run Upgrade Wizard and the source and destination servers must be configured for TCP/IP. Once this is done, IPX can be removed.

D. When Upgrade Wizard prompts for the type of protocol support required on the NetWare 5 destination server

32. What is the easiest way to perform VREPAIR on a server SYS volume?

A. Dismount the SYS volume, load VREPAIR, and select the volume.

B. Load VREPAIR and select the SYS volume. Volumes must be mounted to run VREPAIR.

C. Load SYS:SYSTEM\VREPAIR, switch to the console prompt, dismount the SYS volume, and then switch back to the VREPAIR screen and select the SYS volume.

D. From NetAdmin, highlight the SYS volume in the tree, select Properties, and select Repair Volume.

Refer to the Following Scenario in Answering Questions 33–35

You have been asked to evaluate the performance of a new NetWare 5 installation and make recommendations for improving the server performance. The NetWare 5 server is a 400 MHz Pentium with 64MB of RAM, with a RAID 5 array consisting of five 4-gigabyte drives. The SYS volume is four gigabytes and the remainder of the disk space is configured as second volume. In addition to file service, the server provides DNS and DHCP service for the network.

33. You immediately notice that this server has a high processor utilization rate. What is your first recommendation for improving performance?

   A. Removing DNS and DHCP and placing these services on a separate device

   B. Adding additional server RAM

   C. Adding a second processor to the server

   D. Moving the SYS volume off the RAID array and placing it on a dedicated disk drive

34. After adding server memory, how can you determine if the server is still performing excessive virtual memory swapping? Choose all that apply.

   A. Monitoring the disk activity LED on the server

   B. Checking server processor utilization

   C. Using the SWAP console command to view swap file statistics

   D. Using a SET parameter at the server to set an alert for this condition

35. In an attempt to prevent a critical process from failing on this server, you have decided to load the process in its own protected memory space. How is this accomplished?

A. Simply loading the process. All processes on a NetWare server utilize protected memory space.

B. Creating an NCF file for the process and using the command PROTECT *NCF filename* when starting the process

C. Placing the server in protected mode using a SET command, then loading the process

D. It is not possible to load processes in their own protected memory space.

36. What is the default directory for storing HTML pages on the FastTrack Web server?

A. SYS:NOVONYX\DOCS

B. SYS:WEB\DOCS

C. SYS:FASTTRAK\DOCS

D. SYS:NOVONYX\SUITESPOT\DOCS

37. Which of the following is true about master and read/write replicas?

A. Read/write replicas cannot be promoted to master replicas.

B. Master replicas must be deleted before a read/write replica can be promoted to master.

C. Master replicas must be demoted to read/write before another replica can be designated the master.

D. Promoting a read/write replica to master will result in the previous master being demoted automatically to read/write.

38. Applications, such as queue-based printing, that require IPX, also require:

A. The IPX protocol bound to NetWare 5 servers

B. No special considerations when run on a NetWare 5 server

C. Upgrading to IP versions

D. A legacy 3.x or 4.x server volume to maintain these queues

39. What is a key consideration when designing the file system structure?

A. File system rights flow downward, so rights should be defined at the highest level possible, to reduce management requirements.

B. File system rights are set at each level in the directory, so it doesn't matter what rights are assigned above a directory in the file-system tree.

C. All users are assigned the default rights of Read and File Scan when a directory is created. The Admin should modify these rights as necessary.

D. Shared files that should be available to all users should be placed above the user home directories.

40. When performing a full restore on a server that uses a combination of full and differential backups, which backup sets must be restored?

A. The last full backup and the last differential backup set

B. The last full backup and all differential backup sets created after the full backup

C. Only the last differential backup

D. All of the differential backups taken since the last full backup

41. How can connectivity to the FastTrack Web server be verified?

A. Using the DISPLAY SERVERS and DISPLAY NETWORKS command at the server console

B. Using PING at the workstation and the PING.NLM on the server

C. Using the Administration page to verify that the server is set to On

D. By stopping and restarting the Web server

42. What is the recommended number of replicas for a partition?

A. One

B. Two

C. Three

D. Four

43. What is one of the primary functions of the Service Registry Service?

   A. To transmit Service Advertising Protocol (SAP) messages for available print services
   B. To track printer driver information and allow clients to download drivers
   C. To provide clients with a list of registered NDPS printers
   D. To provide clients with print job status information

44. What is the maximum number of volumes a single NetWare partition can support?

   A. 64
   B. 128
   C. 32
   D. 1

45. In order to back up a NetWare 5 server and its NDS replica, which NLM modules must be loaded on the target server?

   A. SMS and TSA500
   B. TSA500 and NWBACK32
   C. TSA500 and NDSBACKER
   D. TSA500 and TSANDS

46. Users and Groups can be imported into the FastTrack server local-user database if the information is stored in LDIF format. What is LDIF?

   A. Lightweight Directory Interchange Format
   B. LDAP Data Interchange Format
   C. Local Database Information File
   D. Long Data Interface Functions

47. In NDS Manager how may a partition be deleted?

    A. Highlighting the partition and pressing the DELETE key

    B. Deleting all the replicas of the partition

    C. Highlighting the partition and using the right mouse button menu option to delete the partition

    D. Highlighting the partition and using the Merge menu option to merge the partition with its parent

48. After creating an NDPS Manager object, what should you do?

    A. Shutdown and restart the server assigned to this object.

    B. Load the NDPS.NLM on the server assigned to this object.

    C. Unload and reload the NDPS broker associated with the Manager object.

    D. Add the line: NDPSM {NDPS manager name and context} to the AUTOEXEC.NCF file on the server assigned to this object.

49. Which of the following statements regarding the TTS$LOG.ERR file is correct:

    A. This file is stored in the SYS:SYSTEM directory and is used to record transaction tracking errors.

    B. This file is stored in the root of the SYS: volume and is used to record transaction tracking errors.

    C. This file is stored in the SYS:PUBLIC directory and is used to store volume error logs.

    D. This file is stored on the server's DOS partition and is used to record transaction tracking errors.

50. What server console command can be used to recreate the SMS backup queue?

    A. LOAD QMAN –NEW

    B. LOAD SMDR –NEW

    C. LOAD SMS –NEW

    D. LOAD SBCON –NEW

PE 2 EXAM 50-640 QUESTIONS

51. Which of the following are valid destinations when installing the FastTrack server? Choose all that apply.

A. SYS:

B. SYS:NOVONYX

C. SYS:\

D. VOL1:

52. Users at a remote location complain about the amount of time it takes to log on to the network. Your examination reveals that the server at this location has a read-only replica of their partition, and it appears to be synchronized with its master replica at the main office. What change would most likely reduce the amount of time it takes to log on for these users?

A. Promote the read-only partition to either a master or read/write replica.

B. Delete the read-only partition on the server and add a read/write replica.

C. Increase the bandwidth between the remote office and the main office.

D. Reconfigure the remote workstations to use the local server for authentication.

53. Which of the following statements are true in regards to non-NDPS-aware printers?

A. Non-NDPS-aware printers are not supported by NDPS.

B. These printers are only supported when attached directly to a NetWare 5 server.

C. A Novell or third-party gateway can be used to support these printers.

D. A print queue must be created and NDPS will accept jobs from this queue.

54. Which of the following functions are supported by Console One? Choose all that apply.

A. File and folder manipulation on server volumes

B. Creating containers, groups, and users in the NDS tree

C. Changing user passwords

D. Assigning trustee rights to NDS objects

E. Remote-console access to other NetWare servers

55. How are Windows 95/98 TSAs loaded?

A. As part of WSBACK32

B. During the NetWare 5 client installation

C. Via command-line execution at the workstation

D. Via a device driver in the workstation CONFIG.SYS

56. Which object rights can be granted to the trustee of an NDS object?

A. Supervisor, Compare, Read, Write, Add Self, Inheritable

B. Supervisor, Browse, Create, Delete, Rename, Inheritable

C. Supervisor, Read, Write, Create, Erase, Modify, File Scan, Access Control

D. Admin, Browse, Create, Delete, Rename, Inheritable

57. What software does a Windows 95 PC use for remote-node access to a NetWare 5 server?

A. NetWare Client 32

B. Dial-Up Networking

C. Win2NCS

D. NetWare Connect

58. How many levels of security are available to NDPS printer objects?

    A. Two–User and Operator

    B. Three–User, Operator, and Manager

    C. Four–User, Operator, Manager, and Admin

    D. Five–Public, User, Operator, Manager, and Admin

59. Which of these applications in NetWare 5 replaces the INSTALL.NLM used in NetWare 4?

    A. NWCONFIG.NLM

    B. SETUP.NLM

    C. INETCFG.NLM

    D. STARTX.NCF

60. What is the primary function of a DNS server?

    A. To respond to remote host requests for an IP address assignment

    B. Web page hosting

    C. To respond to remote host requests with the IP address of a requested host name

    D. To maintain IP routing tables for Internet access

61. How can you determine if a property right is applicable to a specific object type?

    A. Only rights that apply to the object are displayed in the list of object property rights.

    B. Property rights that do not apply to an object are grayed out in the list of object property rights.

    C. An arrow appears next to property rights that apply to the selected object.

    D. The property rights selections are grayed out when a property that does not apply to the object is selected.

62. Which menu option in NWCCON is used to configure dial-out phone number restrictions?

A. Restrict Service by User

B. Restrict Ports by User

C. Set User Parameters

D. Set Global Parameters

63. Which NLM extends the NDS schema for DNS and DHCP?

A. NWCONFIG

B. DHCPSRVR and NAMED

C. STARTX

D. DNIPINST

64. The Global Options button on the FastTrack Administration page is only used to configure:

A. The directory service settings

B. The Web-server TCP/IP address, and the server and Administration TCP port numbers

C. Cluster management

D. The default location of Web documents

65. What is the primary advantage of the hierarchical structure of NDS?

A. Places users in different containers from their server objects

B. Creates multiple NDS trees within the organization and ties them together

C. Manages both NetWare 3.x binderies and NDS objects from a common interface

D. Creates Administrative roles at different levels of the tree

66. During an NDS Unattended Repair, users complain that they cannot log on to the network. What is the most likely reason for this?

A. The user accounts were corrupt and were deleted by the repair process.

B. The repair process locks the NDS database.

C. The repair process dismounts the SYS volume while running.

D. The server running DSREPAIR contains the master replica for the affected users.

67. During a custom installation of NetWare 5, what action should you take in preparation for creating an NSS volume?

A. Create a NetWare partition large enough for the SYS volume and the NSS volume.

B. Leave sufficient unallocated space for the NSS volume.

C. Create a single NSS partition and create all volumes on this partition.

D. Unload NSS.NLM, create the appropriate volumes, and then load NSS.NLM on the server.

68. What server module must be loaded to support the RCONJ.EXE remote-access utility?

A. LOAD RCONAG6 <*password* > <*IP port*> <*IPX port*>

B. LOAD RCONJ <*password*> <*IP port*> <*IPX port*>

C. LOAD REMOTE <*password*>

D. LOAD NWAGENT <*password*>

69. From within the DNS/DHCP management console, what is the first step in configuring the DHCP service?

A. Create a DHCP subnet.

B. Choose the DHCP server.

C. Import the DHCP database or create a new one.

D. Create a DHCP server object.

70. Which of these default directory rights are included in the list of rights automatically granted to a container?

A. [RWF] to the SYS:PUBLIC of all servers in the container

B. [RF] to the SYS:SYSTEM directory and [C] to the SYS:MAIL directory for all servers in the container

C. [RF] to the SYS:SYSTEM and SYS:PUBLIC directory, and [C] to the SYS:MAIL directory for all servers in the container

D. [RF] to the SYS:PUBLIC and [C] to the SYS:MAIL directory for all servers in the container

71. In the Network Administrator program, changes to the remote access settings for a user apply to what server?

A. The users' default server

B. All NetWare Connect servers

C. Any NetWare Connect servers in the same container as the User object

D. The NetWare Connect server specified in the remote access configuration screen

72. What is one of the primary advantages of an in-place upgrade of an existing NetWare server?

A. No additional hardware is required.

B. The possibility of data loss is minimized, since the data is left intact.

C. File compression and suballocation can be enabled on the existing volumes.

D. Volume block sizes can be adjusted without recreating existing volumes.

73. The Macintosh communications redirector for dial-out connections through the NetWare Connect server is available by what means?

A. Purchase from Apple Computer

B. Download from the Novell Web site

C. Installing the MAC2NCS program from the MAC Client disk shipped with NetWare 5

D. None of the above

Test Yourself:
Practice Exam 2
Answers

Q
&
A

The answers to the questions are in boldface, followed by a brief explanation. The incorrect answer choices are explained in the final paragraph following each correct answer. Some of the explanations detail the logic you should use to choose the correct answer, while others give factual reasons why the answer is correct. If you miss several questions on a similar topic, you should review the corresponding section in the *CNE®* *NetWare® 5 Study Guide* before taking the NetWare 5 Advanced Administration test.

Practice Exam 2 Answers

1. ☑ **A. Upgrading the DS.NLM on all 4.1x servers to version 5.99 or higher.** NetWare® 5 introduces significant changes in the NetWare schema and modifies the way NetWare servers handle key directory service functions. Failure to upgrade the directory service modules on all of your existing NetWare 4.1x servers will result in corruption of the directory service replicas stored on these servers.

    ☒ **B.** This answer is incorrect because NetWare 5 servers can be added to an existing tree, as long as the existing servers in the tree are running the correct directory service version. **C.** This answer is incorrect because it is not necessary to define a context for the NetWare 5 server—it can be placed in an existing context along with the existing servers. **D.** This answer is incorrect because it is not necessary to change the server name when upgrading a NetWare 3.x server. If you would like to change the server name as part of the upgrade, you should do so before starting the upgrade, but you can use the existing server name.

2. ☑ **B. Shut down and restart the server.** The only way to reverse the SECURE CONSOLE command is to down the server and restart. Because of this, it's probably not a good idea to place this command in the server AUTOEXEC.NCF file.

    ☒ **A.** This answer is incorrect because there is not an UNSECURE CONSOLE option. Once the console is secured, it stays secured until the server is rebooted. **C.** This answer is incorrect for the same reason, there is no UNSECURE CONSOLE option in Console One. **D.** This answer is incorrect because the SECURE CONSOLE does not support any command-line options.

3. ☑ **D.** When a single physical network segment is supporting multiple virtual IP networks. A subnet pool tells the DHCP server that the subnets in the pool can be treated as a single physical network. If the available addresses in one subnet are exhausted, then addresses in other subnets in the pool can be assigned when a new IP request is received.

☒ **A.** is incorrect because routed segments connected to the DHCP server cannot use the same IP subnet. **B.** is incorrect because subnet pools cannot be used unless there are multiple virtual IP networks on the physical segments. **C.** is incorrect because the number of devices using the subnet is irrelevant. A large number of devices using a small number of IP addresses can only be handled by using a very short lease time for IP addresses, not by creating an IP address pool.

4. ☑ **B, C, D.** Leaf objects are security equivalent to all container objects that lead from the leaf to the [Root] object, and are security equivalent to the [Root] object as well. All objects are security equivalent to the [Public] trustee. Objects are security equivalent to all objects listed in their Security Equals property page.

☒ **A.** is incorrect because security equivalencies cannot be filtered through an IRF.

5. ☑ **A.** Using the Generate Configuration Report option in NWCCON. This option will allow the installer to review the configuration on screen or print the configuration to a text file.

☒ **B.** is incorrect because the CONNECT_<server name> object Details screen does not provide any configuration information. **C.** is incorrect because the NETINFO.CFG file contains LAN configuration information used by the INETCFG utility and it does not contain NetWare Connect configuration information. **D.** is incorrect because the details display for the NetWare Connect server does not provide server configuration information.

6. ☑ **A, B, D.** After upgrading, you should verify that the logon scripts and drive mappings are correct, as well as that any third-party applications, such as backup or virus-scanning server software, is operating correctly. The upgrade process also updates the printing environment, so you will need to test network printing.

☒ **C.** is incorrect because NetWare 5 does not *require* TCP/IP, and can operate in an IPX-only environment.

7. ☑ **D.** Place multiple files in a volume block. Suballocation allows the operating system to place multiple files in a single block. Without suballocation, a 4K file on a volume with a 64K block size would take 64K (an entire block).

☒ **A.** is incorrect because it refers to a separate volume flag that is used to enable compression on a volume. **B.** is incorrect because the suballocation flag does not affect the number of volumes supported by a NetWare partition. **C.** is incorrect because the suballocation flag does not affect volume block sizes, either. The default volume block size for NetWare 5 is 64K.

8. ☑ **B.** ServerTop. ServerTop provides an X-Windows style interface that allows Java applications to be executed in a style similar to the start button in Windows 95. It provides the desktop for server GUI applications.

☒ **A, C, D.** are incorrect because they are not valid names for NetWare 5's GUI desktop.

9. ☑ **B.** To send DNS updates from a master DNS server to replica DNS servers. Replica DNS servers provide load balancing and eliminate the single point of failure for DNS. DNS updates are made to the master server, and zone transfers automatically replicate these updates.

☒ **A.** is incorrect because this is not the purpose of zone transfers. **C.** is incorrect because this describes DNS forwarding, not zone transfers. **D.** is incorrect because zone transfers are used for replicating DNS entries between master and replica DNS servers, not for converting DHCP host entries into resource records.

10. ☑ **A.** Adding the explicit trustee assignments of an object to the rights of its higher-level containers (minus any IRF blocks) and adding this to the rights granted through security equivalencies, group memberships, and the [Public] trustee. Effective rights are always additive; if rights to the same object are granted by different means, the total of all rights is granted.
☒ **B.** is incorrect because rights to the object's higher-level containers were not included. Effective rights include all of the object's higher containers, to the [Root] object. **C.** is incorrect for both this reason and the failure to add the rights of the [Public] trustee. Although **D.** includes the [Public] and [Root] trustees, it is also incorrect for the same reason **B.** is: the object's higher-level container rights are part of the effective rights for the object.

11. ☑ **D.** All of the above. Remote control network access requires a one-for-one connection. Every simultaneous remote client requires its own dedicated local node. Network node security is an issue with remote control since the network node must be up and running at all times. Remote control requires special software on both the networked PC and the remote client.

12. ☑ **C.** The CONFIG.SYS file on the server requires files=40 and buffers=30 (these values can be higher, but not lower). A new installation of NetWare 5 creates a new CONFIG.SYS with these values.
ý **A.** is incorrect because HIMEM.SYS is an extended memory manager used by DOS. DOS memory managers will prevent NetWare's protected mode OS from accessing all the available memory in the server. **B.** is incorrect because it is not always necessary to have a DOS CD-ROM driver loaded on the server. Most installations can be performed by booting directly from the NetWare 5 CD, or by accessing the CD across the network. **D.** is incorrect because the *lastdrive* statement is not required on the server, unless the NetWare Client for DOS is being used to access a remote CD or server with the OS installation files.

13. ☑ **B.** Internal IP hosts to communicate with other IP networks using the public address of the NetWare server. NAT is a method of connecting local Intranets to the Internet without requiring a public IP address scheme. NAT allows a company to use a local IP address scheme, using one of the IP network addresses reserved for this purpose. A server or router that supports NAT would route all traffic bound for the Internet through its own public address. Dynamic NAT refers to NetWare's ability to route Internet traffic initiated by a local host to and from an Internet public address by dynamically mapping the local host IP address to its primary public IP address. Static NAT, on the other hand, maps individual local IP addresses to secondary public IP addresses bound to the server. Static NAT is required when Internet hosts want to initiate conversations with host devices on the local network.

☒ **A.** is incorrect because NAT is used for converting private IP addresses to and from public IP addresses and has nothing to do with IPX communication. **C.** is incorrect because the question asked specifically about dynamic NAT. Static NAT address tables are required to allow external host access to devices on the local network. **D.** None of the above, is wrong because **B.** is correct.

14. ☑ **C.** Swap files are deleted when a volume is dismounted. If the swap file is on the SYS volume, it will be recreated automatically when the volume is mounted. Swap files on other volumes must be recreated after a volume is dismounted. Note that the parameters for a swap file include a minimum and maximum size. When a volume is mounted, the swap file will be created using the minimum value. As virtual memory is needed to page active processes, the swap file will increase.

☒ **A.** is incorrect because, with the exception of the SYS volume, swap files are not created automatically. **B.** is incorrect because the command to modify swap files is SWAP PARAMETER followed by the volume name and the parameters to be modified. **D.** is incorrect because swap file changes can be made to a dismounted volume. When the volume is mounted, the swap file will be created using the new parameters.

15. ☑ **C.** The address of the interface in the local router connected to the 192.168.1.0 segment. As each segment is defined in DHCP, the default gateway should also be added. This should point to the IP address of the local router on this segment.

☒ **A, B, D.** are incorrect because the default gateway is used to forward packets to any address not on the local segment. Since most TCP/IP hosts do not maintain IP routing tables, they rely on a default gateway to forward IP traffic. After applying the subnet mask to an address, the host determines if a packet should be sent to the local segment or should be forwarded to the gateway for processing. The default gateway must be a gateway (router) on the same local segment as the host.

16. ☑ **C.** Delete the RR and recreate it. Once created, it is not possible to modify the attributes of a resource record. You must delete the record and recreate it.

☒ **A.** is incorrect because the sequence listed will allow you to view the IP address assigned to the record, but you cannot change it. You must highlight the RR, delete it, and create a new one. **B.** is incorrect because, while it may be possible to change the host IP address (if the new address is on the correct subnet and no other device is already using the address), this is certainly not the best way to resolve the problem. **D.** is incorrect because ALIASES can only be used as additional names for a host and they cannot be assigned an IP address of their own.

17. ☑ **D.** 2.168.192.IN-ADDR.ARPA. When IN-ADDR.ARPA zone records are created, the IP address in reversed notation is used as a prefix. If the trailing octets are 0, they are not used.

☒ **A.** is incorrect because the trailing 0 in this network would automatically be dropped when this zone record is created. **B, C.** are incorrect because the address is not listed in reverse notation.

18. ☑ **B.** Audit log files appear as NDS™ objects in the directory tree.
☒ **A.** is incorrect because the auditing function in NetWare 5 can only track access; it cannot restrict network access. Auditing is a useful tool for monitoring network activity and user activity and can detect unauthorized activity after the fact. **C.** is incorrect because audit logs are stored as NDS objects for the specific reason that they can then be managed using NDS security. **D.** is incorrect because auditing is not enabled by default. Enabling auditing can hamper network performance and audit logs can grow rapidly. Auditing is normally enabled on specific portions of the network and for specific periods of time, usually when unauthorized activity is suspected.

19. ☑ **A.** The modem has not been certified for use with NetWare Connect, but a modem script has been provided. NIAS includes modem scripts for a large number of modems, including modems that have not been submitted to Novell_® for certification with NetWare Connect.
☒ **B.** is incorrect; the superscript indicates that the modem has NOT been certified. **C.** is incorrect because every modem listed in NWCCON has a custom modem script designed for it, regardless of its certification status. **D.** is incorrect because Novell provides all of the modem scripts listed in NWCCON. The superscript is used to indicate that the modem itself is not certified.

20. ☑ **A.** Prior to adding a NetWare 5 server to an existing tree, NetWare 4.1x servers need to have Novell Licensing Services installed. NetWare 5 uses a new method of tracking server licenses—it places license information directly into the NDS tree. Although NetWare 4 servers do not use this license information, installing Novell Licensing Services on the existing servers allows them to participate in providing licensing information to NetWare 5 servers.
☒ **B.** is incorrect because there are no special considerations for installing partition replicas in a tree with both NetWare 4 and NetWare 5 servers. **C.** is incorrect for this same reason. **D.** is incorrect because NetWare 4 and NetWare 5 servers do not require a separate context for their server and volume objects.

21. ☑ **C.** Volumes, folders, and files. The network file system uses a hierarchical structure similar to DOS and Windows. The top of the file structure is the network volume. Within the volume, folders contain the individual files. Folders may also be called directories.

    ☒ **A.** is incorrect because it includes partitions. A partition must be created to hold a server volume, but partitions are not part of the network file system. **B.** is incorrect for the same reason. **D.** is incorrect because it includes both partitions and servers. Although servers are used to maintain network volumes, they are also not part of the file system.

22. ☑ **D.** Insufficient number of packet receive buffers will result in dropped connections and network performance degradation. Packet receive buffers are used by the server to temporarily store workstation requests until the server can process it. Incoming requests to a heavily loaded server can be discarded if insufficient packet receive buffers are available. This can result in lost connections or a large number of workstation retransmissions, which can degrade the network.

    ☒ **A.** is incorrect because the best recommendation is to allocate two buffers per workstation. **B.** is incorrect because packet receive buffers are used to buffer inbound data to the server, not outbound data to the workstation. **C.** is incorrect because the server automatically allocates the minimum number of packet receive buffers on startup. As additional buffers are required, the server will allocate them automatically, up to the amount specified in the maximum packet receive setting.

23. ☑ **C.** 80. This is the standard port number used by World Wide Web servers. During setup, you can use this default or assign a different TCP port for Web service.

    ☒ **A, B.** are incorrect as these port numbers are typically used for proxy servers. **D.** is incorrect because although a port number may be entered during setup, the setup defaults to TCP port 80.

24. ☑ **D.** Root, Country, Organizational, Organizational Unit, and Locality. Each of these NDS objects is a container, and partitions can only be created at a container level in the NDS tree.

☒ **A, B, C.** are incorrect because each contains NDS Leaf objects, i.e., objects in the tree that do not contain other NDS objects. You cannot partition the NDS tree at a Leaf object level.

25. ☑ **A.** NetWare 2.x is not supported by the in-place upgrade. You must first upgrade these servers to NetWare 3.1x or higher before upgrading to NetWare 5.

☒ **B, C, and D.** are all supported by the in-place upgrade. The Migration Wizard can be used to migrate NetWare 3.1x servers "across-the-wire" to an installed NetWare 5 server, but it cannot be used to migrate NetWare 4.x servers, since the servers already exist in the NDS tree.

26. ☑ **B.** Disk mirroring uses a single disk controller while disk duplexing uses multiple controllers. Disk mirroring consists of placing a second disk drive on a single controller and then duplicating the data on the primary drive to the secondary drive. Disk duplexing mirrors data to a second drive just like mirroring, but the second drive must be attached to another controller. Disk duplexing provides a higher degree of fault-tolerance because it allows either a disk drive or a controller to fail without the possibility of data loss. Both disk mirroring and disk duplexing are considered RAID Level 1, which only specifies that the primary drive be mirrored to a secondary.

☒ **A.** is incorrect because the definitions of mirroring and duplexing are reversed. **C.** is incorrect because it refers to a different level of RAID. RAID 5 does not use a mirrored drive; it writes data across an array of drives and then stores a checksum value for the write command (this checksum is randomly written on any drive in the array). In the event of a drive failure, the checksum can be used to determine the value of the missing data. **D.** is incorrect because both disk mirroring and disk duplexing provide for fault tolerance in the event of a disk failure.

27. ☑ **B.** The receiver will transmit a request only for the missing packet. Packet bursting allows a sender to transmit several packets without requiring an acknowledgement for each packet. The receiver will send a single acknowledgement for the entire sequence of packets. In the event that a packet is missing, the receiver will request only the missing packet.

☒ **A.** is incorrect because the sender does not have to resend the entire packet burst sequence. The receiver will acknowledge the packet burst and will request only the missing packet. **C.** is incorrect because the receiver does not acknowledge individual packets during a packet burst sequence. To do so would negate the performance increase provided by packet bursting. **D.** is incorrect because packet bursting still sends data in individual packets, but the sender does not wait for an acknowledgement before sending the next packet.

28. ☑ **A, B, C, D, E.** All of the above functions can be performed via a Web browser with administrative access to the FastTrack server. During setup, the installer is prompted for an admin name and password. This name and password must be supplied when connecting to the Administration page. The Administration page includes options for Admin preferences, global settings, users & groups, keys & certificates (SSL), and cluster management.

29. ☑ **C.** The time. NDS uses a timestamp on each database update. In order to apply updates properly, all participating servers must agree on the time.

☒ **A.** is incorrect because network frame types do not have to match, provided a router is used to pass dissimilar frame type traffic between servers. **B.** is incorrect since NDS allows different NDS database versions to synchronize. **D.** is incorrect because NDS does not use sequence numbers for NDS traffic; all NDS traffic is sequenced using timestamps.

30. ☑ **A.** Ignoring the duplicate users and generating an error during subsequent migrations. NDS does not support multiple objects in the same container with the same name. The Upgrade Wizard verification process will inform you prior to the migration if it detects existing objects with the same name as the bindery objects to be migrated. If you persist in upgrading without first deleting or renaming the objects, the Upgrade Wizard will reject the duplicates and generate an error.

☒ **B.** is incorrect because multiple objects with the same name are not allowed in a single context. **C.** is incorrect because there is no mechanism in the Upgrade Wizard to handle duplicate objects, apart from generating an error log. **D.** is incorrect because Upgrade Wizard will not add trustee assignments to an object. Trustee assignments are maintained in the file system, and the Upgrade Wizard treats the duplicate user name as a unique user account, and will not assign file rights of that account to an existing user.

31. ☑ **B.** Only after all the servers are migrated and client software has been updated. NetWare 5 is the only NetWare OS that supports native support for the TCP/IP protocol. The Upgrade Wizard application running at a workstation must use IPX to communicate with the NetWare 3.x servers. Until all the servers are migrated, you will need to use IPX to transfer data from the source 3.1x servers to the Upgrade Wizard workstation. The NetWare 5 server will need to have IPX enabled until the NetWare 5 client (with TCP/IP support) has been loaded on all client PCs.

☒ **A.** is incorrect because NetWare 5 provides IPX compatibility in the TCP/IP protocol stack. Most IPX applications, including NetWare print services, will work in a NetWare 5-pure TCP/IP environment. **C.** is incorrect because removal of IPX support on the NetWare 3.1x servers will result in a communications failure. The NetWare 5 client cannot connect to NetWare 3.1x servers using TCP/IP. **D.** is incorrect because the Upgrade Wizard does not request this information. Prior to running Upgrade Wizard, the installer must configure the workstation for an IPX connection to both the source and destination server. This protocol is used exclusively during the migration process.

32. ☑ **C.** Load SYS:SYSTEM\VREPAIR, switch to the console prompt, dismount the SYS volume, and then switch back to the VREPAIR screen and select the SYS volume. The VREPAIR.NLM is located in the SYS:SYSTEM directory. Dismounting the SYS volume before loading this module will require loading it from another location, such as the server floppy drive. If possible, load the module from the SYS volume, then switch to the console prompt and dismount SYS. You can now switch back to VREPAIR and select the SYS volume. Volumes that are mounted are not available for VREPAIR.

☒ **A.** is incorrect because dismounting the volume will prevent you from being able to load VREPAIR from the default location. **B.** is incorrect because it indicates that the volume must be mounted to perform the repair. Mounted volumes are inaccessible to VREPAIR. **D.** is incorrect because there is no option in a volume's Properties section that supports volume repairs.

33. ☑ **B.** Add additional server RAM. The 64MB of RAM installed in this server is the minimum amount of memory required to load NetWare 5. Given the large size of the NetWare volumes and the additional services running on this server, the OS will be forced to use virtual memory to operate. This significantly affects server performance and the constant swapping of tasks will result in higher processor utilization as well as lower overall throughput.

☒ **A.** is incorrect because, while removing these services would help the server, the root cause of the high processor utilization and poor server performance remains insufficient server RAM. **C.** is incorrect because the addition of a second processor would not significantly improve performance here until the server RAM has been upgraded. **D.** is incorrect because the placement of the SYS volume would not significantly affect server CPU use.

34. ☑ **C, D.** Using the SWAP console command to view swap file statistics. Using a SET parameter at the server to set an alert for this condition. At the console, the SWAP command, with no parameters, will provide you with a real-time display of the number of swap pages in use. The SET statement, SET AVERAGE PAGE IN ALERT THRESHOLD =x, will result in console alerts whenever the number of active swap pages exceeds the value of x.

☒ **A.** is incorrect because the disk activity LED merely indicates that disk activity is occurring. While constant disk activity may be the result of virtual memory swapping, it may also simply be based on file service activity. **B.** is incorrect because server processor utilization may be high for many reasons, only one of which is virtual memory activity.

35. ☑ **B.** Creating an NCF file for the process and using the command PROTECT *NCF filename* when starting the process. When an NCF file is launched using the PROTECT command, a protected memory space will be created. This memory space can be viewed using the PROTECTION command at the server console.

☒ **A.** is incorrect because individual processes do not run in separate protected memory space on a NetWare server. Placing processes in separate memory spaces prevents them from communicating with each other and results in slower server performance. **C.** is incorrect because there is no SET parameter to create or manage separate protected memory spaces. **D.** is incorrect because NetWare 5 provides a means of loading applications into separate memory space using the PROTECT command.

36. ☑ **D.** SYS:NOVONYX\SUITESPOT\DOCS. The installation of the FastTrack server must be done at the root of the server SYS volume. The NOVONYX directory is created automatically and all Web-server applications and data files are stored in directories beneath this directory. The DOCS directory is used to store HTML pages and a set of default pages is placed here during installation.

☒ **A.** is incorrect because the DOCS directory is one level lower in the directory tree. **B.** is incorrect as the 2.0 and 3.0 Web servers shipped with NetWare 4.11 use the SYS:WEB directory, but the FastTrack server does not. **C.** is incorrect because the installation of the FastTrack server does not create a SYS:FASSTRAK directory.

37. ☑ **D.** Promoting a read/write replica to master will result in the previous master being demoted automatically to read/write. In the event that a master replica becomes damaged, promoting a read/write replica to master will automatically demote the damaged master to a read/write replica. This replica will then synchronize with the new master replica.

☒ **A.** is incorrect because read/write replicas can always be promoted to master. **B.** is incorrect because it is not necessary (or advisable) to delete the master replica before promoting another replica. Deleting the master replica will result in a loss of synchronization and would require recreating the replica on the affected server. **C.** is incorrect because there is no process for demoting a master replica prior to designating a new master replica. Simply designating an existing read/write replica as the new master will force the existing master replica to become a read/write replica.

38. ☑ **B.** No special considerations when run on a NetWare 5 server. NetWare 5 servers configured for TCP/IP will still support IPX applications because the TCP/IP modules in NetWare 5 include a Compatibility mode. This mode allows server-based IPX applications to communicate with their client counterparts using the IP protocol. A NetWare 5 version of the client is all that is required for support of IPX applications over TCP/IP.

☒ **A.** is incorrect because the Compatibility mode eliminates the requirement for loading the IPX protocol on the server. **B.** is incorrect because IPX-based applications CAN be supported without upgrading. **D.** is incorrect because it is not necessary to maintain IPX application queues on a NetWare 3.x or 4.x server; these queues and their associated applications can function on a NetWare 5 server, regardless of the protocols loaded on the server.

39. ☑ **A.** File system rights flow downward, so rights should be defined at the highest level possible, to reduce management requirements. Unless blocked by an inherited rights filter (IRF) or an explicit rights assignment, rights to a directory flow down to all its subdirectories. This allows the network Admin to set rights for users and groups at fairly high levels of the directory tree and reduces the need to set rights to subdirectories.

☒ **B.** is incorrect because it states that rights assigned to directories higher in the directory tree do not matter. Rights assigned above the directory are inherited by the directory, unless an IRF is defined to block the inheritance. **C.** is incorrect because users do not get these default rights when a directory is created; rather, the inherited rights determine the rights to the new directory. **D.** is incorrect because shared files should never be placed in a directory above the user home directory. Users will normally have no access to this directory, but would have explicit full access to their personal directory below it. Placing shared files in a directory above the user home directory would require granting the users access to this directory. This access would flow down to all the user directories and would then require an IRF each time a new user directory is added.

40. ☑ **A.** The last full backup and the last differential backup set. Since differential backups do not set the archive bit after backing up a file, each subsequent differential backup since the full backup will include all files that have been modified since the full backup. Restoring the last full backup, followed by the last differential backup, will result in a complete set of restored files.

☒ **B.** is incorrect because it is not necessary to restore all of the differential backup sets created after the last full backup. The most current differential backup will include all the modified files that were backed up by previous differential sets. **C.** is incorrect because full backups clear the archive bit on backed-up files, and the differential backup set will not include files that were not modified since the full backup. For the same reason, **D.** is incorrect, since the differential backups will not include unmodified files.

41. ☑ **B.** Using PING at the workstation and the PING.NLM on the server. When you are troubleshooting the Web server, you can quickly verify connectivity by pinging the server from a workstation and the workstation from the server.

☒ **A.** is incorrect because the DISPLAY SERVERS and DISPLAY NETWORKS commands would not provide any information about the FastTrack server, and cannot assist in verifying connectivity. **C.** is incorrect because any connectivity problems would prevent you from being able to access the Administration page. **D.** is incorrect because stopping and restarting the Web server will not verify connectivity either. Using the Administration page to verify that the server is on and restarting the server are valid troubleshooting steps, but they cannot be used to verify connectivity.

42. ☑   C. Three. Novell recommends no less than three replicas for every partition. As a matter of fact, new servers installed into a partition will automatically get a read/write replica of the partition if there are not three (one master and two read/write) replicas already defined.

    ☒   A. is incorrect because a single (master) replica does not provide any fault tolerance. B. is incorrect because two replicas is not considered sufficient. D. is incorrect because four replicas results in additional NDS synchronization traffic while providing little benefit.

43. ☑   C. To provide clients with a list of registered NDPS printers. SRS maintains and advertises printer registration information. Unlike SAP, which broadcasts services throughout the entire network, SRS responds to the client after a direct query.

    ☒   A. is incorrect because NDPS does not use SAP broadcasts. B. is incorrect because it lists a function of the Resource Management Service (RMS). D. is incorrect because it lists the function of the Event Notification Service (ENS).

44. ☑   C. Each NetWare partition can have up to 32 volume segments. Server volumes can use one or more volume segments. Thus the 32-segment limit to a partition also limits the number of volumes on the partition. This volume-segment limitation is for standard NetWare partitions only, not for NSS partitions.

    ☒   A, B. are in incorrect because of the 32-segment limit of a NetWare partition. Since a segment cannot be divided between volumes, up to 32 segments and 32 volumes can be defined in a single partition. D. is incorrect because up to 32 volumes could be defined on a single partition if 32 segments were first created. Don't confuse partitions and segments with volumes. Up to 64 volumes can be defined on the server. Volumes can be created using one or more segments, which are created on partitions.

45. ☑ **D.** TSA500 and TSANDS. These two target service agents must be loaded on the server in order to back up the server and its NDS replica.
☒ **A.** is incorrect because SMS refers to Novell's Storage Management Service, not the specific agents used to accomplish SMS backups. **B.** is incorrect because NWBACK32 is the name of the workstation utility used to create backup and restore jobs. This application cannot be loaded on a NetWare server. **C.** is incorrect because there is no NetWare NLM module called NDSBACKER. The NLM used to back up NDS partitions is TSANDS.

46. ☑ **B.** LDAP Data Interchange Format. LDIF is the standard file format for exported LDAP data.
☒ **A, C, D.** are incorrect because they do not represent the full name of the LDIF file. Additional information and a description of LDIF file formats can be obtained at http://www.ukoln.ac.uk/metadata/desire/ overview/rev_13.htm.

47. ☑ **D.** Highlight the partition and use the Merge menu option to merge the partition with its parent. The only way to remove a partition properly is by merging it with the parent.
☒ **A, C.** are incorrect because there is no delete option in NDS manager using either the DELETE key or the menu. **B.** is incorrect because it is not possible to delete all the replicas of a partition in NDS Manager. NDS Manager requires that partitions have at least a Master replica, and this replica cannot be deleted. If the partition is merged with its parent, then NDS will automatically remove the partition and its replicas.

48. ☑ **D.** Add the line: NDPSM {NDPS manager name and context} to the AUTOEXEC.NCF file on the server assigned to this object. Creating the NDPS Manager will not automatically instruct the server to load the manager—you must manually add this command. After adding the command, you can switch to the console screen and manually type this command to start the NDPS manager manually.

☒ **A.** is incorrect because shutting down the server and restarting it will not allow the NDPS manager to start, unless the AUTOEXEC.NCF is first updated. **B.** is incorrect because it incorrectly identifies the name of the NDPS Manager module. **C.** is incorrect because the NDPS broker is not a component of the Manager. The NDPS broker sends data to clients and printers but does not communicate directly with the Manager.

49. ☑ **B.** This file is stored in the root of the SYS: volume and is used to record transaction tracking errors. The NetWare 5 OS uses transaction tracking files to maintain NDS and TTS availability is critical to maintaining a healthy directory services database.

☒ **A.** is incorrect because it indicates that the TTS$LOG.ERR is stored in the SYSTEM directory. **C.** is incorrect because it references the wrong directory, and because volume errors logs are stored in SYS:VOL$LOG.ERR. **D.** is incorrect because the server does not store any log files to the DOS partition. Both the TTS$LOG.ERR and the VOL$LOG.ERR files are stored in the root of the SYS volume, and should be reviewed and deleted periodically, as they continue to grow. The NetWare OS will recreate these files when a log entry is required.

50. ☑ **A.** LOAD QMAN –NEW. If Queue Manager (QMAN) is loaded, it must first be unloaded before executing this command. Loading the Queue Manager with the –NEW parameter will allow it to create a new queue. All previous queue jobs will be deleted by this action.

☒ **B.** is incorrect, as this command is used to recreate the SMS group and container objects. **C.** is incorrect because there is no specific NLM called SMS. SMS refers to the entire Storage Management Services functionality built into NetWare 5. **D.** is incorrect because this statement would load the C-Worthy interface at the server to perform backups and restorations of devices running SMS target agents. The –NEW parameter is invalid and would be ignored when loading this application.

51. ☑ **A, C.** SYS: or SYS:\. The installer must select a drive letter mapped to the root of the SYS volume.

☒ **B.** is incorrect because, although the FastTrack Web server installs to the SYS:NOVONYX directory, the installation program creates this directory for you. You must select the root of the SYS volume as the destination for the FastTrack server. **D.** is incorrect because it refers to a volume other than SYS.

52. ☑ **B.** Delete the read-only partition on the server and add a read-write replica. Read-only partitions cannot be used to authenticate to the network. In this instance, users had to cross a WAN link to authenticate to the network.

☒ **A.** is incorrect because read-only partitions cannot be promoted to read/write or master. They must be deleted and recreated. **C.** is incorrect because adding additional bandwidth would not have the same impact as allowing the users to authenticate to the local server. Placing a read/write replica on the local server allows users to authenticate even if the WAN link is unavailable. **D.** is incorrect because there is no option for configuring workstations to use a specific server for authentication. Workstations will always authenticate to the closest master or read/write replica.

53. ☑ **C.** A Novell or third-party gateway can be used to support these printers. Non-NDPS-printers can be supported by gateways. Novell offers a generic gateway in NetWare 5, and third-party gateways are also available.
☒ **A.** is incorrect because at present, very few printers are 100% NDPS aware. Novell is working with printer manufacturers to build NDPS support directly into printers and printer network adapters, but at present, most network printers require a gateway. **B.** is incorrect because gateways support a variety of network connections, not just server-attached printers. **D.** is incorrect because NDPS and the NDPS gateway allows network printers to be configured as NDPS devices without defining a standard NetWare print queue.

54. ☑ **A, B, C, D, E.** All of the above operations can be performed using Console One. At present, the performance of Console One and its lack of complete support for NDS operations limits its functionality, but simple tasks, such as the ones listed here, can be performed directly at the server console.

55. ☑ **B.** During the NetWare 5 client installation. The default client installation setting does not load the Windows 95/98 TSA. The client must be installed using custom options or the NWSETUP.INI file must be modified to change the default settings to install the TSA.
☒ **A.** is incorrect because the WSBACK32 client program can be used to create backup and restore jobs, but it is not part of the TSA. **C.** is incorrect because it is not possible to load the TSA via command line. **D.** is incorrect because there is no DOS device driver that acts as a TSA. For this reason, DOS and Windows 3.x workstations cannot be backed up using NetWare SMS.

56. ☑ **B.** Supervisor, Browse, Create, Delete, Rename, Inheritable. These are the trustee rights that can be granted to an object. These rights determine if a trustee can view objects in the tree, create new objects, delete objects, and rename objects, and whether trustee rights are inherited by objects below the selected container (the Inheritable object right only applies to container objects). The Supervisor right grants all the object rights to the trustee.
☒ **A.** is wrong because these are the individual property rights that can be assigned to a trustee, not the object rights. **C.** is wrong because these are the rights that can be granted at the file system level to files and directories, not the rights to an NDS object. **D.** is incorrect because there is no Admin object right. The NetWare 3.x Supervisor account has been replaced by an account called Admin, but full access to NDS objects and files are still granted using the Supervisor right.

57. ☑ **B.** Dial-Up Networking. The Dial-Up Networking software that ships with Windows 95, Windows 98, and Windows NT is all that is required on the remote client when connecting via PPPRNS.
☒ **A.** is incorrect because it is not necessary to load the NetWare Client 32 on a remote PC when connecting as a remote node. **C.** is incorrect because Win2NCS is used for dial-in access for remote control and dial-out access via server modems, not for remote node access. **D.** is incorrect because NetWare Connect is a component of the NetWare Internet Access Server (NIAS) software. NIAS is bundled with NetWare 5.

58. ☑ **B.** Three—User, Operator, and Manager. There are three roles associated with an NDPS printer object. Users are granted permission to print to the printer, Operators have administrative control of the printer, and Managers have complete control of the printer.
☒ **A.** is incorrect because it does not include the Manager role. **C.** incorrectly lists a fourth Admin security level. **D.** lists two fictitious security levels, Public and Admin.

59. ☑ A. NWCONFIG. This NLM can be used for a variety of tasks, including loading and unloading drivers, installing NetWare license certificates, and configuring volumes.

☒ B. is incorrect because there is no SETUP.NLM in NetWare 5. C. is incorrect because the INETCFG.NLM is used to configure the server network adapters and protocols. This NLM remains unchanged from NetWare 4. D. is incorrect because it refers to the NetWare Control File (NCF) used to start Console One. Console One is not a replacement for the functions available in NetWare 4's INSTALL.NLM.

60. ☑ C. To respond to remote host requests with the IP address of a requested host name. DNS servers perform a lookup for a requested host name, such as http://www.novell.com, and send the actual IP address back to the requesting host (i.e. 192.233.80.9).

☒ A. is incorrect because it refers to the function of a DHCP server. B. is incorrect because it refers to the functions of a Web server. D. is incorrect because it refers to the functions of a router. Typically, internal routers do not maintain Internet routing tables (due to the size and complexity of the Internet). The normal practice is to configure internal routers to maintain tables for a company's WAN, then configure a default route to the Internet for all other traffic.

61. ☑ C. An arrow appears next to property rights that apply to the selected object. Regardless of whether a specific property right applies to an object, it will appear in the list of property rights. Those properties that apply to the object have a right arrow pointing to their name in the list of property rights.

☒ A. is incorrect because all property rights in the NDS schema appear for every object, regardless of whether they apply to the object or not. B. is incorrect because the property object rights are not grayed out and property rights that do not apply to an object can be selected and modified (the modifications will not have any effect). D. is incorrect because the property rights selections are not grayed out either. As with C., selecting an invalid property (that is, one without the arrow to the left of its name) and changing the rights does not have any net effect on the trustee's property rights to the object.

62. ☑ **D.** Set Global Parameters. All of the options listed here are accessed from the Configure Security menu in NWCCON. The global parameters setting allows the administrator to limit dial-out connections to specific phone numbers. These settings can be overridden on a group or individual basis using either the Set User Parameters menu in NWCCON or via container, group, or user settings in the Network Administrator.

☒ **A, B, C.** are incorrect because these security settings in NWCCON do not support dial-out phone number restrictions.

63. ☑ **D.** DNIPINST. This module, when loaded at the server, will add the database object types used by NetWare 5 for DNS and DHCP objects to the NDS schema.

☒ **A.** is incorrect because NWCONFIG has no options for extending the schema. **B.** is incorrect because these modules are used to start the DHCP and DNS services, but they cannot be used to extend the schema. **C.** is incorrect because this command is used to start the Server Top Java interface for Console One. Neither Server Top nor Console One can be used to extend the NDS schema.

64. ☑ **A.** The directory service settings. The only setting under Global Options is Configure Directory Service. The options for directory service are Local Database, LDAP Directory Server, or NDS.

☒ **B.** is incorrect because these settings are configured from the Admin Preferences button. **C.** is incorrect because cluster management has its own button on the FastTrack Administration page. **D.** is incorrect because the default location of Web documents is configured from the FastTrack server information button.

65. ☑ **D.** Creates Administrative roles at different levels of the tree. NDS allows decentralized network management of the network. Administrative roles, such as Help Desk, Password Admins, File System Admins, Container Admins, and NDS partition Admins can easily be created by assigning specific rights to containers and objects in the tree.

☒ **A.** is incorrect because placing users in different containers from their server objects complicates the assignment of rights and is not a recommended practice. **B.** is incorrect because creating multiple NDS trees in the organization would also have a negative effect on network management. Separate NDS trees do not communicate with each other and would have to be managed independently. Multiple user and group accounts would have to be managed for users with access to objects in multiple trees. **C.** is incorrect because NDS does not provide native support for NetWare 3.x binderies.

66. ☑ **B.** The repair process locks the NDS database. During an unattended repair, the NDS replicas stored on a server are locked. Users who attempt to authenticate to the network using the affected server will be locked out until the DSREPAIR process unlocks the database.

☒ **A.** is incorrect because the users were only locked out during the repair process, so their user accounts are not likely to be corrupt. **C.** is incorrect because the DSREPAIR process does not dismount the SYS volume. **D.** is incorrect because users do not have to access the master replica when authenticating to the network; any server with either the master or a read/write replica can authenticate them to the network. The NetWare client attempts to authenticate to the closest server; if this server's database is locked, the user logon will fail.

67. ☑ **B.** Leave sufficient unallocated space for the NSS volume. NSS volumes are not created during the custom installation, but you can leave sufficient free space to create an NSS volume at a later time. The SYS volume must be created during the installation, and must reside on a standard NetWare partition. ☒ **A.** is incorrect because it suggests creating a single NetWare partition for both a standard volume type and an NSS volume. Allocating disk space to a NetWare partition renders this space unavailable to NSS. **C.** is incorrect because, at present, NetWare does not support placing the SYS volume on an NSS partition. **D.** is incorrect because this action will have no effect on NSS volume creation.

68. ☑ **A.** Load rconag6 *<password> <IP port> <IPX port>*. The remote-control agent, RCONAG6, is followed by the remote control password and the port numbers for TCP/IP and IPX. The default ports can be used, unless some other server module is already using these port numbers. The defaults are port 2034 for TCP/IP and port 16800 for IPX. ☒ **B.** is incorrect because RCONJ is used at the workstation, not at the server. **C.** is incorrect because this is the command to load remote support for the old RCONSOLE utility, not RCONJ. **D.** is incorrect because there is not an NWAGENT module in NetWare 5.

69. ☑ **D.** Create a DHCP server object. After the DHCP server object is created, you can configure the DHCP server and add subnets. ☒ **A.** is incorrect because several other tasks have to be performed before a subnet can be defined. **B.** is incorrect because the DHCP server object must be created before the server can be selected. **C.** is incorrect because you cannot import an existing DHCP database or create DHCP objects before the DCHP server object is created.

70. ☑ **D.** [RF] to the SYS:PUBLIC and [C] to the SYS:MAIL directory for all servers in the container. The Read and Filescan right is granted to the SYS:PUBLIC directory and the Create right is granted to the SYS:MAIL directory for the container where a server object resides.

    ☒ **A.** is incorrect because the Write right is not automatically granted to the container for the SYS:PUBLIC directory on any server in the container. **B, C.** are incorrect because no container rights are automatically granted to the SYS:SYSTEM directory of a server.

71. ☑ **B.** All NetWare Connect servers. The Container, Group, and User objects in the NDS tree do not contain server-specific settings. All remote access settings for Containers, Groups, and Users will apply to any NetWare Connect server the user accesses.

    ☒ **A.** is incorrect because the users' default server does not have to be a NetWare Connect server, and remote-access settings are not configured at a server level. **C.** is incorrect because a NetWare Connect server does not have to reside in the same container as a user object. Remote-access settings apply to all remote-access servers in the NDS tree. **D.** is incorrect because there is no option in the remote-access configuration screen to specify the NetWare Connect server.

72. ☑ **C.** File compression and suballocation can be enabled on existing volumes. Both NetWare 4.1x and NetWare 5 support these two extended volume attributes. During the volume upgrades, you can choose to enable file compression and suballocation on a volume-by-volume basis. File compression allows the operating system to track file usage and compress files that have not been accessed in a specified amount of time. The suballocation flag allows the operating system to store multiple small files in a single volume sector, significantly reducing storage requirements on a volume with a large number of files that are smaller than the volume sector size. NetWare volumes support sector sizes from 4K to 64K, and in NetWare 4.1x and 5 the default sector size is 64K, to take advantage of the suballocation bit.

☒ **A.** is incorrect because, while it may be possible to perform an in-place upgrade without adding additional hardware to the server, the processor and memory requirements of NetWare 5 are considerably greater than earlier versions of NetWare, and many servers will require additional hardware. **B.** is incorrect because an in-place upgrade requires extensive modifications to the existing NetWare server volumes and these modifications cannot be easily reversed. The possibility of data loss is greater when doing an in-place upgrade. **D.** is incorrect because volume sector sizes, once defined, cannot be changed. A volume sector size is selected prior to creating the volume, and an in-place upgrade modifies existing volumes–it does not create new ones.

73. ☑ **C.** Installing the MAC2NCS program from the MAC Client disk shipped with NetWare 5.

☒ **A.** is incorrect because Apple Computer does not supply the MAC2NCS redirector for dial-out connections. Dial-in AppleTalk Remote Access (ARAS) support does require additional software available from Apple Computer. **B.** is incorrect because it is not necessary to download the MAC2NCS software since it ships with NetWare 5. **D.** is incorrect because the MAC2NCS redirector is on the MAC Client disk.

Part 9

Test Yourself: Practice Exam 3: Networking Technologies (Exam 50-632)

Test Yourself:
Practice Exam 3
Questions

Q&A

Before you call to register for the actual Networking exam (Exam # 50-632), take the following test and see how you make out. Set a timer for 105 minutes—the same time you'll have to take the live exam—and answer the following 79 questions in the time allotted. Once you've finished, turn to the Practice Exam 3 Answers section and check your score to see if you passed! Good luck!

Practice Exam 3 Questions

1. What type of network allows each workstation to act as a server and share its files and printers?

   A. Peer to peer
   B. Client/server
   C. Server centric
   D. Protocol

2. TDX.Com is a new Internet company with a group of NetWare® 5 servers running the FastWeb server software to provide the Web services to Internet customers. TDX.Com records the length of time that each customer uses when accessing their TDX software and manages charges based on the bytes transferred.

   TDX.Com's marketing department uses an application that creates a newsletter and sends it through the TDX11 server to the fax machines of TDX.Com's customers. What type of service is the TDX11 server providing?

   A. Application
   B. Database
   C. Print
   D. Storage

3. What benefit does STP have over UTP?

   A. STP is cheaper.
   B. STP does not require any grounding.
   C. STP is less susceptible to interference.
   D. STP uses fiber optics.

4. When data is transmitted from a sending node to a receiving node, which of the following best represents what happens to the data at the receiving node?

A. Packets are received at the presentation layer and the headers stripped off, then sent to the data-link layer.

B. Bitstream is received by the data-link layer and the headers stripped off, then sent to the MAC layer.

C. Bitstream is received by the physical layer, the bits assembled into frames and sent to the data-link layer.

D. Packets are received by the transport layer, the packet headers stripped off and sent up to the LLC layer.

5. JNS is an enterprise with four sites. The JNS internetwork will be implemented as shown here. This configuration is a hub and spoke network, where the HQ site is the hub and all other networks are the spokes with direct point-to-point links to the HQ site. RTR1 will have an IP address of 199.5.5.52 on one interface and 199.5.6.81 on the other interface. The subnet masks for all IP addresses at JNS is 255.255.255.0.

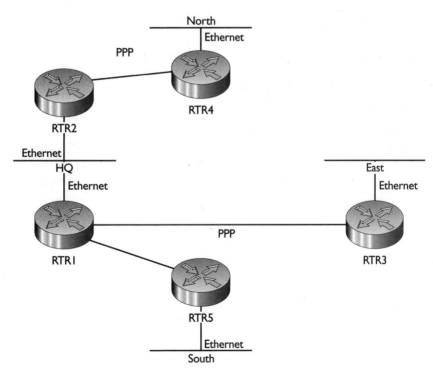

A. What part of the address 199.5.5.52 is the network segment's address?

B. 199.5.0.0

C. 199.0.0.0

D. 255.255.255.0

E. 199.5.5.0

6. The transport layer sends data independent of the lower layers. It is conceivable that packets will take multiple paths through the internetwork and arrive in a different order than they were sent. How does the transport layer know how to put the packets into the correct order?

A. CRC

B. Sequence number

C. Connection identifier

D. Port

7. What is the process of deciphering an encrypted file?

A. Encryption

B. Decryption

C. Compression

D. Expansion

8. Rhonda is attempting to access a file that is located on SERVER1\ CDROM:DIR\FILES. Rhonda receives an error message that the volume is not available. What type of storage is Rhonda attempting to access?

A. Online

B. Nearline

C. Offline

D. Volume

9. TDX.Com's administrator uses an SNMP application to watch the processor utilization on each of the TDX servers. The captured data is then graphed. The administrator makes decisions on whether to upgrade to multiple processors, to add new servers, or to adjust the network server configuration, based on this data. For what type of management is the SNMP data being used?

A. Configuration

B. Fault

C. Security

D. Performance

10. Which of the following is also known as Thin Ethernet?

A. RG-11

B. RG-58

C. RG-59

D. RG-62

11. If NetBIOS is a session-layer API running on a workstation, what layer does it communicate with on a server that supports NetBIOS?

A. NetBEUI

B. Transport

C. Session

D. Application

12. JNS is an enterprise with four sites. The JNS internetwork will be implemented. This configuration is a hub and spoke network, where the HQ site is the hub and all other networks are the spokes with direct point-to-point links to the HQ site. RTR1 will have an IP address of 199.5.5.52 on one interface and 199.5.6.81 on the other interface. The subnet masks for all IP addresses at JNS is 255.255.255.0. All servers and workstations use IPX as well as IP on the JNS network. Pat adds a route to SvrEast and the East segment on RTR1 using IPX. What type of routing has Pat implemented?

    A. Static routing

    B. Dynamic Host Configuration Protocol

    C. Dynamic routing

    D. Domain Naming Service

13. Which of the following mechanisms is used for error control?

    A. CRC

    B. Port

    C. ARP

    D. NDS™

14. Which of the following is an application layer service?

    A. Ethernet

    B. CAT5

    C. SAP

    D. SMTP

15. What presentation layer method changes the amount of data that is transmitted?

    A. Encryption

    B. Bit-order translation

    C. Compression

    D. Decryption

16. What function is necessary when a computer receives multiple packets at the transport layer, but they are multiplexed for two different services?

A. Address/name resolution

B. Flow control

C. Message segment development

D. Segmentation

17. Which of the following best represents a global network?

A. Metropolitan area network

B. Local area network

C. Wide area network

D. Segment

18. TDX.Com is a new Internet company with a group of NetWare 5 servers running the FastWeb server software to provide the Web services to Internet customers. TDX.Com records the length of time that each customer uses when accessing their TDX software and manages charges based on the bytes transferred.

TDX.Com has a SQL service running on the TDX08 server. Currently, a user inputs a query into a Web page. The Web server sends the Web page to TDX08, read by TDX08 as a request, and a query response is sent back to the Web server. The Web server then displays the response in another Web page. TDX.Com is considering migrating the service to Oracle. What type of service is being provided by TDX08?

A. Database service

B. Application service

C. Message service

D. Storage service

19. What is the best reason to select fiber-optic cabling over UTP?

A. Capacity

B. Ease of installation

C. Cost

D. Interference immunity

20. What is the term that defines network structure at the physical layer?

A. Bitstream

B. Cabling

C. Topology

D. Electrical signaling

21. Which of the following connection services manage the rate of data transmission?

A. Sequence control

B. Flow control

C. CRC

D. Error control

22. What is an application layer service that provides file transfer services?

A. NDS

B. SNMP

C. PING

D. NCOPY

23. Which of the following storage services uses a migration process?

A. Online

B. Nearline

C. Offline

D. Hot swap

24. TDX.Com is a new Internet company with a group of NetWare 5 servers running the FastWeb server software to provide the Web services to Internet customers. TDX.Com records the length of time that each customer uses when accessing their TDX software and manages charges based on the bytes transferred.

TDX.Com analyzed their incoming traffic and realized that more than 50 percent of the traffic was initiated from southern California. TDX.Com's Website servers are located in Boca Raton, Florida. In order to provide the majority of their clients with a faster service, TDX.Com decides to open a sister site in southern California. TDX.Com's administrator is concerned that the new servers will not be equivalent to the existing servers because there is no control over how they are installed. What should TDX.Com's administrator implement?

A. Configuration management

B. Fault management

C. Security management

D. Accounting management

25. Which of the following is a wireless media?

A. UTP

B. STP

C. RG-11

D. Radio

26. JNS is an enterprise with four sites. The JNS internetwork will be implemented. This configuration is a hub and spoke network, where the HQ site is the hub and all other networks are the spokes with direct point-to-point links to the HQ site. RTR1 will have an IP address of 199.5.5.52 on one interface and 199.5.6.81 on the other interface. The subnet masks for all IP addresses at JNS is 255.255.255.0. Pat uses the PSTN to connect to the network in order to run the network management system remotely. What type of system is the PSTN?

  A. Packet switched
  B. Circuit switched
  C. Message switched
  D. Cell switched

27. What type of physical topology is characterized by a single cable that all network nodes access and that has terminators at each end?

  A. Ring
  B. Mesh
  C. Bus
  D. Star

28. What mechanism is used to ensure data reliability at the transport layer?

  A. NDS
  B. DHCP
  C. ACK
  D. ARP

29. Which NLM will configure storage volumes on a NetWare 5 file server?

  A. NWINSTALL
  B. NWCONFIG
  C. CONFIG
  D. STORCFG

30. TDX.Com is a new Internet company with a group of NetWare 5 servers running the FastWeb server software to provide the Web services to Internet customers. TDX.Com records the length of time that each customer uses when accessing their TDX software and manages charges based on the bytes transferred.

After the TDX.Com administrator creates the second site in southern California, the TDX.Com marketing group launches a huge push for the TDX.Com applications in the United Kingdom. The marketing group is successful and the TDX.Com Web sites in both southern California and in Florida are inundated with international traffic. The administrator adds a UK site to the network. Even though each site is connected via the Internet, the administrator adds private links between Florida and each of the other sites. What type of network does TDX.Com represent?

A. MAN

B. LAN

C. WAN

D. Segment

31. Cindy sets up a workstation and printer using infrared to the network. The network infrared diode is not within the line of sight of the workstation, but the workstation still connects to the network. How is this possible?

A. It is not possible.

B. The network Infrared diode emits light in multiple directions.

C. The Infrared diode manages bidirectional traffic regardless of the network diode.

D. The infrared light bounces off the walls.

32. Alan has a Token Ring network that he is expanding by adding a second multistation access (MAU) unit. What must he do to make the two MAU units work as a single ring?

A. Connect the ring in port on MAU1 to the ring in port on MAU2, then connect the ring out port on MAU1 to the ring out port on MAU2.

B. Connect the ring in port on MAU1 to the ring out port on MAU1, then connect the ring in port on MAU2 to the ring out port on MAU2.

C. Connect the ring out port on MAU1 to the ring out port on MAU2, then connect the ring in port on MAU1 to the ring in port on MAU2.

D. Connect the ring in port on MAU1 to the ring out port on MAU2, then connect the ring in port on MAU2 to the ring out port on MAU1.

33. JNS is an enterprise with four sites. The JNS internetwork will be implemented. This configuration is a hub and spoke network, where the HQ site is the hub and all other networks are the spokes with direct point-to-point links to the HQ site. RTR1 will have an IP address of 199.5.5.52 on one interface and 199.5.6.81 on the other interface. The subnet masks for all IP addresses at JNS is 255.255.255.0.
    Pat decides to keep the existing point-to-point links, but to add a redundant link between East and South, and another redundant link between South and North. Pat wants to implement a dynamic routing protocol to create the routing tables. What will the routing protocol have to perform because of the redundant routes?

    A. Cost
    B. Route selection
    C. Ticks
    D. Static routes

34. With which layers is the end user most likely to interact?

    A. Lower layers
    B. Middle layers
    C. Upper layers
    D. Only the physical layer

35. What does the application layer use to interact with a workstation's operating system?

    A. SNMP
    B. SAP
    C. OS call interception
    D. NLM

36. Which service does GroupWise® provide?

A. File services

B. Storage services

C. Print services

D. Message services

37. George is installing a network for Private Health Care (PHC). PHC has three nursing care facilities in two states. None of the facilities have an existing network. Instead, PHC has some stand-alone PCs and Apple Macintosh computers and a UNIX host running an accounting package with two serial terminals in a single room at one nursing facility. Data is faxed to the one facility and input to the accounting system.

George has purchased three server machines, network operating software, hubs, workstations, Windows, and printers. What else must George plan to install?

A. Fax server

B. PDA cradles

C. Security system

D. Transmission media

38. When Jack installed a test lab network, he decided to use CAT 5 cabling with RJ-45 connectors. He placed the cable into the hub, but was unable to connect the workstation. What was missing?

A. Modem

B. RJ-45 receptacle

C. NIC

D. Repeater

39. Of the following physical topologies, which offers ease of troubleshooting because each network device has a separate cable to the hub?

A. Cellular

B. Ring

C. Star

D. Mesh

40. JNS is an enterprise with four sites. The JNS internetwork will be implemented. This configuration is a hub and spoke network, where the HQ site is the hub and all other networks are the spokes with direct point-to-point links to the HQ site. RTR1 will have an IP address of 199.5.5.52 on one interface and 199.5.6.81 on the other interface. The subnet masks for all IP addresses at JNS is 255.255.255.0. Pat wants to ensure that whenever a change occurs on the JNS internetwork, the routers are all updated quickly. What is this process called?

A. Route selection

B. Static routes

C. Route discovery

D. Convergence

41. Which of the following layers owns the services that are used by end users?

A. Session

B. Presentation

C. Application

D. None

42. What protocol may use an agent?

A. SNMP

B. SAP

C. DNS

D. DHCP

43. Select the NDS object that is not a printing service element.

A. NDPS Manager

B. NDS Manager

C. PSERVER.NLM

D. PCONSOLE

44. George is installing a network for Private Health Care (PHC). PHC has three nursing care facilities in two states. None of the facilities have an existing network. Instead, PHC has some stand-alone PCs and Apple Macintosh computers and a UNIX host running an accounting package with two serial terminals in a single room at one nursing facility. Data is faxed to the one facility and input to the accounting system.

George informs PHC about the probable requirement of fiber-optic cabling and its associated costs at the main facility. PHC has asked George to keep the costs for transmission media as low as possible. What is the second priority George must take in selecting a transmission media?

   A. Attenuation
   B. Cost
   C. Immunity from interference
   D. Capacity

45. Which of the following services is specific to an Intranet?

   A. Database services
   B. Application services
   C. Web services
   D. Message services

46. Which of the following will alleviate the problem of attenuation?

   A. Repeater
   B. NIC
   C. Modem
   D. RJ-45

47. What type of signal does modulation create?

   A. Digital
   B. Multipoint
   C. Point to point
   D. Analog

48. JNS is an enterprise with four sites. The JNS internetwork will be implemented. This configuration is a hub and spoke network, where the HQ site is the hub and all other networks are the spokes with direct point-to-point links to the HQ site. RTR1 will have an IP address of 199.5.5.52 on one interface and 199.5.6.81 on the other interface. The subnet masks for all IP addresses at JNS is 255.255.255.0.

Pat also wants to use a link-state routing protocol for IP routing. What is the TCP/IP link-state routing protocol?

A. AURP

B. OSPF

C. IGRP

D. NLSP

49. What does the session layer establish between two nodes?

A. Dialog

B. Address

C. Multiplexing

D. Sequencing

50. Which of the following network applications provides access to directory services?

A. NCOPY

B. RCONSOLE

C. NetWare Administrator

D. ARP

51. Database services can be distributed to multiple servers for fault tolerance. When a database is distributed, what process must occur to ensure that the data is updated on each server?

A. File update synchronization

B. Replication

C. Multiplexing

D. Migration

52. George is installing a network for Private Health Care (PHC). PHC has three nursing care facilities in two states. None of the facilities have an existing network. Instead, PHC has some stand-alone PCs and Apple Macintosh computers and a UNIX host running an accounting package with two serial terminals in a single room at one nursing facility. Data is faxed to the one facility and input to the accounting system.

George redesigns the Sun City facility so that the maximum distance between the farthest point and a wiring closet is 89 meters. Since there has never been any network in the facility before, the PHC president has raised the question of whether or not the network will be fast enough for future usage. What transmission media consideration has the president brought up to George?

A. Attenuation

B. Cost

C. Capacity

D. Ease of installation

53. What equipment repeats a signal on a single port?

A. NIC

B. Switch

C. Modem

D. Hub

54. What are the two types of biphase encoding with self-clocking?

A. Manchester

B. NRZ

C. RZ

D. Differential Manchester

55. JNS is an enterprise with four sites. The JNS internetwork will be implemented. This configuration is a hub and spoke network, where the HQ site is the hub and all other networks are the spokes with direct point-to-point links to the HQ site. RTR1 will have an IP address of 199.5.5.52 on one interface and 199.5.6.81 on the other interface. The subnet masks for all IP addresses at JNS is 255.255.255.0. Pat knows that the router works at the network layer, but he also heard that the transport layer has an error-control method. He is concerned that no errors are checked at the routers, but only after data is received by the end node. What function does a network layer perform that will allay Pat's concerns?

A. CRC

B. Windowing

C. Flow control

D. Sequencing

56. Which of the following describes an alternating, two-way communication?

A. Simplex

B. Half-duplex

C. Full-duplex

D. Half-simplex

57. Which of the following is a feature of network management?

A. Replication

B. Application services

C. Security management

D. Migration

58. Which of the following is a transmission medium made of plastic or glass?

A. STP

B. UTP

C. Fiber optic

D. Coax

59. Which OSI layer header does a router use?

A. Data link

B. Network

C. Transport

D. Session

60. What is another name for a signal's clocking system?

A. Phase shift keying

B. Manchester encoding

C. Bit synchronization

D. Idling

61. JNS is an enterprise with four sites. The JNS internetwork will be implemented. This configuration is a hub and spoke network, where the HQ site is the hub and all other networks are the spokes with direct point-to-point links to the HQ site. RTR1 will have an IP address of 199.5.5.52 on one interface and 199.5.6.81 on the other interface. The subnet masks for all IP addresses at JNS is 255.255.255.0.
Pat wants to know how many hops are between the SvrNorth1 server on the North network segment and a workstation on the South network segment. How many hops are there?

A. Two

B. Three

C. Four

D. Five

62. What layer is sometimes implemented with the ability to resume data transmission where it left off if there was an interruption in network service?

A. Application

B. Presentation

C. Session

D. Transport

63. TDX.Com is a new Internet company with a group of NetWare 5 servers running the FastWeb server software to provide the Web services to Internet customers. TDX.Com records the length of time that each customer uses when accessing their TDX software and manages charges based on the bytes transferred.
What type of network management feature is used by TDX?

A. Fault Management
B. Configuration management
C. Security management
D. Accounting management

64. How many categories of twisted-pair cabling has the EIA ranked?

A. Two
B. Three
C. Four
D. Five

65. What is the correct sequence of OSI layers, from the highest to the lowest layer?

A. Application, session, presentation, transport, network, physical, data link
B. Presentation, session, data link, transport, network, physical, application
C. Application, presentation, session, transport, network, data link, physical
D. Presentation, application, transport, session, network, physical, data link

66. What are the two sublayers of the data-link layer?

A. Media access control
B. Transmission control
C. Logical link control
D. Presentation

67. Pat heard that the transport layer handles multiplexing, which lets multiple applications on his NetWare server use the same datastream transmission on the network. He asks his consultant what mechanism makes multiplexing happen. What is the consultant's response?

A. Socket

B. Name resolution

C. Sequencing

D. Windowing

68. Into what format does the presentation layer translate data?

A. Bits

B. Signals

C. Voltages

D. Transfer syntax

69. TDX.Com is a new Internet company with a group of NetWare 5 servers running the FastWeb server software to provide the Web services to Internet customers. TDX.Com records the length of time that each customer uses when accessing their TDX software and manages charges based on the bytes transferred.

The TDX.Com RUNIT application is provided by a separate server. RUNIT is accessed by a hyperlink in the TDX.Com Web site. Although RUNIT appears to be running from the network client, it is being processed on the server. What type of service does the RUNIT server provide?

A. Database service

B. Application service

C. Storage service

D. Web service

70. Which connector has an 8-pin connection?

    A. RJ-45

    B. RS-232

    C. RJ-11

    D. Vampire clamp

71. Which layer on a receiving device communicates with the transport layer on the sending device?

    A. Physical

    B. Data link

    C. Network

    D. Transport

72. Ethernet NIC manufacturers use a method that ensures what quality for the MAC address?

    A. Polling response

    B. Token Ring passing capability

    C. Logical link control

    D. Unique addresses

73. JNS is an enterprise with four sites. The JNS internetwork will be implemented. This configuration is a hub and spoke network, where the HQ site is the hub and all other networks are the spokes with direct point-to-point links to the HQ site. RTR1 will have an IP address of 199.5.5.52 on one interface and 199.5.6.81 on the other interface. The subnet masks for all IP addresses at JNS is 255.255.255.0. Pat is planning to switch some of his servers to IP from IPX. What name resolution service or protocol will no longer be needed for those servers?

    A. DNS

    B. NDS

    C. SAP

    D. DHCP

74. Which of the following specifies that data is read from the last byte received?

    A. Big endian

    B. Bit order translation

    C. Little endian

    D. Sequencing

75. George is installing a network for Private Health Care (PHC). PHC has three nursing care facilities in two states. None of the facilities have an existing network. Instead, PHC has some stand-alone PCs and Apple Macintosh computers and a UNIX host running an accounting package with two serial terminals in a single room at one nursing facility. Data is faxed to the one facility and input to the accounting system.
PHC's main facility is located in Florida. The other two facilities are located in Arizona, with one in Sun City and the other in Flagstaff. Sun City is a relatively new desert community and PHC has a brand new, state-of-the-art facility there. Flagstaff is an older, mountainous, community, and PHC has a smaller facility there. In the Sun City location, George determines that the best place to put wiring closets is 142 meters from the farthest proposed location for a workstation. In the Flagstaff location, George has a maximum distance of 52 meters. What should George be concerned with when he puts wiring in the Sun City location?

    A. Attenuation

    B. Cost

    C. Capacity

    D. Ease of installation

76. Tim has two network segments that he needs to connect together so that SNA can be sent between the two segments. Segment 1 has a mainframe and Segment 2 has a server and workstations. There are other segments that connect to Segment 1 and Tim wants to make sure that only traffic meant for Segment 2 is forwarded to it from Segment 1. Which piece of equipment will do this?

    A. Repeater

    B. Active hub

    C. Passive hub

    D. Bridge

77. Which digital signal encoding technique uses a positive voltage plus a zero voltage to represent data?

    A. Polar encoding

    B. Frequency shift keying

    C. Unipolar encoding

    D. Manchester

78. JNS is an enterprise with four sites. The JNS internetwork will be implemented. This configuration is a hub and spoke network, where the HQ site is the hub and all other networks are the spokes with direct point-to-point links to the HQ site. RTR1 will have an IP address of 199.5.5.52 on one interface and 199.5.6.81 on the other interface. The subnet masks for all IP addresses at JNS is 255.255.255.0. Pat is applying IP addresses manually and knows that they are used for routing data. He heard from his brother-in-law that IP addresses and routing are handled by the physical layer. Which layer handles routing?

    A. Physical

    B. Data-link

    C. Network

    D. Session

79. What can be used to secure a dialog?

    A. CRC

    B. Data transmission

    C. Password

    D. Encryption

Test Yourself:
Practice Exam 3
Answers

Q & *A*

The answers to the questions are in boldface, followed by a brief explanation. The incorrect answer choices are explained in the final paragraph following each correct answer. Some of the explanations detail the logic you should use to choose the correct answer, while others give factual reasons why the answer is correct. If you miss several questions on a similar topic, you should review the corresponding section in the CNE® NetWare® 5 Study Guide before taking the Networking Technologies test.

Practice Exam 3 Answers

1. ☑ **A.** A peer-to-peer network exists when each workstation on the network can also be a server by sharing its files and printers. The peer-to-peer network workstations are both service requestors and service providers. Each workstation becomes a peer of the others since they are all equal in their capabilities. The other type of network is a client/server, or server centric, network. In this arrangement, the server is the only one capable of sharing its files to the workstations. The workstations each act as service requestors, but do not act as service providers. The server is a service provider and is dedicated to the sharing of files, printers and other network resources. The following illustration compares peer-to-peer and client/server.

☒ **B.** Client/server is incorrect because it uses a dedicated server. **C.** Server centric is incorrect because it uses a dedicated server. **D.** Protocol is incorrect because it is the method of communication between network devices.

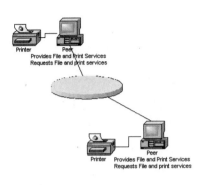 

Peer-to-Peer

Each workstation acts as a file and print server

Client/Server

Each workstation requests services. Only servers provide services.

2. ☑ **C.** The TDX11 server provides a print service. Print service includes fax service as a subset. To an application, a fax machine is similar to a serial printer device. In this way, the application prints to the remote fax machine, but must create a serial connection to it first through a dial-up procedure.

☒ **A.** Application service is incorrect because it makes a remote application appear to be running locally. **B.** Database service is incorrect because a fax does not store data in a structured format like a database. **D.** Storage service is incorrect because the TDX11 server is sending data out, not storing it.

3. ☑ **C.** Shielded twisted-pair (STP) is less susceptible to electromagnetic interference than UTP, or unshielded twisted-pair.

☒ **A.** STP is more expensive than UTP so this answer is incorrect. **B.** STP requires a special grounding that UTP does not require, so this answer is incorrect. **D.** STP uses copper cabling, not fiber optics.

4. ☑ **C.** The data is received at the physical layer in bitstream format, the bits assembled into frames, then sent to the data-link layer. The way that data travels across the transmission media is in the form of bits, in an electronic signal format. This signal format is known as a bitstream.
☒ **A.** is incorrect because only bits are received at the physical layer.
B. is incorrect because the physical layer will be receiving the bitstream.
D. is incorrect because bitstream, not packets, received at the physical layer, not the transport layer.

5. ☑ **D.** The network segment's address is 199.5.5.0. IP addresses include a logical address for the network and for the node. A subnet mask is used to subdivide the address into its network and node portions. The IP address for the network portion consists of all the bits masked by the subnet mask. These bits begin at the leftmost side of the address. The router is given a network and node address for each interface attached to a network segment.
☒ **A.** 199.5.0.0 is incorrect because it does not include all of the network portion of the address. **B.** 199.0.0.0 is also incorrect because it does not include all of the network portion of the address. **C.** 255.255.255.0 is incorrect because it is the subnet mask.

6. ☑ **B.** The transport layer knows how to put the packets in the correct order using the sequence number. Each packet header includes a sequence number, which is a serialized number that is assigned to the packet at the sending computer. When packets are received out of order, the transport layer puts them in order according to the sequence number.
☒ **A.** CRC is incorrect because it is used for error control. **C.** Connection identifier is incorrect because it is used to identify which application, or data conversation, the data is meant for. **D.** Port is incorrect because it is the same as a connection identifier.

7. ☑ **B.** Decryption is the process of deciphering an encrypted file. Different types of encryption have different ways to decrypt a file. Some decryption methods use keys, passwords and other user-supplied authentication. Others are handled transparently to the end user because the operating system, software, or even the directory service will authenticate the user to the file and decrypt it.

☒ **A.** Encryption is incorrect because that is the method of encoding the file so that it cannot be read. **C.** Compression is incorrect because that is a method of reducing the data size before transmission. **D.** Expansion is incorrect because that is the method of increasing the data size to the original transmission size.

8. ☑ **B.** Nearline storage. This is a type of CD-ROM, optical jukebox, or carousel. Nearline storage is not always immediately available, since the storage media can be easily replaced. NetWare mounts CD-ROM drives as volumes. CD-ROMs use different volume names for each CD. The volume names do not reflect whether the volume is a CD or not, so end users do not necessarily know that they are accessing a CD-ROM.

☒ **A.** Online storage is incorrect because it is nonremovable storage media on the server. **C.** Offline storage is incorrect because it refers to tape storage. **D.** Volume storage is incorrect because it is not a storage method but a storage area on a server.

9. ☑ **D.** The SNMP data is being used for performance management, which is the process of balancing network demands with network capabilities. This includes being able to analyze trends, such as the ones created through graphing SNMP data. It also includes the adjustment of various components in order to identify bottlenecks and then remove their impact on the network's performance. Performance management is the delicate balance of enabling network availability during peak demand periods, predicting future demands, and providing for those demands. Performance management tends to be a forgotten task when there are problems on a network.

☒ **A.** Configuration management is incorrect because it is not normally transmitted. **B.** Fault management is incorrect because the utilization metric does not mean the server has faulted. **C.** Security management is incorrect because the data is not being used to change the security on the network.

PE 3 EXAM 50-632 ANSWERS

10. ☑ **B.** RG-58 cabling is better known as Thin Ethernet. RG-58 is a coaxial cable with a 50-ohm rating. It is thinner and more flexible than Thick Ethernet, which explains their nicknames.

☒ **A.** RG-11 is incorrect because it is Thick Ethernet. **C.** RG-59 is incorrect because it is the coaxial cabling used for cable television. **D.** RG-62 is incorrect because it is used for ArcNet.

11. ☑ **C.** NetBIOS running on a workstation would communicate with the session layer on a server. Peer layers communicate between sending and receiving computers. This means that the physical layer on the sending computer communicates with the physical layer on the receiving computer, and the sending data-link layer communicates with the receiving data-link layer, and so on up through the application layer.

☒ **A.** NetBEUI is incorrect since NetBEUI is a transport layer protocol. **B.** Transport is incorrect because the transport layer is transparently accessed by session layer protocols. **D.** Application is incorrect, because the application layer is above the session layer.

12. ☑ **A.** Pat has implemented static routing. Static routing is when a routing table is created by the manual additions of routes to each server or router. Each route that is added to a router or server is placed in a routing table.

☒ **B.** Dynamic Host Configuration Protocol (DHCP) is incorrect because it is a dynamic IP addressing method. **C.** Dynamic routing is incorrect because it requires a routing protocol to establish routes. **D.** Domain naming service is incorrect because it is an IP address-to-IP host mapping service.

13. ☑ **A.** CRC is a mechanism used for error control. A CRC is an algorithm that is performed on the data packet at the sending transport layer. The value of the CRC is placed in the header of the packet. At the receiving node, the same algorithm is performed on the data packet and the results compared to the CRC value. If the results do not match, the data packet is dropped.

☒ **B.** Port is incorrect because it identifies a data conversation. **C.** ARP is incorrect because it is a protocol used for name resolution. **D.** NDS™ is incorrect because it is a directory service.

14. ☑ **D.** Simple Mail Transfer Protocol (SMTP) is an application layer service. This is a message service.

☒ **A.** Ethernet is incorrect because it is a media and topology specification. **B.** CAT5 is incorrect because it is a type of copper cabling. **C.** SAP is incorrect because it is an address/name resolution protocol.

15. ☑ **C.** Compression is the presentation layer method that changes the amount of data that is transmitted. Compression is a method of shortening the amount of data by replacing typical bit sequences with shorter bit sequences. This is similar to replacing the word *and* with the symbol *&*. By replacing each *and* with the symbol, even if it were part of a word (b*and*), the total amount of data is reduced.

☒ **A.** Encryption is incorrect because it does not necessarily change the amount of data, but the translation method. **B.** Bit-order translation is incorrect because it is the method of reading the bits from the first or last received within each byte. **D.** Decryption is the reverse of encryption and may not change the amount of data transmitted.

16. ☑ **C.** The transport layer uses message segment development to reassemble the packets into the two different data conversations.

☒ **A.** Address/name resolution is incorrect because it will map a name to an address. **B.** Flow control is incorrect because it will maintain an optimal flow of data through the network. **D.** Segmentation is incorrect because segmentation is what happens when the message is multiplexed with other data conversations at the sending node.

17. ☑ **C.** A wide area network (WAN) is the best representation of a global network from this list. It is one of three types of networks, namely, a local area network (LAN), a metropolitan area network (MAN), and WAN. These types graduate in size, with the LAN consisting of one or more physical segments that are confined within a building or campus. A MAN consists of two or more LANs within a single metropolitan area. Usually, the term MAN is not used and the WAN terminology is applied to the area instead. A WAN consists of two or more LANs that are geographically distant from each other, but connected through network links.

 ☒ **A.** Metropolitan area network is incorrect because it is limited to a metropolitan area. **B.** Local area network is typically limited to a building or campus. **D.** A segment is a single portion of a network that is limited in size and distance.

18. ☑ **A.** TDX08 provides a database service. Both SQL and Oracle are types of database services that are available commercially. SQL service is available from many different manufacturers, because it is incorporated into database software. Oracle, however, is a proprietary vendor's database management software. A database service is a common service provided via the Internet. It is usually provided in the manner depicted here, where a Web server sends queries to a database server, and then displays the query responses in a Web page to the requesting user.

 ☒ **B.** Application service is not provided by Oracle. **C.** Message services is incorrect because Oracle is not an e-mail application. **D.** Storage services is incorrect because Oracle does not provide server storage.

19. ☑ **D.** Of all the reasons to select fiber-optic cabling over UTP, interference immunity ranks the highest. UTP is very susceptible to interference, while fiber is immune to it.

 ☒ **A.** Capacity is incorrect because it is similar for both types, but fiber is commonly implemented at over 100 Mbps, while UTP is implemented more commonly at 100 Mbps, or less. **B.** Ease of installation is incorrect because UTP is much easier to install than fiber optics is. **C.** Cost is incorrect because UTP is much cheaper than fiber optics.

20. ☑ **C.** The network structure at the physical layer is known as the topology. The topology is the physical shape of the network segment. When drawn out on paper, a layout of the network resembles certain shapes. The ring topology, where workstations are connected to each other and the last to the first, creates a circle, or ring. A topology with a hub in the center and workstations connected to each port represents a star.

☒ **A.** Bitstream is incorrect because it is the electrical signal stream of data transmitted across the cable. **B.** Cabling is incorrect because it does not define the network structure. **D.** Electrical signaling is incorrect because it is the format of the voltage for the bitstream.

21. ☑ **B.** Flow control is a connection service that manages the rate of data transmission. Flow control is the method of managing the data flow between the sending and receiving node. The two nodes agree upon the rate of transmission. Then the data is sent at the rate that the receiving node can accept.

☒ **A.** Sequence control is wrong because it manages the sequence of data received. **C.** CRC is incorrect because it is an error-checking algorithm method. **D.** Error control is incorrect because it is used to check for errors.

22. ☑ **D.** NCOPY is an application layer service that provides file transfer services on NetWare servers.

☒ **A.** NDS is incorrect because it provides a directory service. **B.** SNMP is incorrect because it provides network management messages. **C.** PING is incorrect because it uses ICMP echo responses to determine whether a computer is reachable on the internetwork.

23. ☑ **B.** A nearline storage service uses a migration process, and is one in which the media is not immediately accessible to the end user, yet the end user can utilize the service transparently. An example of this type of nearline service is High Capacity Storage System (HCSS), offered by Novell® for NetWare. HCSS enables end users to transparently store data on optical jukeboxes by extending the volume capabilities to include a designated optical jukebox. Properties are set on files and directories to migrate files to the designated HCSS jukebox after a specified period of time.
☒ **A.** Online is incorrect because it is a nonremovable storage device of the server. **C.** Offline is incorrect because it refers to a tape backup service. **D.** Hot swap storage services is not correct because it is not commonly used terminology.

24. ☑ **A.** The TDX.Com administrator should implement configuration management. Configuration management is a feature of network management that controls the installation options, general configuration, and distribution of operating systems and applications.
The most common form of configuration management is to manage the configuration of workstations. However, server configuration can also be managed to ensure that consistency is held throughout an internetwork.
☒ **B.** Fault management is incorrect because it will not control how the installation is completed. **C.** Security management is incorrect because it does not affect installation. **D.** Accounting management is incorrect because it will not control the way that the servers are installed.

25. ☑ **D.** Radio is a wireless media. Radio waves fall between the 10-Kilohertz and 1-gigahertz range. Radio is susceptible to weather conditions.
☒ **A.** UTP is a copper cable. **B.** STP is a copper cable. **C.** RG-11 is known as Thick Ethernet due to its thick diameter and is a copper coaxial cable.

26. ☑ **B.** The public switched telephone network (PSTN) is a circuit switched network that dedicates a link between a sending and receiving node for the duration of the data transmission. The PSTN establishes a circuit between two nodes. The circuit can include several physical hops between the two nodes, but it is virtually a link that is established between the sending and receiving nodes.

☒ **A.** Packet switched is incorrect because it only dedicates a link for the duration of a single packet transmission. **C.** Message switched is incorrect because it only dedicates a link for the duration of a single message transmission. **D.** Cell switched is incorrect because it only dedicates a link for the duration of a single cell transmission.

27. ☑ **C.** A single cable that all network nodes access and that has terminators at each end, characterizes the bus topology. The physical bus topology is found in Ethernet 10Base5 and 10Base2 technologies. These use coaxial cabling and T-connectors. Each end of the coaxial cable is terminated.

☒ **A.** Ring is incorrect because it forms a ring of nodes, each connected to the next. **B.** Mesh is incorrect because all of a mesh topology's nodes are connected to each other. **D.** Star is incorrect because each node connects to a central station.

28. ☑ **C.** ACK packets are used to ensure data reliability at the transport layer. An ACK packet is sent in response to the receipt of data, if that data is error-free. If an ACK packet is expected by the original sending node, but it is not received, the transport layer can either resend the data or let upper layers know that an error has occurred.

☒ **A.** NDS is incorrect because it is a directory service. **B.** DHCP is incorrect because it is a dynamic addressing protocol. **D.** ARP is incorrect because it is used to resolve names to addresses.

29. ☑ **B.** The NWCONFIG.NLM is the loadable module that will enable an administrator to configure storage volumes on a NetWare® 5 file server. NWCONFIG is initialized during the NetWare 5 file server installation process. The NWCONFIG NLM will enable the installer to create the first NetWare partitions and volumes on the NetWare 5 file server. NWCONFIG can be used after the NetWare server has already been installed to configure the storage volumes. If the NetWare File System 32-bit volumes have been installed, NWCONFIG replaces them with Novell Storage Services 64-bit volumes through an in-place upgrade process.

☒ **A.** NWINSTALL does not exist. **C.** CONFIG displays the current NetWare server configuration, but does not change it. **D.** STORCFG does not exist.

30. ☑ **C.** TDX.Com is a WAN, a large internetwork with multiple LANs that are linked although they are geographically distant. The TDX.Com internetwork was originally a group of LANs that were connected to the Internet. Until the administrator added the links between each site, they were not a true WAN.

☒ **A.** MAN is incorrect because it is limited to a metropolitan area. **B.** LAN is incorrect because it is limited to a building or campus environment. **D.** Segment is incorrect because it is a portion of a network.

31. ☑ **D.** The infrared light bounces off the walls, thus enabling the workstation to connect to the network. Although infrared light works with line of sight, it is not a requirement if the light is able to create a path through reflection. The infrared diodes either emit light or injection laser for data transmission. The receiving port of the infrared interface is a photodiode. Infrared signals do not penetrate opaque surfaces, but are known to bounce off white or highly reflective surfaces.

☒ **A.** It is possible for the workstation to connect to the network under this circumstance through reflection. **B.** A diode emits light in a single direction. **C.** is not correct because the Infrared diode does not manage bidirectional traffic without connecting to the network interface.

32. ☑   **D.** In order to make the two MAUs work as a single ring, Alan must connect the ring in port on MAU1 to the ring out port on MAU2, then connect the ring in port on MAU2 to the ring out port on MAU1. A MAU creates a ring between each computer connected to a port and all the other computers connected to ports. MAUs have two ports, a ring-in port and a ring-out port, as well as ports to which computers can be connected. For two MAUs to create a single ring, the ring in port of each MAU must be connected to the ring out port of the other MAU.

☒   **A.** is incorrect because connecting the two ring in ports essentially sends the data from both MAUs towards each other. **B.** is incorrect because it creates two separate rings. **C.** is incorrect because connecting the two ring out ports essentially sends the data from both MAUs away from each other.

33. ☑   **B.** The routing protocol will have to perform route selection because of the redundant routes. A dynamic routing protocol performs route selection when there is more than one route available to the same destination network. The router bases the route selection decision on the cost metric of a link. A cost metric can be based on the type of link, the length of time it takes to reach a destination network, and/or the number of routers, or hops, that the data passes through. Pat will need the dynamic routing protocol to select the best route whenever there are two routes to the same network.

☒   **A.** Cost is incorrect because cost is a metric applied to the link. **C.** Ticks is incorrect because a tick is $1/18^{th}$ of a second. **D.** Static routes is incorrect because a dynamic routing protocol does not use static routes.

34. ☑   **C.** The end user is most likely to interact with the upper layers of the OSI Protocol stack. The upper layers consist of the session, presentation, and application layers. The application layer provides the network applications that end users use.

☒   **A.** Lower layers is incorrect because the lower layers specify hardware and topology. **B.** Middle layers is incorrect because the middle layers specify logical addressing and datastream, which are transparent to the end user. **D.** The physical layer is incorrect because it specifies the hardware and signaling, which is transparent to the end user.

35. ☑   C. The application layer uses OS call interception to interact with a workstation's operating system. OS call interception is when networking software looks at application calls and makes a determination about whether that call should be forwarded to the network instead. In this way, non-network-aware applications can interact with the network because they do not need to be aware of the network; the networking software handles that for them.

☒   A. SNMP is incorrect because it is a network management protocol. **B.** SAP is incorrect because it is a service advertising protocol. **C.** NLM is incorrect because it represents the type of applications, namely, NetWare loadable modules that run on NetWare.

36. ☑   D. GroupWise® provides message services. Although GroupWise is a separate product from NetWare 5, it is a service that can be installed on NetWare 5. The GroupWise message services integrate with the NetWare 5 operating system and with the Novell Directory Services® tree. GroupWise DLL files extend the NetWare administrator application so that the NetWare administrator can manage the message services.

☒   A. File services is provided by NetWare, not GroupWise. **B, C.** Storage services and print services are also provided by NetWare.

37. ☑   D. George should plan to install transmission media. Since the PHC facilities did not have any LANs prior to George's installation, the facilities are not likely to be cabled. Transmission media is the method by which data is transmitted from one computer to another. To network computers, host devices, communications protocols, and transmission media are required. In the example, George has purchased the servers and workstations, or host devices, and network operating systems that provide communications protocols for both server and clients, but no cabling.

☒   A. Fax server is incorrect because it is not required to network computers. **B.** PDA cradles is incorrect because they are not required for networking. **C.** Security system is incorrect because it is not a required component of networking, even if it is recommended.

38. ☑ **C.** Jack was missing the network interface card (NIC). The NIC is required for a workstation or server to be connected into the network. A NIC is created for certain types of transmission media. Most currently manufactured NICs have a receptacle for the RJ-45 connector, though some are still made with a coax connector for Thin Ethernet. When a new transmission medium is installed on a network, the existing NICs are usually replaced because they are not compatible with the new medium.

☒ **A.** Modem does not connect to the hub. **B.** RJ-45 receptacle is incorrect because it does not necessarily work with Ethernet. **D.** Repeater is incorrect because it does not connect into a workstation.

39. ☑ **C.** The star topology offers ease of troubleshooting because each network device has a separate cable to the hub. One of the main benefits of the star topology is that a cable or port failure will only affect a single workstation. This benefit is directly related to the fact that each network device is connected directly to a hub and does not share any cabling with other network devices.

☒ **A.** Cellular is incorrect because it is a wireless topology. **B.** Ring is incorrect because it does not use a hub in the physical topology. **D.** Mesh is incorrect because every network device is connected to every other network device and there is no hub.

40. ☑ **D.** Convergence is the name given to the time it takes for a routing update to propagate throughout a network. Convergence time increases with the complexity of an internetwork. The update method determines how much time that convergence takes, too. A link-state protocol has a relatively short convergence time because the updates are flooded throughout the internetwork. A distance vector protocol takes much longer to update all network routers with a change, especially as the network gets larger. This is because a change is propagated to each router, stored on it, and then forwarded.

☒ **A.** Route Selection is incorrect because it is the method that a routing protocol uses to select a route when multiple routes exist. **B.** Static routes is incorrect because they are a manually input entry into a routing table. **C.** Route discovery is incorrect because route discovery is the method used to find routes on the internetwork.

41. ☑ **C.** The application layer owns the network services that are used by end users. These services grant network access to the user via the client's request to use a server's service. The application layer provides applications including the LOGIN application and utilities such as FILER in NetWare.

    ☒ **A.** Session is incorrect because it establishes and releases sessions between two nodes. **B.** Presentation is incorrect because it handles data translation. **D.** None is incorrect because the application layer provides the services for end users.

42. ☑ **A.** SNMP may use an agent. An agent is a program interface to the operating system. It watches the activity on the OS and takes action if the activity meets certain criteria. In the case of SNMP, the agent looks for network management information.

    ☒ **B.** SAP is incorrect because it does not use agents, but advertises services. **C.** DNS is incorrect because it does not use agents, but resolves names and addresses. **D.** DHCP is incorrect because it does not use agents, but dispenses dynamic addresses.

43. ☑ **B.** NDS Manager is not an element of a printing service. NDS Manager is an application that manages the way that the directory service database is partitioned, replicated, and distributed across multiple servers.

    ☒ **A.** NDPS Manager is not correct because it is a printing service element that manages the NDPS services from a NetWare server. **C.** PSERVER.NLM is a NetWare loadable module that provides the legacy print-queue-based print services from a NetWare server. **D.** PCONSOLE is an application that is used to view the network printing in progress from a workstation.

44. ☑ **B.** The cost of the transmission media is George's second priority. PHC may not be able to keep the costs low for the cabling, but transmission media costs also include the cost of hubs, routers, NICs, and other infrastructure equipment. For example, if George is tied to fiber-optic cabling at the main facility, he still can opt to have Ethernet 100BaseFL (Ethernet over Fiber) infrastructure equipment put in. George will also be able to evaluate a different set of transmission media at the other two nursing facilities, since those facilities will probably not have identical power problems and require the EMI immunity as a top priority for transmission media.

☒ **A.** Attenuation is incorrect because it is related to the length of the transmission media. **C.** Immunity from interference is not related to costs. **D.** Capacity also is not related to costs.

45. ☑ **C.** Web services are specific to an intranet. Web services exist when a server is installed with Web server software and can deliver HyperText Markup Language (HTML) documents to clients through their Web browser requests. The Web service provided with NetWare 5 is the FastWeb server. It enables a NetWare 5 server to provide HTML browsing for either an intranet or the Internet. Web services are unique in that they provide automatic downloading of files to clients, immediate viewing of those files, and execution of various applications on Web servers using a variety of databases and applications as providers. The Web service can integrate with file services such as File Transfer Protocol (FTP), messaging services such as Simple Mail Transfer Protocol (SMTP), database services such as Structured Query Language (SQL), and applications such as JAVA, which is created just for use on the Web.

☒ **A.** Database services, **B.** application services, and **D.** message services are not intranet specific and can be used on a standard network.

46. ☑ **A.** A repeater is a piece of network equipment that alleviates the problem of attenuation. The actual function of a repeater is to receive signals from the network, copy the signal, and send it on towards its destination. When the repeater copies the signal and sends it on, it is actually creating a new signal. The signal is not attenuated and is able to continue on for another stretch of cable. The repeater effectively doubles the maximum length of the cable.

☒ **B.** NIC is incorrect because it will not affect the cable length, which is the cause of attenuation. **C.** Modem is incorrect because the modem modulates digital signals to analog. **D.** RJ-45 is incorrect because it is a cable connector.

47. ☑ **D.** Modulation creates an analog signal. Modulation is the technique of formatting a signal into an analog communication. Analog signals can be formatted with the characteristics of amplitude, frequency, or phase. The equipment used to create an analog signal is called a modulator/demodulator (MODEM).

☒ **A.** Digital is incorrect because a digital signal is encoded. **B.** Multipoint is incorrect because it describes a connection type, not a signal. **C.** Point to point is incorrect because it describes a connection type and not a signal.

48. ☑ **B.** Open Shortest Path First (OSPF) is the TCP/IP link-state routing protocol. It is a link-state protocol that was developed for use with TCP/IP. Link-state protocols use a hello packet to announce a router's presence on the internetwork. They use link-state advertisement (LSA) packets to flood the internetwork with updates. The link-state advertisements are small and flooded to all routers and are able to greatly shorten the convergence time.

☒ **A.** AppleTalk Update-Based Routing Protocol (AURP) is wrong because it is used with AppleTalk. **C.** Interior Gateway Routing Protocol (IGRP) is wrong because it is not a link-state protocol. **D.** NetWare Link State Protocol (NLSP) is wrong because it is used with IPX.

49. ☑ **A.** The session layer establishes a dialog between two nodes. The dialog is basically a data conversation between two nodes. The dialog is established independently of the physical media and logical addressing.

☒ **B.** Address is incorrect because the session layer is independent of addressing. **C.** Multiplexing is incorrect because it is a transport layer mechanism. **D.** Sequencing is incorrect because it is a transport layer mechanism.

50. ☑ **C.** The NetWare Administrator is a network application that provides access to directory services. NetWare Administrator runs on a workstation and accesses the Novell Directory Services tree.

☒ **A.** NCOPY is incorrect because it is a file transfer application. **B.** RCONSOLE is incorrect because it is a remote terminal application. **D.** ARP is incorrect because it is an address resolution protocol.

51. ☑ **B.** Replication ensures that data is updated on each server and is the creation of multiple database replicas on distributed database servers. It further maintains the data by enabling the replication updates of data records within the database. A database service must be programmed to enable distribution in order for replication to work appropriately. Non-network-enabled databases cannot be replicated. An example of a replicated, distributed database is the database that contains the Novell Directory Services tree. The application that manages the NDS database replication is the NDS Manager, shown in the following illustration.

☒ **A.** File update synchronization is used between a server and a workstation for "checked-out" files. **C.** Multiplexing is a service offered at the transport layer. **D.** Migration is performed by HCSS on a nearline storage device.

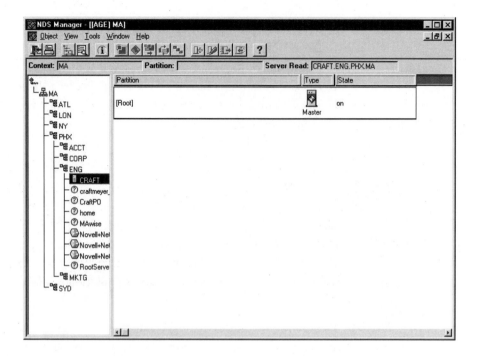

52. ☑ **C.** The president is concerned about the capacity of the transmission media. Capacity refers to the amount of data that the transmission media can support. Capacity metrics are measured in hertz, or cycles per second. Capacity is also known as throughput. If the transmission medium does not support sufficient throughput for the applications used on the network, the transmission medium becomes a bottleneck.

☒ **A.** Attenuation is incorrect because the length of the cable has been fixed. **B.** Cost is incorrect because the PHC president was asking about speed of data transmission. **D.** Ease of installation is incorrect because it does not affect the throughput of the network.

53. ☑ **B.** A switch repeats a signal on a single port. The switch maintains a table of which MAC addresses exist on each port. When a signal is received from a port, the switch looks at the MAC address and forwards the signal to the correct port. The switch is similar to a hub in appearance, but the hub is a multiport repeater. When a signal is received on a hub, the hub repeats the signal on every port.

☒ **A.** NIC is incorrect because it does not repeat signals. **C.** Modem is incorrect because it does not repeat signals. **D.** Hub is incorrect because it repeats on all ports.

54. ☑ **A, D.** Manchester and differential Manchester are both types of biphase encoding techniques. Biphase encoding techniques require a transition for each bit, which makes the signal self-clocking. Other encoding types that do not have self-clocking must use another clocking mechanism, which can create overhead.

☒ **B.** NRZ is incorrect because it does not have a self-clocking technique, nor is it a biphase encoding technique. **C.** RZ is incorrect because it is not a biphase encoding technique.

55. ☑ **A.** The network layer performs a Cyclic Redundancy Check (CRC) error check. A CRC is an algorithm that is performed on a packet. The value of the algorithm is added into the header of the packet. The receiving node performs the same algorithm and compares its value to the value that was in the header. If the value is not the same, the packet is considered in error and is discarded. Otherwise, the packet can be forwarded to the next node.

☒ **B.** Windowing is wrong because it is a form of flow control, not error control. **C.** Flow control is wrong because it does not perform error checking. **D.** Sequencing is wrong because it does not perform error checking.

56. ☑ **B.** Half-duplex is an alternating, two-way communication. Each participant in a half-duplex session acts as both a transmitter and receiver. The data can only travel in a single direction at any one point in time. This means that each device takes turns in sending data.
☒ **A.** Simplex is incorrect because it provides a one-way communication. **C.** Full-duplex is incorrect because it provides simultaneous two-way communication. **D.** Half-simplex is incorrect because there is no such thing as half-simplex.

57. ☑ **C.** Security management is a feature of network management. Security management is the protection from unauthorized use or harm of the various internetwork components and their data. Security management is an intrinsic quality of network operating systems. It includes the execution of a password protection policy, the creation and management of access rights to files and directories, and the physical security of each network device.
☒ **A.** Replication is incorrect because it is the process that is used to distribute a database across multiple servers. **B.** Application services is incorrect because it is a service that is provided to workstations. **D.** Migration is incorrect because it is a process used to move files to a nearline storage device.

58. ☑ **C.** Fiber optic media is made of either plastic or glass. The fiber optic media has a light-conducting glass or plastic fiber core. In the loose configuration, the fiber optic core is surrounded by a liquid gel and a plastic outer encasement. In the tight configuration, the fiber optic core is surrounded by a plastic sheath, which is then surrounded by strength wires, and that is surrounded by an outer plastic encasement.
☒ **A.** STP is incorrect because it is made of copper. **B.** UTP is incorrect because it uses copper. **D.** Coax is incorrect because it is made of copper.

59. ☑ **B.** A router uses the network layer header of data packets. When a router receives data, it looks at the network layer header and finds the network layer address for the destination. The router reads its routing table to select the best path towards the destination and then forwards the packet to the next router in the path.

There are two ways that a routing table can be created on the router. The first is through the manual configuration of static routes. The second is through the implementation of a dynamic routing protocol.

☒ **A.** Data link is incorrect because the router looks at the network layer. **C.** Transport is incorrect because the router does not translate above the network layer. **D.** Session is incorrect because the router does not translate data above the network layer.

60. ☑ **C.** Another name for a signal's clocking system is bit synchronization. This is a timing or clocking system for a signal. It is used for synchronous communications to ensure that the communicating nodes both know when the data stops and starts. If an encoding type has a guaranteed state change, it is considered self-clocking and uses less overhead than other encoding types. Other bit synchronization types include oversampling and a separate clocking signal.

☒ **A.** Phase shift keying is incorrect because it is a modulation technique. **B.** Manchester encoding is incorrect because it is a digital encoding scheme. **D.** Idling is a period of time that the connection is not being used.

61. ☑ **C.** There are four hops between the server SvrNorth1 on the North network and a workstation on the South network segment. Because a NetWare server acts as a router, it can be a hop in the path. However, because the server in this case is the source, it is not considered a hop. Data follows a path through RTR4 to RTR2, RTR2 to RTR1, RTR 1 to RTR5, at which point it is routed to the segment.

☒ **A.** Two is wrong because there are more than two routers in the path. **B.** Three is wrong because there are more than three routers in the path. **D.** Five is wrong because there are less than five routers in the path.

62. ☑ C. Some implementations of the session layer are able to resume data transmissions where they left off if there is an interruption in network service. The session layer handles the establishment of the dialog, the transmission of data, and the release of the session. If implemented, this is managed at the session release.

    ☒ A. Application is incorrect because that provides applications to end users. B. Presentation is incorrect because it handles data translation. D. Transport is incorrect because it does not handle dialogs.

63. ☑ D. TDX.Com uses the accounting management feature of network management. Accounting management is a feature that tracks various costs of network utilization. Typical costs are the bytes transferred or stored on a hard drive, the hours logged into a network, or the time used in processing. Although TDX.Com uses accounting management for basing charges, it can also use the accounting management feature to determine at what threshold it will require a larger server, more processing power, or another server added to its Web site. Accounting management in NetWare 5 is managed on a server basis, which enables different servers to have different accounting thresholds.

    ☒ A. Fault management is incorrect because it refers to the review and prevention of faults. B. Configuration management is incorrect because it refers to maintaining a consistent configuration throughout an internetwork. C. Security management is incorrect because it refers to establishing network security.

64. ☑ **D.** The Electrical Industries Association (EIA) has ranked five types of copper, twisted-pair wiring. These are listed in the following table.

EIA Category	Common form	Throughput	Usage
Category 1	CAT1	Less than 4 Mbps	Low speed data and voice
Category 2	CAT2	Less than 4 Mbps	Low speed data and voice
Category 3	CAT3	10 to 16 Mbps	Data
Category 4	CAT4	Up to 100 Mbps	Data—supports 100BaseT4
Category 5	CAT5	Up to 100 Mbps and above	Data—supports 100BaseTx

☒ Answers **A**, **B**, and **C**. list incorrect numbers of categories of EIA twisted-pair cabling.

65. ☑ **C.** The OSI reference model's layers, placed in the correct order from highest to lowest, are application, presentation, session, transport, network, data link, and physical. Using the mnemonic device, *All people seem to need data processing,* the initial letter of each word stands for the layers in the sequence, from Layer 7 (application) to Layer 1 (physical).

66. ☑ **A, C.** The data-link layer's sublayers are media access control (MAC) and logical link control (LLC). The data-link layer was subdivided into two sublayers to provide for greater functionality at that layer. The MAC sublayer of the data-link layer specifies the hardware address and logical topology. The LLC sublayer specifies the control services for data flow.
☒ **B.** Transmission control is incorrect because it is the name for TCP, the transport layer protocol in TCP/IP. **D.** Presentation is incorrect because it is the sixth layer of the OSI reference model.

67. ☑ **A.** The consultant responds that multiplexing uses a socket. Multiplexing is the method whereby multiple applications can use the same datastream transmission on the network. The applications each use a separate port to identify the application the data is destined for. When multiple applications are using the same datastream, the data at the sending node is interwoven so that it creates a single, seamless transmission. At the receiving node, the data is reassembled into the packets and forwarded to their appropriate applications based on the sockets used. Other names used for sockets are ports or connection identifiers.

    ☒ **B.** Name resolution is wrong because it maps addresses to host names. **C.** Sequencing is wrong because it reorders packets based on a sequence number. **D.** Windowing is wrong because it is a method of flow control.

68. ☑ **D.** The presentation layer translates data into the transfer syntax. The transfer syntax is actually the mutually agreed upon format of the data.

    ☒ **A.** Bits is incorrect because bits are transmitted at the physical layer. **B.** Signals is incorrect because they are the format of bits at the physical layer. **C.** Voltages is incorrect because that is a specific format of bits at the physical layer.

69. ☑ **B.** The RUNIT server provides application services. Application services are set up in a way where all or most of the processing occurs on the server for that application.

    The benefits of application services are that they can enable applications to run on workstations with little or no impact to the workstation's other activities. Additionally, some application servers can provide higher-level applications to a workstation that would not be capable of using that application natively. Those application services that are provided via the Internet are typically built to provide applications with good service even over very poor bandwidth conditions.

    ☒ **A.** Database services is incorrect because it will appear to be running on the server. **C.** Storage service is incorrect because it requires a server to store files. **D.** Web services is incorrect because they appear to be running on the server.

70. ☑ **A.** A registered jack 45 (RJ-45) connector uses an 8-pin connection and is a common connector for unshielded twisted-pair wiring on an internetwork.

The RJ-45 connector is similar to an RJ-11 connector which is used for standard telephones. The RJ-11 connector only has a 4-pin connection. Since most network cabling uses four pairs of wires, an 8-pin connection is required.

☒ **B.** RS-232 is incorrect because it uses either a 9-pin or 25-pin connector. **C.** RJ-11 is incorrect because it uses four pins and sometimes six pins. **D.** Vampire clamp is incorrect because it does not use a pinout system.

71. ☑ **D.** The transport layer on the receiving device communicates with the transport layer on the sending device. This is called peer layer communication. Peer layers communicate through using headers on the data packets.

On the sending node, data is received from an upper-layer protocol. The layer packages the data into small packets and adds a header to the packets. The data is then forwarded to the next layer down.

☒ **A, B, C.** All are incorrect because none is a peer layer of the transport layer.

72. ☑ **D.** Ethernet NIC manufacturers use a method to ensure that MAC addresses are unique. MAC addresses must be unique on the network. The Institute of Electrical and Electronics Engineers (IEEE) assigned to each NIC manufacturer unique bytes of the NIC address, which is six bytes in length, to the first three positions in the address. The NIC manufacturer must create unique addresses for the remaining three bytes of the address in order to ensure that all MAC addresses are unique, even when multiple manufacturers' NICs are on the network.

☒ **A.** Polling response is wrong because Ethernet is a contention media access method. **B.** Token Ring passing capability is wrong because Ethernet uses contention media access. **C.** Logical link control is incorrect because it is a data-link sublayer.

73. ☑ **C.** Service Advertising Protocol (SAP) will no longer be needed for the servers that are changed from IPX to IP. Each server maintains a SAP table based on the SAP updates received from neighboring servers and routers. Each server also broadcasts its table to its neighbors every 60 seconds. The SAP table contains the names and addresses of each service available on the internetwork.

☒ **A.** Domain naming service (DNS) is incorrect because provides address/name resolution for TCP/IP. **B.** NDS is incorrect because it is a directory service. **D.** DHCP is incorrect because it is a dynamic addressing protocol for TCP/IP.

74. ☑ **C.** The little endian method specifies that data is read from the last byte received, or the "little end." Little endian is a byte order translation method used by Intel processors.

☒ **A.** Big endian is incorrect because it specifies that data is read from the first byte received. **B.** Bit-order translation is incorrect because it specifies bits, not bytes. **D.** Sequencing is incorrect because it is a transport layer mechanism to reorder packets into messages.

75. ☑ **A.** George should be concerned with attenuation of the signal when he installs cabling at the Sun City location. Transmission media all have a published standard for a maximum cabling length. When a cable is longer than the maximum, the signal traveling on the cable becomes attenuated, or stretched out and flattened in an electronic way.

Attenuation makes it easy for the signal to be confused. The only way to alleviate the problems with attenuation is to place a repeating device (repeaters, active hubs, and switches all perform repeating) at the maximum point of one of the cable lengths (inclusive of the patch panel cabling length or drop cabling length). The repeater will copy the signal and send it out at full strength. Some transmission media types have rules regarding how many repeaters may be used along a segment and how many workstations may be placed on each. These issues must also be taken into account when reviewing the transmission media needs.

The maximum length for many cabling types is 100 meters, so attenuation is more of a concern at the Sun City facility than in Flagstaff. A different approach for George may be to simply decide where the Sun City cabling closets can be placed, or whether or not additional closets are needed.

☒ **B.** Cost is incorrect because the length of the cable is not directly related to cost. **C.** Capacity is incorrect because capacity is not mentioned. **D.** Ease of installation is not correct because the installation performance is not related to cable length.

76. ☑ **D.** A bridge can forward data to Segment 2 and ensure that the data is only that data intended for Segment 2. A bridge is a device that reads the MAC sublayer header of each packet that it receives. It looks at the destination MAC address. The bridge maintains a table for MAC addresses for each segment. Then the bridge makes a forward/don't forward decision based on the MAC address.

☒ **A.** Repeater is incorrect because it will forward all data. **B.** Active hub is incorrect because it will forward all data. **C.** Passive hub is incorrect because it will forward all data.

77. ☑ **C.** Unipolar encoding uses a positive voltage plus a zero voltage to represent data. Unipolar encoding uses only one voltage type, either a positive voltage or a negative voltage, along with a zero voltage. In this way, it stays to one side of the zero voltage line. The positive voltage represents a bit and the zero voltage represents the other value bit. Whether or not the zero voltage represents a one or a zero depends on the implementation.
☒ **A.** Polar encoding is incorrect because it uses both a negative and a positive voltage, but no zero voltage. **B.** Frequency shift keying is incorrect because it is an analog formatting technique. **D.** Manchester is incorrect because it uses mid-bit transitions to represent data.

78. ☑ **C.** Routing takes place at the network layer. Routing is the movement of data between two network segments. Routers read the logical addressing information that is contained in the network layer headers. This information includes the destination network and node address, as well as the source network and node address. The router reads the destination network and node and determines whether the packet should be forwarded or discarded. If it should be forwarded, the router compares the destination information with the data contained in the routing table to find out the next router in the path to the destination network.
☒ **A.** Physical is incorrect because it handles the bitstream. **B.** Data link is incorrect because it handles hardware addressing and media access. **D.** Session is incorrect because it provides an establishment and management of an end-to-end connection.

79. ☑ **C.** A password and valid ID can be used to secure a session layer dialog. At the beginning, or establishment of a dialog, a valid ID and password can be entered. Only when the ID and password are correct would the dialog be established.
☒ **A.** CRC is incorrect because CRC is used to control errors. **B.** Data transmission is incorrect because it is not used for security. **D.** Encryption is incorrect because data is encrypted at the presentation layer.

Part 10

Test Yourself: Practice Exam 4: NDS™ Design and Implementation (Exam 50-634)

Test Yourself: Practice Exam 4 Questions

Q&A

Before you call to register for the actual NDS™ Design and Implementation exam (Exam # 50-634), take the following test and see how you make out. Set a timer for 105 minutes—the same time you'll have to take the live exam—and answer the following 68 questions in the time allotted. Once you've finished, turn to the Practice Exam 4 Answers and check your score to see if you passed! Good luck!

Practice Exam 4 Questions

1. What are two reasons a network solution should be proposed?

   A. It is a new technology.
   B. It solves a problem that currently exists.
   C. It is cheap.
   D. It provides a way to meet a business requirement.

2. What is the first phase of the Systems Design Life Cycle?

   A. Implementation
   B. Analysis and specification
   C. Maintenance
   D. Design

3. Which of the following elements is not a requirement of the network solution?

   A. NDS tree
   B. Applications
   C. CPU utilization
   D. Servers

4. Which of the following defines the Z.E.N.Works workstation name?

   A. User object
   B. Server object
   C. Win95 user package
   D. Windows NT policy package

Refer to the Following Scenario
When Answering Questions 5–9

Tim is a network consultant hired to review the NDS tree design for Acme Co. He discovers a problem with the names of the servers and immediately decides to change them in a naming standards document. Tim decides not to change the Acme user account naming standard because it prevents duplicate names for multiple users with the same first and last names that are placed in the same container.

5. Which user account naming standard example based on the name Robert T. Jones represents a standard that would prevent duplicate names?

A. Robertjones

B. Rjones

C. Robjon01

D. Robertj

6. Tim creates a naming standards document for Acme. In it he includes which of the following information?

A. Naming standard definitions for network resources and accounts

B. List of the data required for each named resource

C. Example of a name for each resource and account

D. All of the above

7. Tim finds that two printers in Acme's tree have different common names, but he cannot move them into the same context. Which two of the following names would cause this problem?

A. Prt-bldg1

B. Prt_bldg1

C. Prt bldg1

D. Prt/bldg1

8. Tim is asked by Acme to migrate some user accounts from two Unix boxes. He reviews the list of users in the two files he is given, and states that some cannot be migrated. What reason might this be?

   A. There are duplicate names using different cases, such as Jjones and JJONES.
   B. There are names with underscores, such as J_jones.
   C. There are names using spaces, such as J jones.
   D. There are names using dashes, such as J-jones.

9. Tim has named the production tree ACME and the lab tree AcmeLab. He decides that, for the lab to be truly effective for experiments, it must mirror the ACME-tree hierarchy. The production ACME tree has the Organization name of Acme. What should the Organization name be for the AcmeLab tree?

   A. AcmeLab
   B. Acme
   C. ACME1
   D. O=Acme1

10. What utility is used to partition the NDS tree and create replicas?

   A. NetWare Administrator
   B. NDS Manager
   C. FILER
   D. Explorer

Refer to the Following Scenario When Answering Questions 11–17

Warren is implementing a NetWare network for TFX, Inc. He is planning on installing a single NDS tree with servers at each site. When Warren conducts visits to each of TFX's three sites, he discovers that none of the sites has WAN connections to the others. Warren persuades TFX, Inc.'s management to install WAN links before NetWare® 5 is implemented. Not only will TFX have three sites with NetWare servers and interconnecting WAN links, it will have a single NetWare administrator.

11. TFX, Inc. has several business units. Administration is located in each site, Accounting and HR are located in HQ, which is a single site, and Sales is located in two sites. In his single NDS tree design, which model or models should Warren use?

    A. Administrative model
    B. Geographical model
    C. Divisions model
    D. Hybrid model

12. When Warren develops the NDS naming standards, he remembers that he will have to set at least two bindery contexts, for Sales and Administration, so that a bindery application will be available for them. How will this affect the NDS naming standards?

    A. Two names in the same container cannot be the same.
    B. Two names in different containers cannot be the same.
    C. Two names in different bindery contexts cannot be the same.
    D. Two names in the same container must be the same.

13. Warren installs all the servers in all the sites for TFX, Inc. as objects in the Organization container of the NDS tree. After the network clients are installed and people start logging into the network, he discovers that the first server he installed is consistently at 100-percent CPU utilization. What can Warren do to resolve the utilization problem?

    A. Partition the NDS database
    B. Create multiple read/write replicas of the master replica
    C. Move the server to a different site
    D. Add more Organizational Units to the NDS tree

14. Warren creates the partition scheme shown in the following illustration. If each master server has only a read/write or master replica of the root partition and not any other partitions, what is automatically created on the master servers?

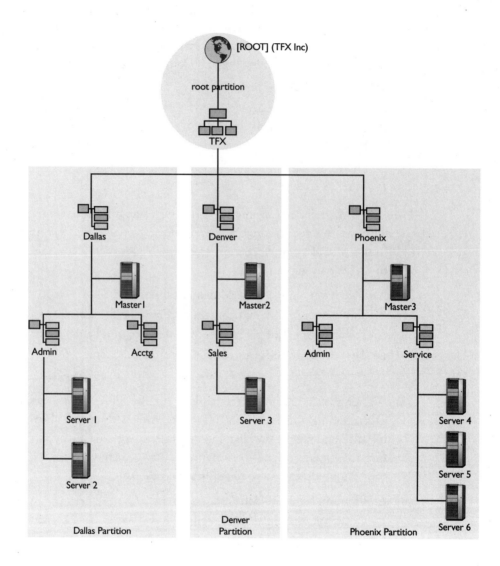

A. Read/write replicas of the other partitions

B. Master replicas of the other partitions

C. Read-only replicas of the other partitions

D. Subordinate references of the other partitions

15. Warren initially creates a single master replica each of the Dallas, Denver, and Phoenix partitions. What can he provide by creating two read/write replicas for each partition?

    A. Maximum bandwidth

    B. Decreased performance

    C. Bindery services

    D. Fault tolerance

16. Warren has installed only IPX on the TFX servers. What protocol should Warren look for when he reviews the WAN utilization-by-time synchronization traffic?

    A. NTP

    B. NNTP

    C. SAP

    D. SPX

17. Warren learns that TFX is acquiring another company, Sandscapes. Which utility does Warren use to merge TFX's and Sandscapes's NDS trees?

    A. MERGE

    B. NDSMERGE

    C. DSMERGE

    D. NWMERGE

18. Which of the following objects can assist a mobile user in accessing resources?

    A. Alias

    B. Container policy package

    C. Volume

    D. Server

19. What will the cost-benefit analysis include?

A. A design schedule

B. An implementation schedule

C. The estimated decrease in maintenance costs

D. A list of risks

20. Which of the following objects is optional in the NDS tree?

A. [Root]

B. Country

C. Organization

D. None of the above

21. Select the option that has the design phase components in the correct order.

A. Propose a generic solution, design a specific solution, propose alternative solutions

B. Propose alternative solutions, design a specific solution, propose a generic solution

C. Propose a generic solution, propose alternative solutions, design a specific solution

D. Propose alternative solutions, propose a generic solution, design a specific solution

22. Accessus.com is a new company on the Internet. It currently rents a service that provides its Internet Web site. It plans on installing a NetWare network of its own, both for its Web site and for the employees. Because of the Internet usage, the protocols used must include TCP/IP. Which design component will this affect?

A. NDS tree design

B. Server design

C. Application design

D. None of the above

23. How many replicas are automatically created by NetWare if there are enough servers?

A. One

B. Two

C. Three

D. Four

Refer to the Following Scenario When Answering Questions 24–28

Galax Industries is installing a NetWare network. The administrator, Hallie, is creating the accessibility plan for end users. When Hallie reviews the application needs, she asks the question "Are there data and applications that everyone will need access to?" The answer to the question is "Yes, there are several."

24. What other question will she need to ask about the shared applications?

A. Which shared applications have hardware or operating system requirements?

B. Do any partitions have more than 3500 objects?

C. Will administration be centralized or distributed?

D. Are there more than 30 servers?

25. Hallie must determine to which physical resources end users need access. Which of the following represents physical network resources? Choose all that apply.

A. Applications

B. Login scripts

C. CD-ROM

D. Printer

26. When Galax Industries prepares for placing container policy packages in the tree, they are unsure which Organizational Units should contain them. Hallie discovers that each workgroup will need identical settings for the container policy package. Given the network configuration shown in the following illustration, select the OUs that would be the best option for holding the container policy packages.

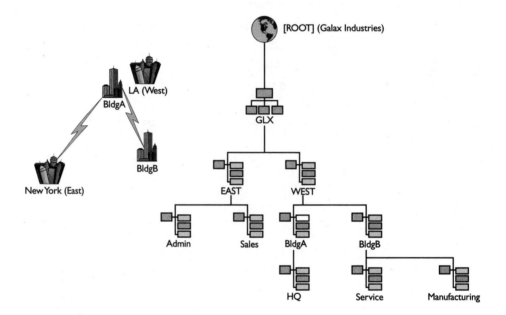

A. GLX

B. BLDGA, BLDGB, EAST

C. BLDGB, EAST, WEST

D. EAST, WEST

27. Hallie discovers that there are four printers used by the accounting group and two of them are used by the administrators. Both accounting and administrator user objects are in the admin container. The two printers that the administrators do not use are check printers and must be kept very secure. What should Hallie do to ensure that printers are accessible by the correct users? Choose all that apply.

A. Place printer objects in the GLX container.

B. Create two groups, one for the two check printers, and one for the other printers with the correct users in each group.

C. Grant access to the check printers only to the check group, but grant access to the other printers to the other group.

D. Run the secure printer utility on the print server.

28. One of Galax's servers, located in the HQ Organizational Unit, is supposed to be highly secured. The president of Galax has asked Hallie to ensure that she alone will have access to the server, its volumes and data. What can Hallie implement to ensure this?

A. Directory map objects

B. Alias objects

C. IRF

D. Profile script

29. Grace already has a NetWare 4.11 network that she is hoping to upgrade to NetWare 5. In defining the solution, she is creating the design and implementation schedule. What task should she exclude because it is already done?

A. Design of the NDS tree

B. Design of the NetWare servers

C. Design of the printers

D. None of the above

30. Which type of server is a time consumer and not a time provider?

    A. Single-reference time server

    B. Primary time server

    C. Reference time server

    D. Secondary time server

31. What utility is used to create and name Organizational Units?

    A. OU Creator

    B. NetWare Administrator

    C. NDS Manager

    D. FILER

32. Which of the following NDS objects has an associated login script property?

    A. Group

    B. Alias

    C. User policy package

    D. Organization

33. Sam has a user who telecommutes, teleconferences, and works in a virtual office. What type of user is this?

    A. Local user

    B. Wide area user

    C. Remote user

    D. System administrator

34. What phase troubleshoots performance problems?

    A. Project approach

    B. Design

    C. Implementation

    D. Manage and monitor

35. What is the first thing that a NetWare systems designer should analyze?

    A. Installation process

    B. Business requirements

    C. Resource needs

    D. Length of the installation project

36. What is a justification for a network solution?

    A. Increase time it takes to access files

    B. Increase the cost of printing

    C. Increase users' productivity

    D. Increase the complexity of network access

37. What can a naming standards document prevent?

    A. Network installation

    B. Duplicate names

    C. Access to resources

    D. Security violations

38. What are three design considerations that should be taken into account when designing an NDS tree? Choose all that apply.

    A. Whether administration will be centralized or distributed

    B. The network infrastructure, including WAN links

    C. Location of network resources and their associated users

    D. Cabling type; whether using copper or fiber

39. What design enables user to log on, get into files, and use network resources?

    A. Cost-benefit analysis

    B. NDS design

    C. Accessibility plan

    D. Risk assessment

40. What must be completed prior to creating the Novell Directory Services® tree?

   A. Tree design

   B. Gathering of information about the environment

   C. Insertion of Organizational Unit objects

   D. Installation of the first NetWare server

41. Before moving from the pilot to the full deployment during the implementation phase, what action must be taken?

   A. Design a specific solution.

   B. Gain customer acceptance.

   C. Retire the solution.

   D. Prepare a schedule.

Refer to the Following Scenario When Answering Questions 42–44

Accessus.com is a new company on the Internet. It currently rents a service that provides its Internet Web site. It plans on installing a NetWare network of its own, both for its Web site and for the employees. The owner, Jill, wants all end users to use network printers to realize the savings from sharing those resources.

42. In order to distribute the printers without dedicating print servers the administrator would purchase networkable printer-sharing devices that use either DLC or TCP/IP protocols. What design component does this decision affect?

   A. NDS tree design

   B. Server design

   C. Workstation design

   D. Printer design

43. Accessus.com administrator Taylor must create a design and implementation schedule. Which tasks should she include?

A. Organize and educate the team

B. Create a naming standard

C. Design the NDS tree

D. All of the above

44. Which of the following tasks should Taylor list first?

A. Designing the NDS tree

B. Designing servers

C. Creating the naming standard

D. Designing workstations

45. What is the maximum number of objects that should be in any single partition?

A. 100

B. 1500

C. 350

D. 3500

Refer to the Following Scenario to Answer Questions 46–50

Justine is rolling out a NetWare network and she is trying to decide which of four candidates to place on the NDS design team. George is the receptionist and uses a computer simply to access the company's Intranet phone list. Chris is the mainframe backup operator and handles tape changes and backup problems on the mainframe from a dumb terminal. Yvette is a network specialist and originally contracted the network cabling. Julie is the company trainer and holds classes and develops training materials, as well as publishes them on her own Intranet server.

46. Since Justine makes the decisions about whom to place on the NDS design team, which role is she most likely fulfilling?

A. IS manager
B. Workstation specialist
C. Printing specialist
D. Testing-lab coordinator

47. Justine decides that Frank, a consultant whose specialty is NetWare installation and NDS design, will be the NDS expert. Which of the following tasks will Frank be responsible for?

A. Install servers
B. Maintain WAN links
C. Match the design to the corporate structure
D. Create login scripts to access applications

48. Justine must now decide who will be the workstation specialist. Her candidates are network specialist Yvette, Greg, who handles installations, moves, adds, and changes for workstations, Danny, who performs all hardware repair and maintenance, and printer support, and Vesna, who automates applications so that they can be installed via software distribution. Whom should Justine select for the workstation specialist?

A. Yvette
B. Greg
C. Danny
D. Vesna

49. Justine assigns George, who handles hardware maintenance and printers, as the printing specialist. What is George's responsibility?

A. Verifying that printer drivers are installed and configured correctly
B. Checking network bandwidth utilization
C. Obtaining resources for the lab
D. Managing the cost and schedule of the project

50. Justine has decided to act as both the IS manager and the testing-lab coordinator. The team is complete and they begin the first phase, the project approach. Which of the following is *not* a document that the team will have to collect during this phase?

A. Company background information

B. Organization chart

C. Sales brochure

D. WAN topology

51. Which phase of the NetWare NDS design cycle includes the task to train the project team?

A. Project approach

B. Design

C. Implementation

D. Manage and monitor

52. What is required on a source server when it performs transitive synchronization for a replica list?

A. IP protocol

B. IPX protocol

C. IP and IPX protocols

D. SPX protocol

53. Which of the following tasks in the design and implementation schedule can rectify a pilot implementation, should problems occur?

A. Notification

B. Installation of infrastructure components

C. Contingency plan

D. Educate the pilot group

54. What NDS mechanism enables an administrator to use the same volume name on all the servers?

A. Volumes are not recognized as objects in NDS.

B. Volume names are treated as file names, which can be identical.

C. Volume names are concatenated with the NDS tree name to create unique names.

D. Volume names are concatenated with their server name to create unique names.

55. If a network has a primary time server, what other two types of time servers can the network have? Choose all that apply.

A. Single reference

B. Reference

C. Secondary

D. None of the above

56. Which type of login script is the most difficult to administer?

A. Organization container login script

B. Organizational Unit container login script

C. Profile login script

D. User login script

57. Which of the following are costs that should not be listed in the cost-benefit analysis?

A. Costs for new hardware or hardware upgrades

B. Costs for software or software upgrades

C. Salary or contracting costs for implementation team members

D. Costs for personal, long distance calls for traveling team members

58. Which of the following naming standards, based on the name of Terence Edwin Jackson, adds security to the network for user accounts?

A. TEJ

B. TERENCE

C. TJACKS01

D. 01HTJ9987

59. What is the default time configuration for a new NetWare installation?

A. Reference servers with secondary servers

B. Reference servers with primary servers

C. Single-reference servers with primary servers

D. Single-reference servers with secondary servers

60. What administrative role manages NetWare configuration, volumes, directories, and files as its core capability?

A. Enterprise administrator

B. Password administrator

C. Server administrator

D. Backup administrator

61. AllTek has 43 servers across three sites and decides against using NTP. What scheme is their best option for time synchronization?

A. All servers are set up as single-reference servers.

B. All servers are set up as primary servers.

C. Some servers are set up as reference (some as primary and the remainder as secondary servers).

D. The default time configuration

62. Which of the following tasks includes creating a login script?

    A. Design the NDS tree

    B. Manage NetWare

    C. Plan time synchronization

    D. Plan the user environment

63. Given the network in the following illustration, what are the lowest-level containers that should have separate partitions?

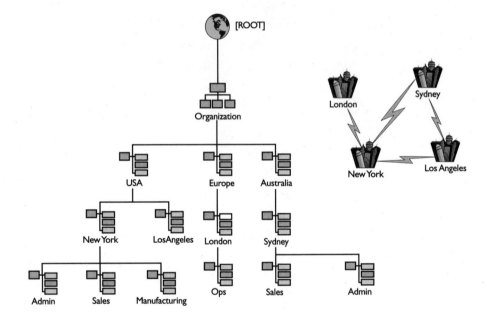

    A. Organization (top level)

    B. USA, Europe, and Australia (second level)

    C. New York, Los Angeles, London, and Sydney (third level)

    D. Admin, Sales, Ops, and Manufacturing (fourth level)

64. What step in defining and justifying a network solution can a network administrator ignore?

A. Define the initial solution

B. Create a design and implementation schedule

C. Sell the solution

D. None of the above

65. What options does Z.E.N.works give for naming Windows 98 workstations? Choose all that apply.

A. User

B. Computer

C. Application

D. RAM

66. What protocol does NetWare use by default to communicate time synchronization information?

A. SAP

B. IPX

C. SPX

D. NCP

67. What is the default value for the number of incorrect login attempts for a user object?

A. Two

B. Three

C. Four

D. Five

68. AllTek has 43 servers across three sites and decides against using NTP. Although it has discarded the NTP scheme, it retains it as an option because there is a rumor that NTP time synchronization will be a requirement if AllTek merges with a company called NewEdge. If AllTek and NewEdge merge, what type of NTP server does AllTek need to exchange time updates with NewEdge's NTP server?

A. Server

B. Peer

C. Primary

D. Reference

Test Yourself:
Practice Exam 4
Answers

Q & A

The answers to the questions are in boldface, followed by a brief explanation. The incorrect answer choices are explained in the final paragraph following each correct answer. Some of the explanations detail the logic you should use to choose the correct answer, while others give factual reasons why the answer is correct. If you miss several questions on a similar topic, you should review the corresponding section in the *CNE® NetWare® 5 Study Guide* before taking the NDS™ Design and Implementation test.

Practice Exam 4 Answers

1. ☑ **B, D.** Two reasons a network solution should be proposed are that it solves a problem that currently exists and that it provides a way to meet a business requirement. A business requirement is something that enables business to occur in a faster, better, or cheaper way, such as reducing loss in productivity or increasing customer support options.
☒ **A.** It is a new technology is incorrect because the age of the technology is irrelevant to helping the Organization in any way. **C.** It is cheap is incorrect because the cost of a solution is also irrelevant to helping the Organization in any way.

2. ☑ **B.** Analysis and specification is the first phase of the SDLC model. This phase marks the beginning of the project, including the project scope and requirements identification.
☒ **A.** Implementation is incorrect because a project cannot start until the requirements have been identified. **C.** Maintenance is incorrect because you cannot maintain a network that has not been installed. **D.** Design is incorrect because a design is dependent upon the project scope.

3. ☑ **C.** CPU utilization is not a requirement of the network solution. The utilization of a CPU would not be a known factor until after the solution was implemented.
☒ **A.** NDS tree is incorrect because it is a required component of the network solution. **B.** Applications is incorrect because it is also a required component of the network solution. **D.** Servers is incorrect because servers are also a required component of the network solution.

4. ☑ **C.** The Win95 user package defines the Z.E.N.works workstation name. The user package is used to import workstations. When workstations are imported they require a predefined naming standard in order to be added to NDS as objects.

☒ **A.** User object is incorrect because the User object is not directly involved with the import of the workstation. **B.** Server object is incorrect because the Server object is not involved with the import of the workstation. **D.** Windows NT policy package is incorrect because the workstation policy packages are only applied after a workstation has been imported into NDS and already has a name.

5. ☑ **C.** The user account robjon01 represents a naming standard that would prevent duplicate names. The naming standard is the first three letters of the first name plus the first three letters of the last name and two digits to serialize the account if there are people whose user accounts would be the same without the digits.

☒ **A.** Robertjones is incorrect because any two people with the same first and last names would have duplicate account names. **B.** Rjones is incorrect because anyone whose first name began with R and last name was Jones would have duplicate account names. **D.** Robertj is incorrect because anyone whose first name was Robert and last name began with J would have duplicate account names.

6. ☑ **D.** The naming standards document that Tim created for Acme should include the naming standards for network resources and accounts, a list of the data required for each named resource, and an example of a name for each resource and account.

☒ The answers for **A**, **B**, and **C.** are all incorrect because all of them should be in the naming standards document.

7. ☑ **B, C.** The two names Prt_bldg1 and Prt bldg1 cannot be placed in the same container unit in an NDS tree. NDS lets an administrator create names with either spaces or underscores for objects in the tree. However, NDS interprets the space and the underscore as the same character. This means that if Prt_bldg1 and Prt bldg1 were placed in the same NDS container, they would not have unique, distinguished names.

☒ **A.** Prt-bldg1 is incorrect because the dash is unique in NDS. **D.** Prt/bldg1 is incorrect because NDS does not let you use the slash character in object names.

8. ☑ **A.** Tim cannot migrate any of the user accounts that are duplicates differentiated only by case since NDS is not case sensitive. This means that a user account with the name Jjones is interpreted exactly as a user account with the name JJONES. NDS will preserve the case used when the object is originally created or renamed, so it is seen that way in the NetWare Administrator, but no two objects can have the same name, regardless of the case.

☒ **B.** There are names with underscores, such as J_jones, is incorrect because underscores can be used in NDS. **C.** There are names using spaces such as J jones, is incorrect because spaces can be used in NDS account names. **D.** There are names that use dashes, such as J-jones, is incorrect because those names can be used in NDS.

9. ☑ **B.** In order to mirror the production ACME tree, the Organization name for each tree can be identical. Since the Organization name for the production tree is Acme, the lab tree's Organization name should also be Acme.

☒ **A.** AcmeLab is incorrect because it will not mirror the production tree. **C.** ACME1, is incorrect because there is no need to serialize the names of objects between two different NDS trees except for servers. **D.** O=Acme1 is incorrect because this is a typeful name for a serialized Organization name.

10. ☑ **B.** The NDS Manager utility is used to partition the NDS tree and create replicas. This utility displays the container objects of the tree and the servers contained in the tree so that an administrator can create partitions or replicas and place them on servers throughout the NDS tree.

☒ **A.** NetWare Administrator is incorrect because it is used to manipulate objects within the NDS tree, not to manipulate the database containing the tree. **C.** FILER is incorrect because it is used to manipulate files on NetWare volumes. **D.** Explorer is incorrect because it is a Windows utility used for file manipulation.

11. ☑ **B, D.** Warren should use the geographical model for the NDS tree design. Alternatively, Warren can use the hybrid model, since TFX, Inc. has some business units that do not span the WAN.

In the geographical model, the upper layers of the NDS tree represent the sites that are separated by WAN links. The lower layers can be further separated into containers that represent the Organization.

In the hybrid model, the upper layers represent the sites that are separated by WAN links and any business units that are wholly contained within a site and do not span the WAN.

☒ **A.** Administrative model is incorrect because there will be a single NetWare administrator and no need to separate the containers. This would then span the WAN and be a performance problem. **C.** Divisions model is incorrect because there are two divisions, Administration and Sales, that are located in more than one site. These divisions will span the WAN and be a performance problem.

12. ☑   **C.** Multiple bindery contexts on a server will force naming standards in order to ensure that no two names in different bindery contexts are the same. A NetWare₆ 5 server can have up to 16 bindery contexts set on it. This creates a virtual bindery on the server. The names in the virtual bindery must be unique.

☒   **A.** Two names in the same container cannot be the same is incorrect because this is a standard NDS rule. **B.** Two names in different containers cannot be the same is incorrect because those two containers may not be the ones used for the bindery context. **D.** Two names in the same container must be the same is incorrect because this is unacceptable in an NDS tree.

13. ☑   **A.** Warren can partition the NDS database to reduce the utilization on the first installed server. The first server installed in the NDS tree holds the master replica of the [Root]. As more objects are added to the NDS tree, the utilization increases on the server. Since Warren added the servers into the same container, there are only three default replicas of the master replica. They each contain all the objects in the tree and would then become very large as objects are added.

☒   **B.** Create multiple read/write replicas of the master replica is incorrect because they will not reduce the utilization on the first server. **C.** Move the server to a different site is incorrect because that will not change the utilization. **D.** Add more Organizational Units to the NDS tree is incorrect because the additional objects may increase the utilization, not reduce it.

14. ☑   **D.** Each of the master servers has subordinate references of the other partitions automatically created on them. A subordinate reference is a pointer to a child replica. It is created when a server has a copy of the parent replica but not of the child replica.

☒   **A.** Read/write replicas of the other partitions is incorrect because those must be defined at the time the tree is partitioned. **B.** Master replicas of the other partitions is incorrect because there can only be a single master replica for each partition. **C.** Read-only replicas of the other partitions is incorrect because read-only replicas must be specifically created by an administrator.

15. ☑ **D.** Creating two read/write replicas for each partition will provide fault tolerance. At least one additional read/write replica will ensure that if a problem occurs with the master replica, users can still authenticate and access network resources.

☒ **A.** Maximum bandwidth is incorrect because additional read/write replicas will not add any network bandwidth. **B.** Decreased performance is incorrect because the additional read/write replicas may increase performance. **C.** Bindery services is incorrect because bindery services are provided by the SET BINDERY CONTEXT command on a server.

16. ☑ **C.** Warren should look for the traffic that is created by the SAP protocol. Service Advertising Protocol (SAP) is the protocol used to update time on NetWare servers using IPX.

☒ **A.** Network Time Protocol (NTP) is incorrect because it is used for time updates on NetWare servers using the IP protocol suite. **B.** Network News Transport Protocol (NNTP) is incorrect because it is used for Usenet news, not time updates. **D.** Sequenced Packet Exchange (SPX) is incorrect because it provides a reliable, connection-oriented datastream.

17. ☑ **C.** Warren uses the DSMERGE utility to merge the TFX and Sandscapes NDS trees. This utility is provided as part of NetWare 5.

☒ Answers **A**, **B**, and **D.** are all incorrect because none (MERGE, NDSMERGE, NWMERGE) exists as a utility in NetWare 5.

18. ☑ **A.** An alias object can assist a mobile user in accessing resources. It can be created for a mobile user and placed in those containers to which the user may travel. The administrator may choose to implement NetWare 5's contextless login to eliminate the need to provide an NDS context when logging in. The NDS catalog service will present a list of user objects if there is more than one with the same common name for the end user to select from. Also, Client 32 can be configured with locations for mobile users and login scripts can be customized to support mobile users.
    ☒ **B.** Container policy package is incorrect because it will not affect a mobile user. **C.** Volume is incorrect because it will not assist a mobile user. **D.** Server is incorrect because it will not assist a server.

19. ☑ **C.** The cost-benefit analysis should include an estimated decrease in maintenance costs to occur after the network solution is in place, a benefit of implementing the network solution.
    ☒ **A.** A design schedule is incorrect because that is a separate document. **B.** An implementation schedule is incorrect because that, too, is a separate document. **D.** A list of risks is incorrect because the risk assessment is a separate document from the cost-benefits analysis.

20. ☑ **B.** The Country object is an optional container object in the NDS tree. The Country object is meant for global networks and is located directly beneath the [Root] when it is implemented.
    ☒ **A.** [Root] is incorrect because a [Root] is always part of an NDS tree. **C.** Organization is incorrect because an NDS tree always has at least one Organization object. **D.** None of the above is incorrect because a Country object is optional.

21. ☑   **C.** The correct order of the design phase components is:
Propose a generic solution
Propose alternative solutions
Design a specific solution
The design phase begins after the analysis and specification phase. The solutions proposed use the goals and objectives of the project as guidelines.
☒   **A.** This answer is incorrect because the final step is to design a specific solution. **B.** This answer is also incorrect because the final step is to design a specific solution. **D.** This answer is incorrect because the first step is to propose a generic solution.

22. ☑   **B.** The protocol usage of TCP/IP will affect the server design component of the network solution for Accessus.com. TCP/IP must be installed and configured on each server on the network. Because some servers will be dedicated for employees and visitors to the Web site, the protocol decision may specify that only Internet Web site servers use TCP/IP and others use another protocol, or the decision may specify that all servers use TCP/IP.
☒   **A.** NDS tree design is incorrect because its design does not depend on protocols. **C.** Application design is incorrect because applications are typically not protocol dependent. **D.** None of the above is incorrect because the protocol usage will affect how a server is designed.

23. ☑   **C.** NetWare automatically creates three replicas of each partition if there are enough servers to house them on the network. An administrator can use NDS Manager to create more replicas if more are needed for a partition. Or, if the network did not have enough servers when the original partition was created, new replicas can be created.
☒   Answers **A, B,** and **D.** are incorrect because NetWare will create 3 replicas automatically if there are a sufficient number of servers.

24. ☑ **A.** Hallie should ask some further questions about the shared applications, including "Which shared applications have hardware or operating system requirements?" Other questions that she may ask include "Which shared applications must be launched manually by the end user?" and, "Which shared applications must be launched automatically for the end user?"

    ☒ **B.** Do any partitions have more than 3500 objects is incorrect because that is a question to be asked about partitioning and replication. **C.** Will administration be centralized or distributed is incorrect because that is a question to be asked to determine Organizational Unit separations. **D.** Are there more than 30 servers is incorrect because that is a question to help with time configuration.

25. ☑ **C, D.** Two physical network resources are CD-ROMs and printers. A physical network resource falls into one of two categories:

    - ■ Networked resources   printers, scanners and other equipment that attach to the network and provide a service to network users

    - ■ Network storage devices   CD-ROMs, NetWare volumes, jukeboxes, and other equipment that can be considered an online, offline, or nearline storage device

    ☒ **A.** Applications is incorrect because they are not physical resources. **B.** Login scripts is incorrect because they are not physical resources.

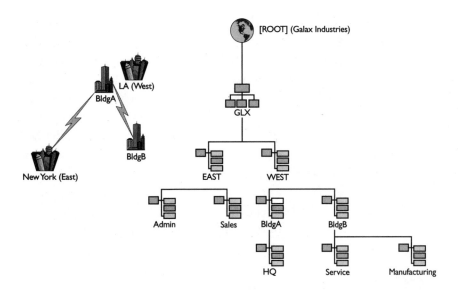

26. ☑ **B.** The three Organizational Units that are best suited for the container policy package are BLDGA, BLDGB and EAST. Even though the policy packages will be identical, a container policy package should not span a WAN link. In the illustration, the network is depicted with a WAN link between BLDGA and BLDGB, as well as between BLDGA and EAST. This means that those would be the highest level containers in which to place the policy packages.

☒ **A.** GLX is incorrect because it spans the WAN and because it is not an Organizational Unit, but the Organization. **C.** BLDGB, EAST, and WEST is incorrect because WEST spans a WAN link. **D.** EAST and WEST is incorrect because WEST spans a WAN link.

27. ☑ **B, C.** Hallie should set up two groups. For example, CHKPTRS and ACCTPTRS. In the CHKPTRS group, Hallie should add the accounting users who are allowed to access the check printers. In the ACCTPTRS group, Hallie should add the accounting and administrator users who are allowed to use the other two printers. Hallie should then change the security on the CHKPTRS group to ensure that it has access to the check printers. Hallie should then change the security on the ACCTPTRS group so that it has access to the accounting printers, but is restricted from using the check printers.

    ☒ **A.** Place printer objects in the GLX container is incorrect because the printers should be placed close to the users that will be using them. **D.** Run the secure printer utility on the print server is incorrect because there is no such utility.

28. ☑ **C.** Hallie can implement an Inherited Rights Filter (IRF) or for the server. In order to ensure that the supervisor right is not inherited, Hallie would first explicitly grant supervisor rights of the server object to the administrator object with which she logs in. Then Hallie would create an IRF for the server that removes the supervisor right. The IRF will filter out only inherited rights, so Hallie's object will not be affected.

    ☒ **A.** Directory map objects is incorrect because they ease administration for file access. **B.** Alias objects is incorrect because they do not add any security to servers. **D.** Profile script is incorrect because a profile script is used as an additional login script that may run after the container script.

29. ☑ **D.** Grace should not exclude any of the design tasks listed. An upgrade design and implementation schedule should revisit the design of network components that already exist. If there are any problems being experienced on the network, the design tasks can focus on resolving those problems. If there are new goals or changes made to the network, the design tasks can plan to incorporate those changes as they occur.

☒ **A.** Design of the NDS tree is incorrect because the NDS tree structure should be reviewed, validated, or redesigned. **B.** Design of the servers is incorrect because servers should be designed to include NetWare 5 features such as Z.E.N.works, NDPS, NSS, or FastWeb server. **C.** Design of the printers is incorrect because printers should be designed to include NetWare 5 features such as NDPS.

30. ☑ **D.** The secondary time server is a time consumer. Servers can be either time providers or time consumers. A time consumer is a server that receives time updates from the network and does not provide any time updates to the network.

☒ **A.** Single-reference time server is incorrect because it is a time provider. **B.** Primary time server is incorrect because it is a time provider. **C.** Reference time server is incorrect because it is a time provider.

31. ☑ **B.** The NetWare Administrator utility is used to create and name Organizational Units. An Organizational Unit (OU) can be created under the Organization or any other Organizational Unit. To create a new OU, select the Organization or Organizational Unit and press the INSERT key. Then select Organizational Unit from the list of available objects and click OK. Give the Organizational Unit the name, according to the naming standard, and press the CREATE button.

☒ **A.** OU Creator is incorrect because there is no such NetWare utility. **C.** NDS Manager is incorrect because it is used to manage the partitioning and replication of the NDS database. **D.** FILER is incorrect because it is used to manage files on NetWare volumes.

32. ☑ **D.** The Organization NDS object has an associated login script property. This login script is a container login script. From an end user's perspective, the container script for the container holding the user object will load first immediately after logging in.

☒ **A.** Group is incorrect because there are no login script properties for group objects. **B.** Alias is incorrect because there are no login script properties for aliases. **C.** User policy package is incorrect because a user policy package does not have a login script.

33. ☑ **C.** Sam's telecommuting user is known as a remote user. Remote users work in areas that are remote from a network office. Remote users are becoming more common as telecommuting gains greater acceptance by the corporate world.

☒ **A.** Local user is incorrect because this user is not in a local office. **B.** Wide-area user is incorrect because there is no such term. **D.** System administrator is incorrect because telecommuting does not imply additional security access.

34. ☑ **D.** The manage-and-monitor phase of the NetWare NDS design cycle includes the task to troubleshoot performance problems. Specifically, network management tasks fall under the monitor NetWare portion of this phase. Monitoring performance, faults, and events can enable NetWare to meet changes within the enterprise, such as large groups of users added, moved, or changed.

☒ **A.** Project approach is incorrect because NetWare is not available during this phase. **B.** Design is incorrect because NetWare is not in the production environment during this phase. **C.** Implementation is incorrect because NetWare has not been fully rolled out and accepted until implementation has been completed.

35. ☑ **B.** The first thing that a NetWare systems designer should analyze is the business requirements of the enterprise that is installing NetWare. These drive NetWare's choice of goals for the installation project and include performance, fault tolerance, and accessibility, among others.

☒ **A.** Installation process is incorrect because the goals of the project based on the requirements of the enterprise will determine the installation process. **C.** Resource needs is incorrect because the project's goals will determine whether more resources or fewer are needed. **D.** Length of the installation project is incorrect because the length will be determined by the requirements of the enterprise.

36. ☑ **C.** One justification for a network solution would be to increase users' productivity. The way that the productivity could be increased is by the faster, less complex access to network resources. A justification for any network solution usually affects the total cost of ownership of the network, reducing that cost for the business. Cost of ownership is not simply the price of a piece of equipment or software. Instead, cost of ownership involves the upkeep, administration, management, productivity losses and other support expenditures. Note that a justification for network solution always is related to business, not technology.

☒ **A.** Increase time it takes to access files is incorrect because it will adversely affect the user's productivity. **B.** Increase the cost of printing is incorrect because it will adversely affect the business. **D.** Increase the complexity of network access is incorrect because it will adversely affect users' productivity.

37. ☑ **B.** A naming standards document can prevent duplicate names. A common problem is that people share first and/or last names. User accounts are usually based on the user's actual name, so duplicates can occur if they are not planned for.

☒ **A.** Network installation is incorrect because a naming standards document does not prevent a network installation. **C.** Access to resources is incorrect because a naming standards document does not prevent resource access. **D.** Security violations is incorrect because naming standards do not prevent security violations.

38. ☑   **A, B, C.** Three design considerations to take into account are how administration will be performed, the network infrastructure including WAN links, and the location of network resources and their associated users. The use of centralized administration allows a more centralized type of tree, but when distributing administration, each administrator will be granted a different section of Organizational Units to administer. The network infrastructure affects the top layer of OUs, since any slow links should separate Organizational Units. The location of network resources and their associated users should all be placed closely together in the NDS tree.
    ☒   **D.** Cabling types is incorrect because the cabling types used should not affect the NDS tree design.

39. ☑   **C.** The design for users to be able to log on, get into files and use network resources is called an accessibility plan. This plan details the users' needs for network resources and the method that will be used to grant them access.
    ☒   **A.** Cost-benefit analysis is incorrect because that is a document used to determine the costs and benefits of the proposed network solution. **B.** NDS design is incorrect because that document designs the NDS tree Organization. **D.** Risk assessment is incorrect because it is a document to specify the risks of a network solution.

40. ☑   **B.** The first thing that must be completed prior to creating the NDS tree is the gathering of information about the environment. This step establishes the business drivers, the WAN links, the Organizational structure, and the user's requirements. These all affect the decisions made when designing the tree.
    ☒   **A.** Tree design is incorrect because the design should be created prior to the first NetWare server installation and NDS tree creation. **C.** Insertion of Organizational Unit objects is incorrect because they are added after the tree has been initially created. **D.** Installation of the first NetWare server is incorrect because that is the action that creates the NDS tree.

41. ☑ **B.** Before moving from the pilot to the full deployment, you must gain customer acceptance. This happens twice during the implementation phase: first, to move from pilot to full deployment, and second, to end the implementation phase and move to the maintenance phase.

    ☒ **A.** Design a specific solution is incorrect because it is part of the design phase. **C.** Retire the solution is incorrect because it is part of the maintenance phase. **D.** Prepare a schedule is incorrect because it is part of the analysis and specification phase.

42. ☑ **D.** This decision affects the printer design component. The business requirement to share network resources and reduce expenses is easily translated to sharing printers with networkable printer-sharing devices.

    ☒ **A.** NDS tree design is incorrect because it is unaffected by printer sharing devices. **B.** Server design is incorrect because it is not directly affected by printer sharing devices. **C.** Workstation design is incorrect because it is not affected by shared printers.

43. ☑ **D.** All of the above. Taylor should include the tasks to organize and educate the team, create a naming standard and design the NDS tree. Each of these tasks is in the order that it should be executed. The first is to organize and educate the team. Next, a naming standard should be designed by the team. The naming standard would be used in the NDS tree design.

44. ☑ **C.** The task of creating the naming standard should be listed first. The naming standard is used in the design of the NDS tree and the design of the servers and the design of the workstations. If it is not created first, the other design tasks suffer.

    ☒ **A.** Designing the NDS tree is incorrect because its structure depends on the naming standard. **B.** Designing servers is incorrect because their names depend on the naming standard. **D.** Designing workstations is incorrect because workstation names depend on the naming standard.

45. ☑ **D.** The maximum number of objects that should be in any single partition is 3500. After that, the administrator should split the partition. This is not a hard and fast rule. There can be more than 3500 objects in a partition. The problem is that when there are more than 3500 objects, the partition takes longer to synchronize. This type of performance problem can be alleviated by splitting the partition into two or more smaller partitions.

    ☒ Answers **A, B,** and **C.** are all incorrect because the threshold number is 3500 objects within a partition.

46. ☑ **A.** Justine is most likely fulfilling the IS manager role on the NDS design team. The IS manager role is the one that makes decisions and is accountable for the design of the NDS tree. As the IS manager, Justine is not only responsible for selecting team members, but coordinating the project, securing resources, and managing the schedule and budget for the project.

    ☒ **B.** Workstation specialist is incorrect because this person manages the workstation client software, not the team. **C.** Printing specialist is incorrect because he or she manages the printer design. **D.** Testing lab coordinator is incorrect because he or she sets up a test network and runs tests on it.

47. ☑ **C.** Frank will be responsible for matching the design to the corporate structure. The NDS expert role is both the NDS tree designer and an assistant to the IS manager. The NDS expert will assist in selecting team members and communications with the company, as well as be responsible for the design of the NDS tree and overall design of the NetWare network.

☒ **A.** Install servers is incorrect because that is a server specialist's task. **B.** Maintain WAN links is incorrect because that is a connectivity specialist's task. **D.** Create login scripts to access applications is incorrect because that is an application specialist's task.

48. ☑ **B.** Greg is the best choice for workstation specialist. Greg's job is to install workstations, move them, and make changes to them. The job makes Greg an expert on the current workstation configuration and installation process.

☒ **A.** Yvette is incorrect because her experience is in infrastructure network support. **C.** Danny is incorrect because his experience with workstations has nothing to do with installation of their software or their configuration. **D.** Vesna is incorrect because she has no experience in the installation process of the entire workstation. However, she would make a good second choice if Greg were unavailable.

49. ☑ **A.** George will be responsible for verifying that printer drivers are installed and configured correctly. The printing specialist is also responsible for setting up printers, ensuring that bindery services are set up for anything that requires bindery-based printing, and setting up the point-and-print functionality for 32-bit clients.

☒ **B.** Checking network bandwidth utilization is incorrect because that is a connectivity specialist task. **C.** Obtaining resources for the lab is incorrect because that is a testing-lab coordinator task. **D.** Managing the cost and schedule of the project is incorrect because that is the IS manager's task.

50. ☑ C. The team will not have to collect a corporate sales brochure. A corporate sales brochure is not likely to add any value to the design of the NDS tree or the mission of the NDS design project.

☒ A. Company background information is incorrect because it provides insight into the corporate mission and helps guide the project.
B. Organization chart is incorrect because it assists in designing the lower layers of the NDS tree. D. WAN topology is incorrect because it assists in designing the upper layers of the NDS tree.

51. ☑ A. The project approach phase in the NetWare NDS design cycle includes the task to train the project team. Training the team is a necessary task to ensure that valid decisions are made during the design phase.

☒ B. Design is incorrect because the team must be trained before designing NDS. C. Implementation is incorrect because the team must be trained before implementing NDS. D. Manage and monitor is incorrect because the team must be trained before managing NDS.

52. ☑ C. Both the IP and IPX protocols are required on a source server when it performs transitive synchronization for a replica list. A replica list is the group of all servers that contain a replica of a single partition. Transitive synchronization is the process of a source server updating other servers' replicas with either the IP or the IPX protocol, depending on which protocol the other servers are using. Using this method, the source server uses two protocols and the other servers can use either IP or IPX, or both. The replicas remain synchronized between servers that cannot communicate natively.

☒ A. IP protocol is incorrect because the source server requires both IP and IPX. B. IPX protocol is incorrect because the source server requires both IP and IPX. D. SPX protocol is incorrect because both IP and IPX are required on the source server.

53. ☑ **C.** The contingency plan is intended to rectify a pilot implementation if there are problems during the pilot. This is actually a set of tasks meant to uninstall and undo an implementation. If there has been some critical implementation requirement that has been overlooked, the contingency plan can prevent productivity loss.

☒ **A.** Notification is incorrect because it is a task to simply notify users that the implementation will begin. **B.** Installation of infrastructure components is incorrect because it installs and doesn't uninstall. **D.** Educate the pilot group is incorrect because it does not rectify problems with the pilot.

54. ☑ **D.** In NDS, a volume name is concatenated with its server's name to create a unique name. Since server names are required to be unique on the internetwork and volume names are required to be unique on each server, the final volume name is unique within NDS. For example, every NetWare server has a SYS volume. No server can have more than one volume named SYS. Each server's SYS volume is then named SERVER_SYS within the NDS tree.

☒ **A.** Volumes are not recognized as objects in NDS is incorrect because volumes can be seen in the NDS tree as objects. **B.** Volume names are treated like file names which can be identical is incorrect because volume names are not treated like file names. **C.** Volume names are concatenated with the NDS tree name is incorrect because they are concatenated with the server name.

55. ☑ **B, C.** Both the reference and secondary servers can exist on a network with primary servers. The reference server participates in a time-polling process with a loaded favorability towards its own time at about 16 to 1, when compared to a primary server. The secondary server does not participate in updating time on the network.

☒ **A.** Single reference is incorrect because it will only exist on networks with secondary servers. **D.** None of the above is incorrect because both reference and secondary servers can exist with primary time servers.

56. ☑ **D.** A user login script is the most difficult to administer. It is a common rule to avoid using any personal login scripts because users are automatically granted the ability to change them. Instead, container scripts make it easy to review, edit and troubleshoot because there are very few of them and container script commands are executed first.

When users create and use individual scripts, a diverse environment exists. Nobody's drive mappings are the same. Nobody's print captures are the same. It is difficult to communicate with end users because there is not a common environment to use as a point of reference. Further, if there are problems with the login scripts themselves, not only must a container login script be analyzed, but also the user login script and, if it is assigned to the user, a profile login script.

☒ **A.** Organization container login script is incorrect because a container script is easiest to administer. **B.** Organizational Unit container login script is incorrect because it is easiest to administer. **C.** Profile login script is incorrect because these scripts are applicable to groups of users and by default, users cannot make changes to them.

57. ☑ **D.** The cost-benefit analysis should not list costs for personal long-distance calls for traveling team members. Corporate policies vary as far as what types of calls will or will not be covered. In most cases, they cover corporate calls, or are lumped into a per diem, or daily, charge. The cost-benefit analysis should include such per diem charges for each team member that travels.

☒ **A.** Costs for hardware or hardware upgrades is incorrect because those costs should be calculated. **B.** Costs for software or software upgrades is incorrect because those costs should also be calculated. **C.** Salary or contracting costs for implementation team members is incorrect because those costs should also be calculated in the cost-benefit analysis.

58. ☑ **D.** The naming standard 01HTJ9987 adds security to the network. This naming standard is based on the employee number or some other unpublished scheme. This method of naming users makes it difficult for hackers to guess a user's account name.

☒ **A.** TEJ is incorrect because a user's initials are either known or fairly easy to guess. **B.** TERENCE is incorrect because a user's first name is usually known. **C.** TJACKS01 is incorrect because this is a standard naming convention, and easy to guess.

59. ☑ **D.** The default time configuration for new NetWare installations is the setting of the first server as a single-reference server and all subsequent servers as secondary servers.

☒ **A.** Reference servers with secondary servers is incorrect because this configuration is not the default. **B.** Reference servers with primary servers is incorrect because this configuration is not the default. **C.** Single-reference servers with primary servers is incorrect because primary servers do not work with single-reference servers.

60. ☑ **C.** The server administrator role manages the configuration, volumes, directories, and files on a server. This encompasses the end users' rights to files and directories, the server configuration, migration and compression, file deletion and salvage, performance management, and any other task that directly affects a single server. The server administrator is given full administrative authority over an NDS server object.

☒ **A.** Enterprise administrator is incorrect because this role has access to the entire tree, and is not limited to server objects. **B.** Password administrator is incorrect because a password administrator does not have access to server objects. **D.** Backup administrator is incorrect because the backup administrator's access to a server object is limited to only the rights necessary to back it up.

61. ☑ C. The best option for AllTek's time synchronization scheme is to install some servers as reference time servers, some as primary time servers, and the remainder as secondary servers. Novell® recommends that any network with more than 30 servers should have a custom configuration.

☒ A. All servers are set up as single-reference servers is incorrect because this is an invalid time configuration. **B.** All servers are set up as primary servers is incorrect because this is an invalid time configuration. **D.** The default NetWare configuration is incorrect because AllTek has more than 30 servers. A network with more than 30 servers should have a custom configuration, not a default configuration, for time.

62. ☑ D. Creating a login script is part of the task of planning the user environment. This task is in the design phase of the NetWare NDS design cycle. Login scripts define the user environment at the moment login begins. They can include drive mappings, printers, NDS context, and access requirements for other network resources.

☒ A. Design the NDS tree is incorrect because it refers to the Organizational layout of the tree and the naming conventions. **B.** Manage NetWare is incorrect because the login script should be in place before NetWare needs to be managed. **C.** Plan time synchronization is incorrect because time synchronization is the strategy applied to the server environment, not the user environment.

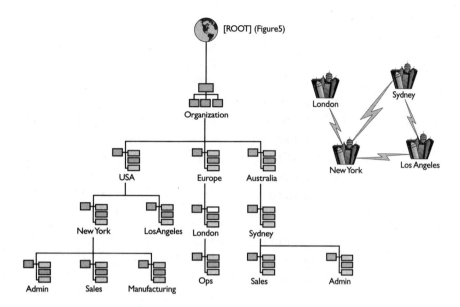

63. ☑ **C.** The lowest level that should absolutely have separate partitions is the third-level, with containers that include New York, Los Angeles, London, and Sydney. In the illustration, each city location is shown with a WAN link connecting it to other city locations. To avoid spanning the WAN, each city location should have a separate partition. Further partitions can be created, but the absolute requirement should be to avoid spanning the WAN.

☒ **A.** Organization is incorrect because that partition would span the WAN. **B.** USA, Europe and Australia, is incorrect because the USA partition would span the WAN. **D.** Admin, Sales, Ops and Manufacturing is incorrect because none of these absolutely requires a separate partition from the information given.

64. ☑ **D.** None of these three steps can be ignored by a network administrator. A network administrator should define a solution, create a schedule, and sell the solution to management. The final selling step is the point at which management approves the network solution so that the resources can be gathered and the project begun.

A. Define the initial solution is necessary because the administrator cannot implement any solution that is not defined. **B.** Create the design and implementation schedule is necessary because they provide an estimate of the project's duration and associated costs. **C.** Sell the solution is necessary because the solution must be approved by management before it can be implemented.

65. ☑ **A, B.** Both User and Computer are options for Z.E.N.works Windows 98 workstation object names. The User represents the user's account name that is associated with the workstation object. The Computer represents the NetBIOS name for the Windows 98 PC.

☒ **C.** Application is incorrect because it is not a workstation object name option. **D.** RAM is incorrect because it is not a workstation object name option.

66. ☑ **A.** NetWare uses by default the Service Advertising Protocol (SAP) to communicate time synchronization information. Because it is a broadcast protocol, SAP's information is directed to all network nodes. Although SAP can transmit information quickly, the network traffic overload is inefficient.

☒ **B.** IPX is incorrect because IPX handles routing of data. **C.** SPX is incorrect because SPX specifies a connection-oriented datastream. **D.** NCP is incorrect because NCP is the core services protocol for NetWare.

67. ☑ **B.** A user object has the default value of three (3) incorrect login attempts. When a user attempts to log in the fourth time incorrectly, the default behavior is to lock the account so that it cannot be used. NetWare counts the incorrect logins as consecutive attempts during a default Bad Login Count Retention Time value of 15 minutes.

☒ **A, C,** and **D.** are incorrect because the default value is 3. This does not prevent an administrator from changing the user's account values to something else.

68. ☑ **B.** The only types of NTP servers that exchange time updates are peers. This will require that not only is AllTek's server configured as a peer, but also that NewEdge's server is configured as a peer.

☒ **A.** Server is incorrect because an NTP server does not exchange time updates. **C.** Primary is incorrect because a primary server is a NetWare time server. **D.** Reference is incorrect because a reference server is a NetWare time server.

Part 11

Test Yourself:
Practice Exam 5:
NetWare Service
and Support
(Exam 50-635)

Test Yourself:
Practice Exam 5
Questions

Q&*A*

Before you call to register for the actual Service and Support exam (Exam #50-635), take the following test and see how you make out. Set a timer for 120 minutes—the same time you'll have to take the live exam—and answer the following 79 questions in the time allotted. Once you've finished, turn to the Practice Exam 5 Answers section and check your score to see if you passed! Good luck!

Practice Exam 5 Questions

1. IBM calls a hub designed for use in a Token Ring network an *MSAU*, which is an acronym for:

    A. Multiple Sequential Access Unit
    B. Modulated Station Access Unit
    C. Multiple Station Access Unit
    D. Managed Sequential Access Unit

    ### Use the Following Scenario for Questions 2–9
    Mark has been put in charge of coming up with a disaster recovery strategy for his company. The company wants to ensure that there is minimal downtime under several different scenarios.

2. All volumes are mounting correctly, but some users are reporting that they can no longer access directories and files that they used to be able to access. What action should Mark take to restore the users' access to their files and directories?

    A. Restore the volumes in question
    B. Restore the directory from the last day that users were able to access the directories and files
    C. Run VREPAIR on the volume in question
    D. Run DSREPAIR

3. In order to have full confidence in a backup system, what is essential?

    A. Buy the most expensive hardware and software because the most expensive is generally the best

    B. Backup the entire system twice daily

    C. Do a test restoration of files to a non-production volume from time to time

    D. Only use backup software developed by Novell®

4. In order to make sure that his backups are reliable, what must Mark do?

    A. He must use a new tape every time.

    B. He must back up every file every day.

    C. He must make sure file compression is turned off.

    D. He must make sure verify-after-write is enabled.

5. The server room at Mark's site is unexpectedly flooded when a water pipe bursts in the building. The server is destroyed, and installing the disk array into another server proves unsuccessful. The hard disks in the array will not even power up. What can Mark do to recover data that had not yet been backed up?

    A. Send the disk array to a data recovery company, where the hard disk platters will be placed into new mechanisms, and data recovery attempted

    B. Nothing, the data is lost forever

    C. Remove the hard disk platters, and put them into new mechanisms

    D. Send the disk array to a data recovery company, where a laser beam will be used to recover data from the hard disk platters

6. Mark wants his server to perform to the best of its ability, given its hardware. What utility or utilities should Mark use to check out the performance of the server so that he can make setting changes to enhance the performance of the server?

    A. There is really no need to do this, as NetWare will automatically configure itself optimally for the hardware that it is installed on.

    B. Mark could copy and print large files and track the time that it takes to complete the operations under different settings.

    C. Mark could use the MONITOR utility provided with NetWare to observe the performance of the server in real time.

    D. Mark could buy a third party performance monitoring program.

7. Mark wants to make sure that enough RAM is available to load and run virus scanning NLMs on the server. He can reserve RAM for loading NLMs

by using a SET command or by using MONITOR to reduce minimum file cache buffers and what other file cache buffers?

    A. Minimum directory cache buffers

    B. Maximum directory cache buffers

    C. Maximum file cache buffers

    D. Minimum NLM RAM buffers

8. Mark notices that the server is responding slowly to directory searches. To speed up the process, Mark can use a SET command or the change settings in MONITOR.NLM to decrease:

    A. Directory cache allocation wait time

    B. The priority of other default system processes

    C. The priority of third-party NLMs

    D. Directory cache buffers

9. Mark wants to keep an eye on the network by running LANalyzer on a workstation. Mark should be concerned if the utilization gauge consistently reads above 50 percent. What does this indicate?

    A. More than half of the server's processing capacity is being used.

    B. The network is only being used to half of its potential.

    C. The network may run out of bandwidth during peak demand periods.

    D. More than half of the server's RAM is being used.

Use the Following Scenario for Questions 10–11

The company wants to make sure that the important data on the servers are not destroyed by viruses, and asks Joe how to keep viruses from infecting the files on the server.

10. When should Joe install server virus scanning and cleaning software?

    A. Immediately, using software from a reputable third-party company with a good reputation for responding quickly to new viruses

    B. Immediately, using software that is included with NetWare

    C. After he firsts suspects that a fellow employee is trying to deliberately infect files on the server

    D. When the company decides to link its e-mail system to the Internet

11. Considering that his company has several hundred workstations, how should Joe protect those workstations from viruses?

    A. Trust the virus scanning software on the servers

    B. Personally scan each workstation with a virus-checking program on a bootable floppy disk

    C. Use a software package that allows remote installation and updates of workstation virus-scanning software

    D. Write-protect the workstation hard drives

Use the Following Scenario for Questions 12–16

Joe's company needs to keep proprietary files and information on the servers, and wants to ensure that the information can be accessed only by authorized employees of the company.

12. Joe wants to make sure that the members of each workgroup only see the files and directories that they are authorized to see. What is the best way to do this?

    A. Keep each workgroup's files on a separate server

    B. Make each employee sign a promise to only look at the files that they know they are supposed to be looking at

C. Make sure that file and directory rights are set correctly using NetWare Administrator

D. Make sure that a supervisor watches what each member of the workgroup is doing at all times

13. To ensure the physical security of the servers, Joe should keep the server room:

A. Easily accessible, but keep an eye out for suspicious people

B. Locked and accessible only to authorized employees with keys or lock combinations

C. Accessible to employees of the company, but not non-employees

D. Accessible only to himself

14. What should Joe do to keep unauthorized people from logging into the network?

A. Require unique user IDs and passwords for each person who logs in

B. Set group passwords that any member of a workgroup may use to log into the network

C. Require user IDs, but not passwords

D. Require user IDs and passwords only for people who need to access proprietary information

15. When designing the password policy, what requirement should Joe include?

A. That it be short and easy to remember, so that customers do not forget it

B. That it never expire, so that he will not have to burden customers with the inconvenience of changing them periodically

C. That it be displayed on the customer's monitor, to aid the customer in logging in

D. That it be 10–14 characters in length, use some symbol characters (like $%), expire periodically, and not be reusable more than once

16. Joe knows that it is also a good idea to keep 1–2 weeks worth of backups in case a customer needs restored a previous version of a file. Where should Joe store the backup tapes?

A. In the server room, where it is easily accessible

B. Locked in his desk

C. On shelves outside the server room where customers can find the backup tape that they need and hand it to Joe

D. At a secure, offsite location

17. What would be the best course of action if a volume would not mount after a server reboot?

A. Run DSREPAIR on the volume

B. Run VREPAIR on the volume

C. Restore the volume from a backup

D. Contact a data recovery service to repair the volume

Use the Following Scenario for Question 18

Joe uses Novell's recommended method of troubleshooting when solving network problems. He takes the following steps to do so:

1. Tries a quick fix/gathers basic information
2. Develops a plan to isolate the problem
3. Executes the plan
4. Ensures user satisfaction
5. Documents the solution and takes steps to avoid a recurrence

18. One day, a customer is unable to log into the network. Other customers in that area are able to log in without any problem. Joe suspects that the customer is typing in an incorrect password, or that there is a problem with the login script. Resetting the password only takes 2–3 minutes, while analyzing the login script may take half an hour or more. What should Joe do when troubleshooting the problem?

A. Reset the customer's password and then analyze the login script before asking the customer to try to log in again

B. Reset the customer's password and ask the customer to try logging in before analyzing the login script

C. Analyze the login script before resetting the password

D. Ask the customer to log in under another customer's ID

19. In order to recover from a true disaster, such as fire, flood, or tornado, where should backup tapes be stored?

A. In a fireproof box

B. In a fireproof, waterproof box

C. Offsite

D. In a different part of the building

Use the Following Scenario for Questions 20–22

Joe's company wants to make sure that he has access to all of the information and tools that he needs to be effective as a network administrator. To that end, it purchases a monthly subscription to the CD-based *Novell's Support Connection* (formerly known as *Novell Support Encyclopedia Professional/NSEPro*), then purchases a copy of *Microhouse's Support Source* (formerly known as *Microhouse Technical Library*) on CD, and makes sure that Joe has a reliable connection to the Internet from which he can access Novell's support web site, http://support.novell.com where he will find the online content, files, and forums that were once found on NetWire on CompuServe.

20. Joe's customers have been experiencing intermittent problems with printing and he wants to research the problem quickly. How should he start?

A. Look at the Support Source CD

B. Call Novell's technical support line

C. Search the Support Connection CD

D. Post the problem on a forum on Novell's web site

21. Joe's search of the Support Connection CD shows that the problem can be fixed by installing a newer version of the Novell Client than is currently installed on the workstations at Joe's company. Where should Joe should get the updated client installation files?

A. From the Support Connection CD

B. From Novell's Web site

C. From the Support Source CD

D. By calling Novell's technical support line and asking them to send him the installation files for the new client

22. After using the login script to install the new client software on the workstations, the printing problem is eliminated. However, several hundred workstations with a particular brand of network card seem to require more than one login attempt before successfully attaching to the network. Joe searches the Support Connection CD and Novell's web site, and even calls Novell's technical support line, but finds no reference to this problem. What is his next step?

A. Replace the network cards in all affected workstations

B. Uninstal the new client software

C. Search the Support Source CD

D. Post the issue on a forum on Novell's Web site to see if anyone has had this problem and fixed it

Refer to the Following Scenario in Answering Question 23

Gary works for a company that will be expanding to a new building that has no existing network cabling or infrastructure. The company has asked Gary to design the network in the building taking into consideration current technology, as well as the jobs that people using the network will be asked to perform. Being a new, relatively inexperienced CNE, Gary asks you for some advice. Gary knows that the people in his company use the network in a fairly traditional way. They share files, print, and run applications from the server. Gary does not expect that there will be a need to transmit digital audio or video over the network.

23. Given the fact that the network will not need to transmit digital audio or video, around what transmission speed should Gary design the network?

A. 10 Mbps

B. 16 Mbps

C. 100 Mbps

D. More than 100 Mbps

Use the Following Scenario for Questions 24–30

Gary knows that networks following the Ethernet standards are the most prevalent, and wants to consider whether or not to design the network around Ethernet standards.

24. Assuming that Gary decides to use Ethernet for the network and that he uses Ethernet_II and Ethernet 802.2 as his frame types, what is the minimum number of network cards that he will have to install on the server?

A. Two network cards, one for each frame type

B. Four network cards, one for each frame type, and one for each protocol

C. Two network cards, one for each protocol

D. One network card, bound to both frame types

25. Since Gary has decided to design the network around a 100Mbps-transmission speed, which type of Ethernet cabling should he consider?

A. 10Base5 (ThickNet) Ethernet

B. 10Base2 (ThinNet) Ethernet

C. 10BaseT (twisted-pair) Ethernet

D. 100BaseTX (twisted-pair) Ethernet

E. 100BaseT4 (twisted-pair) Ethernet

26. Gary would like the network to communicate efficiently with the Internet, as well as with the existing company network, which is a mixture of NetWare 5 and NetWare 4.x servers. What frame type(s) should Gary plan to use on the network?

A. Ethernet_II (TCP/IP)

B. Ethernet 802.2 (IPX/SPX)

C. Ethernet 802.3 (IPX/SPX)

27. If a workstation stops communicating with the rest of the network and Gary determines that the software on the workstation is installed and configured correctly, what kind of cabling problems would *not* apply to Ethernet cable?

A. A bad LocalTalk connector

B. A loose connection

C. Interference from a source of electromagnetic energy

D. A cable break

28. Although Gary has noted that the 100 Mbps speed of Ethernet's 100BaseTX meets his requirements, he wonders if a Token Ring-based network would offer any compelling advantages over 100BaseTX. Which of the following describes an advantage that a Token Ring network has over a 100BaseTX network?

A. The network cards, hubs, and cabling that make up a Token Ring network are less expensive and easier to find than 100BaseTX components.

B. Token Ring networks are more efficient because workstations on a Token Ring network may only transmit when in possession of a token so there will be none of the data packet collisions that occur when two Ethernet-based workstations try to transmit simultaneously.

C. Token Ring networks are easier to wire than 100BaseTX networks.

D. Token Ring networks are faster than 100BaseTX networks.

29. Gary knows that Fiber Distributed Data Interface (FDDI) fiber-optic networks are relatively expensive, but wonders if there are any advantages to FDDI that would justify spending the extra money necessary to implement an FDDI network. Which of the following are advantages of FDDI networks?

A. FDDI networks are very fast—100 Mbps.

B. FDDI can transmit signals at a very long distance—hundreds of miles.

C. FDDI cable is much harder to tap into than coaxial or twisted-pair cable, making it more secure.

D. FDDI cable is not susceptible to electromagnetic interference because it uses light rather than electrical impulses to transmit information.

30. Jim has been asked to build a new server that will host the company's e-mail. Although he has decided on the other specifications of the server, he

is not quite sure what type of hard-drive setup would be the best, given the heavy demands that he expects will be made on the server. Jim first reviews the basics about hard drives. Jim is concerned about what would happen if the electricity in the server room were unexpectedly lost. What will happen to information on the hard drive if electrical power to the server is lost?

A. It will not be lost because the magnetic charges making up the data do not have to be electrically refreshed after they have been written to the platter.

B. It will be lost because the magnetic charges making up the data must be electrically refreshed after they have been written to the platter.

C. It can be recovered from the RAM on the server.

D. It can be recovered from the hard-drive controller card.

31. The circular platter of a formatted hard disk is divided, much like a dartboard, into concentric rings and pie-shaped wedges. What are the rings and wedges called?

A. Grooves and segments

B. Loops and whorls

C. Tracks and sectors

D. Paths and subdivisions

32. How would you find the location of a break in an FDDI cable?

A. Use a laser light detector to find where the light is escaping at the broken end of the cable

B. An FDDI cable analyzer will be able to determine the distance to the break based on analysis of the test pulse that is sent down the cable and partly reflected back to the analyzer.

C. Look for kinks in the insulation that surrounds the glass core

Use the Following Scenario for Questions 33–39

Having reviewed the characteristics of hard disks versus other types of storage media, Jim has determined that a hard disk or array of hard disks will be the best form of data storage for the server. Now he must consider which type of hard drive interface would be the best.

33. Jim knows that he must make sure that the SCSI bus is properly terminated so that signals generated by the controller and hard drives do not bounce back and forth across the SCSI cable. What should Jim look for in checking for proper termination?

A. Each device, including the controller card, should have terminating resistors, jumpers, or switches activated.

B. Each device except for the controller card should have terminating resistors, jumpers, or switches activated.

C. Only the controller card needs to have terminating resistors, jumpers, or switches activated.

D. The controller card, which should be at one end of the SCSI cable, and the drive at the far end of the cable should have terminating resistors, jumpers, or switches activated.

34. Jim finds some drives and controller cards in storage. By searching his Support Source CD, he determines that several drives and controllers support the ST412/ST506 standard and several drives and controllers support the Enhanced Small Device Interface (ESDI) standard. Why shouldn't Jim use ST412/ST506 or ESDI drives or controllers in the new server?

A. ST412/ST506/ESDI devices, designed for the original PC, XT, and AT computers, have a very slow data-transfer rate.

B. ST412/ST506/ESDI devices do not hold much data by modern standards.

C. ST412/ST506/ESDI devices are no longer available and cannot be replaced.

D. All of the above

35. Jim knows that Integrated Drive Electronics (IDE) and Small Computer System Interface (SCSI) are the modern standards for hard drives and controllers. Which of the following would be an advantage to IDE drives/controllers versus SCSI?

A. IDE drives/controllers transfer data faster than SCSI.

B. IDE drives/controllers allow more devices on the bus than SCSI.

C. IDE drives/controllers are less expensive than SCSI.

D. IDE drives/controllers do not use the system CPU to process I/O requests.

36. Jim would like to use a high-speed tape backup unit on the server and would like to use an external model that can easily be moved to another server if necessary. What additional advantage would SCSI offer over IDE?

A. SCSI tape backup units are less expensive than IDE units.

B. SCSI controllers conform to the Tape Backup Device (TBD) standard.

C. SCSI controllers generally have an external port to which an external tape backup can be easily attached, while IDE controllers have no such external port.

D. SCSI allows two or more servers to share a single external tape backup device simultaneously.

37. Jim orders the SCSI drives necessary for a RAID 5 array. When the drives arrive, Jim takes them to the workbench to configure the SCSI ID number for the controller and for each drive. What ID numbers are typically given to the controller and to hard drives?

A. The controller is typically set to 0, the first hard drive to 1, and the second hard drive to 2.

B. The controller is typically set to 7, the first hard drive to 0, and the second hard drive to 1.

C. The controller is typically set to 1, the first hard drive to 2, and the second hard drive to 3.

D. The controller is typically set to 7, the first hard drive to 6, and the second hard drive to 5.

38. Jim wants the server to recognize the SCSI drives so that he can format them. With IDE drives, he generally goes into the BIOS setup program which "autodetects" the drive or allows him to specify the number of heads, cylinders, and sectors per track. What must Jim do to get the server to recognize the SCSI hard drives?

A. Use the same "autodetect" feature of the system BIOS

B. Use the software provided by the SCSI controller manufacturer to format the drive at a low level, after which it can be partitioned using FDISK or NetWare's setup program

C. Run NetWare's VREPAIR utility

D. Use the FORMAT command from a bootable DOS floppy

39. To make sure that there is no extra room taken up by excess cable in the server case, Jim stacks the hard drives vertically in the case and orders a SCSI cable with only enough space between each connector to reach the next hard drive in the chain. The system will not reliably recognize all of the drives. What did Jim do wrong?

A. Jim should have lined up the drives horizontally rather than vertically.

B. Jim should have purchased a cable that meets SCSI specifications from a reputable manufacturer, such as Adaptec or Belkin.

C. Jim did everything right—there's probably a problem with the SCSI controller.

D. Jim should get a separate controller card for each drive, each with its own cable.

40. Which of the following is *not* an advantage to FDDI cabling?

A. FDDI cabling is thin and light compared to other types of cabling.

B. Because data in an FDDI scheme flows in two counter-rotating rings, a faulty station can be easily bypassed by the other stations making up the ring.

C. FDDI cabling can be used as a bar code scanning device.

D. If a break occurs in an FDDI cable, there are tools available that will tell you where the break has occurred.

Use the Following Scenario for Questions 41–47

Jim's supervisor is concerned by the cost of the server, and wonders if perhaps the company could save some money by not using Redundant Array of Inexpensive Disks (RAID) on the server. He knows that, with RAID, data is written onto two or more disks in such a way that the data can be recovered from the good disks if any one disk fails. However, the supervisor asks Jim to explain why the server should not have only one hard drive and depend on the tape backup for recovery.

41. Since Jim's supervisor is impressed with the capabilities of MO drives, he wonders whether MO drives should be used instead of standard hard drives in the servers. Jim replies that MO drives should probably not be used since

they cost much more than standard hard drives. What other reason does he give for not using MO drives?

A. MO drives are less reliable than hard drives.

B. MO drives are slower at read/write operations than hard drives.

C. MO drives are not supported under NetWare 5.

D. MO drives cannot be set up in a RAID configuration.

42. Next, Jim's supervisor asks Jim about the different RAID "levels." He wants to know which RAID levels would be usable by the NetWare server. Which of the following levels of RAID should Jim explain are generally usable by a NetWare server?

A. Level 0

B. Level 1

C. Level 2

D. Level 3

E. Level 4

F. Level 5

43. Jim's supervisor asks him to explain the difference between mirroring and duplexing. How does Jim respond?

A. Duplexing refers to two hard disks, mirroring to more than two.

B. Mirroring refers to two hard disks, duplexing to more than two.

C. Mirroring uses a separate controller for each hard disk or array of hard disks.

D. Duplexing uses a separate controller for each hard disk or array of hard disks.

44. Jim wants to put a CD-ROM drive on the server so that he can easily install CD-based software updates as they become available. Which type of CD-ROM drive does NetWare support?

A. SCSI

B. IDE

C. Novell

D. SCSI and IDE

45. Jim wonders if he should use a SCSI CD-ROM drive instead of IDE, given the greater performance of SCSI over IDE. What would you tell him?

A. Use SCSI if the drive will be sharing a CD-ROM as a NetWare volume

B. Use IDE—SCSI CD-ROM drives are prohibitively expensive

C. Use whichever is cheapest

46. Jim's supervisor wonders if an MO disk is more durable than tape or hard disks for data storage. Jim replies that MO disks are:

A. Less durable because strong light will tend to erase the disks

B. More durable because the surface of the disk must be heated to 200-or-more degrees before the magnetic polarity of an individual bit can be changed

C. Less durable because MO disks are more likely to be erased by nearby magnetic or electrical fields

D. More durable because MO disks write with a stronger magnetic impulse

47. Jim's supervisor wonders if MO drives have an advantage over tape drives as a backup medium. What is the main advantage that MO drives have?

   A. MO drives can access data randomly, unlike a tape, which must be advanced or rewound to find individual files.
   B. MO drives are physically smaller than tape drives.
   C. MO drives can also read CD-ROMs.

Use the Following Scenario for Questions 48–58

Dave has been asked to set up Novell's DOS client on some older PCs with limited memory. The PCs will be used for collecting data from some manufacturing machinery, which is designed to be monitored by a DOS program.

48. In which of the following places would Dave *not* find the files needed to install the DOS client?

   A. On the NetWare CD
   B. On diskettes that he could create with the INSTALL.NLM on the server
   C. At http://support.novell.com
   D. On MS-DOS 5.0 or higher installation diskettes

49. The DOS client installation program asks if Dave wants to install support for MS Windows? Which version(s) of MS Windows would be supported if Dave tells the program to install support for MS Windows?

   A. Windows NT
   B. Windows 3.1
   C. Windows 95
   D. Windows 98

50. Dave knows that several files must be loaded into memory before any network drivers are loaded. Having done some further research, he finds that the files load in what order?

A. IO.SYS, MSDOS.SYS, COMMAND.COM, CONFIG.SYS, AUTOEXEC.BAT

B. COMMAND.COM, MSDOS.SYS, IO.SYS, CONFIG.SYS, AUTOEXEC.BAT

C. IO.SYS, COMMAND.COM, MSDOS.SYS, CONFIG.SYS, AUTOEXEC.BAT

D. MSDOS.SYS, IO.SYS, COMMAND.COM, CONFIG.SYS, AUTOEXEC.BAT

51. Dave is attempting to install an ISA-bus Network Interface Card (NIC) into one of the PCs and knows that the NIC will need to be set to a unique IRQ, but is unsure which Interrupts/IRQs are not being used by other devices in the PC. What program could Dave run to find out which IRQs are already being used?

A. Memmaker.exe

B. Config.exe

C. IRQset.exe

D. Msd.exe

52. Dave has successfully configured all of the DOS workstations and has set them up to run continuously. He decides to use NetWare's watchdog feature to alert him if a workstation stops communicating with the server. How should Dave tell the server to send an alert to the server console screen when a workstation stops responding to the server?

A. Dave should configure the server by running the WATCHDOG.NLM.

B. Dave should modify the server object in NDS™.

C. Dave should use the SET CONSOLE DISPLAY WATCHDOG LOGOUTS=ON command at the server console.

D. Dave should include the SEND WATCHDOG ALERT in the NET.CFG file on each workstation.

53. Dave has been asked to make one of the networked workstations "diskless," that is, able to log into the server without booting from a floppy or hard disk. How is this accomplished?

    A. By purchasing a special motherboard for the workstation

    B. By using a command at the server console to initialize the workstation through the network

    C. By putting a boot Programmable Read-Only Memory (PROM) chip onto the socket found on compatible NICs

    D. By connecting the workstation via serial cable to another workstation that boots from a hard or floppy disk

54. Dave would like to be able to keep an eye on the communications between the server and workstations. What would be the best way to observer network packet traffic at the server?

    A. Load MONITOR.NLM

    B. Load TRAFFIC.NLM

    C. Use the SET TRACKING=ON command at the console prompt

    D. Use the TRACK ON command at the console prompt

55. In the process of setting up a new DOS workstation, Dave notes that the workstation freezes whenever the mouse is moved and that the NIC driver is setting the NIC to use IRQ 3. Further investigation using MSD reveals that the COM port used by the mouse is also trying to use IRQ 3. Attempts to change the card to another IRQ by modifying NET.CFG have failed. Dave therefore needs to set the NIC to use a different IRQ by some other method. Since there are no DIP switches or jumpers on the card, what should Dave do to set the NIC to a different IRQ setting?

    A. Install a boot PROM

    B. Buy a different NIC that is preset to a different IRQ

    C. Find a driver for the NIC that will address it on a different IRQ

    D. Use the SETUP program on the floppy, included with most NICs

56. Dave wants to make sure that the PCs have enough memory installed to run the monitoring program that keeps an eye on the workstations' manufacturing machines. The documentation that comes with the monitoring program states that the program requires 392K of base memory and three megabytes of extended memory to run properly. Based on these specifications, what should be the minimum amount of RAM memory installed in each workstation?

A. 4000K

B. 395K

C. 4096K

D. 3392K

57. After configuring a PC to attach to the network, Dave finds that it is unable to run the program that monitors the manufacturing machines. Dave suspects that there may not be enough conventional memory (the base 640K) free to run the program after the network drivers have been loaded. What DOS command would be the best to determine where network drivers are loading and how much conventional memory is available for running the monitoring program?

A. MSD

B. MEM /C | MORE

C. CHKDSK

D. MEM

58. Dave is conscientious about adhering to licensing requirements, and wants to make sure that each workstation has a legitimately licensed copy of DOS. If he gets a copy of MS-DOS for each computer, what would be the best version to choose?

A. 6.52

B. 7.0

C. 6.0

D. 6.22

59. In the PC memory model, the first 640 K of memory, also called *conventional memory*, can be used for running programs. For what are the memory addresses from 641 K–1024 K, also called *upper memory*, reserved?

A. Keyboard buffers

B. Hard disk buffers

C. Video and other hardware

D. Mouse drivers

60. How is data on a hard drive stored?

A. Optically; a laser beam reads the information

B. Magnetically, on reels of tape

C. Magnetically, on a spinning platter

D. Magnetically, on a voice coil

Use the Following Scenario for Questions 61–64

Joe has been asked by his company to design a new server room that will be an ideal environment for the company's servers.

61. What level of coolness should the room maintain?

A. Maintain the same temperature as the other rooms in the building

B. Maintain a warmer temperature than the other rooms in the building

C. Maintain a temperature cooler than the other rooms in the building

D. Maintain a constant cool temperature

62. How should Joe ensure there is ventilation of air?

A. Link it to outdoor air to ensure adequate oxygen

B. Filter and dehumidify it

C. Filter it and maintain constant humidity

D. Humidify it to promote electrical conductivity

63. Joe knows that Electro-Static Discharge (ESD) can damage components and that a workbench with properly grounded wrist straps should be installed. Joe should, however, post a warning on the workbench that a grounded wrist strap is not to be used when repairing which of the following items?

A. Printers

B. Laptops

C. Monitors

D. Keyboards

64. Joe should design the wiring plan so that network and power lines:

A. Share the same conduits to maximize the available space

B. Are kept as far from each other as practicable

C. Use the same grade of cable

D. Always traverse the shortest distance between two points to avoid wasting cable

65. Troubleshooting Token Ring network problems is very similar to troubleshooting Ethernet network problems—you should check for loose connectors, cable breaks, and correct I/O settings. What is one difference between Token Ring boards and Ethernet NICs that you should keep in mind when troubleshooting?

A. Token Ring board drivers may load even if they are the wrong drivers for that particular card. Ethernet NIC drivers almost always return an error message if you try to use the wrong driver.

B. Token Ring boards are much more sensitive to electromagnetic interference than are Ethernet NICs.

C. Token Ring boards need to be tuned properly with an MSAU tuner.

D. Token Ring boards have a manual reset button next to the connector where the cable plugs in that should be depressed as part of the troubleshooting process.

Use the Following Scenario for Questions 66–75

Leslee is responsible for setting up and maintaining network printers for several hundred users that work at one of her company's larger sites. These responsibilities include physically setting up the printers as well as setting up the NDS objects that make up network printing in NetWare 5. Finally, Leslee is responsible for troubleshooting the NetWare 5 print process when there is a problem with printing.

66. Leslee needs to set up a new networked printer that will be shared by several members of a workgroup. Which of the following methods could not be used to share a printer under NetWare 5?

A. Hook the printer to a workstation via a parallel cable and share the printer by running NPRINTER.EXE or, under Win95/98, NPTWIN95.EXE, found in the SYS:\Public\Win95 on the server

B. Hook the workstations' and printer's serial port to a multiport LAN modem and run SPRINTER.EXE or SPTWIN95.EXE on the workstations

C. Hook the printer to a server via a parallel cable and share the printer by running PSERVER.NLM at the server

D. Hook the printer to a network cable by installing a printer LAN card, such as a Jetdirect card

67. Which of the following is not one of the NDS objects that must be created for shared printers under NetWare 5?

A. Print Host

B. Printer

C. Print Queue

D. Print Server

68. Leslee determines that all other members of the workgroup can print to the printer, meaning that Tim's printing problem is most likely related to something on his workstation. What should be the next thing that Leslee determines?

A. Whether the problem is hardware-related or software-related

B. Whether Tim's workstation is set to the correct print driver

C. Whether Tim is designated as an Operator of the Print Queue object

D. Whether there is a problem with Tim's LPT1: port

69. Brian, another user at the site, must use a plotter that only supports a serial cable connection. What is one of the most important things for Leslee to remember in configuring the connection to a serial print device?

A. The cable should measure 15 feet, or less.

B. A parallel to serial adapter will have to be placed on the workstation.

C. The print device will have to be connected to a modem.

D. Leslee must configure the serial port on the workstation to match the baud rate, parity, data bits, stop bits, and flow control settings of the print device.

70. Users in the accounting workgroup are unable to see their printer, an HP Laserjet with JetDirect card, or to send print jobs to it. Leslee suspects that the network cable going to the JetDirect card may have been damaged when some additional cables were run through the cable conduit over the weekend. What would be the fastest way to determine if the network cable to the printer was damaged?

A. Plug a cable from a workstation with a known good connection into the printer, power the printer off and back on, test printing

B. Try to ping the printer

C. Visually inspect the cable

D. Plug the cable into another port on the hub

71. What must be done to maintain the ink jet printers?

A. Refill the ink cartridges with refill kits every couple of weeks

B. Clean the print nozzles with acetone every couple of weeks

C. Turn the printer off when not in use

D. Use new ink cartridges made by the manufacturer of the printer when the ink in a cartridge goes dry

72. If the paper in a laser printer jams frequently, what should you do?

A. Disassemble and clean the printer, adjust the tension on the rollers

B. Change the toner cartridge

C. Call a certified technician to clean the printer and adjust the tension on the rollers

D. Replace the paper tray

73. Print jobs from the payroll department are not being printed. In troubleshooting the problem from a workstation, Leslee notes that the workstation shows the jobs leaving the spooler and being sent to the NetWare queue. Where could Leslee look to check the status of jobs in the NetWare print queue?

   A. The print queue object in NetWare Administrator, or by running PCONSOLE.EXE from a command prompt

   B. The print server or printer objects in NetWare Administrator

   C. The print queue or print server objects in NetWare Administrator

   D. The print server object in NetWare Administrator, or by running NPRINTER.EXE from a command prompt

74. Another printer has stopped printing. When Leslee checks the print queue object in NetWare Administrator, she notes that the jobs are entering the queue, but are never leaving the queue. None of the jobs has been placed on hold by a user or operator. What should be the first thing that Leslee tries when attempting to solve the problem?

   A. Inserting and printing a job from PCONSOLE

   B. Checking the free space on the volume hosting the print queue

   C. Turning the printer off and back on, then restarting PSERVER.NLM

   D. All of the above

75. Leslee needs to add another NetWare print server to the network, but does not want to use the NetWare 5 server, which is already highly utilized. She has a DOS workstation that could be used to host a NetWare print server. Is it possible to do so?

   A. Yes, NetWare 5 includes a utility called PSERVER.EXE that will allow a DOS workstation to host a NetWare print server.

   B. No, a DOS workstation may not host a NetWare print server.

    C. Yes, if she can find (and is licensed to use) the PSERVER.EXE utility that came with NetWare 3.x.

    D. Yes, if she can find (and is licensed to use) the PSERVER.EXE utility that came with NetWare 4.x.

76. Is configuration of a Token Ring network card just as easy as configuration of an Ethernet card?

    A. No, a Token Ring card, like an Arcnet card, must be set to a unique address using DIP switches.

    B. Yes, IRQ, DMA, and I/O settings must be configured using jumpers or a configuration program based on the existing settings that are already in use on a given workstation.

    C. No, a Token Ring card uses two interrupts, where an Ethernet card uses one.

    D. No, a Token Ring card must be configured by the server.

77. How does FDDI transmit information?

    A. Converts light pulses into audible sound waves, then back into light pulses at the other end

    B. Transmits laser or LED-generated light pulses along a strand of glass fiber

    C. Transmits laser or LED-generated light pulses through the air to a receiver on a distant building or tower

    D. Converts light pulses into radio waves, then back into light pulses at the other end

78. Why is RAID preferable to restoring from tape?

    A. RAID is less expensive.

    B. Data on the RAID array is updated continuously and allows missing data to be recovered much more quickly than when restoring data from tape.

    C. RAID is easier to set up.

    D. Data on the RAID array is recoverable using the DOS BACKUP utility.

79. You want to recover a database file for a customer, but the SALVAGE utility is unable to restore it. You run VREPAIR, but find that the file still is not recoverable. What third-party utility does Novell recommend for recovering the file?

A. Norton Utilities for NetWare

B. Ontrack Data Recovery for NetWare

C. PowerQuest Partition Magic

D. Nuts&bolts NetWare Utilities

Test Yourself: Practice Exam 5 Answers

Threch he answers to the questions are in boldface, followed by a brief explanation. The incorrect answer choices are explained in the final paragraph following each correct answer. Some of the explanations detail the logic you should use to choose the correct answer, while others give factual reasons why the answer is correct. If you miss several questions on a similar topic, you should review the corresponding section in the *CNE® NetWare® 5 Study Guide* before taking the Service and Support test.

Practice Exam 5 Answers

1. ☑ **C.** Multiple Station Access Unit is the MSAU hub.
   ☒ **A, B, D.** are incorrect because they are not correct names for a Token Ring hub.

2. ☑ **D.** Run DSREPAIR. This utility, provided with NetWare, will fix most problems with the NDS™ database that keeps track of users' rights to directories and files on NetWare volumes. Once NDS is repaired, the users will likely be able to access their directories and files. In some cases, it might be necessary to reassign rights after repairing NDS.
   ☒ **A.** is incorrect because restoring a volume would replace the files and directories, but would not restore users' rights to the files. **B.** is incorrect because it is generally not necessary to restore NDS; repair is generally all that is needed. **C.** is incorrect because VREPAIR will fix file system errors, but not errors in NDS, which keeps track of user rights.

3. ☑ **C.** Do a test restoration of files to a non-production volume from time to time. This will prove that files are actually being backed up and can be recovered.
   ☒ **A.** is incorrect because the most expensive solution is not necessarily the best. **B.** is incorrect because two backups are not necessary if the backup hardware and software is working properly. **D.** is incorrect because Novell's backup software provides minimal features and does not, by default, allow you to schedule daily backups.

4. ☑ **D.** He must make sure verify-after-write is enabled. This means that the backup software will read each file after writing it to the tape and repair any errors found. This is necessary because write errors when backing up to tape are actually fairly common.

☒ **A.** is incorrect because it is not necessary to use a new tape each time. **B.** is incorrect because a weekly full backup with daily incremental backups is generally sufficient and would not result in a significantly greater restoration time. **C.** is incorrect because turning file compression on will reduce the time that it takes to write each file to tape and, with verify-after-write enabled, you can still be confident that the backup is reliable.

5. ☑ **A.** Send the disk array to a data recovery company, where the hard disk platters will be placed into new mechanisms and data recovery attempted. This will be done in a clean room environment to ensure that no dust particles adhere to the platter surface and cause a head crash.

☒ **B.** is incorrect because at least some data is probably recoverable. **C.** is incorrect, unless Mark has access to a clean room environment. (Professionals would undoubtedly have more success, even if Mark does have access to a clean room.) **D.** is incorrect because, according to current information, lasers are not used in data recovery.

6. ☑ **C.** Mark could use the MONITOR utility provided with NetWare to observe the performance of the server in real time. By noting the areas where the server's resources are being utilized most, Mark can focus his efforts on improving the use of those resources.

☒ **A.** is incorrect because, although NetWare does a very good job of configuring itself for the platform on which it's installed, a skilled CNE can improve the performance beyond that which a default installation allows. **B.** is incorrect because large file copies and prints would tie up network bandwidth and would be very time consuming. **D.** is incorrect because the MONITOR utility provided with NetWare generally gives more than enough information for optimizing server resources.

7. ☑ **B.** Maximum directory cache buffers. Since the system sets aside and never reallocates the RAM given to maximum directory cache buffers, it may be necessary to reduce these buffers in order to reserve the space to load NLMs.
☒ **A.** is incorrect because directory cache buffers are reduced by lowering the maximum, not the minimum. **C.** is incorrect because file cache buffers are "given back" to enable NLMs to load. Therefore, they are controlled by the minimum setting, not the maximum. **D.** is incorrect because it is not a valid buffer setting according to current information.

8. ☑ **A.** Directory cache allocation wait time. This will tell NetWare to wait a shorter amount of time before allocating more RAM to the directory cache. With more RAM dynamically allocated to directory caching, directory searches will be processed more quickly.
☒ **B, C.** are incorrect because the speed of directory searches is much more dependent on RAM for caching than on free CPU cycles. **D.** is incorrect because reducing directory cache buffers would make directory searches slower by taking away RAM from the directory caching process.

9. ☑ **C.** The network may run out of bandwidth during peak demand periods. The utilization gauge in LANalyzer shows the percentage of network bandwidth that is being used. A baseline of more than 50 percent could quickly turn into very little available bandwidth during peak periods.
☒ **A, D.** are incorrect because the utilization gauge shows network bandwidth usage, not server processing or RAM usage. **B.** is incorrect because low utilization on a network is a good, not bad, thing.

10. ☑ **A.** Immediately, using software from a reputable third-party company with a good reputation for responding quickly to new viruses. Ask some fellow network administrators whose software they have had the best success with.
☒ **B.** is incorrect because NetWare does not include virus scanning software. **C.** is incorrect because a virus infection will likely be introduced by someone who is not deliberately infecting files—they will probably be unaware that the file that they copy to the server is infected. **D.** is incorrect because viruses need not come through internet e-mail, but can come from infected floppies or even commercial software.

11. ☑ C. Use a software package that allows remote installation and updates of workstation virus-scanning software. There are several good programs available that allow you to manage deployment and updates from a central location.
☒ A. is incorrect because a virus could destroy data on a workstation without being detected by the scanning software on the server. B. is incorrect because it would be impractical to personally scan several hundred workstations. D. is incorrect because a write-protected workstation hard disk would be unusable.

12. ☑ C. Make sure that file and directory rights are set correctly using NetWare Administrator. NetWare Administrator gives you ultimate control over files and directories—not only what people can see based on their user ID, but also which files they can overwrite or copy.
☒ A. is incorrect because it is generally a waste of resources to set up a server for each workgroup. B. is incorrect because even if employees conscientiously kept their promise, they might accidentally look into a restricted area. D. is incorrect because it is not reasonable to expect the supervisor of a workgroup to visually enforce network security.

13. ☑ B. Locked, and accessible only to authorized employees with keys or lock combinations. Physical access does need to be given to trusted employees with a legitimate need for that access.
☒ A. is incorrect because simply keeping an eye out for suspicious people is not adequate. C. is incorrect because not all employees should be allowed physical access to the servers, only specified employees. D. is incorrect because other trusted employees may need to access the servers when Joe is unavailable.

14. ☑   **A.** Require unique user IDs and passwords for each person who logs in. Both a unique ID and password are essential to network security. Remember that rights to files and directories are assigned by user ID and unique passwords restrict the use of that ID to a single person.

☒   **B.** is incorrect because allowing more than one person to use a password makes it impossible to determine exactly which individual is logging in at any given time. **C.** is incorrect because passwords are necessary to restrict login to a specified individual. **D.** is incorrect because IDs and passwords are essential to protecting access to the network itself, not just to proprietary information. After all, the first step towards getting to sensitive information is getting on the network itself.

15. ☑   **D.** That it be 10–14 characters in length, use some symbol characters (like $%), expire periodically, and not be reusable more than once. It sounds somewhat draconian, but long passwords that use symbol characters are the only passwords that will survive a dictionary attack by a hacker who uses software that randomly tries common words for passwords when attempting to break in. Passwords must also expire periodically, and not be reusable because the longer that a password is in use, the more likely it is to be discovered.

☒   **A.** is incorrect because short, easy passwords are also easy for hackers to guess. **B.** is incorrect because the need for security outweighs the convenience of a non-expiring password. **C.** is incorrect because a password should never be accessible to anyone but the person who uses it.

16. ☑   **D.** At a secure, offsite location. The location must be secure, because access to your backup tapes is, in effect, access to your files. The location should be offsite so that you can restore the tapes even if the server room is destroyed by fire, flood, or some other disaster.

☒   **A.** is incorrect because a fire, flood, etc. that destroyed servers would likely also destroy the backup tapes in the server room. **B.** is incorrect because Joe's desk is still too close to the server room to keep the tapes from being damaged by anything that would destroy the servers. **C.** is incorrect because shelves outside the server room would not be secure and also would be too close to the servers.

17. ☑ **B.** Run VREPAIR on the volume. This utility, provided with NetWare, will repair most minor file errors and will generally allow you to mount the volume.

☒ **A.** is incorrect because DSREPAIR is used to correct Directory errors. **C.** is incorrect because it would take a long time to restore the volume from a backup and, with VREPAIR, restoring from backup is usually unnecessary. **D.** is incorrect because a data recovery service is very expensive and is generally used only as a last resort when all else has failed.

18. ☑ **B.** Reset the customer's password and ask the customer to try logging in before analyzing the login script. It is almost always best to try a quick fix first. If it works, you'll save a great deal of time; if the quick fix doesn't work, you won't have wasted much time. Good troubleshooting technique also demands that you only try one solution at a time and see if that solved the problem before moving on to the next possible solution.

☒ **A.** is incorrect because Joe should see if resetting the password fixed the problem before trying another solution. **C.** is incorrect because analyzing the login script will take much more time than a password reset, and it is generally better to try the quick solution first. **D.** is incorrect because asking the customer to log in under another user's ID does not solve the underlying login problem.

19. ☑ **C.** Offsite. Though an unpleasant thought, a true disaster might wipe out the whole site.

☒ **A.** is incorrect because even if the box is fireproof, it may still get hot enough inside the box to destroy tapes or MO disks. **B.** is incorrect for the same reason. **D.** is incorrect because a fire could quite conceivably destroy the contents of the entire building.

20. ☑ C. Search the Support Connection CD. This would probably be the fastest way to determine if the printing problem is a known issue and, if so, the solution to the problem.

☒ A. is incorrect because the Support Source CD is mainly a collection of information about specific types of network cards and other hardware. B. is incorrect because a call to Novell's technical support line is generally not a quick way to solve a problem. One should consider a call only if all else fails. D. is incorrect because it might take several days to get a response to a question posted on a Web forum.

21. ☑ A. From the Support Connection CD. The Support Connection CD also contains files released within the last month. Files on the web site may be newer, but can take a long time to download. Unless an updated file on the web contains a fix for a specific problem, it is generally faster to use the files found on the Support Connection CD.

☒ B. is incorrect because a download of files from the web site will probably take much longer than retrieving the files from the Support Connection CD. C. is incorrect because the Support Source CD does not contain Novell® Client installation files. D. is incorrect because of the unnecessary time and expense that would be incurred by calling Novell and having installation files shipped to you.

22. ☑ D. Posting the issue on a forum on Novell's Web site to see if anyone has had this problem and fixed it. Since the new client solves the printing problem and does not disable the workstations, posting the issue on a forum and waiting a reasonable amount of time for a response would be a good start.

☒ A. is incorrect because it would be better to see if a fix exists that does not involve removing network cards from all of the workstations. B. is incorrect because uninstalling the new client software will reintroduce the printing problem. C. is incorrect because the Support Source does not contain information about the interaction between network cards and Novell client software.

23. ☑ **C.** 100 Mbps. Transmission speeds of greater than 100 Mbps are generally only needed when digital audio or video need to be sent over the network and cabling and hardware that transmits at speeds greater than 100 Mbps is very expensive.

☒ **A, B.** are incorrect because while 10 Mbps and 16 Mbps are adequate for most networking tasks, the hardware that can handle 100 Mbps does not cost significantly more money. **D.** is incorrect because the needs of the network users do not justify the much higher cost of the hardware that can handle speeds greater than 100 Mbps.

24. ☑ **D.** One network card, bound to both frame types. A single network card may be bound to up to four frame types simultaneously.

☒ **A.** is incorrect because you do not need a separate network card for each frame type. **B.** is incorrect because you do not need separate network cards for both a frame type and its corresponding protocol. **C.** is incorrect because up to four protocols can be bound simultaneously to a network card through a corresponding frame type.

25. ☑ **D.** 100BaseTX (twisted-pair) Ethernet. This has become the de facto standard for 100 Mbps network. The Category 5 cable, network cards, hubs, and routers that are compatible with this standard are all readily available and readily low in cost.

☒ **A, B, C.** are incorrect because 10Base5 (ThickNet) Ethernet, 10Base2 (ThinNet) Ethernet, and 10BaseT (twisted-pair) Ethernet have a maximum transmission rate of 10 Mbps. **E.** is incorrect because although the 100BaseT4 (twisted-pair) Ethernet standard can use slightly cheaper Category 3 cable, the network cards, hubs, and routers that conform to the standard are more difficult to find, and more costly.

26. ☑ **A, B.** Ethernet_II should be used so that the network can communicate using TCP/IP, the language of the Internet. Ethernet 802.2 should be included so that the server can communicate with older, IPX/SPX-based hardware and software.

☒ **C.** is incorrect because, although Ethernet 802.3 is an IPS/SPX frame type, it does not provide automatic check summing (an error-checking procedure) of packets as Ethernet 802.2 does.

27. ☑ **A.** A bad LocalTalk connector. LocalTalk connectors are used on AppleTalk, not Ethernet networks.
☒ **B, C, D.** are incorrect because loose connections, electromagnetic interference, and cable breaks are all problems that can occur with Ethernet cabling.

28. ☑ **B.** Token Ring networks are more efficient because workstations on a Token Ring network may only transmit when in possession of a token, so there will be none of the data packet collisions that occur when two Ethernet-based workstations try to transmit simultaneously. However, since Token Ring only transmits at 16 Mbps, the increased efficiency is overshadowed by the 100 Mbps speed of 100BaseTX.
☒ **A.** is incorrect because Token Ring network cards and cabling are generally made by fewer manufacturers, making Token Ring components more expensive and more difficult to find. **C.** is incorrect because, in general, Token Ring networks are not easier to wire than 100BaseTX networks. **D.** is incorrect because, as pointed out earlier, 100BaseTX transmits at 100 Mbps and Token Ring at 16 Mbps.

29. ☑ **A, B, C, D.** All of the above statements are true of FDDI.

30. ☑ **A.** It will not be lost since the magnetic charges making up the data do not have to be electrically refreshed after they have been written to the platter. RAM chips must be electrically refreshed to retain the information stored on them, but hard drives do not need to be refreshed.
☒ **B.** is incorrect because the information on the hard drive will not be lost due to power failure alone. **C, D.** are incorrect because the information cannot be recovered from the RAM on the server or from the hard drive controller card.

31. ☑ **C.** Tracks and sectors. The tracks and sectors help the read/write head of the hard disk to know its position over the surface of the platter.
☒ **A, B, D.** are incorrect because they are not the accepted terms for the divisions on the platter.

32. ☑ **B.** An FDDI cable analyzer, also called a *Time Domain Reflectometer* (TDR), will be able to determine the distance to the break based on analysis of the test pulse that is sent down the cable and partly reflected back to the analyzer.

☒ **A.** is incorrect because light may not be escaping a broken FDDI cable if the insulation is still intact. **C.** is incorrect because FDDI cable is often run through conduit or underground, where it would be impossible to visibly check the cable insulation.

33. ☑ **D.** The controller card, which should be at one end of the SCSI cable, and the drive at the far end of the cable should have terminating resistors, jumpers, or switches activated. The devices on each end of the SCSI cable/bus need to have termination activated. The termination at each end prevents the signals generated by devices from bouncing endlessly along the cable.

☒ **A.** is incorrect because only the devices on the ends should be terminated. **B.** is incorrect because the controller card, which is at one end of the SCSI bus, will be terminated. **C.** is incorrect because the controller card is not the only device that needs to be terminated—the device at the other end of the SCSI cable needs to be terminated as well.

34. ☑ **D.** All of the above. ST412/ST506/ESDI devices are much slower at reading, writing, and transferring data than modern hard drives; they were also limited in most cases to 80MB of storage space and are no longer manufactured or sold.

35. ☑ **C.** IDE drives/controllers are less expensive than SCSI. Manufacturers are able to cut costs on IDE drives by integrating the controller circuitry onto the hard-drive circuit board and using the system CPU to process I/O requests.

☒ **A.** is incorrect because IDE drives/controllers generally don't transfer data faster than SCSI. **B.** is incorrect because IDE can generally only support two devices on each bus, while SCSI can support seven or more. **D.** is incorrect because IDE does use the system CPU to process requests, SCSI does not.

36. ☑ **C.** SCSI controllers generally have an external port to which an external tape backup can easily be attached, while IDE controllers have no such port. For this reason, IDE tape backup devices are generally only available as internal units (although some have been designed to use the system parallel port).

    ☒ **A.** is incorrect because SCSI tape backup units are generally more expensive than IDE units. **B.** is incorrect since there is no such standard as TBD. **D.** is incorrect because SCSI does not allow two or more servers to share a single tape backup unit simultaneously.

37. ☑ **B.** The controller is typically set to 7 the first hard drive to 0, and the second hard drive to 1. Since SCSI device requests are prioritized by number with 0 being the highest priority, the first hard drive or boot hard drive is typically assigned ID 0, and the controller card itself, ID 7.

    ☒ **A, C, D.** are incorrect because priority would not be given to the first hard drive under those configurations.

38. ☑ **B.** Use the software provided by the SCSI controller manufacturer to format the drive at a low level, after which it can be partitioned using FDISK or NetWare's setup program. The low-level formatting software is often built into the BIOS on the SCSI controller and can be accessed with a keyboard command sequence, such as ALT A, at boot.

    ☒ **A.** is incorrect because the system BIOS will not generally recognize a SCSI drive until the drive has been formatted at a low level with manufacturer-provided software. **C.** is incorrect because VREPAIR is used to repair NetWare volumes, not to format or recognize SCSI drives. **D.** is incorrect because the DOS FORMAT command will not recognize a SCSI drive until it has been formatted at a low level with manufacturer's software.

39. ☑ **B.** Jim should have purchased a cable that meets SCSI specifications from a reputable manufacturer, such as Adaptec or Belkin. Since a ribbon cable must conduct electrical signals to specified voltages, it is important that the cable be the right length and that there be the right amount of space between each connector.

☒ **A.** is incorrect because the position of the drives would not affect the conductivity of the signals across the SCSI cable. **C.** is incorrect because Jim should not have used a cable that did not meet SCSI specifications. **D.** is incorrect because it is not necessary to have a separate controller card for each hard drive.

40. ☑ **C.** FDDI cabling can be used as a bar code scanning device. This is not true since media must be connected to an input/output device in order to function as such, since bar codes are a form of digitized data.
☒ **A, B, D.** would not be correct responses, as they are all legitimate advantages to FDDI cabling.

41. ☑ **B.** MO drives are slower at read/write operations than hard drives. Although MO drives are approaching hard-drive speeds, they are still slower, particularly because most models must erase a bit before writing to it.
☒ **A.** is incorrect because MO drives have proven to be at least as reliable as hard drives. **C.** is incorrect because MO drives can be used with NetWare 5. **D.** is incorrect because MO drives can be set up in a RAID configuration.

42. ☑ **A, B, F.** are correct. With Level 0, blocks of data are sent sequentially to one drive after another. In this way, no single drive falls behind in writing data. However, since Level 0 does not duplicate any data, it provides no protection if a drive fails, and is therefore not used very often. Level 1 mirrors or duplexes data by writing *all* data to every drive in the array. However, Level 1 tends to be slower than other RAID levels because the task of writing data is not shared among several drives. Level 5 is the most common implementation of RAID on NetWare servers. With Level 5, blocks of data are sent sequentially to one drive after another as they are in Level 0, but each individual drive also contains the error-correcting parity information needed to rebuild a new drive if any single drive goes bad. Level 5 gives the best combination of protection and low down time if a drive goes bad.
☒ **C, D, E.** are incorrect. Level 2 RAID is not used because it is designed for systems that use hard disks that do not have built-in error detection.

Since all currently manufactured SCSI hard disks have built-in error detection, it would not make sense to use Level 2. Level 3 RAID is incompatible with NetWare because it sends information to each drive a bit at a time, rather than a block at a time. NetWare can read blocks of data as small as 4KB in size, but cannot read individual streams of bits from drives in sequence. Level 4 RAID is not used. Under the Level 4 scheme all error-correcting parity information is kept on one hard drive dedicated to that purpose, and the entire server tends to be slowed down as it waits for the parity drive to "catch up" with the rest of the system.

43. ☑ **D.** Duplexing uses a separate controller for each hard disk or array of hard disks. In this way, you are protected from controller failure as well as hard-disk failure—an extra measure of protection.
☒ **A, B.** are incorrect because they are not accurate definitions of duplexing and mirroring. **C.** is incorrect because mirroring uses only one controller, not a separate controller for each hard disk.

44. ☑ **D.** SCSI and IDE. NetWare includes drivers for both types of CD-ROM drives.
☒ **C.** is incorrect because Novell does not manufacture CD-ROM drives.

45. ☑ **A.** Use SCSI if the drive will be mounting a CD-ROM as a NetWare volume. A shared IDE CD will tie up the server CPU, SCSI will not; therefore, SCSI should always be used if a CD will be shared.
☒ **B.** is incorrect because the difference in cost between SCSI and IDE is not large enough to outweigh the effect of an IDE drive tying up the server CPU. **C.** is incorrect because SCSI should be used for the reasons stated previously.

46. ☑ **D.** More durable because the surface of the disk must be heated to 200-or-more degrees before the magnetic polarity of an individual bit can be changed. This makes MO disks one of the most durable forms of storage available.

☒ **A.** is incorrect because strong light will not erase MO disks. **C.** is incorrect because MO disks are not more likely to be erased by nearby magnetic or electrical fields. **D.** is incorrect because the strength of the magnetic impulse used to write the data does not make MO disks more durable.

47. ☑ **A.** MO drives can access data randomly, unlike a tape, which must be advanced or rewound to find individual files.
☒ **B.** is incorrect because MO drives are generally larger than tape drives. **C.** is incorrect because MO drives generally cannot read CD-ROMs.

48. ☑ **D.** On MS-DOS 5.0 or higher installation diskettes. MS-DOS did not include a DOS NetWare Client.
☒ **A, B, C.** are incorrect because they describe places where DOS NetWare installation files can be found.

49. ☑ **B.** Windows 3.1 would be supported by the DOS client installation program.
☒ **A, C, D.** are incorrect because clients for other versions of Windows have their own installation files and programs and are not supported by the DOS client installation.

50. ☑ **A.** IO.SYS, MSDOS.SYS, COMMAND.COM, CONFIG.SYS, AUTOEXEC.BAT is the correct load order.
☒ **B, C, D.** are incorrect because DOS workstations do not load files in the orders described in those answers.

51. ☑ **D.** Microsoft Diagnostics (Msd.exe) is included with later versions of MS-DOS and will tell you which interrupts are already in use.
☒ **A.** is incorrect because Memmaker is used to optimize memory.
B, C. are incorrect, unless the NIC manufacturer includes programs by those names with the card.

52. ☑ **C.** Dave should use the SET CONSOLE DISPLAY WATCHDOG LOGOUTS=ON command at the server console. A message will then be displayed at the server console when the server does not receive any packets from the workstation after 15 minutes.

    ☒ The options described in **A, B, D.** are incorrect because they don't exist in current versions of NetWare.

53. ☑ **C.** By putting a boot Programmable Read-Only Memory (PROM) chip onto the socket found on compatible NICs. This will allow the workstation to "boot" from the PROM without a floppy or hard disk.

    ☒ **A.** is incorrect because it is not necessary to purchase a special motherboard. **B.** is incorrect because it is not possible to initialize the workstation from the server through the network. **D.** is incorrect because connecting the workstation to another via serial cable would not make it possible for the diskless workstation to boot up.

54. ☑ **D.** Use the TRACK ON command at the console prompt. This will display information on incoming and outgoing packets at the server console. They will look similar to the following:

    IN [00002345:0000AF43D482] 11:06:12am Get Nearest Server

    OUT [00002345:0000AF43D482] 11:06:14am Give Nearest Server

    ☒ **A, B, C.** are incorrect because they do not describe valid ways of observing packet traffic at the server console.

55. ☑ **D.** Use the SETUP program on the floppy included with most NICs. In fact, the SETUP program included with most NICs will usually find an unused IRQ automatically and modify NET.CFG, if necessary.

    ☒ **A.** is incorrect because installation of a boot PROM will not allow you to change the IRQ on a NIC. **B.** is incorrect because it is not necessary to buy another NIC when you can change the IRQ on the existing one. **C.** is incorrect because a different driver is not usually available.

56. ☑   C. 4096K. Even though the program only requires 3392K of RAM, more RAM is needed for DOS, network and video, and other drivers. Therefore, four megabytes would probably be the minimum. Also, because of the way memory chips and motherboards are designed, memory can usually be installed only in the following progression (by megabyte): 1,2,4,8,16,20,32…

☒   **A.** is incorrect because four megabytes of memory = 4096K, not 4000K. **B.** is incorrect because three megabytes = 3072K, not 3K. **D.** is incorrect because additional memory is needed for DOS and various drivers.

57. ☑   B. MEM /C | MORE gives more information than the standard MEM command. The /C option tells you exactly how much conventional and high memory each driver is using. The | MORE extension will pause the display after each screen of information; without it, vital information might scroll past before you can read it.

☒   **A.** is incorrect because it does not provide as much information as MEM /C. **C.** is incorrect because CHKDSK is designed to give detailed information about hard disks, not about RAM memory usage. **D.** is incorrect because the MEM command without the /C option does not generally give enough information for memory troubleshooting.

58. ☑   D. 6.22 was the last version of MS-DOS that was released as a stand-alone product (DOS 7 was incorporated into Windows 95/98) and includes memory optimization and other utilities that provide the best tools for configuring workstations.

☒   **A.** is incorrect because there was no version 6.52 of MS-DOS. **B.** is incorrect because DOS 7 is integrated into Windows 95/98 and cannot be installed separately to a workstation. **C.** is incorrect because version 6.0 contained some bugs that were fixed in the 6.22 release.

59. ☑   C. Video and other hardware uses this address space and it is not generally available for running programs.

☒ **A, B, D.** are incorrect because upper memory was not designed for keyboard or hard disk buffering or for mouse drivers.

60. ☑ **C.** Magnetically, on a spinning platter. The spinning platter is coated with a metallic compound that can hold a magnetic charge.
☒ **A.** is incorrect because optical storage is used in CD and DVD media. **B.** is incorrect because reel-to-reel tape is not used in hard drives, but is used in tape drives. **D.** is incorrect because a voice coil is a component of a hard drive, not a method of storage.

61. ☑ **D.** Maintain a constant cool temperature. Because computer chips generate a great deal of heat and that heat can damage or destroy server components, a server room must be kept at a constant cool temperature.
☒ **A, B.** are incorrect because a room temperature that is comfortable to humans is generally warm enough for a server to overheat, especially if a cooling fan fails. **C.** is incorrect because it doesn't stipulate a constant cool temperature, and it is important that the temperature in the room not fluctuate by more than a few degrees at a time to prevent condensation and the expansion and contraction of components.

62. ☑ **C.** Filter it and maintain constant humidity because filtering the air will remove contaminants that could clog server fans and a constant humidity will help prevent static electricity.
☒ **A.** is incorrect because outside air has both contaminants and varying humidity. **B.** is incorrect because dehumidified air increases static electricity. **D.** is incorrect because the water in humid air can condense on components and damage them.

63. ☑ **C.** Monitors. Monitors store electricity in capacitors, even when the monitor is turned off and unplugged, so the monitor will start up quickly. The amount of electricity stored in the capacitors can be enough to injure or even kill a person wearing a grounded wrist strap.
☒ **A, B,** and **D.** are incorrect because these devices do not store electricity in capacitors as monitors do.

64. ☑ **B.** Are kept as far from each other as practicable. This will help to prevent power-line electromagnetic interference with the network transmissions.

☒ **A.** is incorrect because using the same conduits would put the network and power cables too close to each other. **C.** is incorrect because electrical cable is not designed to carry network transmissions. **D.** is incorrect because separation and grouping of cables will prevent a "shortest distance" design.

65. ☑ **A.** Token Ring board drivers may load even if they are the wrong drivers for that particular card. Ethernet NIC drivers will almost always return an error message if you try to use the wrong driver.

☒ **B.** is incorrect because Token Ring boards are not more susceptible to electromagnetic interference than Ethernet NICs. **C.** is incorrect because Token Ring boards do not need to be tuned. **D.** is incorrect because Token Ring boards do not have manual reset buttons.

66. ☑ **B.** Hook the workstations' and printer's serial port to a multiport LAN modem and run SPRINTER.EXE or SPTWIN95.EXE on the workstations. LAN modems are designed to be shared by multiple workstations on the LAN, not to share printers via a printer connection.

☒ **A, C, D.** are incorrect because they all describe valid methods of connecting printers to the network.

67. ☑ **A.** Print Host is not the correct term for any of the NDS objects that need to be created when sharing a printer under NetWare 5.

☒ **B, C, D.** are the three objects that must be created and linked for network printing to work properly under NetWare 5.

68. ☑ **A.** Whether the problem is hardware-related or software-related. For example, if Tim can see servers and printers from his workstation, then the network hardware is probably OK and there may be a software or configuration problem. If Tim cannot see servers and printers from his workstation, then he is either not logged in properly, or there is a hardware problem with the NIC, cabling, or port on the hub.

☒ **B.** is incorrect because Leslee should first determine if the problem is hardware-related or software-related before checking the print driver.

C. is incorrect because Tim only has to be designated a User of the Print Queue object, not an Operator, to be able to print to that particular printer. D. is incorrect because a problem with the LPT1: port should only affect printers hooked to the workstation via parallel cable, not networked printers.

69. ☑ D. Leslee must configure the serial port on the workstation to match the baud rate, parity, data bits, stop bits, and flow control settings of the print device. The print device, in this case, the plotter, will not work unless all of these settings match.

☒ A. is incorrect because serial print cables may be much longer than 15 feet. B. is incorrect because a parallel to serial adapter does not have to be placed on the workstation. C. is incorrect because although a modem may be used for long-distance serial printing, a modem is not required and is rarely used in practice.

70. ☑ A. Plug a cable from a workstation with a known good connection into the printer, power the printer off and back on, test printing.

☒ B. is incorrect because a device may still intermittently respond to ping interrogations even when the cable is damaged. C. is incorrect because the damage to a cable may not be visible. D. is incorrect because testing the port on the hub would come later in the troubleshooting process, after verifying that the printer and cable were OK.

71. ☑ D. Use new ink cartridges made by the manufacturer of the printer when the ink in a cartridge goes dry. Third-party cartridges or refill kits may contain ink that will eventually gum up the print nozzles.

☒ A. is incorrect because refill kits should not be used. B. is incorrect because print nozzles should not have to be cleaned if the correct ink cartridges are used consistently. C. is incorrect because it is actually better for most ink jet printers to stay on and "warmed up."

72. ☑ C. Call a certified technician to clean the printer and adjust the tension on the rollers. The technician should also be able to determine if anything else needs to be done to make the printer more reliable.

☒ **A.** is incorrect because you should not disassemble and adjust a laser printer unless you are a certified technician. **B.** is incorrect because a bad toner cartridge usually has no effect on paper jams. **D.** is incorrect because incorrect roller tension or dirty rollers are more likely to cause paper jams than a bad paper tray.

73. ☑ **A.** The print queue object in NetWare Administrator, or by running PCONSOLE.EXE from a command prompt. A look at either will show if there are any jobs in the NetWare queue, and the status of each job.

☒ **B.** is incorrect because individual jobs cannot be viewed from the print server or printer objects in NetWare Administrator. **C.** is incorrect because print jobs cannot be viewed from the print server object in NetWare Administrator. **D.** is incorrect because print jobs cannot be viewed from the print server object in NetWare Administrator, nor by running NPRINTER.EXE from a command prompt.

74. ☑ **C.** Turning the printer off and back on, then restarting PSERVER.NLM. Since the jobs are reaching the queue, the problem is probably either a connection problem or that the printer or PSERVER are hung up and need to be restarted.

☒ **A.** is incorrect because we already know that jobs are reaching the queue—they are just not being printed. **B.** is incorrect since jobs would not even make it to the print queue if there were inadequate space on the volume hosting the print queue.

75. ☑ **C.** Yes, if she can find (and is licensed to use) the PSERVER.EXE utility that came with NetWare 3.x. However, this would definitely not be the best option in a NetWare 5 environment. It would be better to add the necessary RAM to the NetWare 5 server.

☒ **A.** is incorrect because NetWare 5 does not include the PSERVER.EXE utility. **B.** is incorrect because a DOS NetWare print server program does exist. **D.** is incorrect because PSERVER.EXE was not included with NetWare 4.x.

76. ☑ **B.** Yes, IRQ, DMA, and I/O settings must be configured using jumpers or a configuration program based on the existing settings that are already in use on a given workstation.
☒ **A.** is incorrect because a Token Ring card does not need to be set to a unique address as Arcnet cards do. **C.** is incorrect because a Token Ring card only uses one interrupt. **D.** is incorrect because a Token Ring card is not configured by the server.

77. ☑ **B.** Transmits laser or LED-generated light pulses along a strand of glass fiber.
☒ **A.** is incorrect as the light pulses are not converted into sound waves. **C.** is incorrect as the light pulses are not sent through the air. **D.** is incorrect as the light pulses are not converted into radio waves.

78. ☑ **B.** Data on the RAID array is updated continuously and allows missing data to be recovered much more quickly than when restoring from tape. When restoring from tape, the NetWare server software must be re-installed from scratch before any data is restored, which results in a much longer down time. With RAID, recovery is generally as easy as replacing the bad drive and allowing the RAID array to rebuild the data on the new drive.
☒ **A.** is incorrect because RAID is generally not less expensive than a tape backup solution. **C.** is incorrect because RAID is typically not easier to set up than a tape backup. **D.** is incorrect because data on a RAID array is not accessible by the DOS backup utility.

79. ☑ **B.** Ontrack Data Recovery for NetWare.
☒ **A, C, D.** are incorrect as they describe products that do not exist, according to current information.

Part 12

Test Yourself:
Practice Exam 6
NetWare:
Integrating
Windows NT
(Exam 50-644)

Test Yourself:
Practice Exam 6
Questions

Q&A

Before you call to register for the actual NetWare: Integrating Windows NT exam (Exam #50-644), take the following test and see how you make out. Set a timer for 90 minutes—the same time you'll have to take the live exam—and answer the following 66 questions in the time allotted. Once you've finished, turn to the Practice Exam 6 Answers section and check your score to see if you passed! Good luck!

Practice Exam 6 Questions

1. If you have Windows NT workstations accessing a Novell® NetWare server what protocol would be the most likely to be used?

A. NetBEUI

B. TCP/IP

C. NWLINK IPX/SPX

D. ODI

2. If your network required support for DOS drivers as well as for Plug-n-Play, what operating system would you choose for your workstations?

A. Windows NT Workstation

B. Windows 3.11 for Workgroups

C. Windows 95

D. Windows NT Server

3. What groups are used to assign access rights to resources located on the local Windows NT machine?

A. Global

B. Local

C. NetWare

D. Domain

4. What type of policy is used to control specific user activities in Windows NT and can be used in conjunction with user profiles to control most facets of the user's interaction with Windows NT?

A. System

B. Account

C. User rights

D. Audit

5. What is the formula used to calculate the number of trusts for each domain in the complete trust model?

A. 2^n-2

B. $n(n-1)$

C. $n(n+12)$

D. 6^n+10

6. Which NLM's job is it to scan the NDS™ database for object modifications such as creation or deletion of objects, and to attribute value changes?

A. NDS.NLM

B. NDSDM.NLM

C. DMNDS.NLM

D. DOMAIN.NLM

7. What provides the file structure and defines the attributes that can be assigned to individual files and directories?

A. Operating system

B. Folder system

C. Permissions

D. File system

8. What type of group can contain users from the entire domain?

   A. Local

   B. Global

   C. Network

   D. No group has users from the entire domain

9. Where must system policy files be stored on a Windows NT server so access is automatic?

   A. *<winnt_root>*\SYSTEM32\REPL\EXPORT\SCRIPTS

   B. *<winnt_root>*\SYSTEM\REPL\IMPORT\SCRIPTS

   C. *<winnt_root>*\SYSTEM32\REPL\IMPORT\SCRIPTS

   D. *<winnt_root>*\SYSTEM32\REPL\IMPORT

10. With Windows NT Workstation in a NetWare network, what prevents having one account on the workstation and one within NDS?

    A. NwAdmin

    B. Workstation Manager

    C. Remote Control Agent

    D. SMS

11. What is the executable for the Integration utility?

    A. INTEGRATE.EXE

    B. INT.EXE

    C. IGRATE.EXE

    D. NTIGRATE.EXE

12. Which of the following protocols would you NOT use in a WAN environment?

    A. TCP/IP

    B. IPX/SPX

    C. NetBEUI

    D. AppleTalk

13. What acronym can be used to remember the method for assigning permissions to local groups, assigning global groups to these local groups, and then assigning the users to these global groups?

A. AGLP

B. AGPL

C. APGL

D. LPGA

14. What Registry subkey contains information on the hardware?

A. HKEY_LOCAL_MACHINE

B. HKEY_HARDWARE_PROFILE

C. HKEY_LOCAL_USER

D. HKEY_CURRENT_CONFIG

15. Where is the 32-bit version of the NetWare Administrator utility on a NetWare server?

A. SYS:PUBLIC\WIN95

B. SYS:PUBLIC

C. SYS:PUBLIC\WIN32

D. SYS:PUBLIC\WINNT

16. What is one prerequisite to installing the Novell Administrator for Windows NT?

A. Client for NetWare Networks on PDC

B. Client for Microsoft Networks on PDC

C. NetWare Client for Windows NT on PDC

D. NetWare Client for Windows 32 on PDC

17. How are the configuration files from previous versions of Windows consolidated with Windows 95 and Windows NT?

A. Everything is in a new database known as the Registry.

B. Everything is now in the WIN.INI.

    C. They are not consolidated and are the same as Windows 3.1.

    D. Everything is now in the SYSTEM.INI.

18. Which file system would you want to use with Windows NT if you want to have the maximum security available?

    A. HPFS

    B. NTFS

    C. FAT 16

    D. FAT 32

19. What utility is used to manage user accounts in a workgroup environment?

    A. User Manager For Domains

    B. User Manager

    C. Server Manager

    D. Disk Administrator

20. What is a link between two domains that permits the sharing of resources and account information?

    A. PDC and BDC working together

    B. A trust relationship between two domains

    C. Global grouping of objects on the network

    D. Shares setup pointing to the other domain

21. What are the two ways to launch the Integration utility?

    A. From NWADMIN

    B. From the G: drive no matter what the drive mappings are

    C. From the command line as a stand-alone application

    D. From the System Tray

22. Which three components make up a hive in the Registry?

    A. Key

    B. Subkey

    C. Value

    D. Superkey

23. With a Windows NT Server and Windows 95 as your client workstation, how many accounts would you need to have in a domain environment if you worked at various workstations?

    A. Two

    B. One

    C. Three

    D. Four

24. Where is the information stored for a local group on a Windows NT workstation in a domain environment?

    A. Only on the BDCs

    B. On the PDC

    C. On the workstation

    D. Local groups do not exist on Windows NT workstation

25. What is the name of the executable run to install the NetWare Client for Windows NT only?

    A. WINSETUP.EXE

    B. SETUP.EXE

    C. SETUPNW.EXE

    D. INSTALL.EXE

26. Which of the following is NOT an option on the password tab in User Properties?

    A. No password required

    B. Generate a random password

    C. Require password change at every logon

    D. Don't allow user to change password

27. What utility do you use to manage and maintain hard drives on a Windows NT computer?

    A. Disk Manager

    B. Disk Administrator

    C. User Manager

    D. Server Manager

28. If you have multiple domains in your network and want the servers to communicate with each other what is needed between the domains?

    A. A simple connection via a hub, switch, or router

    B. The same administrator password on both domains

    C. A trust relationship between the domains

    D. This is not possible.

29. How many domains exist in a single master domain model?

    A. One

    B. Two or more

    C. Three or more

    D. Four or more

30. Where do you edit system policies with Z.E.N.works?

    A. System Policy Editor

    B. Server Manager

    C. User Manager

    D. NWADMIN32

31. In addition to Windows NT User assignments, what else can NetWare Administrator manage from Windows NT?

A. NetLogon processes

B. Group objects

C. SIDs

D. Permissions to the WINNT folder

32. In what folder is User Manager found under Start Menu and Programs?

A. Accessories

B. Administrative Utilities

C. Administrative Tools

D. Admin Tools

33. In Windows networking, what do you need if you want others to be able to access a file or folder?

A. This happens automatically so nothing is needed.

B. You must copy the contents to the other computers.

C. A share is setup to allow other computers to access the file or folders.

D. As long as you have a network medium all files are accessible by default.

34. If you want to prevent users from accessing the file on your Windows NT workstation by booting to a floppy disk, what should you do?

A. Use the domain model for your network.

B. Use the FAT file system for your workstation.

C. Use the NTFS file system for your workstation.

D. Add third-party software that does not allow access unless the workstation boots from the hard drive.

35. In what model do the user accounts reside within the account domain? In what model do the network resources reside within the resource domains?

A. Single domain

B. Single master domain

C. Multiple master domain

D. Complete trust

36. Once the NT Configuration object is configured what must be done so users may take advantage of the configuration object?

   A. E-mail the object to each user.

   B. Add the proper command to the logon script.

   C. Associate the object with the user, group, or container.

   D. Drag and drop the object onto the user, group, or container.

37. What utility is used to add computers to the domain?

   A. User Manager

   B. Server Administrator

   C. Server Manager

   D. Domain Manager

38. Where are the user-account database and security settings maintained in a Windows NT domain?

   A. Member server

   B. Backup domain controller

   C. Primary domain controller

   D. Master server

39. In order to monitor and log a user's actions on the network what do you implement?

   A. User logging

   B. Audit trails

   C. SID searching

   D. Domain model

40. What is the maximum number of domains in a complete trust model?

   A. One

   B. 10

   C. 11

   D. Unlimited number

41. What utility lets an administrator control the icons and shortcuts on the desktop?

A. Workstation Manager

B. Novell Application Launcher

C. Scheduler

D. User Manager

42. What Windows NT server stores the original or copies of the directory database?

A. Member server

B. Master server

C. Domain controller

D. Workstation

43. What is an advantage of having a directory of user and security information on a network?

A. A directory provides a backup of all the data on a server.

B. Administrators can manage and maintain the network from a single location.

C. A directory provides users with a map of the network.

D. A directory doesn't provide any advantages.

44. What types of policies control the activities a user account can perform on a computer?

A. System

B. Account

C. Audit

D. User rights

45. Which form does the administration take in a single master domain model?

A. Centralized

B. Decentralized

    C. Both centralized and decentralized

    D. Neither centralized nor decentralized

46. What is a collection of computers without a centralized server and that have been logically grouped together for the purpose of sharing resources?

    A. Domain

    B. Workgroup

    C. Workstation

    D. Server group

47. When a primary domain controller (PDC) fails, what has to be done so administrative changes can be made?

    A. The administrator has to administer with a BDC.

    B. The administrator must install a new PDC on the network.

    C. No administration can occur unless the original PDC is brought back online.

    D. The administrator must promote a BDC to a PDC so administrative changes can be made.

48. Which event would you audit in secure environments to track the individuals who made changes to the network security policies?

    A. Use of User rights

    B. Process tracking

    C. Security policy changes

    D. File and object access

49. Which domain is the account domain?

    A. Trusted

    B. Master

    C. Trusting

    D. Secondary

50. What is the main advantage of being able to administer the Windows NT configuration from within NWADMIN32?

   A. Centralization
   B. Multiple user accounts
   C. Lower cost of hardware
   D. This cannot be done

51. What is the one major benefit of a domain model over a workgroup model?

   A. Centralized management of user accounts
   B. Multiple SAMs
   C. More than one user-database to manage
   D. Multiple points of administration

52. What type of server is used primarily to provide application, file, or printer services to the network and does not provide user authentication services?

   A. Primary domain controller
   B. Backup domain controller
   C. Member server
   D. Workstation

53. Which of the following is not one of the three types of user profiles?

   A. Local
   B. Roaming
   C. Global
   D. Mandatory

54. Which domain model has a trusting relationship and is trusted with every other domain on the network?

   A. Single domain model
   B. Single master domain model

C. Multiple master domain model

D. Complete trust model

55. Which of the following is true about integrating and administering Windows NT from NetWare NDS?

A. You would have to use two different account managers: the User Manager for domains, application for Windows NT and the NetWare Administrator for NDS accounts.

B. You would double your workload by maintaining two separate directory databases.

C. You would have to manually migrate users from Windows NT to the NDS database.

D. The margin for error is lower due to the fact that administration is centralized.

56. What do two computers need to have in common in order to communicate on the network?

A. The type of network adapter

B. The network protocol

C. The operating system

D. The drivers

57. When a new account is created what is assigned to the user account and used by the system as an identifier?

A. A security ID

B. Read permissions to the WINNT directory

C. A username

D. A password

58. What do you have to specify in the User configuration to use roaming profiles?

A. Nothing

B. The path to the local profile on the workstation so it will be copied to the server

C. The path to the profile on the server or location where the profile is found

D. Click the roaming profiles option in User Manager for Domains.

59. If you have the three domains of Sales, Marketing, and Engineering, and have a trust between Sales and Marketing and a trust between Marketing and Engineering, what relationship would there be between Sales and Engineering?

A. Since there are two trusts, a third automatically forms between the Sales and Engineering domains.

B. The one-way trusts become two-way trusts and a one-way trust forms between Sales and Engineering.

C. There is no trust relationship between Sales and Engineering.

D. None of the above

60. What defines the NDS object and the various properties that are associated with that object?

A. NT Configuration Object

B. Schema

C. Extension

D. Snap-In

61. With NDS for NT, how are NT Objects created by default within the NDS Tree?

A. They are not created by default.

B. The Domain Object Wizard creates them.

C. The Administrator uses the Auto Import feature within NWADMIN.

D. The Administrator must create one and then the rest will migrate based on the first object.

62. What happens if a Windows NT user account has the same name as an existing NDS user account?

A. The account will not be migrated.

B. The NDS account information will be deleted.

C. You will be given three choices: Don't Move, Overwrite, and Create As.

D. You will be given three choices: Don't Move, Associate With, and Create As.

63. Which property page allows you to specify that you want passwords to be synchronized between the Windows NT Domain and NDS?

A. Domain Access

B. Members of the Domain Object

C. Domain User Settings

D. Replica Advisor

64. When preparing for an unattended installation, what utility can be used to specify properties for various workstations?

A. Novell Client Install Manager

B. Novell Client Install Setup

C. Novell Client Install Configuration

D. Novell Installation Configuration

65. Which of the following can be used to get help about the Novell Client for Windows NT? (Choose all that apply.)

A. SETUPNW.EXE /?

B. Readme Files

C. Technical Support

D. Help and About in the Client Screen

66. What type of dynamic user would be created if the administrator wants the user account to be created on the NT Workstation at login and deleted at logout?

A. NonVolatile User

B. Temporary User

C. Volatile User

D. Admin User

CERTIFIED NOVELL ENGINEER℠

Test Yourself:
Practice Exam 6
Answers

Q&A

The answers to the questions are in boldface, followed by a brief explanation. Some of the explanations detail the logic you should use to choose the correct answer, while others give factual reasons why the answer is correct. If you miss several questions on a similar topic, you should review the corresponding section in the *CNE® NetWare® 5 Study Guide* before taking the Integrating Windows NT test.

Practice Exam 6 Answers

1. ☑ **C. IPX/SPX.** The NWLink IPX/SPX Compatible protocol is Microsoft's version of IPX/SPX and is NDIS compliant. Network Device Interface Specification is to Microsoft Networking what Open Data-Link Interface (ODI) is to Novell Networking; they are both specifications that allow the binding of multiple protocols (or Ethernet Frametypes, in the case of NetWare) to a single network card. NWLink is a transport protocol that relies on a redirector, such as Novell's 32-bit client for Windows, to access file or print services located on a NetWare-based network. However, because of the widespread use of mixed networks, NWLink is one of the protocols selected by default during the installation of Windows NT.
    ☒ **A.** NetBEUI doesn't exist in a Novell environment. **B.** TCP/IP would work as long as the Novell® server was set up with TCP/IP. In this question we didn't see any indication of this. The proprietary protocol is NWLINK IPX/SPX for Novell so we know this should work with the information we have. **D.** is not correct since ODI is not a protocol.

2. ☑ **C.** Windows 95 supports DOS-level drivers as well as Plug-n-Play technology. When you compare Windows NT Workstation with Windows 95, you might conclude that Windows NT is an upgraded version of Windows 95. However, there are as many differences as there are similarities. In the area of hardware support, Windows 95 provides support for MS-DOS device drivers and plug-and-play technology, whereas Windows NT does not. However, Windows NT does include support for multiple processors—two in an out-of-box installation—while Windows 95 can handle only one.
    ☒ **A.** and **D.** Windows NT Workstation and Server are both incorrect, for the above-mentioned reasons. **B.** Windows 3.11 was designed for networking, but in a peer-to-peer environment like Windows 95.

3. ☑ **B.** Local groups are used to assign access rights to resources located on the local Windows NT machine. For example, if you installed a new printer on the engineering department's server, you could create a local group and assign permissions to access the printer to that group. At this point, taking into account the permissions assignment rule of assigning permissions to groups and placing users in groups, you would grant membership to the local group for each user. If at some point you needed to modify permissions to access the printer, you could merely change the local group's permissions and the modification would affect all members in the group.
☒ **A.** Global groups are very similar to local groups, except they gather user accounts from the entire domain. The information pertaining to a global group is stored in the Directory database on the domain controllers. **C.** NetWare is incorrect because Windows NT groups do not exist in NetWare. **D.** Windows NT provides for three built-in, or default, global groups: Domain Administrators, Domain Guests, and Domain Users. Domain Administrators grants and revokes access rights on domain accounts.

4. ☑ **A.** System policy. User profiles not only establish default settings for new user accounts, but they also control environmental settings. In contrast, system policies are used to control specific user activities in Windows NT and can be used in conjunction with user profiles to control most facets of the user's interaction with Windows NT. Some of the more commonly used features of system policies are listed below:

- Permit users to connect and/or remove printer connections through Print Manager
- Disable the RUN command on the Start menu
- Require users to process the logon script before initiating any other processes
- Control automatic program execution through the Startup folder
- Lock and unlock specific program groups
- Specify what types of changes a user can make to an unlocked program group
- Disable the Save Settings menu option in Program Manager, File Manager, and Print Manager

☒ **B.** Accounts, **C.** User rights, and **D.** Audit, are incorrect because they are available options in Windows NT, but do control the facets of the users' interaction with Windows NT.

5. ☑ **B.** In order to calculate the number of trusts needed for each domain, you would use the formula $n(n-1)$, where n is the number of domains. By looking at the formula, you can tell that the number of trust relationships can become quite large after a period of time.

   ☒ **A, C, D.** are incorrect since they will not calculate the correct answer.

6. ☑ **B.** The NDS Event Monitor is an NLM (NDSDM.NLM) that is implemented on a NetWare server. Its job is to scan the NDS™ database for object modifications such as creation or deletion of objects and attribute value changes. When it detects that an object has changed, it then transfers the changes to the NDS Object Replication Service, which we discuss in the next section. The NDS Event Monitor can also ensure that synchronization with a Windows NT system is completed even if the Windows NT system or its connection fails. When a failed Windows NT system comes back on-line, the NDS Event Monitor will submit the appropriate changes to the Windows NT system. This ensures that the NetWare network and the Windows NT network are synchronized with each other while also providing fault tolerance. The administrator can configure how often NDS events are synchronized with a Windows NT system through the Novell Administrator. This feature is important, as it can significantly cut down on network traffic between the two systems.

   ☒ **A.** NDS.NLM is the NDS itself, so it is incorrect. **C.** DMNDS.NLM, and **D.** DOMAIN.NLM, do not exist.

7. ☑   **D.** File system. Just as a protocol is necessary for communication to take place, the operating system must have a method to manage and store data on the hard disk. A file system provides the file structure and defines the attributes that can be assigned to individual files and directories. Windows NT includes three file systems: CDFS, FAT, and NTFS whose use is based upon your file storage needs. When you install Windows NT, you are required to choose the file system or systems that you wish to deploy. However, Windows NT not only includes the capability to install multiple file systems, but also provides the Disk Administrator utility to manage and maintain your file system. Since CDFS is the CD-ROM file system, which permits read-only access, it will not be discussed further.

☒   **A.** The Operating System contains the file system information so this answer is not specific enough. **B.** Folder system is a made-up term for purposes of this practice test. **C.** Permissions have nothing to do with general file system configuration.

8. ☑   **B.** Global groups are very similar to local groups, except they gather user accounts from the entire domain. The information pertaining to a global group is stored in the directory database on the domain controllers. Because of this, only user accounts from the domain can be stored in a global group. This also means that global groups cannot contain local groups or other global groups. However, a trusted domain can use global groups, making it easy to allow administrators from one domain to assign access rights to users in another domain. This task is performed by adding global groups to local groups and allowing the global group to inherit rights from the local group.

☒   **A.** Local groups do not contain users from the entire domain. Local groups are used to assign access rights to resources located on the local Windows NT machine **C.** There is no such thing as a network group. **D.** is false because global groups contain users from the entire domain.

9. ☑ **C.** *<winnt_root>*\SYSTEM32\REPL\IMPORT\SCRIPTS. Remember that the Registry stores information for each user's hardware and software configuration settings. When you create a system policy, the configuration settings are stored in a file called NTCONFIG.POL. This file must be stored in the NETLOGON share, which is a shared directory located in the *<winnt_root>*\SYSTEM32\REPL\IMPORT\SCRIPTS directory. By placing NTCONFIG.POL in the NETLOGON share, you are enabling a standard policy for every Windows NT computer in the domain. However, the system policy used by a workstation is based on the user's logon domain and not the computer's domain. This has been known to cause confusion, as most people forget that the computer can be set up as part of one domain while the user can log onto a different domain.

☒ **A, B, D.** are incorrect because the other paths do not contain the .pol file needed for policy and also are not shared by default as the netlogon share.

10. ☑ **B.** Workstation Manager. The nice part about integrating the workstation into NDS is that you don't need one password for the NT workstation and another for logon to the NetWare network. With NDS integration it is easy to keep these two components synchronized. With the two-account situations existing with an NT workstation on a NetWare network, you can use NetWare's Workstation Manager to automatically generate accounts on the workstation when the user logs onto the network. Without this feature you would have to create one account on the workstation and one in NDS. The centralized administration of policies, profiles, and workstation components makes it easy to handle a diverse network environment.

☒ **A.** NwAdmin, **C.** Remote Control Agent, and **D.** SMS are incorrect because these options will not automatically create an account.

11. ☑ **C.** IGRATE.EXE. When you first begin the process of integrating a Windows NT network into a NetWare network, you must synchronize the existing users between both networks. The Novell Administrator includes an integration utility, IGRATE.EXE, that takes the existing user and group information from the Windows NT SAM database and imports them into NDS. Subsequently, it then takes existing user and group information from NDS and synchronizes it with the Windows NT system. After a successful integration, any modifications are handled by the NDS Event Monitor and the NDS Object Replication Service components of the Novell Administrator.

☒ **A, B, D.** The other executables do not exist.

12. ☑ **C.** NetBEUI. The main shortcoming with NetBEUI is that it is not a routable protocol. This means that a second protocol that is routable (such as IPX or IP) will become necessary to encapsulate NetBEUI packets if your network traffic has to cross a router. Another problem with NetBEUI is that there are only a few platforms, primarily Windows and OS/2, that support it. This limits your connectivity options for current and future network growth.

☒ **A.** TCP/IP, **B.** IPX/SPX and **D.** AppleTalk, are incorrect because they are routable and can operate in WAN environments.

13. ☑ **A.** AGLP. Just as with NetWare network resources, Microsoft Windows NT domain resources should have groups assigned permissions to use them, rather than individual user accounts. However, don't forget that NT domains have two main types of groups, local and global. Additionally, don't confuse an NT global group with an NDS global group, which is nothing more than a group composed of users from multiple NDS contexts. With NT domains, the recommended method of assigning permissions to domain resources can be remembered with the acronym AGLP: 1) add user *A*ccount to a 2) *G*lobal group, which is added to a 3)*L*ocal group 4) to which you assign *P*ermissions.

☒ **B.** AGPL, **C.** APGL and **D.** LPGA are wrong because they do not represent acronyms in the Windows NT security system.

14. ☑ **A.** HKEY_LOCAL_MACHINE. The first subtree, HKEY_LOCAL_MACHINE, contains all of the computer's hardware information. Applications, device drivers, and the operating system use this information when they need to access data on a particular device. When a Windows NT machine boots, the boot process determines which device drivers to load by referencing this subtree.

☒ **B.** HKEY_HARDWARE_PROFILE doesn't exist within the Registry. **C.** The HKEY_USERS subtree contains the system default settings and the security settings for each user. This information is used by the operating system to determine what each user is allowed to view and access on the computer. Examples of the data stored in this subtree are default user settings, network settings, and control panel settings. When a user logs on to a Windows NT machine, this data is copied into the HKEY_ CURRENT_USER subtree. **D.** The HKEY_CURRENT_CONFIG subtree stores the active hardware profile. This subtree obtains its initial data from the HKEY_LOCAL_MACHINE subtree when the user logs on and maintains it for the active hardware profile.

15. ☑ **C.** SYS:PUBLIC\WIN32. The 32-bit NetWare Administrator runs on an NT workstation. The same file can be used by Windows 95 and 98 as well as Windows NT. The filename is NWADMN32.EXE and it is located in the SYS:PUBLIC/WIN32 directory. NWADMIN32 allows administration of the User objects in the directory tree.

☒ **A, B, D.** The other paths are incorrect since the NWADMN32 executable is not located there by default.

16. ☑ **C.** NetWare Client for Windows NT on PDC. Before you install the Novell Administrator for Windows NT, you must meet some system requirements.

For the Windows NT network, the following is necessary:

■ Windows NT server functioning as a PDC. The NetWare Client for Windows NT must be installed on the PDC.

■ IPX protocol installed on the PDC. IPX is the native protocol of NetWare. (This step is necessary only if the NetWare® 5 server is not using pure IP.)

■ Access to a user account with administrative privileges to the domain

☒ **A, B, D.** These clients run on the PDC do not enable the installation of Novell Administrator for Windows NT.

17. ☑ **A.** Everything is in a new database known as the Registry. Earlier versions of Windows stored operating system information in text files that were given special extensions based on the type of file, such as configuration (CFG), initialization (INI), or system (SYS). These files were stored in a variety of locations, and if you needed to make a change you would have to locate the appropriate file. The current version of Windows changed the way that Windows stores system information by consolidating the numerous configuration files into a single database called the Registry. By doing so, Windows centralizes the location of operating system settings and user information.

☒ **B.** WIN.INI and **D.** SYSTEM.INI are still used, but aren't equipped with what is needed for configuration settings. These are used for backwards compatibility. **C.** is incorrect. The way Windows 3.1 stores these files is not similar to the way NT stores this information.

18. ☑ **B.** Windows NT File System (NTFS) allows an administrator to assign different permissions to file, directories, or folders. There are sharing permissions and directory permissions.

☒ **A.** HPFS is incorrect because it isn't supported under Windows NT 4.0 as it was in 3.51. **C.** FAT 16 and **D.** FAT 32 are incorrect because they only give you limited file attributes. This is due to the fact that FAT supports only read-only (RO), system (S), hidden (H), and archive (A) attributes. Even if you set a file as read only, it is still possible to modify the file by turning off the read-only attribute. This poses a problem in environments that require a medium-to-high level of security, yet at the same time provides for low overhead as there are fewer security settings that need to be stored.

19. ☑ **B.** User Manager. When you create a new user account on the local machine, you use the User Manager utility. However, in order to create a new user account on a domain, you must use the User Manager for Domains utility. While the look and feel of both applications is similar, the location of their respective databases is different. The User Manager utility maintains all accounts in a database that reside on the workstation. With the User Manager for Domains utility, the directory database resides on a domain controller. However, you can modify the directory database only on the PDC because it contains the master copy. The master database is then replicated, or copied, to the BDCs.

☒ **A, C, D.** are incorrect because server manager and disk administrator do not have anything to do with user or account management. The User manager for domains is not for workgroups.

20. ☑ **B.** A trust relationship between two domains. Since trust relationships are an integral part of most Windows NT networks, it's necessary to have a thorough understanding of how they work with the different domain models. Recall that a domain is composed of network servers and computers that have been logically grouped together for the purpose of sharing resources. A trust relationship, or simply trust, is a communications and administrative link between two domains that permits the sharing of resources and account information. Without the implementation of trust relationships, individual domains have no method of communicating with each other and, therefore, no method of sharing resources.

☒ **A, C, D.** The other answers are invalid because they have nothing to do with a link between two domains.

21. ☑ **A, C.** You may launch the integration utility either from the NetWare Administrator or from the command line as a standalone utility. When the utility is started, you are presented with a dialog box. From this utility, you can perform the following integration tasks:

- Integrate NDS User to Windows NT
- Integrate Windows NT Users to NDS
- Synchronize existing Windows NT users with existing NDS users

☒ **B, D.** are not correct since you cannot launch the integration utility from them.

22. ☑ **A, B, C.** A hive is made up of three components: keys, subkeys, and values. A hive also has two files associated with it: a data file and a log file. A key is similar to a folder in the file system, but instead of holding subdirectories and files it holds subkeys and values. Subkeys are analogous to subdirectories and aid in breaking down the Registry into a more organized structure. Values are comparable to files and just as files have attributes associated with them, so do values. These attributes are composed of a name, a data type, and a configuration parameter. The name is used as a label, or variable, just as you would name a file. The data type can be compared to an extension on a file and is used to associate a specific data type with the value. The configuration parameter is the actual data, or value, that is used.

☒ **D.** Superkey does not exist.

23. ☑ **B.** One. An advantage to a centralized directory database is that it eliminates the need for maintaining separate accounts on each workstation, as is required by the workgroup model. This drastically cuts the time and coordination required to maintain multiple databases on a network. A second benefit is that users are required to log on only once to access any of the resources on the network. This single-point logon cuts down on the number of accounts and passwords that users need to remember, again unlike the workgroup model.

☒ **C, D.** The other answers are not correct for obvious reasons. If you had to maintain three or four accounts, the network design is very poor. With Windows NT Workstation in a workgroup environment it would be possible for maintaining that many accounts. **A.** Having to have two is not correct.

24. ☑   **C. On the workstation.** Since local groups permit access only to local resources, the group's information is stored in the local machine's account database. This has the advantage of offloading some of the burden from the domain's directory database. However, local groups can assign rights and permissions only to resources that reside on that particular machine. It cannot grant rights or permissions to global resources. In addition, you are limited to assigning only users and global groups to a local group—that is, you cannot assign a local group to another local group. However, you can include users and global groups from any domain in the network in which a trust relationship has been established.

☒   **A. Only on the BDCs,** and **B. On the PDC,** are incorrect because they show domain controllers which can hold local accounts, but this would do no good for the workstation. **D. Local groups do not exist on Windows NT workstation,** is false.

25. ☑   **C. SETUPNW.EXE** To install the NetWare client for Windows NT you use the SETUPNW.EXE from the PRODUCTS/WINNT/I386 directory on the CD. The CD is an auto-run and will come up with the WINSETUP.EXE, which then allows you to select what you want to install. When the Windows NT selection is chosen, then the SETUPNW.EXE is executed. You will follow various prompts and then have to reboot when the client is installed. With the unattended installation there are some switches to accomplish the type of installation you want. The /U switch is for the unattended install. Along with this switch is the /ACU switch for automatic client upgrades.

☒   **A, B, D.** The other executables do not exist in the directory for the client for Windows NT.

26. ☑ **C.** Require password change at every logon. The password tab allows you to specify how the password synchronization phase is completed. The options are as follows:

- No password required (**A.**). This option will remove the password from both accounts, and may jeopardize network security.

- Generate a random password (**B.**)

- Use new password. If enabled, you will need to enter and confirm the new password.

- Require password change at next login.

- Don't allow user to change password (**D.**). This option is generally used for a Guest account.

☒ **A, B,** and **D.** are incorrect because they are options on the password tab, as shown above.

27. ☑ **B.** Disk Administrator is used to manage and maintain the hard drives on a Windows NT computer. Some of the functions of Disk Administrator are:

- Create and delete partitions
- Create and delete logical drives
- Create, delete, format, and label volumes
- Change drive letter assignments
- Create and delete stripe sets (fault tolerance)
- View drive information

☒ **A.** Disk Manager does not exist in a Windows NT environment. **C.** User Manager is for administering the user database. **D.** Server Manager, only available on NT servers, is used for other server administration jobs like PDC and BDC promotion and demotion.

28. ☑ **C.** A trust relationship between the domains. You can establish multiple domains in a Windows NT network, but in order for them to communicate you will need to implement a trust. Trusts in Windows NT are built to allow one domain to access resources located on another domain. When you establish a trust relationship, you can set up a one-way trust, a two-way trust, or a complete trust. Because of the complexity of the domain model, it is much more difficult to plan and implement than the workgroup model. However, because the domain model can support a larger number of users, it is usually the model of choice.

    ☒ **A** is not correct due to the fact you need the trust relationship. **B.** is not correct and can be a security risk depending on your organization. **D.** is not correct because it IS possible with a trust relationship.

29. ☑ **B.** In a single master domain model, there are two or more domains. One domain functions as the master domain and contains the user accounts for the domain. Since user and computer accounts reside in the master domain, it is also called the account domain. All other domains, which contain resources such as files and printers, are resource domains in this model. Each resource domain communicates with the master domain through one-way trust relationships. The account domain is considered the trusted domain and all resource domains are considered the trusting domains.

    ☒ **A.** One is too few. **C.** Three or more, and **D.** Four or more, are incorrect because they are too many.

30. ☑ **D.** NWADMIN32. The key to successful management of workstations with Z.E.N.works and NetWare Administrator is association with the appropriate objects. NetWare5 enables you to have NT policies and profiles integrated into the NDS.

    ☒ **A.** System Policy Editor allows for configuration of system policies, but is not integrated with Z.E.N.works. **B, C.** Server Manager and User Manager have no bearing on system policies.

31. ☑ **B.** In addition to Windows NT User objects, NetWare Administrator can also handle Windows NT Group assignments. In order to make a Windows NT Group assignment to a Windows NT User object, whether or not they are integrated into NDS, you would pull up the Details of the Windows NT Group object and make your assignments through the Members page. Here, you simply click the Add button to add Windows NT User objects to the Windows NT Group object.

☒ **A, C.** NWADMN cannot manage the NetLogon process or SIDs. **D.** Permissions cannot be directly assigned from NWADMN.

32. ☑ **C.** Administrative Tools. As we mentioned earlier in the chapter, the WinLogon process requires a valid username and password in order to grant a user access to the Windows NT machine's resources. Microsoft has provided the User Manager utility to manage and maintain user accounts. There are actually two versions of the User Manager utility; one for Windows NT Workstation and Windows NT servers that are installed as stand-alone servers (User Manager), and another for Windows NT Server, which is installed as Domain Controller (User Manager for Domains). The only difference between the two versions is that the User Manager for Domains utility also administers user accounts on the network. User Manager is accessed under the Administrative Tools folder from Start | Programs.

☒ **A.** Accessories is not correct, but is an available folder. **B, D.** Administrative Utilities and Admin Tools are not default folders available with Windows NT.

33. ☑ **C.** A share is set up to allow other computers to access the file or folders. Windows NT allows you to share resources through shares and permissions. A share makes the resource available to other users located on the local machine or over the network. However, shares alone do not allow access to files or printers. Instead, shares are combined with permissions, which define what type of access to the resources each user or group of users is permitted.

☒ **A.** is not correct since you need to set up a share for others to access the resource. **B.** Copying the components takes the networking out of the network. **D.** is also wrong because you need to establish a share for the file or folder.

34. ☑ **C.** Use the NTFS file system for your workstation. While the mandatory logon process is one of the security implementations used in Windows NT, it cannot prevent access to files on the local computer by itself. This is especially true when the FAT file system is in use on the computer.

There is no provision for file-level access controls with the FAT file system. While you can secure FAT directories over the network using shares, you cannot secure FAT files and directories from local access. Even if there were a method to prevent unauthorized access to these files, the user could simply reboot the machine with an MS-DOS bootable disk and bypass the mandatory logon process. However, by using another implementation of the Windows NT security system, the NTFS file system, you are able to initiate file-level access. NTFS not only allows you to set permissions on a file-level basis, but it also prevents access using the MS-DOS bootable disk trick. Since MS-DOS uses the FAT file system, it cannot read data on an NTFS partition. Windows NT does not allow for the creation of an NTFS bootable disk, which further prevents access to files stored by NTFS.

☒ **A.** and **D.** are incorrect because domain model has nothing to do with access controls, and getting third-party software is not a good solution for any network. **B.** is incorrect because there is no provision for file-level access controls with the FAT file system. While you can secure FAT directories over the network using shares, you cannot secure FAT files and directories from local access.

35. ☑ **C.** Multiple master domain. The multiple master domain model is much more complicated than the single master domain model. In this domain, user accounts still reside in the account domain and network resources in the resource domains. However, you are basically taking the single master domain and multiplying it. In order to communicate among the single master domains, a two-way trust must be established between each master domain to every other master domain.

☒ **A.** Single domain, and **B.** Single master domain are incorrect because they have the main permission close to home. **D.** Complete trust is wrong because it has trusts going in many directions.

36. ☑ **C.** Associate the object with the user, group, or container. Once you have the NT Configuration object configured the way you want it, you have to associate with your user, group, or container. To do this you use the Associations tab in the Details window for the NT Configuration object.
☒ **A.** E-mailing the object to each user is not possible. **B.** The logon script does not allow a command to associate a configuration object. **D.** Dragging and dropping the object over the user is not possible, either.

37. ☑ **C.** Server Manager is available only on Windows NT Server, but it allows you to configure domains and manager computers connected to the server. Some of the functions of Server Manager include:

■ Add and remove computers from a domain

■ Display users connected to a particular computer on the domain

■ Send messages to users connected to the domain

■ Display open and shared resources, such as files or printers

■ Promote a backup domain controller to a primary domain controller

■ Manually synchronize servers with the primary domain controller

■ Manage and maintain directory replication

☒ **A.** User Manager is incorrect because it is for handling users, not computers. **B.** Server Administrator and **D.** Domain Manager do not exist.

38. ☑ **C.** Primary domain controller. In the domain model, the user account database and security settings are maintained on a central server, called the primary domain controller. Since the user-account database and security settings reside in a single location rather than being spread throughout the network, administration is centralized. This form of network administration is more desirable to companies since it takes fewer individuals to maintain the network.
☒ **A.** Member server is not correct because member servers provide no residency for user-account and security information. **B.** Backup domain controller is not correct because it is not the central location of the database, but a backup of the domain database in case of primary controller failure. **D.** Master server does not exist in a Windows NT domain and therefore is not correct.

39. ☑ **B.** Audit trails. Audit trails are used to monitor a user's activities on the network. When the mandatory logon process authenticates a user's credentials, an access token is attached to the user's process. The access token contains the user's SID and each group SID to which the user belongs. Through these SIDs, the Windows NT security system can maintain a log of the user's activities while they are logged onto a Windows NT network. Audit trails cover all security-related activities, including other system events, which are then placed into logs that are viewable by the administrator.

☒ **A.** User logging, **C.** SID searching, and **D.** Domain model are incorrect because they have nothing to do with tracking user actions.

40. ☑ **C.** Eleven. Remember that a Windows NT domain is limited to 128 inbound trusts. In order to calculate the number of trusts needed for each domain, you can use the formula *n(n-1)*, where *n* represents the number of domains. With the formula you can see that if you use the complete trust model, you will be limited to only 11 domains. It is for this reason that Novell and Microsoft agree that you should use the complete trust model only when the number of domains in the network is relatively small.

☒ **A, B.** do not follow from the formula n(n−1). **D.** is incorrect based on the formula.

41. ☑ **B.** The Novell Application Launcher (NAL) gives the network administrator a powerful tool for application management, which includes managing the desktop icons. There are two ways to use NAL. There is the standard NAL that incorporates a window of its own on the desktop with the applications for the user, and there is the NAL Explorer, which allows you to incorporate icons on the Start Menu and the desktop.

☒ **A, C, D.** The other three options are components or utilities that do different things. Workstation Manager handles interactions with policies, User Manager is a tool used to manage user in Windows NT, and the Scheduler allows processes and actions to be scheduled on the workstation.

42. ☑   **C.** Domain Controller. When a Windows NT server stores the original or copies of the directory database, it is a domain controller. If it contains the master copy of the directory database, it is a PDC. With domains, there can be only one PDC at any given time on the network. Hence, all other controllers are BDCs. If a Windows NT server machine does not store a copy of the directory database, it is called a member server.

☒   **A.** The member server has nothing to do with Windows NT accounts. **B.** The master server does not exist. **D.** Workstation is not a server.

43. ☑   **B.** Since the master copy of the directory database resides on the PDC, administrators can manage and maintain the network from a single location. This allows the administrator to make one change on the network rather than at several different points on the network. Changes are then propagated throughout the network by directory replication.

☒   **A.** is incorrect since a directory does not provide a backup of the data on the server. **C.** is not correct since there's no map of the network. **D.** is not correct because having a directory does provide the advantage of a single place for administration.

44. ☑   **D.** User rights policies control the activities a user account can perform on a computer. These types of activities range from accessing the computer from the network to loading/unloading device drivers, and are normally associated with an administrative account. In order to access the User Rights Policy dialog box you must select the User Rights option from the Policies pull-down menu in User Manager for Domains.

☒   **A.** System, **B.** Account, and **C.** Audit are incorrect because they are either the wrong policy type or wrong utility.

45. ☑ **C. Both centralized and decentralized.** Resource administration in the single master domain model can be either centralized or decentralized, giving added flexibility in tailoring a network. However, if you choose to decentralize your resource administration, you must keep in mind that resource administrators have no control over global group membership. Therefore, it is important that there is some coordination and trust between account administrators and resource administrators in order to keep a secure network.

☒ **A, B.** are not comprehensive answers since the administration can be either centralized or decentralized. **D.** is false since the reverse is true.

46. ☑ **B. A workgroup is a collection of computers that have been logically grouped together for the purpose of sharing resources.** However, a workgroup is a peer-to-peer arrangement that does not require a central server to provide access to network resources. Instead, the individual workstations bear the responsibilities of account administration, resource management, and security policies, by maintaining their own security database locally, also known as the Security Accounts Manager (SAM).

☒ **A.** isn't correct because the domain model has a central server and is not a peer-to-peer arrangement. **C.** and **D.** are not correct because a workstation in one computer in a network and a server group don't exist.

47. ☑   **D.** The administrator must promote a backup domain controller (BDC) to a PDC so administrative changes can be made. One of the problems associated with PDCs is server failure. When a PDC fails or communication to the PDC is lost, no administrative changes can be made. To rectify this potential problem, a BDC can be promoted to a PDC, at which time the PDC is automatically demoted to a BDC. The process of promoting a BDC to a PDC is not automatic, but must be manually performed by an administrator. If you have advance notice that a PDC must be taken offline, such as for preventive maintenance, you can demote a PDC to a BDC, then promote a BDC to a PDC. However, you cannot demote a PDC to a member server without reinstalling the Windows NT server software. This is primarily because the structure of the Registry is slightly different between a domain controller and a member server. Even though you cannot demote a PDC to a member server, a PDC can still function as a file, print, or application server. While there are minor differences in the Registry structure, those areas that are affected do not interfere with the functionality of these types of services.

☒   **A.** and **C.** are incorrect because they are false statements. **B.** is wrong since a BDC can be promoted.

48. ☑   **C.** Tracking security policy changes is used in secure environments to track the individuals who made changes to the network security policies.

☒   **A.** Use of User rights, **B.** Process tracking, and **D.** File and object access are incorrect because they do not audit changes in network security policies.

49. ☑   **A.** Trusted domain. Since the resource domain trusts the account domain, the resource domain is said to be the trusting domain. The account domain then becomes the trusted domain.

☒   **B, D.** Master and secondary domains are not considered to be the account domain. **C.** The trusting domain is incorrect because the trusting domain is the resource domain.

50. ☑ **A.** Centralization. Being able to centralize administration makes the job much easier.

☒ **B.** Multiple user accounts would not be an advantage, **C.** Lower cost of hardware is a plus but not an advantage for an administrator. **D.** is not correct since administering the Windows NT configuration can be done.

51. ☑ **A.** Centralized management of user accounts. One of the advantages to a centralized directory database is that it eliminates the need for maintaining separate accounts on each workstation, as is required by the workgroup model. This drastically cuts the time and coordination required to maintain multiple databases on a network. A second benefit is that users are required to log on only once to access any of the resources on the network. This single-point logon cuts down on the number of accounts and passwords that users need to remember, again unlike the workgroup model.

☒ **B, C, D.** The other answer choices are wrong because they do not focus on centralization.

52. ☑ **C.** A member server is used primarily to provide application, file, or printer services to the network. The most common use of a member server is to support applications services, such as the Microsoft BackOffice product family. In this regard, a member server is similar to a domain controller. However, member servers do not store copies of the directory database and therefore cannot provide logon authentication services for the domain. While at first glance this may seem to be a disadvantage, it isactually a benefit if you plan on using application services that require a lot of processing power or will be heavily accessed. Without the extra overhead of providing logon authentication, a member server can use the additional resources for other services.

☒ **A.** Primary domain controller, and **B.** Backup domain controller, provide authentication services. **D.** Workstations are not servers.

53. ☑ **C.** Global.

☒ **A.** Local user profile, **B.** Roaming user profile, and **D.** Mandatory user profile, are the three types of user profiles that can be used by the administrator to control a user's environmental settings.

54. ☑ **D.** Complete trust model. With the complete trust model there is a two-way trust between every domain on the network.

☒ **A, B, C.** The other answers are incorrect since they do not have two-ways trusts between each connection.

55. ☑ **D.** The margin for error is lower due to the fact that administration is centralized. NetWare 5 allows you to centrally administer the two systems from NDS using the NetWare Administrator application. This not only reduces the workload on the administrator, but decreases the potential for errors. If you make a mistake using NetWare Administrator, you know the mistake was replicated to the Windows NT domain. However, rectifying the mistake is easy because once you correct the error using NetWare Administrator, it is automatically corrected on the Windows NT domain. In this case, you are spared having to look at both systems to determine which one contained the error in the first place.

☒ **A, B, C.** The other answer choices are wrong since they do not focus on centralization.

56. ☑ **B.** The network protocol. Just as human beings must have a common language in order to successfully communicate with each other, machines must use a common protocol to exchange information. When data is passed between computers, it is packaged in a specific manner that is dependent upon the protocol used for the transmission. Unless the sender and the receiver are using the same protocol, the receiver will be unable to interpret the information.

☒ **A, C.** It doesn't matter if the computers have the same network adapters, or the same operating system. **D.** The drivers only matter for each individual workstation.

PE 6 EXAM 50-644
ANSWERS

57. ☑ **A.** A security ID. Each time you create a user or group account in a Windows NT domain, the account is assigned a security identifier (SID). The SID is a unique number that is assigned once and is never reused. This means that if you accidentally delete an account, you will not be able to reassign the SID even if you recreate the account with the same settings. If the account were assigned ownership of any shared resources, an account deletion would remove access to those resources. SID assignment is an automatic process that is completed by the Windows NT operating system and is not used by the system administrator.

☒ **B, C, D.** The other answer choices are wrong because they are not automatically created when the user is created.

58. ☑ **C.** The path to the profile on the server or location where the profile is found. A roaming user profile is used to allow the user's environment to follow him across the network. In order to perform this function, the profile must be stored on the network in a location where the user account expects to find it. You do this by accessing the user account properties from User Manager for Domains, then setting the profile path to the location of the user profile. Once the profile path is set, you need to ensure that the profile directory has been shared and that the user account has read, write, and modify permissions to the profile directory itself. Without these settings, the user account cannot load or modify the profile information from the network.

☒ **A, B, D.** The other answer choices are false statements or do not relate to this situation.

59. ☑ **C.** There is not a trust relationship between Sales and Engineering. In this scenario, Marketing uses the resources in both the Sales and Engineering domains and is therefore the trusted domain. Sales and Engineering become the trusting domains. There are two one-way trusts established, one between Marketing and Sales, and one between Marketing and Engineering. Even though the Marketing domain is the trusted domain to both Sales and Engineering, it does not follow that access to resources will be granted to Sales and Engineering.

☒ **A, B.** The first two answers are wrong since there is no trust relationship. **D.** is not right since C is correct.

60. ☑ **B.** Schema. NDS is an extensible database that allows you to add additional schema extensions. A schema defines the NDS object and the various properties that are associated with that object. NDS is an object-oriented database that allows you to include objects that are not developed yet. In order for NetWare to manage Windows NT objects, you must provide it with a blueprint of the objects, or extend its awareness to include them. This is performed through the installation of Novell Administrator for Windows NT by administrators with the supervisor's right to the [Root] object.

☒ **A, C.** NT configuration object and extension do not exist. **D.** A snap-in is an add-in for NWADMN.

61. ☑ **B.** The Domain Object Wizard creates them. NDS for NT has a Domain Object Wizard, which creates the objects needed within NDS. The Domain Object Wizard also extends the schema. The Domain Object Wizard starts automatically when the NT Server is rebooted the first time after NDS for NT is installed.

☒ **A.** is not correct since the objects are created by the DOW. **C.** and **D.** are not right since the Administrator does not use NWADMIN or create an object manually.

62. ☑ **D.** You will be given three choices: Don't Move, Associate With, and Create As. When this happens, you will be prompted with a screen giving you a list of duplicate accounts along with the options to not move, associate the accounts or create a different account.

☒ **A,** is not correct since the account will be migrated if chosen. **B.** is wrong since the NDS account information will not be deleted. **C.** also wrong since there is no Overwrite option.

63. ☑ Domain Access. In the Domain Access Property Page there is a place to mark Force Password Sync.

☒ **B, C,** and **D.** are incorrect because they are different property pages dealing with non password-related functions.

64. ☑   Novell Client Install Manager. The Novell Client Install Manager allows for configuring properties for various workstations, preventing you from having to set up each individual unattended installation.
☒   **B, C,** and **D.** are not correct because they are invalid terms for the utility.

65. ☑   **A, B, C.** SETUPNW.EXE /?, readme files and tech support are three available options for getting help on the client.
☒   **D.** is incorrect because there is no Help and About option in the Client Screen.

66. ☑   **C.** Volatile User. A volatile user is created by the client at login and deleted at logout. This prevents a large number of users in User Manager on the workstation, and it prevents someone from logging into the workstation without being logged into NDS first.
☒   **A.** is incorrect because the NonVolatile user remains in the SAM on the workstation. **B.** is wrong because the Temporary User does not exist. **D.** is wrong because the Admin user would not work, since it already exists and is not a dynamic user.

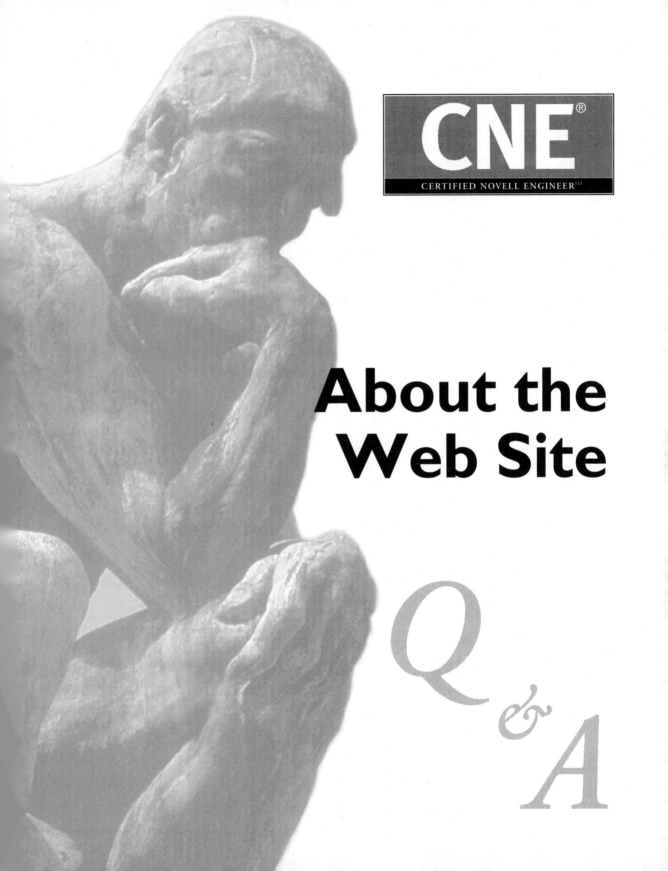

CNE®

CERTIFIED NOVELL ENGINEER℠

About the Web Site

Q & A

Access Global Knowledge

As you know by now, Global Knowledge is the largest independent IT training company in the world. Just by purchasing this book, you have also secured a free subscription to the Global Knowledge Web site and its many resources. You can find it at http://access.globalknowledge.com

You can log on directly at the Global Knowledge site, and you will be e-mailed a new, secure password immediately upon registering.

What You'll Find There. . .

The wealth of useful information at the Global Knowledge site falls into three categories:

Skills Gap Analysis

Global Knowledge offers several ways for you to analyze your networking skills and discover where they may be lacking. Using Global Knowledge's trademarked Competence Key Tool, you can do a skills gap analysis and get recommendations for where you may need to do some more studying. (Sorry, it just might not end with this book!)

Networking

You'll also gain valuable access to another asset: people. At the Access Global site, you'll find threaded discussions, as well as live discussions. Talk to other Network+ candidates, get advice from folks who have already taken the exams, and get access to instructors and MCTs.

Product Offerings

Of course, Global Knowledge also offers its products here, and you may find some valuable items for purchase—CBTs, books, or courses. Browse freely and see if there's something that could help you take that next step in career enhancement.

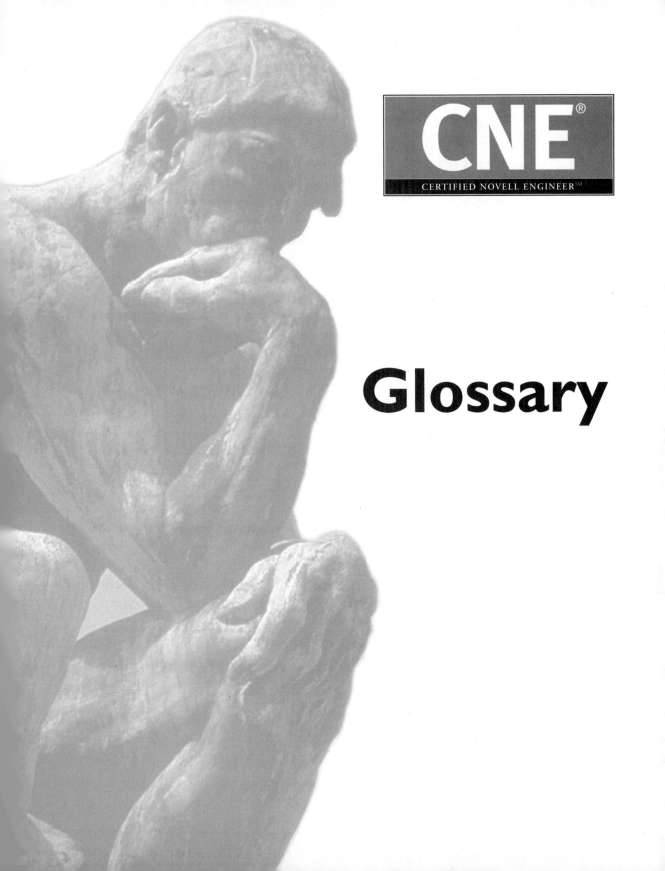

CNE®
CERTIFIED NOVELL ENGINEER℠

Glossary

ACCESS CONTROL ENTRIES (ACE)   Specifies auditing and access permissions for a given object for a specific user or group of users.

ACCESS CONTROL LIST (ACL)   File and print servers also check the access control list (ACL) of each resource before allowing a user to access a file or use a printer. If the user, or a group to which the user belongs, is not listed in the ACL, the user is not allowed to use the resource.

ACCESS MASK   Every ACE must have an access mask. An access mask tells the ACE which attributes are available for a particular object type. The ACE can then grant permissions based on that mask. For example, a file can set Read, Write, Execute, Delete, Take ownership, and Change permissions because an access mask defines these attributes. (See also **Access Control Entries**.)

ACCESS METHODS   The rules governing the use of the physical network by various devices.

ACCOUNT LOCKOUT   Can be set to lock out an account after a certain number of unsuccessful logon attempts. (Three bad attempts is a common choice.) This prevents hackers from breaking into your account.

ACCOUNT POLICIES   Set from the User Manager to change how passwords are used. This is where you can set the account lockout policy to help prevent your system from being hacked into.

ACROSS-THE-WIRE MIGRATION   This upgrade method can take the bindery and volume information from multiple NetWare 3.1x servers and upgrade them to another, more powerful, server that has had NetWare 5 already installed.

ADMINISTRATOR ACCOUNT   One of the two built-in NT user accounts. The administrator account manages the workstation's user accounts, policies, and resources. This account cannot be locked out or disabled. The Administrator account even has control over the files owned by other users. (See also **guest account**.)

ALERTER   Service used by the Server and other services. This service broadcasts the logged on user name in the NetBIOS name table, which can be considered a security breach.

ALERTS   Critical security controls that help perform real-time monitoring. Enabled by configuring the Performance Monitor.

APPLICATION LAYER   (1) OSI layer that provides a consistent way for an application to save files to the network file server or print to a network printer. (2) TCP/IP layer that is the highest layer in the TCP/IP model. It is used by applications to access services across a TCP/IP network. Examples of applications that operate at this layer are a Web browser, file transfer program (FTP), and a remote login program.

APPLICATIONS   There are two types of applications: simple and complex. A simple application is one that does not require any configuration on the workstation in order to run. A complex application may require registry entries, INI file changes, text file changes, and multiple files to be copied.

ASSETS   Anything that is of value and needed for the operation of the corporation.

ATM (ASYNCHRONOUS TRANSFER MODE)   A cell-switching protocol. ATM uses cell switching which is marked by its small, fixed length cells. (See **also Ethernet, Token Ring,** and **FDDI.**)

AUDITING POLICIES   An important component of the Monitoring Security Effectively controls. Auditing measures the system against a predefined system setting to ensure that no changes have occurred. The Windows NT security system uses the SIDs contained in the access token to log user activity, a process known as auditing. (See **also security identifier (SID)**).

AVAILABILITY   Ensuring that information and vital services are accessible when required.

BACKUP ADMINISTRATOR   Usually used in large LAN and or WAN environments. This position is used for backing up and restoring the network data.

BACKUP DOMAIN CONTROLLERS (BDC)   After a domain has been created, the entire account database is basically mirrored on each BDC, and the PDC keeps the information updated within five minutes by default. (See also **PDC**.)

BASEBAND   A type of signal transmission that allows only one frequency to carry information on the cable. (See also **broadband**.)

BINDERY-STYLE LOGON   Require a user to attach or log on to a server before gaining access to services on the server.

BINDING   The linking of network components on different levels to enable communication between those components.

BITS   Information is transmitted in bits on an Ethernet network. A bit is the smallest amount of information that can be represented. A bit is represented as a single binary digit that can be either a 1 or a 0. A sequence of bits is called a frame.

BLOCK SUBALLOCATION   Disk space is divided into blocks just as memory is divided into blocks.

BRIDGES   Used to connect similar LAN segments. Bridges look at the destination and source address of a network packet and decide whether to pass that packet on to the LAN segment. A bridge can be used to filter out traffic for a local subnet and prevent it from passing onto an unnecessary LAN segment.

BROADBAND   Signal transmission that can support more than one signal on the cable by using frequency division techniques. (See also baseband.)

BUS TOPOLOGY   When the computers in your network are all connected in a row along a single cable or segment. (See also star topology and ring topology.)

C2   A security evaluation level assigned to a specific product, by the National Computer Security Center (NCSC), a division of the National Security Association (NSA), after a period of detailed product review and attestation. The C2 level of "trust" is one level that can be granted to an evaluated product. The defined levels of trust, in increasing levels of trust (or security), are D, C1, C2, B1, B2, B3, and A1. NT 3.5 with the Service Pack 3.0 has the C2 level of trust.

CALLBACK SECURITY   Security feature implemented within RAS. When a user is configured to use callback and dials in to a RAS server, the server disconnects the session, and then calls the client back at a preset telephone number or at a number provided during the initial call.

CELLULAR TOPOLOGY   Wireless topology in which the network is comprised of multiple areas, called cells, that are serviced by a wireless hub. Wireless communication takes place between the network devices and the hubs.

CHANGE CONTROL   Manages any negative affects that changes can have on the network so that they are minimized.

CHILD PARTITION   A partition that is below another partition in the tree is called a child of the partition above it, which is the parent partition. (See also parent partition.)

CIFS (COMMON INTERNET FILE SHARING)   An enhanced version of SMB services that is available for use over the Internet. (See also SMB.)

CLIENT 32   A 32-bit software application that is available for DOS, Windows 3.1x, Windows 95/98, and Windows NT 4.0 workstations.

CLIENT/SERVER MESSAGING   One program on one computer talking to another program (usually on another computer).

CLIENT/SERVER MODEL   Model in which data is requested by the client from the server. The server fulfills this request and sends the data to the client. The client does any processing that it wishes on the data and sends the modified data back to the server.

COAXIAL (OR COAX) CABLE   One of the three types of physical media that can be used at the OSI Physical Layer. A coaxial has one strand (a solid-core wire) that runs down the middle of the cable. Around that strand is insulation. There are two different types of commonly used Ethernet coaxial cables: thickwire and thinwire. (See also twisted-pair cable and fiber-optic cable.)

COMPUTER BROWSER   Default service that maintains an up-to-date list of computers and provides the list to applications when requested. Provides the computer list displayed in the Select Computer and Select Domain dialog boxes; and in the main Server Manager window.

CONFIDENTIALITY   The protection of information in the system so that unauthorized persons cannot access it.

CONSOLE WORKSTATION   The machine that is used to submit the backups and restoration jobs. (See also host server and target.)

CONTAINER ADMINISTRATOR   In a large LAN or a WAN environment, you may want to divide the management of administration among several container administrators. These administrators have full control over their containers but not outside their container.

CONTAINER OBJECT   A container object in NDS is like a directory (or folder) in a directory tree. It can contain leaf objects or other container objects. Container objects are used to organize the tree structure. (See also leaf object.)

CONTEXTLESS LOGIN   With contextless login you can authenticate from any point on the network simply by typing your login name and password, without knowing the location of your User object in the NDS tree.

CORRECTIVE SECURITY CONTROLS   Used to correct security holes that have been exploited.

COUNTRY OBJECT   Special container object for country locations. Country objects can be placed only in the root. (See also [Root].)

CSNW   One of the two installable network components, CSNW is the client redirector and NWLink is the IPX/SPX-compatible network transport protocol. (See also NWLink.)

CRYPTOGRAPHY   See public key cryptography, secret key cryptography, and symmetric cryptography.

DATA LINK LAYER   OSI layer that handles many issues for communicating on a simple network.

DATA STRIPING   Process that allocates data evenly among the drives, improving reliability and access times. (See also RAID.)

DECISION TREE   A query-like structure that graphically represents the filter expression. In a decision tree, statements are linked together by colored AND, OR, and NOT tabs. Combined, these statements specify the kinds of data you want to capture or display. (See also filtering.)

DETECTIVE SECURITY CONTROLS   Ascertain when security holes are in the process of being exploited.

DIAL-UP NETWORKING (DUN)   Dialing-out service that is set up when RAS is installed as a service. DUN allows you to connect to any dial-up server using the Point-to-Point protocol (PPP) as a transport mechanism allowing for TCP/IP, NetBEUI or IPX/SPX network access over your analog modem, ISDN, or X.25 Pad devices.

DIAL-UP NETWORKING SERVER Allows Windows 98 to host a single dial-up network connection. Any client with support for PPP can dial-in using either IP, IPX, or NetBEUI as their connection protocol. Windows 98 can then act as a server sharing its files and printers just as it does on a LAN, or it can act as a gateway for an IPX or NetBEUI network.

DIRECTORIES Organizational units for file storage. (See also files.)

DIRECTORY REPLICATION An NT default service that makes an exact copy of a folder and places it on another server.

DIRECTORY REPLICATOR Default service that replicates directories and the files in the directories between computers.

DIRECTORY SYNCHRONIZATION The NT process of synchronizing the Backup Domain Controllers with the Primary Domain Controller on a periodic basis. (See also Backup Domain Controller and Primary Domain Controller.)

DIRECTORY TREE An NDS directory tree is a database of objects. Every object in a directory has a relationship to every other object in the directory.

DISASTER RECOVERY PLAN (DRP) Plan for recovery of necessary systems and data to support the core processes necessary to run the business. (See also Business Recovery Plan.)

DISCRETIONARY ACCESS Access control when the person who created the file or folder is the owner and is responsible for securing those files and folders.

DISK ADMINISTRATOR A program that creates and manages partitions.

DISK CACHE MANAGER Manages disk caching by reducing the amount of I/O traffic to your hard drive. It does this by storing frequently used data in physical memory rather than having to read it each time from your hard drive.

DISK CACHING   Storing frequently used data in physical memory rather than having to read it each time from your hard drive.

DISK DUPLEXING   Disk duplexing uses two disk drives just like disk mirroring does; however, instead of using one controller for both disks, disk duplexing uses two controllers, one for each disk. Using a second controller offers a higher degree of fault tolerance over disk mirroring because if one controller should fail, the system continues on with the other controller and hard disk. (See also RAID and disk mirroring.)

DISK MIRRORING   Disk mirroring (RAID Level 1) uses two disk drives attached to one controller. When disk mirroring is used, NetWare issues two write instructions, one to each disk when a write request is made. (See also RAID and disk duplexing.)

DISK THRASHING   (See thrashing.)

DISTINGUISHED NAME   A distinguished name begins with a leading period, starts with the common name of the resource, and then lists each container unit up the tree to the [Root]. Each object has a unique distinguished name in the tree. A distinguished name can locate an object no matter what the current context is set at. (See also relative distinguished name.)

DMA (DIRECT MEMORY ACCESS)   A process whereby some devices can directly access memory on the system without the intervention of the CPU.

DNS ZONE FILE   Contains one host name, one IP address, and a record type.

DOMAIN   A group of computers containing domain controllers that share account information and have one centralized accounts database. The four domain models—single domain, complete trust, master domain, and multiple-master domain—represent various stages of growth and decentralization. The multiple master domain is actually two or more master domain models joined by a two-way trust. (See also domain model.)

DOMAIN MODEL Under the domain model, a Windows NT Server acts as a domain controller. The domain controller authenticates users into the domain before they can access resources that are a part of the domain. (See also Domain Controller.)

DOMAIN CONTROLLER Serve two purposes in the NT environment: to authenticate users and grant them access to other resources within the network. (See also **Primary Domain Controller** and **Backup Domain Controllers**.)

DOMAIN NAME SERVICE (DNS) Performs name resolution of host names to IP addresses. DNS was created because numerical IP addresses are too difficult for humans to remember.

DYNAMIC HOST CONFIGURATION PROTOCOL (DHCP) Assigns TCP/IP configuration parameters on networked clients.

DYNAMIC ROUTING Protocols that advertise the routes they are familiar with and pass on the metrics, number of other routers, or hops, required to get from their host to another network, either directly or indirectly through another router.

EFFECTIVE RIGHTS The actual rights that an object has, by determining which rights have been inherited, which have been filtered, and which have been directly granted to the object or granted through Security Equivalence.

ELECTRONICS COMMUNICATIONS PRIVACY ACT (ECPA) Prevents you from eavesdropping on the activities of an intruder, even if you own the system, unless you post a message to indicate that all activities are subject to being monitored.

EMERGENCY REPAIR DISK (ERD) Can be used to restore a Windows NT system back to the configuration it had the last time you updated your Emergency Repair Disk. This disk can repair missing Windows NT files and restore the registry to include disk configuration and security information.

ENCAPSULATION   The process of encoding data for transmitting it across the network.

ENCRYPTED AUTHENTICATION   Methods for secure network transmission that include the simple Password Authentication Protocol (PAP) which permits clear-text passwords and the Shiva Password Authentication Protocol (SPAP) used by Windows NT workstations when connecting to a Shiva LAN Rover.

ENTERPRISE ADMINISTRATOR   Has the highest level of security. The rights for this administrator start at the [Root] of the NDS tree and flow through all objects and the file system.

ETHERNET   A baseband, CSMA/CD (Carrier Sense, Multiple Access / Collision Detection) transmission protocol. A type of network cabling and signaling specification originally developed by Bob Metcalfe while working for Xerox in the early 1970s. Ethernet is a baseband, CSMA/CD (Carrier Sense, Multiple Access / Collision Detection) transmission protocol. (See also baseband and broadband.)

EVENT LOG   Default service that records system, security, and application events in the Event Log.

EVENT NOTIFICATION SERVICE (ENS)   Provides event notification for print jobs and status.

EVENT VIEWER   The tool within Windows NT used to review audited events. Event Viewer has three logs that record system, security, and application related events, known as the System log, the Security log, and the Applications log, respectively.

FASTTRACK WEB SERVER   Available from NetScape as part of the Novell and NetScape partnership that created Novonyx. It enables a NetWare 5 server to perform Web services on the network.

FAT (FILE ALLOCATION TABLE) FILE SYSTEM   The FAT file system is predominantly used for other operating systems such as Windows 3.x and Windows 95. To support backward compatibility, Windows NT fully supports the FAT file system. This is also because of FAT's universal acceptance and accessibility through other operating systems. Does not support Windows NT security features and does not offer any of the robust NTFS features. (See also NTFS.)

FAT32   The Windows 98 32-bit upgrade to the FAT file system that originally came from DOS. The benefits of FAT32 include optimal use of disk space and larger partition sizes than the maximum 2 GB (gigabyte) size allowed by FAT. *Note: Windows 98 supports only FAT and FAT32 files systems and Windows NT does not support FAT32.*

FAULT TOLERANCE   Recovery from operational failure control due to the system's ability to withstand hardware failures and software errors. Windows NT provides fault tolerance by allowing the redundancy of data by simultaneously writing files to multiple disks, and by replicating the contents of file directories to other servers on the network.

FDDI (FIBER DISTRIBUTED DATA INTERFACE)   Follows the IEEE 802.5 standard for accessing the network just like Token Ring. However, unlike the Token Ring topology, FDDI uses two fiber-optic cables in a dual counter rotating ring configuration and operates at 100Mbps instead of the 4Mbps or 16Mbps as used in Token Ring. (See also Ethernet, Token Ring, and ATM.)

FIBER-OPTIC CABLES   One of three types of physical media that can be used at the Physical Layer to carry digital data signals in the form of modulated pulses of light. An optical fiber consists of an extremely thin cylinder of glass, called the core, surrounded by a concentric layer of glass, known as the cladding. There are two fibers per cable—one to transmit and one to receive. (See also coaxial cable and twisted-pair cable.)

FILE COMPRESSION   Factor in disk space optimization that makes the most efficient use of hard disk space.

FILES   Files are data units such as graphics, documents, executable applications, and text files.

FILTERING   An effective security monitoring control that allows the system administrator to specify expressions to capture data either by protocol or network address. The filter expressions are represented by a decision tree. (See also decision tree.)

FINGER   Tool used to gather information about users on any machine running a finger server.

FIREWALL   Software that prevents unauthorized traffic between two networks by examining the IP packets that travel on both networks. Firewalls look at the IP address and type of access the packet requires (such as FTP or HTTP) and then determine if that type of traffic is allowed.

FTP PUBLISHING SERVICE   Default service that, in Windows NT 4.0, FTP is part of Internet Information Server (IIS).

FULL-DUPLEX DIALOGS   Used by OSI Session Layer to let data flow in both directions simultaneously.

FULL SYNCHRONIZATION   In a full synchronization, the PDC sends a copy of the entire user accounts database to a BDC.

FULLY QUALIFIED DOMAIN NAME (FQDN)   Identifies the type of service by preceding the domain name with a service name.

GARBAGE COLLECTION   A routine that is run when memory is deallocated.

GATEWAY   A device that enables two dissimilar systems that have similar functions to communicate with each other.

GLOBAL GROUPS   Created on domain controllers and used to assign local permissions to domain users. The sole purpose of a global group is to gather users together at the domain level so that they can be placed in the appropriate local groups. (See also local groups.)

GROUP ACCOUNTS   Accounts used for grouping together users who perform the same function or require access to the same resources. If it were not for group accounts, you would have to grant access to resources on a per-user basis.

GUEST ACCOUNT   One of the two built-in NT user accounts. The guest account is for the one-time or occasional user. (See also administrator account.)

HALF-DUPLEX DIALOGS   Used by OSI Session Layer to allow data to flow in two directions, but only one direction at a time. With half-duplex dialogs, replies and acknowledgements are possible.

HARDWARE   Registry subtree that contains information about the hardware that is detected upon system startup. Such information might include device settings, interrupts, and information about hardware components.

HARDWARE ABSTRACTION LAYER (HAL)   The layer between the operating system and the hardware located in the computer. Separates the Kernel from the hardware to provide an intermediary layer, so that the Windows NT Kernel does not have to perform communication with the hardware. HAL is what makes NT portable to other architectures

HARDWARE COMPATIBILITY LIST (HCL)   A compilation of computer systems and hardware that have been tested for compatibility with Windows NT.

HOST SERVER   A NetWare server that is running the backup program. (See also target and console workstation.)

HOT FIX   Method whereby, transparent to the user, when an error occurs because of a bad sector, the file system moves the data that was located in this sector (if possible) to another sector, and labels the original sector as bad. A feature of NTFS and SCSI hardware, but not the FAT file system.

HTTP (HYPERTEXT TRANSFER PROTOCOL) The protocol that you use to connect to the Internet to view Web pages.

IMPERSONATION Technique for a server process to access objects that it doesn't have permissions to. If the client process has proper access permissions, the server process impersonates the client process in order to access the object.

INHERITED RIGHTS FILTER (IRF) The system used to prevent rights from flowing down the tree from a parent container object. The IRF lists those rights that should not be inherited.

IN-PLACE UPGRADE Method of upgrading to NetWare 5.0 that will overwrite the system files on an existing server and upgrade the bindery and file system to an NDS structure.

INTEGRATED SERVICES DIGITAL NETWORK (ISDN) Connections that take place over digital lines and provide faster and more reliable connectivity. The primary benefit of ISDN is its speed and reliability. ISDN is commonly found in two speeds: 64kbps and 128kbps.

INTEGRITY The protection of information in the system from unauthorized, unanticipated, and unintentional modification ensuring data is accurate and complete.

INTERNET LAYER TCP/IP layer that is responsible for handling the communication from one computer to another computer. It accepts a request to send data from the Transport layer. The Internet layer consists of two protocols, the Internet Protocol (IP) and the Internet Control Message Protocol (ICMP Internet Mail Service (IMS). The Internet Mail Service enables users on Microsoft Exchange Server to send messages to, and receive messages from, users on the Internet.

INTERNETWORKS Repeaters, bridges, and routers are devices used to link individual LANs together to form larger internetworks. (See also repeaters, bridges, and routers.)

INTERNET PROTOCOL (IP)   Provides packet delivery for all other protocols within the TCP/IP suite.

IP ADDRESS   Uniquely identifies a computer on the network. It is 32 bits long, with four octets separated by dots (.). This number is then converted to binary and used as a unique identifier.

IPX/SPX   Protocol used to connect Novell Networks.

IT SECURITY CONTROL MODEL   The relationship between corporate business objectives and IT Security controls or Windows NT Security features. An effective security model has three objectives: confidentiality, integrity, and availability.

LARGE INTERNET PACKETS (LIP)   New feature in NetWare 5.0 that allows the maximum size of internetwork packets to be larger than in previous versions of NetWare.

LAST KNOWN GOOD CONFIGURATION   Allows the user to restore the system to the last working system configuration. When used, it discards any changes to the configuration since the last working system configuration.

LEAF OBJECT   Represents resources in the NDS tree. A leaf object does not contain any other objects.

LEGAL NOTICE   Corporation-specific message that appears whenever a user logs on the system warning them that only authorized users may access the system and that they are being monitored. Set through the Registry Editor or System Policy Editor. (See also Registry Editor and System Policy Editor.)

LOCAL AREA NETWORK (LAN)   A collection of computers connected in a geographically close network.

LOCAL GROUPS   Defined on each machine and may have both user accounts and global groups as members but cannot contain other local groups. (See also global groups.)

LOCAL SECURITY AUTHORITY   The heart of the NT security subsystem. It creates security access tokens, authenticates users, and manages the local security policy.

LOGICAL LINK CONTROL LAYER   One of the sublayers of the Data Link Layer. It controls the establishment and maintenance of links between communicating devices. (See also Media Access Control Layer and Data Link Layer.)

LOGICAL MEMORY ADDRESSING   Logical memory addressing allows NetWare to efficiently use memory because fragmentation of memory is minimal, which results in faster memory response.

LOGIN SCRIPT   Enables authentication for access to any NetWare 5 server, printers, and other network resources.

LOGON SCRIPTS   Used to start applications or set environment variables for a computer upon startup.

LOOSELY CONSISTENT   The NDS Directory is what is know as a "loosely consistent" database, which means the database maintains its integrity even if there are slight differences in replicas for a short period of time. NDS does continuously check all replicas, however, to see if objects in those replicas have been added, deleted, or modified. NDS then makes changes to the appropriate replicas to make sure that they all contain the most up-to-date information. This process is called *NDS* synchronization.

MAC (MEDIA ACCESS CONTROL)   A networked computer's unique address of its network interface card (NIC). Data is transported over networks in packets that always contain the source and destination MAC addresses. A bridge reads this information off the packets it receives to fill its routing table.

MANDATORY LOGON   NT uses mandatory logon to force everyone to logon before it grants access to the system.

MANDATORY PROFILE   Used when the administrator needs to ensure that the user obtains the same workstation configuration every time they log into the network.

MASTER REPLICA   Created automatically when you create a partition. There can be only one master replica of any given partition.

MEDIA ACCESS CONTROL LAYER   One of the sublayers of the Data Link Layer. It controls how multiple network devices share the same media channel. (See also **Logical Link Control Layer** and **Data Link Layer**.)

MESH TOPOLOGY   Network topology most prevalent in Wide Area Networks, since its redundancy provides a high level of reliability. In a full mesh topology, each network device is connected to each of the other network device.

MESSENGER   Default service that sends and receives messages sent by administrators or by the Alerter service. This service is stopped when the Workstation service is stopped.

MICROSOFT CHALLENGE HANDSHAKE AUTHENTICATION PROTOCOL (MS-CHAP)   An encrypted login protocol used by remote users.

MIRRORING   Enables Windows NT to read files from, and write files to, two disks simultaneously. Entire disks (or sets of disks) can be mirrored or just partitions on each disk. If one drive fails, the second continues to function as normal.

MOBILE CLIENT   A workstation or laptop used by a user that works from remote locations. Mobile clients are generally laptop or notebook computers with modems installed on them.

MONITORING CONTROLS   Include violation and exception reporting which help management determine whether their systems are being compromised.

MULTIPOINT CONNECTION   A connection that allows multiple network devices to exist on the physical media simultaneously. Network connections are typically multipoint connections.

NBSTAT   Tool used to display the contents of the remote computer's NetBIOS name table. The information listed in the NetBIOS name table can be used to determine the Domain name or workgroup the machine is in and the currently connected users. The information may also be used to uncover the Administrator's account, due to the fact that account SIDs are displayed in the name cache.

NDPS (NOVELL DISTRIBUTED PRINT SERVICES)   Printing service created by Novell in partnership with Hewlett-Packard and Xerox, NDPS incorporates new technology functions.

NDS SECURITY   Implemented by assigning trustee rights to the NDS objects, or the properties of those objects.

NDS SYNCHRONIZATION   Process in which NDS continuously checks all replicas to see if objects in those replicas have been added, deleted, or modified. NDS then makes changes to the appropriate replicas to make sure that they all contain the most up-to-date information.

NETBEUI (NETBIOS EXTENDED USER INTERFACE)   NetBEUI, the built-in protocol of Microsoft networking, supports communication in a Microsoft-only environment when the network is small and composed of a single network segment. NetBEUI is a non-routable protocol, meaning that its packets contain no routing information and cannot pass through routers into other network segments. NetBEUI protocol is best suited for Local Area Networks that do not connect to the Internet. (See also NetBIOS.)

NETBIOS Protocol used when Microsoft networking is required in a large multi-segment network. NetBIOS has many similarities to NetBEUI except for the fact that it can be routed into other network segments when combined with either the TCP/IP or NWLink protocols in a form known as an encapsulated protocol. (See also NetBEUI and NWLink.)

NET LOGON Default service that performs authentication of account for primary domain and backup domain controllers, and also keeps the domain directory database synchronized between the primary domain controller and the backup domain controllers of he domain. For other computers running Windows NT, supports pass-through authentication of account logons. Used when the workstation participates in a domain.

NETSTAT Tool used to display the status of the TCP/IP stack including what ports are open and what connections are active.

NETWARE APPLICATION LAUNCHER (NAL) The component of Z.E.N.works that handles application management and software distribution. NAL centralizes application administration by creating application objects in Novell Directory Services (NDS). The application objects can then be secured using NDS security. (See also Z.E.N.works.)

NETWARE CONNECT A remote dial-in connectivity software product from Novell that is now part of NetWare Internet Access Server (NIAS).

NETWORK DDE Default service that provides a network transport as well as security for DDE (Dynamic Data Exchange) conversations.

NETWORK DDEDSDM Dynamic Data Exchange Share Database Manager manages the shared DDE conversations. It is used by the Network DDE service.

NETWORK INTERFACE CARD (NIC) Also called an adapter card or interface card, it is installed in a computer to allow it to communicate with other computers over a network. A NIC changes the parallel signals inside the computer into serial signals that go over the network cable.

NETWORK LAYER   OSI layer that manages addressing and delivering packets on a complex internetwork such as the Internet. Internetworks are joined by devices known as routers, which utilize routing tables and routing algorithms to determine how to send data from one network to another.

NETWORK MONITOR   Tool used to monitor packets of information that are sent from or received by the computer where you are running the program, including broadcast and multicast frames. The Microsoft System Management Server includes an advanced Network Monitor tool, which allows you to capture frames sent to and from any computer on the network, edit and transmit frames on the network, and capture frames from remote computers running Network Monitor Agent on the network.

NLMS (NETWARE LOADABLE MODULES)   Applications that run on a NetWare server.

NOVELL DIRECTORY SERVICES (NDS)   The service used by NetWare to organize resources throughout an entire network. It is a database of user IDs and resources. NDS stores network resources in a tree structure that is similar to a directory tree.

NTFS (NEW TECHNOLOGY FILE SYSTEM)   The file system exclusive to Windows NT 4.0. Utilizes Windows NT file and directory security features so it is more secure than FAT.

NT LM SECURITY SUPPORT PROVIDER   Default service that provides Windows NT security to RPC (Remote Procedure Call) applications that use transports other than named pipes.

NWADMIN   The single point of administration for User objects is the NetWare Administrator program, also referred to as NWAdmin.

NWLINK   Microsoft's implementation of the IPX protocol that allows connectivity between the Windows NT and the Novell NetWare environments. (See also CSNW.)

OBJECT RIGHTS   Object rights enable a trustee to perform actions on an NDS object. The object rights are Browse, Create, Delete, Rename, and Supervisor.

ORGANIZATION OBJECT   A high-level container object placed directly in the root or under country units. This object usually represents the company. (See also [Root] and container object.)

ORGANIZATION UNIT OBJECT   Container objects placed below the Organization level unit. This creates a subgroup within the tree in order to organize the network resources.

OSI (OPEN SYSTEMS INTERCONNECTION)   Defines the rules for communication between network devices.

PACKET   Small, manageable pieces of data that are transmitted over the network.

PACKET BURST   Data transmission in which a whole group or "burst" of packets can be sent at once. An acknowledgement still has to be sent, but only one acknowledgement for a group of packets versus one acknowledgement for each packet.

PACKET RECEIVE BUFFERS   Store incoming data until the server can process it. Two parameters that can be set in the packet receive buffer are the maximum and minimum packet receive buffer, referring to how much space is allocated to store data.

PARENT PARTITION   A partition that is above another partition in the NDS directory tree is called a parent of the partition that is below it. (See also child partition.)

PARTITIONING The process of dividing the database into multiple parts. This is beneficial because when one server with a part of the NDS database (called a *replica*) on it goes down, the resources in that replica can still be accessed.

PASS-THROUGH AUTHENTICATION Occurs when you choose a domain to log on to from your NT computer, but your computer doesn't have an account in that domain.

PASSWORD ADMINISTRATOR Used in organizations that utilize a help desk. This administrator has limited rights for User objects, groups, login scripts, and passwords.

PERFORMANCE MONITOR Configured to monitor system performance, to gather vital information on system statistics, and to analyze and graphically display information. Can also be configured to send alerts when a hacker may be attempting to compromise security. There are four ways to view the information gathered by the Performance monitor: chart, alert, log, and report.

PHYSICAL LAYER Bottom OSI layer that is only concerned with moving bits of data on and off the network medium. The Physical Layer does not define what that medium is, but it must define how to access it.

PING (PACKET INTERNET GROPER) A standard TCP/IP network utility that sends packets from one machine to another in order to determine if there is a valid network route between them.

PLUG-AND-PLAY The operating system can automatically detect when a new device is attached to the computer, even if the computer is currently running, and complete the hardware installation.

POINT-TO-POINT CONNECTION A connection that allows only two network devices to exist on the physical media simultaneously. A remote access connection is an example of a point-to-point connection.

POINT-TO-POINT PROTOCOL (PPP)   Enables links between two points with no devices in between.

POINT-TO-POINT PROTOCOL MULTI-LINK PROTOCOL (PPP-MP)   An Internet standard allowing multiple protocols, such as NetBEUI and IPX, to be encapsulated within IP datagrams and transmitted over public backbones such as the Internet.

POINT-TO-POINT TRANSMISSION (PPT)   Many computer networks use point-to-point transmission methods, where there may be one to dozens of points between the two ends (email is a good example of this). Each point is only concerned with transferring data from itself to the next point downstream.

POINT-TO-POINT TUNNELING PROTOCOL (PPTP)   Microsoft PPTP is a transport mechanism under which remote users can connect to corporate networks through secure channels creating connections commonly referred to as Virtual Private Networks (VPNs). There are two implementations of PPTP today, one is a North American version featuring 128-bit encryption and the other is an exportable version with 40-bit encryption. (See also Virtual Private Networks.)

PREEMPTIVE MULTITASKING   Process that lets the operating system judge when an application has to relinquish system time to another process.

PRESENTATION LAYER   OSI layer that ensures that data sent by the Application Layer and received by the Session Layer is in a standard format and if not, it converts the data.

PRIMARY DOMAIN CONTROLLER (PDC)   The central server in the network that maintains the security database for that domain.

PRINT DEVICE   The actual hardware that prints the document. The three basic types of print devices are raster, PostScript, and plotter.

PRINT DRIVER   The software that allows an application to communicate with printing devices. Print drivers are composed of three files, which act together as a printing unit: printer graphics driver, printer interface driver, and characterization data file.

PRINT JOB   Source code consisting of both data and commands for print processing. All print jobs are classified into data types. The data type tells the spooler what modifications need to be made to the print job so it can print correctly on the printing device.

PRINT MONITOR   Controls access to the printing device, monitors the status of the device, and communicates with the spooler, which relays this information via the user interface. Controls the data going to a printer port by opening, closing, configuring, writing, reading, and releasing the port.

PRINTER POOLING   An efficient way to streamline the printing process. It sends print jobs to a pool of printing devices, in which only one printing device actually prints the document.

PRINT PROCESSOR   Completes the rendering process. (See also rendering.)

PRINT ROUTER   Routes the print job from the spooler to the appropriate print processor.

PRINT SPOOLER   A service that actually manages the print process.

PRINTING SOFTWARE   Considered the printer. A printer is software that manages a specific printing device (or devices, in case of printer pooling). The printer determines how the print job gets to the printing device, via parallel port, serial port, or via the network.

PRINTER   See printing software.

PRIVACY ACT   See Electronics Communications Privacy Act (ECPA).

PROACTIVE ADMINISTRATION   The collection of tasks that attempts to prevent errors and avoid problems on the network. Proactive administration results in less reactive administration. (See also reactive administration.)

PROPERTY RIGHTS   Property rights allow a trustee to access the values of the properties information stored within NDS. The property rights are Compare, Read, Write, and Add or Delete Self, and Supervisor.

PROTECTED MEMORY SPACE   Memory set aside for applications or NLMs that might not be stable. Protected memory space is separate from the server kernel, which means that if the application or NLM that is loaded in the protected memory space fails, it will not affect the server. This keeps the server from crashing or abending due to unstable applications or NLMs.

PROTOCOLS   Languages used by computers. In order for two computers to talk to each other they must speak the same language (use the same protocol).

PROXY SERVER   A local server between the client workstation and the Internet itself.

PUBLIC KEY CRYPTOGRAPHY   Consists of a public key and a private key. The public key is given freely to anyone that needs it, and the private key is kept secret by the keys' owner and is stored in the user's security file.

RAID (REDUNDANT ARRAY OF INEXPENSIVE DISKS)   Enables a system to segment data and store pieces of it on several different drives, using a process known as data striping. (See also data striping.)

RAM (RANDOM ACCESS MEMORY)   Physical memory where programs and modules are loaded that are used on the server.

REACTIVE ADMINISTRATION   The collection of tasks that fix problems as they arise. It is "reactive" to the situation at hand. (See also proactive administration.)

READ-ONLY REPLICA   Receives updates from master and read/write replicas, but does not allow their NDS objects to be modified. (See also master replica and read/write replica.)

READ/WRITE REPLICA   Copies of the master replica that also send out the changes made to the NDS objects that they contain. (See also master replica.)

REGEDT32.EXE   Executable that launches the Registry Editor. (See also Registry and Registry Editor.)

REGISTRY   A powerful database that controls your computer by containing all your system and program configuration parameters. Contains the SAM and configuration data for applications, hardware, and device drivers. The Registry also contains data on user-specific information including settings from user-profiles, desktop settings, software configurations, and network settings.

REGISTRY EDITOR   A Microsoft tool for searching the Registry. Both the new tool, Regedit.exe, and the traditional registry editor, Regedt32.exe, are included. Some of the new features of Regedit.exe include improved search capabilities and a Windows Explorer interface. (See also Registry.)

RELATIVE DISTINGUISHED NAME   A relative distinguished name lists the path from the current context to the object, does not contain a leading period, and can have an ending period. The relative distinguished name can be confusing because it starts with the object that it is trying to reach although it is intended to lead to that object from the current context. Remember that this type of name is locating a resource in a context relative to the current context. (See also distinguished name.)

REMOTE ACCESS SERVICE (RAS)   Enables users to connect over a phone line to your network and access resources as if they were at a computer connected directly to the network.

REMOTE CONTROL   A program that grants a user remote control so they can administer a server. This variation of external networking allows the client to take full control of the machine; all input devices, like the keyboard and mouse, are routed to the remote client.

REMOTE NODE   The external networking method employed by Windows NT Remote Access Services (RAS). The remote node method allows a remote client machine to dial into a server and attach itself to the network using various protocols. (See also Remote Access Service.)

REMOTE PROCEDURE CALL (RPC)   Used by programmers to create an application consisting of multiple procedures; some run on the local computer, and others run on remote computers over a network. RPCs allow commands to be sent from one system to execute programs on another system.

REMOTE PROCEDURE CALL (RPC) LOCATOR   Default service that allows distributed applications to use the Microsoft RPC service and manages the RPC Name Service database. The server side of distributed applications registers its availability with this service. The client side of distributed applications queries this service to find available server applications.

REMOTE PROCEDURE CALL (RPC) SERVICE   Default service that is the RPC subsystem for Windows NT. It includes the endpoint mapper and other related services.

RENDERING   The process of translating print data into a form that a printing device can read.

REPEATER   Connects network cables by regenerating signals so they can travel on additional cable lengths.

REPLICA   Copies of partitions. (See also partitioning.)

RESOURCE   An entity that exists on the network. A service provides access to the resource.

RESOURCE DOMAINS   Process of sharing resources, like printers and files, within a domain. Administered by the Resource Domain Controller.

RESOURCE MANAGEMENT SERVICE (RMS)   Allows centralized printing resources such as print drivers, PDF (printer definition) files, and banners, to be downloaded to clients or printers.

RIGHTS   The term used for security access to various network resources.

RING TOPOLOGY   When the computers in a network form an electrical loop with their connecting cable. (See also bus topology and star topology.)

RISK   The measurement of exposure to possible harm or loss. The threat could be from a variety of sources, including market forces, disgruntled employees, competitors, or one's own inefficient/outdated processes.

ROAMING PROFILE   Workstation settings stored on the network to give a user the same environment, regardless of which workstation they're logged into.

ROAMING USER   A user who logs on to the network at different times from different computers.

[ROOT]   The top of the NDS tree. There is only one root object. It is created during the first server installation into the NDS tree. The [Root] can contain only Country objects or the Organization object. It does not contain any leaf objects other than Alias objects, if the Alias represents a Country or an Organization.

ROUTERS   Use the destination network address to see where a packet should go. (See also routing.)

ROUTING   Process of forwarding a packet from one segment to another segment until it arrives at its final destination. A router makes decisions as to where to send network packets by looking at the network addresses of the packets it receives before passing them on.

ROUTING TABLE   Used by bridges to determine whether data is destined for the local network.

SAM (SECURITY ACCESS MANAGER)   A database that maintains all user, group, and workstation accounts in a secure database. (2) Registry subtree that contains all account and security information for local users on a non-domain controller and for all users in the current domain on a domain controller.

SCHEMA   NDS schema is the structure of objects that can be stored within the directory tree.

SECRET KEY CRYPTOGRAPHY   Secret key encrypts and decrypts messages using a single secret key called a bulk encryption key in the Key Management Server. Two examples of secret key cryptography are DES and CAST. The Key Management Server supports CAST 40 and CAST 64. DES and CAST 64 are available only in North America.

SECTOR   The smallest storage unit on a hard disk. A typical sector holds 512 bytes of data.

SECURE ATTENTION SEQUENCE   Invoked at logon by pressing CTRL+ALT+DELETE, this feature requires the user to acknowledge the notice by clicking the OK button in the message box before continuing.

SECURITY   Registry subtree that contains security information for the local machine on non-domain controllers and for the entire domain on domain controllers.

SECURITY DESCRIPTORS   Describes the security attributes for an object, and has the following parts: Owner security ID: identifies the owner of the object, which allows that person to change the permissions for the object; Group security

ID: only used by the POSIX subsystem ; Discretionary access control list (ACL): identifies the groups and users who are allowed and denied access.

SECURITY EQUIVALENCE   The ability to grant an object all the rights that another object has, simply by making them equivalent.

SECURITY ID (SID)   Used to uniquely identify each user, NT Workstation, and Server on the network.

SECURITY LOG   A report where suspicious information can be filtered and tracked.

SECURITY REFERENCE MONITOR   Verifies that the user has permissions to access the requested object, and then performs that action.

SERVER   Default service that provides remote procedure call RPC support, and file, print and named piping sharing using SMB services.

SERVER ADMINISTRATOR   This administrator can change passwords, group memberships, and login scripts.

SERVER ALERTS   Used to send notification messages to users or computers. Server alerts are generated by the system, and relate to server and resource use. They warn about security and access problems, user session problems, printer problems, and server shutdown because of power loss when the UPS service is available.

SERVER MANAGER   A utility not only for managing servers, but for managing workstations and the domain. Allows the administrator to control most domain activity, including domain administration, setting up shares, configuring replication settings, modifying services, and monitoring user connections.

SERVICE REGISTRY SERVICE (SRS)   Holds and advertises printer registration information (device type, address, and device-specific information) for public access servers so that users and administrators can find them.

SERVICES   Processes that run in the background of a Windows NT environment and may be started automatically at boot time or manually started and stopped by the Administrator or Server Operators. Services provide access to resources on the network. (See also resource.)

SESSION LAYER   OSI layer that manages dialogs between computers. It does this by establishing, managing, and terminating communications between the two computers. (See the three types of dialogs that the Session Layer uses: simplex dialogs, half-duplex dialogs, and full-duplex dialogs.)

SHARE   Created by granting a particular resource a share name. This name is what other users or devices recognize as the entity with which they have permission to access. (See also share-level security.)

SHARE-LEVEL SECURITY   Used to give other users access to your hard drive via the network. The four types of share permissions are No Access, Read, Change, and Full Control.

SIMPLE NETWORK MANAGEMENT PROTOCOL (SNMP)   An Internet standard for monitoring and configuring network devices. An SNMP network is composed of management systems and agents.

SIMPLEX DIALOGS   Used by the OSI Session Layer to allow data to flow in only one direction. Since the dialog is one way, information can be sent, but not responded too, or even acknowledged.

SLIP (SERIAL LINE INTERNET PROTOCOL)   An older protocol used to carry TCP/IP over low-speed serial lines.

SMB (SERVER MESSAGE BLOCK)   Services that form the backbone of Microsoft networking in the Windows NT environment. All file and printer sharing in Windows NT operate using the SMB services.

SOFTWARE   Registry subtree that contains software configuration information pertaining to the local computer.

SPOOLER   Provides print spooler services.

STAR TOPOLOGY   In a star topology, all computers are directly cabled to a hub. (See also bus topology and ring topology.)

STAR BUS TOPOLOGY   If you replace the computers in a bus topology with the hubs from star topology networks, you get a star bus topology.

STAR RING TOPOLOGY   Also called star wired ring. The smaller hubs are internally wired like a ring and connected to the main hub in a star topology.

STORAGE MANAGEMENT SERVICES (SMS)   The combination of services that Novell NetWare 5 has bundled as a backup-and-restore product for simple to complex networks.

SUBNET MASK   Used to hide part of the IP address in order to distinguish the network from the host on the network.

SUBORDINATE REFERENCES   Created automatically by NDS when a server's hard drive holds a replica of a partition, but not a replica of its child partition.

SWAP FILE   A temporary file that stores information from RAM that is not being used at this moment in time but will be needed in the future. This is quicker and more efficient than unloading and loading a file or module. (See also virtual memory.)

SWITCH   A common solution to traffic problems, a switch calculates which devices are connected to each port.

SYMMETRIC CRYPTOGRAPHY   So named because both the sender and receiver use a single key.

SYN FLOOD ATTACK   A flood of TCP connection requests (SYN) that can be sent to a server, effectively tying it up and causing the server to respond with a reset to all further connection requests.

SYSTEM   Registry subtree that contains all data that is essential for starting the system.

SYSTEM POLICY EDITOR   Tool that provides the ability to configure and maintain the environment and actions of users, groups and computers. Controls the same configurations as the Registry Editor. (See also Registry Editor.)

SYSTEM USER ACCESS FORM   Defines the appropriate level of access depending on the user's job responsibilities.

SYSTEMS SECURITY AUDIT   An independent examination designed to determine whether adequate controls exist to ensure the following corporate IT objectives: effectiveness, efficiency, compliance, reliability of information, confidentiality, integrity, and availability.

TARGET   The NetWare server or workstation that is to be backed up. (See also host server and console workstation.)

TCP/IP (TRANSMISSION CONTROL PROTOCOL/INTERNET PROTOCOL)   An industry-standard suite of protocols designed for local and wide-area networking. Widely used for Internet communication.

TEARDROP AND TEARDROP 2 ATTACKS   Attacks that can cause a system to halt by using up all available memory in the kernel.

TELNET   Terminal emulation for character-based communicating.

TFTP   Tool that allows unauthenticated file transfer to any tftp server.

THRASHING   Refers to the noise made when you have exceeded the amount of physical RAM in the system, your paging file is becoming full, and the system is looking for more available memory.

TIME SYNCHRONIZATION   Process that NetWare servers use to coordinate and agree on a correct time.

TOKEN RING   Token Ring networks do not use a shared access architecture. Instead, they use a token-passing media access method that is defined by the IEEE 802.5 standard. Unlike Ethernet networks, Token Ring networks pass a token from station to station. Instead of having the nodes listen to the network as to when it is safe to transmit, the node must first be in possession of the token to transmit. (See also Ethernet, ATM, and FDDI.)

TRACERT   Traces the path that a packet follows to its destination server.

TRANSPORT LAYER   OSI layer that ensures reliable delivery of data to its destinations. The Transport layer consists of two protocols, the Transmission Control Protocol (TCP) and the User Datagram Protocol (UDP).

TRIGGER   Conditions that must be met before an action occurs.

TRIVIAL FILE TRANSFER PROTOCOL (TFTP)   Similar to the file transfer protocol, but does not require user authentication.

TRUST   A communications and administrative link between two domains that permits the sharing of resources and account information. There are two possible trust configurations, the one-way trust and the two-way trust. In a one-way trust, one domain trusts the users in the other domain to use its resources. A two-way trust is actually comprised of two one-way trusts. Each domain trusts the user accounts in the other domain.

TRUSTED DOMAIN   Domain in which your workstation doesn't have an account. A user in one domain also can be authenticated to another domain by establishing trust relationships. (See also trust.)

TRUSTEE   Any object within NDS that is granted rights to another object. (See also rights.)

TRUST RELATIONSHIP   A one-way administrative and communicative link between two domains allowing one domain (the trusting domain) to honor authentication requests from users of another domain (the trusted domain). (See also trust and trusted domain.)

TWISTED PAIR   The most common Ethernet implementation used today. (See also coaxial cable and fiber-optic cable.)

TYPEFUL NAME   A distinguished name that includes the attribute abbreviation along with the name of the object. (See also distinguished name and typeless name.)

TYPELESS NAME   A distinguished name without the attribute abbreviations. (See also distinguished name and typeless name.)

UNC (UNIVERSAL NAMING CONVENTION)   Each computer in the domain or workgroup is given a "friendly name," which Windows NT converts into the TCP/IP address, MAC address, or other identifiable means of routing the information. The syntax for the UNC name is \\copmutername\sharename. A full UNC consists of the server's name and the name of the share on the server that you wish to use. The names are then put together in the format of \\<Server Name>\<Share Name>\ to form a UNC.

UPS (UNINTERRUPTABLE POWER SUPPLY)   A device consisting of a standalone power source (a battery or a generator) and circuitry which will automatically and instantaneously switch from building power to backup power in the case of an outage.

USER ACCOUNT   Represent users who access the resources on the domain. User accounts do not have to represent individuals; they can also be accounts for services, such as a SQL Server account.

USER MANAGER FOR DOMAINS   The administrative tool used to manage user accounts, groups, and policies. You can copy, rename, or delete user accounts with User Manager. The User Manager for Domains contains three policies that can be customized for different security needs, Account Policies, User Rights, and Auditing Policies. (See also account policies, user rights, and auditing policies.)

USER MODE   Often referred to as non-privileged processor mode, this is where most of Windows NT code is located. This is also where applications and the various subsystems are run. User Mode is designed to prevent applications from bringing down the operating system.

USER OBJECT   Represents a person who accesses the network.

USER PROFILE   User profiles allow the administrator to control a user's environmental settings from the network. Environmental settings include items such as the user's desktop configuration, startup applications, and automatic network connections. These types of configuration settings are typically set by the user according to personal preferences, and are retained in configuration files known as user profiles.

USER RIGHTS   Allow you to control which operations a user or group performs. Each right enables the user to perform specific operations on the computer.

VIRTUAL FILE ALLOCATION TABLE (VFAT)   With the Windows 95 operating system, enhancements were made to FAT, and the new version was called Virtual File Allocation Table (VFAT). VFAT enables the use of long filenames, while maintaining the 8.3 naming convention for older applications viewing the same file.

VIRTUAL LANS (VLANS)   Restrict where the data can travel by configuring communications equipment to route data across specific paths.

VIRTUAL MEMORY   An extension of RAM that allows items stored in RAM to be swapped to the hard drive. This frees up RAM for other purposes and can make the server more efficient. (See also swap file.)

VIRTUAL MEMORY MANAGER (VMM)   Responsible for the use of virtual memory and the paging file in the system.

VIRTUAL PRIVATE NETWORKS (VPNS)   Networks that use the connections already established by the protocols as its medium for transmission.

VOLATILE USER   The volatile user is removed from the workstation after logging out of the network.

WINDOWS NT DIAGNOSTICS   Utility to view various system, resource, and environment information. Also used to monitor possible breaches of security.

WIRELESS BRIDGE   Provides wireless connectivity of remote Ethernet networks and is fully transparent to network protocol and applications.

WIRELESS CONNECTIVITY   Can be achieved through the use of existing cellular telephone links.

WORKGROUP   A collection of computers that have been logically grouped together for the purpose of sharing resources.

Z.E.N.WORKS (ZERO EFFORT NETWORKS)   Novell's network management utility.

ZONE TRANSFERS   Configuration updates to replica servers are called zone transfers.

Custom Corporate Network Training

Train on Cutting Edge Technology   We can bring the best in skill-based training to your facility to create a real-world hands-on training experience. Global Knowledge has invested millions of dollars in network hardware and software to train our students on the same equipment they will work with on the job. Our relationships with vendors allow us to incorporate the latest equipment and platforms into your on-site labs.

Maximize Your Training Budget   Global Knowledge provides experienced instructors, comprehensive course materials, and all the networking equipment needed to deliver high quality training. You provide the students; we provide the knowledge.

Avoid Travel Expenses   On-site courses allow you to schedule technical training at your convenience, saving time, expense, and the opportunity cost of travel away from the workplace.

Discuss Confidential Topics   Private on-site training permits the open discussion of sensitive issues such as security, access, and network design. We can work with your existing network's proprietary files while demonstrating the latest technologies.

Customize Course Content   Global Knowledge can tailor your courses to include the technologies and the topics which have the greatest impact on your business. We can complement your internal training efforts or provide a total solution to your training needs.

Corporate Pass   The Corporate Pass Discount Program rewards our best network training customers with preferred pricing on public courses, discounts on multimedia training packages, and an array of career planning services.

Global Knowledge Training Lifecycle   Supporting the Dynamic and Specialized Training Requirements of Information Technology Professionals

- Define Profile
- Assess Skills
- Design Training
- Deliver Training
- Test Knowledge
- Update Profile
- Use New Skills

College Credit Recommendation Program   The American Council on Education's CREDIT program recommends 53 Global Knowledge courses for college credit. Now our network training can help you earn your college degree while you learn the technical skills needed for your job. When you attend an ACE-certified Global Knowledge course and pass the associated exam, you earn college credit recommendations for that course. Global Knowledge can establish a transcript record for you with ACE, which you can use to gain credit at a college or as a written record of your professional training that you can attach to your resume.

Registration Information

COURSE FEE: The fee covers course tuition, refreshments, and all course materials. Any parking expenses that may be incurred are not included. Payment or government training form must be received six business days prior to the course date. We will also accept Visa/MasterCard and American Express. For non-U.S. credit card users, charges will be in U.S. funds and will be converted by your credit card company. Checks drawn on Canadian banks in Canadian funds are acceptable.

COURSE SCHEDULE: Registration is at 8:00 a.m. on the first day. The program begins at 8:30 a.m. and concludes at 4:30 p.m. each day.

CANCELLATION POLICY: Cancellation and full refund will be allowed if written cancellation is received in our office at least six business days prior to the course start date. Registrants who do not attend the course or do not cancel more than six business days in advance are responsible for the full registration fee; you may transfer to a later date provided the course fee has been paid in full. Substitutions may be made at any time. If Global Knowledge must cancel a course for any reason, liability is limited to the registration fee only.

GLOBAL KNOWLEDGE: Global Knowledge programs are developed and presented by industry professionals with "real-world" experience. Designed to help professionals meet today's interconnectivity and interoperability challenges, most of our programs feature hands-on labs that incorporate state-of-the-art communication components and equipment.

ON-SITE TEAM TRAINING: Bring Global Knowledge's powerful training programs to your company. At Global Knowledge, we will custom design courses to meet your specific network requirements. Call 1 (919) 461-8686 for more information.

YOUR GUARANTEE: Global Knowledge believes its courses offer the best possible training in this field. If during the first day you are not satisfied and wish to withdraw from the course, simply notify the instructor, return all course materials, and receive a 100% refund.

In the US:

CALL: 1 (888) 762-4442

FAX: 1 (919) 469-7070

VISIT OUR WEBSITE:

www.globalknowledge.com

MAIL CHECK AND THIS FORM TO:

Global Knowledge

Suite 200

114 Edinburgh South

P.O. Box 1187

Cary, NC 27512

In Canada:

CALL: 1 (800) 465-2226

FAX: 1 (613) 567-3899

VISIT OUR WEBSITE:

www.globalknowledge.com.ca

MAIL CHECK AND THIS FORM TO:

Global Knowledge

Suite 1601

393 University Ave.

Toronto, ON M5G 1E6

REGISTRATION INFORMATION:

Course title _____

Course location _____ Course date _____

Name/title _____ Company _____

Name/title _____ Company _____

Name/title _____ Company _____

Address _____ Telephone _____ Fax _____

City _____ State/Province _____ Zip/Postal Code _____

Credit card _____ Card # _____ Expiration date _____

Signature _____